# Nine from Aberdeen

# Nine from Aberdeen

By

Jeffrey M. Leatherwood

CAMBRIDGE
SCHOLARS
PUBLISHING

Nine from Aberdeen, by Jeffrey M. Leatherwood

This book first published 2012. The present binding first published 2013.

Cambridge Scholars Publishing

12 Back Chapman Street, Newcastle upon Tyne, NE6 2XX, UK

British Library Cataloguing in Publication Data
A catalogue record for this book is available from the British Library

Copyright © 2013 by Jeffrey M. Leatherwood

All rights for this book reserved. No part of this book may be reproduced, stored in a retrieval system, or transmitted, in any form or by any means, electronic, mechanical, photocopying, recording or otherwise, without the prior permission of the copyright owner.

ISBN (10): 1-4438-4723-2, ISBN (13): 978-1-4438-4723-0

DEDICATED TO COLONEL THOMAS J. KANE

AND ALL THE MEN WHO SERVED

# TABLE OF CONTENTS

# ACKNOWLEDGEMENTS

This publication began as my master's thesis at Western Carolina University in February 2003. Thinking back to those early days in graduate school, I can recall despairing over finding an "original" topic. Yet, I had entertained no plans to add to the vast body of World War II literature, even though my grandfather, Woodrow Leatherwood, had served with distinction as an infantryman in Europe. But, while re-watching one of my favorite British series, *Danger UXB*, two questions sprang to mind: had there been American bomb disposal squads during the war? And if so, were there any published materials on the subject?

As it turned out, the answers were yes and no respectively. Brief mentions in two official Ordnance histories, plus a few memoirs published in England were the only proofs that Americans had engaged in this perilous work on foreign shores. I sent a query to the Royal Engineers Association (REA). Their secretary at that time, Mr. Gary Woodman-Simmons, kindly sent a scanned color photograph of an American lieutenant, Ronald L. Felton, who wore a British bomb disposal patch on his U.S. Army uniform sleeve. From the REA's existing records, I soon learned that Felton had been one of nine Army ordnancemen sent to England in order to become our first bomb disposal instructors.

Sensing a marvelous story in the making, I proceeded onward with these nine names. However, a genealogical record search confirmed that the "Nine from Aberdeen," as I termed these pioneers, were no longer living. However, Command Sergeant Major James H. Clifford, Army EOD's top-ranking noncom, had just completed a short biographical essay on Colonel Thomas J. Kane for the Army Historical Foundation.

I contacted CSM Clifford shortly before his deployment to Afghanistan and Iraq, and found in him a worthy colleague with shared interests in military history. Over the months, we remained in contact, and upon his return to Fort Gillem, Georgia, Jim Clifford contributed a large portion of Kane's papers found within the 52nd EOD Army Group's archives. Since his retirement from service in 2005, Jim Clifford has served as a military consultant for *The Hurt Locker*. Whereas I only write about EOD history, Jim Clifford and his fellow soldiers have *lived* it.

I also pursued the Ron Felton story and located his two daughters, Sandra Font and Marsha Frost. Felton had passed away in 1993, but

Marsha has served as the "keeper of the flame," preserving her father's memory while promoting a sense of community among Felton's comrades and their wives. In autumn of 2003, Marsha and Larry Frost were my gracious hosts in Virginia during an important research visit to the U.S. Army's Ordnance Museum's special collection at Aberdeen Proving Ground. My indebtedness to Marsha cannot be expressed sufficiently, and I hope this book will justify her patient expectations.

Through Marsha Frost, I contacted two surviving members from her father's 12th Ordnance Bomb Disposal Squad. T/Sgt. James "Mac" McCluskey and T/5 Alfred "Al" Gardner were frequent telephone interviewees in 2003-04. Mac and Al also connected me with Dolores "Dee" Kramer, wife of the late T/Sgt. George G. Kramer, also from 12th Squad. Gardner's old friend, T/Sgt. Bob Kuehner (11th & 57th Squads), kindly shared his written reminiscences as well as out-of-print books.

Marsha Frost also introduced me to Joseph C. Pilcher Jr., a retired Army officer whose father traveled with hers to England in early 1942. While in Bristol, the elder Pilcher nearly lost his life while observing Royal Engineers tackling a German bomb. During his convalescence, Joseph forged a lifelong friendship with Felton, later standing as his best man. Pilcher came to witness terrible battles across France, Belgium, and Germany, but rarely discussed his wartime experiences. I would like to thank Joe and Leena for sharing the captain's precious scrapbook, as well as their continued friendship and encouragement. I am also grateful to Jesse Pilcher for sharing memories concerning his beloved older brother.

In the meantime, the Royal Engineers Association had put me in contact with Professor John P. Hudson and Major Thomas D. Sharman; two of the Royal Engineers responsible for establishing both the U.S. Army and Navy Bomb Disposal Schools, thus cementing our international EOD community. I would like to thank Tom Sharman and John Hudson, as well as other British correspondents who have offered their insights.

Apart from the REA, three other organizations aided my initial research in 2003-04. Thanks to a travel grant from Western Carolina University's Graduate School, I was able to visit Aberdeen Proving Ground's Ordnance Museum in October 2003. I would like to thank Dr. Peter Kindsvatter, Dr. William Atwater, and Mr. Tim Tidwell for granting access to rare files, including Col. Kane's bomb disposal journal. Aberdeen's archive holdings also include papers from Lt. Col. John E. Feldman, one of Kane's trusted officers and a founding member of the National EOD Association, the last group I would like to acknowledge at this time.

Lt. Col. Robert Leiendecker, a retired EOD officer, has served as the NATEODA's chief historian. He has encouraged many EOD lore seekers, beginning with Sergeant First Class Samuel Hooper, who circulated his short EOD history back in 1981. Hooper, who is sadly no longer with us, blazed a trail for other researchers to follow. Back in 2003, Bob and Peg Leiendecker extended their kind hospitality while I researched through NATEODA's World War II document collection. "EOD Bob" has since remained in touch over the years, contributing answers to my technical questions or checking on proper dates. I would also like to thank Ron Felton Jr. for arranging my first meeting with the Leiendecker family.

Two senior NATEODA members, Henry "Bud" Englehardt and Fred J. Puckett, also served under Kane during his latter career in the 1950s. They shared their membership rolls, which allowed me to contact many other World War II disposaleers. At this point, I would also like to salute the late Lt. Col. Walter "Wally" Korsgard, as well as Captains W.G. "Scotty" Calder and Guenther "Gunner" Froebel. If I have neglected to mention any other NATEODA members who contributed to this long-term project, then I must apologize in advance for my oversight.

Through NATEODA's channels, I also exchanged calls and letters with Col. Kane's two daughters, Mary Jo Romba and Kay Levering. Through them, I learned at least two of the "Nine's" wives were still living in 2003-04. Dorothy Parsons and Alice Nass each gave their blessings to my endeavor, on behalf of their late husbands, Col. Frank Parsons and Lt. Col. Wally Nass. I should also like to recognize Maria W. Feldman, widow of Lt. Col. John E. Feldman, O.B.E., for sharing details about her husband's friendship with Kane. Sadly, Maria passed away in 2007.

Perhaps the most enigmatic member of the "Nine," Richard "Dick" Metress left no known children, and his wife, Anita, has vanished from the historical record. However, over the years, I have chipped away at the stone, aided by Dick's living relatives in New Jersey and Virginia. Dr. Patrick Metress, Dick's cousin, contributed general details about life in Pearl Ridge, while Carol Carlo, Metress' niece, provided some insights into their immediate family. Maybe, one day, we will know the full story.

I successfully defended my thesis in 2004, and my panelists; David Dorondo, James Lewis, and Gerald Schwartz, recommended expanding it into a full book. By that point, I had participated in the Barnes Club Conference at Temple University, where the late Russell F. Weigley offered some encouraging commentary. While at West Virginia University, Elizabeth Fones-Wolf encouraged me to write a seminar paper on Vietnam EOD, which may someday come to light. WVU also prepared me to become a well-rounded military history instructor. I would like to thank my history department mentors, especially Liz Fones-Wolf and Maj. Charles D. Dusch (presently at the USAF Academy) for this honor.

After completing my doctorate in 2009, I returned to this project anew. Having signed a publishing contract with Cambridge Scholars Publishing, I could spend more time developing my short chapters on North Africa and the Mediterranean Theater. At this point, I relied on Lt. Col. Richard W. Walkup, a career officer who had served in North Africa, Sicily, and Italy in the 235th BD Company before its reorganization into separate squads. I also solved the mysterious October 1943 disappearance of Walkup's commanding officer, Capt. F. H. Dillon. I would also like to thank Maj. Ed Dillon (USAF) for his insights about the Dillon family.

Bomb disposal in the Pacific Theater has proved the most challenging subtopic, owing to imperfect record-keeping and long distances between field units and headquarters. During the Aleutian Islands campaign, T/5 Clarence Fulcher endured Alaska williwaws and Japanese attacks as a bomb disposal technician. I would like to single out the whole Fulcher clan for sharing their stories with me. Before his death in 2010, T/5 Ernie Neeper happily discussed his island-hopping across the Southwest Pacific. In summer 2011, I contacted Ernie's squad commander, 1st Lt. Carmel "Carl" Cirocco, who helpfully cleared up my lingering questions regarding his mission on Luzon in the Philippines. I would like to thank Carl and Alex Cirocco for their kind support. I also would also like to salute Capt. George "Clifford" Sarauw's surviving relatives for sharing pictures and documents concerning his final mission in the Ryukyu Islands.

My book would never have bounded over its last hurdles in 2011 without the timely efforts of three fellow EOD historians. Jim Clifford has already received honorable mention, but I would like to thank him once again for contributing a thoughtful afterword on Kane's legacy. T. Dennis Reece, author of *Captains of Bomb Disposal*, selflessly loaned his Ordnance documents and photographs from his father's personal collection. Capt. Thomas R. Reece served with the Ninth U.S. Army Air Force, and his experiences have inspired me to incorporate the Air Force's bomb disposal history, broadening my original scope significantly. Lastly, I would like to recognize Mike R. Vining and Donna Ikenberry. Mike, a retired sergeant major, has devoted much of his time to obtaining and scanning historical documents and photographs related to EOD history.

And finally, to cut a lengthy acknowledgement short, I would like to credit my editors and publishers at Cambridge Scholars Publishing for their professional help on my first book. I would also like to thank the National Archives and Double Delta for several last-minute photographs. Finally, I would like to thank my wife, Jennifer Beck, for her support.

Jeffrey M. Leatherwood 3/31/2012

# POSTSCRIPT

Since the first publication of *Nine from Aberdeen*, new efforts to memorialize fallen World War II disposaleers have been spearheaded by the National EOD Association. Moreover, Lt. Col. Robert Leiendecker has released his long-awaited sourcebook on WWII bomb disposal operations from 1940 to 1949, which includes many rare photographs. Once more, I am indebted to Bob for his permission to add new pictures to this book's considerable number of images.

For the upcoming softcover edition, I have also made a few minor revisions without altering the spirit or essence of the original text. Thanks to the CSP team, Graeme Nicol, Chris Humphrey, Carol Koulikourdi, and Amanda Millar, *Nine from Aberdeen* has enjoyed a good first run in hardcover. I am also grateful to my readers, who have helped to spread the word about the heroic U.S. Army bomb squads of World War II.

Sadly, two of the war veterans who were alive at the time of publication, 1st Lt. Carl Cirocco (109th BD Squad) and T/5 Alfred Gardner (12th BD Squad), have since passed on. Instead of altering the book's text to reflect these tidings, I have elected to use this postscript as a reminder to fellow historians. Our cherished "Greatest Generation" is passing all too rapidly, and soon, our Korean and Vietnam War veterans will follow them. We cannot afford to take these soldiers for granted, and their deaths should be taken as clarion calls for renewed interest in traditional military history.

Finally, I would like to announce the March 2013 dedication of a new Kane Hall at Ft. Campbell, Kentucky – now home to the 52nd EOD Group. At this time, I would like to salute all officers, NCOs, and enlisted men responsible for this noble act of historic preservation. I am also humbled to have been instrumental in some small way toward this great accomplishment. Thomas J. Kane's legacy of professionalism, expertise, and cooperation between the services will live on in today's EOD branch.

Jeffrey M. Leatherwood 2/26/2013

# INTRODUCTION

Dating back to the Revolutionary War, the United States Army's Ordnance Corps has governed both arms and ammunition. Over the decades, Ordnance assumed responsibility for researching and designing new instruments for war. During the Twentieth century, the branch came to supervise the manufacture and issuance of military equipment in general. Naturally, in performing their duties, some ordnancemen habitually operated under battle conditions. Two government histories have dealt with the story of Ordnance in World War II. However, this book concerns just one very special Ordnance branch established in 1942. For the next three years, across every combat theater involving Americans, the U.S. Army Ordnance Bomb Disposal services disarmed, removed, and disposed of bombs, artillery shells, and other explosive hazards.[1]

Unexploded ordnance has always posed a hazard in modern warfare, especially after the introduction of artillery shells and landmines with timed fuzes. At first, delayed explosions arose from happenstance. During the Napoleonic Wars, "dud" artillery shells sometimes fizzled out, only to detonate moments later. During the American Civil War, explosive mines were refined by a Confederate officer, Col. Gabriel Rains, whose naval mines became known colloquially as "Rains Torpedoes." However, as the Confederacy crumbled in early 1865, Rains adapted floating mines for ground warfare. Confederate sappers quickly began sabotaging railroads, bridges, and river fords across Georgia and the Carolinas. That April, Union XIV Corps uncovered the first instances of camouflaged "subterra" mines, lurking under driftwood at Sister's Ferry, Georgia. Maj. Gen. J. C. Davis of XIV Corps viewed such tactics as proof of the embattled South's "low and mean spirit of warfare."[2]

During the Franco-Prussian War of 1870-71, German artillery shells and grenades sometimes failed to detonate, creating post-war problems for the French countryside. One period Fleet Street newspaper published *Rural Felicity a la Français*, a humorous anecdote detailing a Parisian gentleman's visit to his country cousin's war-torn estate. Quite alarmed by grim souvenirs from Germany's invasion, the Parisian nonetheless voted his kinsman's residence a fine place to fish for "dead Prussians and *unexploded bombs*." The author has emphasized these last two words.[3]

By World War I, unexploded bombs (UXBs) had become serious concerns, as early aircraft and dirigibles were developed for strategic bombing. Germany's bombers and zeppelins portended a new era over English skies. After several German bombs failed to detonate on impact, British Royal Engineers developed a "low-tech" system of sandbags and controlled detonations. In the trenches, meanwhile, untrained volunteers were often sent to remove ordnance, whether inert or hazardous. Just as the Great War ended in 1918, the Imperial German forces had begun using a variety of delayed-action bomb fuzes, a sign of darker times to come.[4]

The "London Blitz" of 1939-41 marked the origins of "bomb disposal." British authors have since published worthy accounts tracing its early stages of development. However, despite America's unquenchable thirst for World War II culture, U.S. filmmakers and scholars alike have overlooked nearly two thousand men who performed the same tasks for the United States Army. Whereas the British Royal Engineers have justly been immortalized in books, documentaries, television, and even the cinema, the U.S. Army's "disposaleers" are largely forgotten today, despite suffering 10 percent casualties in the European Theater (ETO) alone. Born seventy years ago, their obscure branch became a progenitor of today's Explosive Ordnance Disposal (EOD) services.[5]

*Nine from Aberdeen* presents a cross-section of Army (and Air Force) bomb disposal organizations, from their original conception for national defense to their introduction in all major combat theaters. This book covers a wide breadth of war experiences, but three hundred pages cannot hope to do full justice to the eight original bomb disposal companies, not to mention over two hundred "squads separate" serving across the globe. By highlighting some of the most audacious exploits of these bomb disposal men, I hope to challenge our concept of "war heroes."

Hollywood has long conditioned Americans – even its educated historians – to view World War II through recognizable icons and well-known archetypes, like hard-charging grunts or dashing fighter pilots. Crawling into a muddy shaft to disarm an unexploded bomb might lack the same visual appeal of a lone soldier storming a pillbox on some foreign beachhead. However, ordnance disposal requires a special kind of courage all its own. Since the continental United States never suffered a major bombing raid, citizens scarcely paid attention to their Army bomb disposal services. Domestic activities were mostly limited to instructing civil defense workers and law enforcement agencies. Therefore, most U.S. Army bomb disposal men, together with their brethren in the Navy, realized their fullest potential outside the country. This has continued to be true of EOD service members in all of America's latter-day conflicts.

By 1945, bomb disposal officers and their enlisted soldiers had gained reputations for coolness under fire. At their best, ordnance disposaleers combined the hardiness of infantrymen, the instincts of cavalry scouts, and ingenuity of combat engineers. Quite a number of disposaleers won Bronze and Silver Stars for valor or gallantry under fire, whilst others received Soldier's Medals for averting catastrophes in non-combat situations. Oftentimes, their tough jobs were made even more difficult by "friendly" ordnance, as the Allies began duplicating enemy methods, particularly with regards to delayed-action bombs and aerial mines.

* * *

Nine years in the writing, this book dovetails with *The Hurt Locker*'s controversial victory in the 2010 Academy Awards. Kathryn Bigelow's production professed to show typical EOD technicians in Iraq. Based on technical merits, *Locker* has some verisimilitude. CSM James Clifford, the film's military consultant, served thirty years in EOD. However, many EOD veterans took umbrage over the screenplay's overt characterization of ordnance disposal soldiers as "adrenaline junkies." In all fairness, Clifford later said of his Hollywood experience: "I did not participate in the filming or post-production efforts; I shared ideas but made no decisions." Despite its mixed reception, *The Hurt Locker* has injected EOD into the public consciousness. Now, the time has come for interested readers to assess the Army EOD branch's fascinating origins, peeling back layers of time and challenging popular misconceptions.[6]

Thus, if we reject such Hollywood stereotypes, how then do we explain the sort of man who specializes in such a thankless, hazardous field as ordnance disposal? Nearly all the Army's bomb disposal soldiers were white males, many hailing from industrial Northeastern states, such as New York, New Jersey, or Pennsylvania. But as media programmers should know, demographics alone cannot define a given group of people. Is it perhaps a question of religion? Overwhelmingly, most bomb disposal men belonged to recognizable faiths; Protestants, Catholics, even Jews. During World War II, there indeed were few "atheists in foxholes," or bomb-shafts, for that matter. One bomb squad officer, Edward J. Barry, once described what it was like "down there… looking at a damn bomb… wondering whether it's going to go off when you handle it… you hope *somebody's* looking over your shoulder." Nearer to the mark, perhaps, but as skeptics might point out with some veracity, many other soldiers confronted by danger have expressed similar feelings. So what makes these particular men so special?[7]

Based on their own words, I believe these ordnancemen were motivated by a desire to use their talents in the cause of victory. They were all volunteers who knew what they were getting into. Until Korea, they received no special hazard pay. Yet, they took pride in their work. Each disarmed bomb, every cleared airfield or beachhead represented a small victory. Cpl. Edward Furey (236th BD Company) took heart in doing something "worthwhile" in North Africa. After rendering safe a bombed Corsica airstrip within six hours, 1st Lt. Richard Hughes and his 57th BD Squad felt that they were "actually helping to win the war."[8]

Bill Mauldin, one of America's best-loved war correspondents, walked many of the same battlegrounds combed by Army bomb disposal men. Observing front-line combat soldiers, Mauldin described a "family complex" among such elite groups as infantrymen, paratroopers, and bomber crews. Dangerous professions such as these create tight-knit groups, who engage in all sorts of ribbing and kidding around. However, as Mauldin warned his readers, "no outsiders may join." Using similar terms, a wartime Ordnance magazine profiled its own "rugged breed," bomb disposal men. According to *Firepower*, disposaleers were "an exclusive set" that nevertheless treated "each other like newlyweds." While some soldiers proved their courage by killing their enemies, "bomb killers" showed their best quality when "playing checkers with death." As a historian, I feel strongly inclined to add Army bomb disposal squads to Mauldin's choice list of World War II fraternities, even if they have yet to receive their own *Band of Brothers* treatment.[9]

* * *

This book is chiefly a work of traditional military history, with a few nods toward its academic offspring, "war and society" and "war and memory." But it is not "just another World War II story." Simply put, *Nine from Aberdeen* addresses a long-overdue aspect of that great conflict. Apart from brief mentions in two post-war Ordnance Branch histories, very little coverage has emerged in existing histories concerning these elite specialists. Why is this so? Primary documents from the Ordnance Bomb Disposal School at Aberdeen Proving Ground indicate that the War Department did not fully comprehend the possibilities of bomb disposal, which they envisioned as a stateside defense force. However, unlike their British counterparts, American "disposaleers" mainly fulfilled their missions overseas, where they received less wartime coverage for saving lives. Secrecy also governed their technical operations, based on precedents of German espionage in Great Britain.

We can find other reasons for Bomb Disposal's near-obscurity from surviving unit histories and after-action reviews. In 1943, the Army began replacing cumbersome bomb disposal companies with seven-man teams called "squads separate." Such compact units were routinely overlooked by corps and army commanders, who often credited the Engineers for work done by ordnancemen. Lastly, when bomb squads were not chasing UXBs or retrieving enemy ordnance samples, they were often relegated to basic ordnance tasks, such as ammunition collection.

This writing will hopefully integrate the Army EOD story into military history at large. In World War II, ordnancemen followed the nine Principles of War as recognized by military scientists and most scholars of warfare. Such principles include the self-explanatory factors of Mass, Objective, Offensive, Surprise, Economy of Force, Maneuver (sometimes called Mobility), Security, Simplicity, and Unity of Command.

Thomas J. Kane, the United States Army's "founding father" of EOD, personified the concept of unity in command. There has never been much doubt as to Kane's centrality to the bomb disposal origin story. While still a major, Kane was selected by the Ordnance Department in 1941 to instruct civilians and soldiers in then-current bomb disposal methods. Kane's successes in the continental U.S. persuaded his superiors to place him in charge of an urgent training mission to England in January 1942. Kane then assumed the post of commandant of the new Ordnance Bomb Disposal School, where he recruited a "brain-trust" of innovative officers and promising NCOs based at Aberdeen Proving Ground. Promoted to full colonel by 1943, Kane also carried out important observation missions for the War Department, culminating with a globe-trotting inspection tour of the Middle and Far East. During subsequent visits to the United Kingdom, Kane developed close friendships among the British Royal Engineers, who acknowledged him as their trusted equal. In 1944, Kane reached his zenith as the European Theater's chief bomb disposal officer, answerable to Gen. Dwight D. Eisenhower.

Kane's original detachment, the eponymous *Nine from Aberdeen*, served as the Army Bomb Disposal School's first instructors, developing comprehensive training programs with assistance from their British allies. Using the principle of simplicity, stateside ordnance instructors reached a wide audience of civil defense workers, uniformed servicemen, as well as members of the general public. Later on, Kane's officers set up smaller overseas facilities in England, France, Italy, and even the Pacific Theater, where they instructed other servicemen in recognizing and alerting Ordnance to hazardous items. This new skill, bomb reconnaissance, proved to be a lifesaver in rear areas as well as the battlefront.

Bomb disposal and reconnaissance likewise contributed toward the military principle of security. UXBs and mines had a proven record of demoralizing the military and destabilizing civilian infrastructure. Honing their skills during stateside air raid drills, U.S. Army bomb technicians were noted for their cool reactions during ammunition explosions. Ordnancemen also removed UXBs and mines from rear areas, saving human lives, securing property, and preserving landmarks.

In 1942, the War Department envisioned the standard company as sufficient strength for stateside operations. However, when companies were sent overseas, they were deemed too unwieldy for field operations. In order to free up resources, the Ordnance Department embraced the concepts of maneuver and economy of force. Existing companies were phased out, and separate squads were developed to cover more ground with fewer men and vehicles. Aberdeen Proving Ground organized and trained 219 seven-man bomb squads for mobility and precision.

Three of Kane's original instructors led squads in each major theater of the war. In 1943, Capt. Ronald L. Felton of Pennsylvania deployed with his $12^{th}$ BD Squad in the Mediterranean Theater. In 1944, Capt. Joseph C. Pilcher of New York led the $17^{th}$ BD Squad across France, Germany, and Czechoslovakia. Capt. Richard E. Metress of New Jersey commanded the $209^{th}$ BD Squad during the final Philippine Islands campaign of 1945. Their individual experiences comprise just a few among many instances of sacrifice, dedication, and outright heroism from the hundreds of Army bomb disposaleers who served during World War II.[10]

Usually, a squad deployed to a theater where they remained until the end. However, on a few rare occasions, bomb disposal units would redeploy to a different front of the war. In a modern conflict characterized by bureaucratic administration and large-scale troop movements, few remarked the passing of these seven-man ordnance disposal squads. While it is true that many "bomb killers" never exchanged shots with the enemy, they still performed a necessary and dangerous service to further the war effort. Kane's special ordnancemen enabled the Allied ground and air forces to achieve the goals of mass, offensive, and even surprise. Bomb disposaleers were always willing to provide close infantry support and even acted as auxiliary infantrymen at the "fluid front."[11]

However, "bomb disposal" soon became a misnomer, as aerial bombs represented but a tip of the proverbial iceberg. As a new service, Kane's graduates had to constantly demonstrate their usefulness. In North Africa, they cleared minefields, a task usually delegated to combat engineers. In Sicily and Italy, bomb disposal men searched enemy airfields and towns for booby traps, and participated in assault landings at Salerno and Anzio.

Disposaleers in the Mediterranean gathered intelligence on new Axis weaponry in time for D-Day. Prior to Normandy, bomb disposal men inn England briefed combat divisions on new German mines and explosives. Several squads took part in the first landings and the Allied breakout. Others scouted for V-1 rocket launch sites in the French countryside. By late 1944, Ernie Pyle noted relatively high casualties suffered by the bomb disposal squads since Normandy. Yet such losses were rivaled by those incurred in the Pacific Theater, where shortages of naval personnel often required the Army to fulfill missions without the benefit of specialized naval ordnance training.[12]

*Nine from Aberdeen*'s opening chapter briefly addresses the wartime origins of bomb disposal in Great Britain, plus the mounting need for a similar program in the United States. Even so, Chapter One mainly focuses on the backgrounds and experiences of Kane's training mission to England. Chapter Two describes the U.S. Army's various military and civilian ordnance programs, as well as the Bomb Disposal School's role in preparedness for possible enemy bombardment. Characteristics of both enlisted and commissioned personnel are encapsulated. It likewise summarizes the training, equipage, and other aspects of the U.S. Army's bomb disposal units, who began departing for overseas duty by late 1942.

Chapter Three underscores the lack of bomb disposal support in the opening stages of Operation *Torch*, and the steps taken by Col. Thomas Kane and other Ordnance officers to redress imbalances in North Africa. By the time of Operation *Husky*, the Sicily campaign, bomb disposal units were available in sufficient quantities to make an impact on U.S. Army operations. Early missions in Tunisia and Sicily are narrated by members of two bomb disposal companies and several "orphaned" squads. Eventually, squads replaced companies as the preferred special unit.

Chapter Four picks up these threads with the "forgotten" Italian Campaign of 1943-45. On the peninsula, American disposaleers set a new benchmark by supporting amphibious landings at Salerno and Anzio. Several U.S. bomb squads helped to consolidate the British Eighth Army's advance in Southern Italy during late 1943. Owing to shortages of Royal Engineers, the Yanks were needed to clear Foggia's abandoned hangars and airstrips, which were laced with mines and UXBs. Led by Lt. Ronald "Jobe" Felton, $12^{th}$ BD Squad safely deloused one of the area's largest airfields. They later received Bronze Stars. Foggia later provided significant air bases for Allied bombing raids against Hitler's precious oil fields in Romania. Thus, judicious use of bomb squads enabled the Allies to utilize both mass and offensive against Germany.[13]

Mediterranean-based ordnancemen collected intelligence and weaponry samples that foretold many dangers awaiting the Allies on beachheads in France. Chapter Four shows some rare insights into the daily routines of bomb disposal men at Sardinia and Corsica. While these two islands might sound uneventful, they were by no means inactive outposts. They experienced danger and hardship, as well as camaraderie and even romance. Some units even joined in the follow-up invasion of Southern France before rejoining their brethren in Northern Italy.

Chapters Five and Six cover the entire European Theater, from preparations for Normandy all the way to the Allied crossing of the Rhine. Col. Kane, having conducted two ordnance surveys for civilian and military readiness, went to England in early 1944. He brought with him a cadre of talented bomb disposal officers, including Capt. John E. Feldman, who collaborated with British technicians on the V-1 and V-2 rocket problems. Feldman, regarded as "Kane's Brains," developed portable tools for general Allied use, such as the "Flit-Gun" and the "Rocket Wrench."

Col. Kane went on to supervise a central bomb disposal headquarters, coordinating dozens of separate squads who supported Army and Air Force operations from D-Day to V-E Day. Kane also recognized the need for post-war ordnance removal in Western Europe. Following the liberation of France, he transformed the 234$^{th}$ Bomb Disposal Company into a bomb disposal school at Le Mans for the Free French military. Meanwhile, his field units continued to march alongside infantry, witnessing the Battle of the Bulge and the Roer River campaign.

Capt. Joseph Pilcher's 17$^{th}$ BD Squad shortly after D-Day, actively supporting two U.S. Army Corps during breakouts at St. Lo and Carentan. During the Paris campaign, Capt. Pilcher was awarded a Silver Star for defuzing and clearing an unexploded artillery shell at Vire River. Venturing under enemy fire in near-darkness, Joe Pilcher removed a hazard that would have impeded V Corps' river crossing. In February 1945, Pilcher supported another crossing: 78$^{th}$ Infantry Division's mission to capture Schwammenauel Dam, a strategic German structure controlling the flow of the Roer River. Allied commanders feared the dam might be destroyed, flooding the entire region. As key members of a "T-Section" responsible for removing any demolition charges, Pilcher and his cohorts assaulted the upper dam. They surprised the German defenders, who fought back with a vengeance. Though at least one of Pilcher's comrades suffered battle wounds, the remaining disposaleers ultimately killed or drove off most of the dam's garrison. However, because Capt. Pilcher's "T-Section" was attached to the 303$^{rd}$ Engineer Battalion, Ordnance received very little credit for their active part in this mission.[14]

Chapter Seven encompasses the Pacific Theater, from the first two companies dispatched to Hawaii and Guadalcanal, all the way to separate squads landing on Okinawa, the gateway to Japan. Unfortunately, this aspect of bomb disposal research has been challenged by missing documents and fragmentary accounts. Early on, the War Department's "Germany First" strategy forced the Pacific-based disposaleers to spread out across the theater's various departments. This chapter highlights one overlooked campaign, the Aleutian Islands, where some of America's first bomb disposal casualties occurred. Special emphasis is likewise given to MacArthur's Philippines Campaign, where more wartime information was kept by the $6^{th}$ U.S. Army. Several bomb disposal squads performed errands of mercy for the Filipino people, later receiving citations from a grateful independent government. Japan's *Fu-Go* balloons, launched against the North American mainland, are briefly addressed in this chapter.

One of the notable units serving in the Philippines, the $209^{th}$ Bomb Disposal Squad was one of the last commissioned for wartime duties. Capt. Richard "Dick" Metress, a former training officer at Aberdeen Proving Ground, volunteered to lead this new team rather than sit out the entire war in safety. Metress and his soldiers cut their teeth on Japanese ordnance in the devastated city of Manila. On the still-occupied Southern Philippine island of Mindanao, Dick's team later encountered Japanese depth charges being employed as landmines. Such booby-traps might be detonated by a trigger plate or set off by a Japanese engineer with access to a detonator switch. Despite a lack of training in naval ordnance, Dick Metress and his men bravely cleared the path for U.S. infantrymen during the final campaign in the Philippines. By July 1945, the U.S. Sixth Army managed to surround and capture most of the Japanese defenders on Mindanao, thanks to this courageous handful of ordnance soldiers.[15]

Chapter Eight wraps up the post-war reconstruction efforts in Germany and Japan, examining the relationships between the occupying American disposaleers and their wary neighbors. Both nations had trained bomb disposal technicians of their own. This book concludes with the fates of Col. Kane and his original companions from 1942, and how their legacy has shaped the founding of modern Explosive Ordnance Disposal.

Readers may note only passing mentions of Navy and Marine Corps bomb disposal units. This is not to downplay the contributions of either service branch. United States Army (and Air Force) bomb disposal squads performed a vast majority of ground ordnance operations in World War II, thereby providing the author with the broadest number of case examples. Navy sections were usually limited to ports and vessels, while Marines sent small contingents of disposaleers to the Pacific Theater alone.

Since World War II, "bomb disposal" has evolved to become today's American EOD branch, with overall training supervised by the Navy. Korea and Vietnam marked the modern EOD service's coming of age. Today, EOD removes conventional military explosives from active battlefields, provides national security against terror bombings, and fosters humanitarian goals through the United Nations, such as the U.N. Landmine Commission and other worthy initiatives.[16]

In 1969, Ordnance inducted Thomas J. Kane as one of its first Hall of Fame honorees, citing his fifteen years of leadership in war and peace. Tragically, Kane had passed away four years earlier, but his devoted officers continued to host veterans meetings well into the later decades. As recently as March 2004, the 52nd EOD Group dedicated Kane Hall at Ft. Gillem, Georgia, inviting the colonel's surviving daughters to officiate. When the 52nd EOD Group relocated to Ft. Campbell, Kentucky, they were forced to abandon the first Kane Hall in the wake of base closures. However, in early 2013, plans were announced for a new Kane Hall.[17]

## Notes

---

[1] In World War II, Army Ordnance subsumes not only the ground forces, but also the U.S. Air Force, then under the Army's direction. For more detailed ordnance histories, see the following works: Constance Green M., Peter C. Root, and Harry C. Thomson, *The Ordnance Department: Planning Munitions for War,* Washington D.C.: Department of the Army, 1955; Lida Mayo, *The Ordnance Department: On Beachhead and Battlefront*, Washington D.C.: Department of Defense, 1991. (Charles G. Pritchard, "Ammunition Forward: the U.S. Ordnance Corps at Kunu-Ri, Korea." *Army Magazine*, March 2002).

[2] Maj. Gen. Jefferson C. Davis to Gen. William T. Sherman, 23 March 1865, from *War of the Rebellion*, Vol. 47a, Chap. 59, No. 62; See also Milton F. Perry, *Infernal Machines: the Story of Confederate Submarine and Mine Warfare* (Baton Rouge: Louisiana State University Press, 1965).

[3] "Rural Felicity a la Français," from *Judy, or the London Serio-comic Journal* (Fleet Street, London: Vol. 9, 23 August 1871, 181.)

[4] Paul Deichmann, "Luftwaffe Methods in the Selection of Offensive Weapons, Volume 1," from *USAF Historical Studies*, No. 187 (Manhattan, Kansas: MA/AH Publishing, Sunflower University Press, c. 1985), 5; Ernst A. Marquard, "Luftwaffe Methods in the Selection of Offensive Weapons, Volume 2," USAF *Historical Studies*, No. 187 (Manhattan, Kansas: MA/AH Publishing, Sunflower University Press, c. 1985), Appendix III.

[5] Out of 972 American bomb disposal officers and men actively serving in the European Theater, 111 were killed or seriously wounded during or immediately after World War II. At least 47 U.S. Army officers and technicians are listed on the U.S. EOD Memorial as official casualties, while many others are still awaiting

confirmation. At least fifteen of these soldiers were slain in the Pacific Theater; one of them lost onboard a sinking vessel torpedoed by the Japanese. Incidentally, though some casualties are still officially listed as "missing in action," no records verify BD personnel ever becoming prisoners of war. MIA statistics usually imply no human remains were actually found during or after the war. (Lida Mayo, *The Ordnance Department: On Beachhead and Battlefront*, Washington D.C.: Department of Defense, 1968, 348; Mike R. Vining, *Explosive Ordnance Disposal Memorial – U. S. Army,* EOD Memorial Commission, 9 April 2011; www.eodmemorial.org/army.html.)

[6] One retired Army EOD officer, Robert Leiendecker, criticized *The Hurt Locker* for both its technical flaws and misleading storyline. However, it may have inspired Rep. Ginny Browne-Waite (R-FL) to sponsor a U.S. House Resolution, H.R. 1294, in the 111th Congress. She proposed that the first Saturday in May should be recognized as the National EOD Day, recognizing this "noble and self-sacrificing profession." However, the actual anniversary for Army EOD is February 16, 1942, when the Ordnance Bomb Disposal School began service. (Colonel Olaf P. Winningstad to U.S. Army Ordnance School, memorandum, 19 January 1942; U.S. War Department to the Adjutant General, *Ordnance Training Center General Order #7*, 4 February 1942; *History of Bomb Disposal in the U.S.A,* Aberdeen Proving Ground, 1942, 1-3; Tom Sharman, letters to author, 8 August 2003, 26 August 2003; Kane, *Bomb Disposal School History*.)

[7] Edward J. Barry, interview conducted by G. Kurt Piehler and Shaun Illingworth in New Brunswick, New Jersey, on October 23, 1998, transcript by Shaun Illingworth, Edward J. Barry and Sandra Stewart Holyoak, Rutgers Oral History Archives of World War II.

[8] *Detonator*, newsletter, U.S. Army Bomb Disposal School: Aberdeen Proving Ground, Maryland; 17 September 1943; *Detonator*, newsletter, U.S. Army Bomb Disposal School: Aberdeen Proving Ground, Maryland, 22 October 1943; 57th Ordnance Bomb Disposal Squad (Separate), unit histories, February 1943 to June 1945.

[9] Bill Mauldin, *Bill Mauldin's Up Front,* New York: Henry Holt, 1945, 58; "Bomb Disposal," from *Firepower* (Washington D.C.: Army Ordnance Association, August- September 1945), 8-9.

[10] Pilcher and Felton's names were misprinted slightly in some official documents. This work reflects their proper middle names, and not the incorrect ones used in other ordnance histories. (Thomas J. Kane to U.S. War Department, *Bomb Disposal, U. S. A.*, [unpublished report] c.1942; Ordnance Bomb Disposal School Headquarters, *BD Officer Roster*, 26 November 1942; Ordnance Bomb Disposal School Headquarters, *BD Officer Roster*, 26 October 1943; Ordnance Bomb Disposal School Headquarters, *List of B.D. Officers Assigned to Companies & Staff*, 26 October 1943).

[11] Shortly before CSM James Clifford retired in 2005, the U.S. Army created the Combat Action Badge to recognize soldiers directly exposed to enemy attack in Afghanistan and Iraq. According to Clifford, "many higher level leaders were of the mind that you had to be shot at or get blown up by an IED to get the award."

Senior EOD leaders argued successfully for their branch's eligibility for this badge, reasoning that "an EOD soldier encountering UXO (unexploded ordnance) or IEDs (improvised explosive devices) is tantamount to any other soldier's contact with the enemy." Clifford went further, stating that "if an EOD soldier who successfully defeats an IED is not qualified for the Combat Action Badge, then neither is an American sniper who stealthily kills an enemy soldier." Several years afterward, Jim remarked: "While our soldiers were serving in Iraq and Afghanistan, we were fighting that battle for them back in the States." Clifford humbly credits his one-time commander, Col. Michael J. Davis (52nd Ordnance Group) for the closing arguments that secured this honor for EOD soldiers. (James Clifford, e-mail to author, 16 March 2011.)

[12] Ernie Pyle, "Ordnance Keeps Army in Trim," 10 August 1944.

[13] John Strawson, The *Italian Campaign.* (New York: Carroll & Graf Publishers, 1988), 136-7.

[14] Russell Weigley, one of America's premier military historians, based his account of Schwammenauel Dam upon these incomplete records. (Russell F. Weigley, *Eisenhower's Lieutenants* 603; Hooper, 20-1).

[15] Since World War II, all EOD service personnel have cross-trained in Navy and Air Force weaponry, to prevent future inter-service problems.

[16] The Department of Defense Humanitarian Mine Action provides EOD training for third-world nations like Vietnam, where unexploded ordnance continues to claim lives. In 2001 alone, the U.S. funded $81.8 million toward international programs. Nevertheless, the United States has yet to ratify the United Nations treaty banning antipersonnel mines. Moreover, the Bush and Obama administrations have resisted all international calls to cease manufacture and sales. The U.S. possesses the third largest stockpile in the world, remaining a major exporter of landmines. (http://www.icbl.org/lm/2002/appendices/unmas.html)

[17] Edward Brock, "Ordnance Group Gets New Hope," from *Clayton News Daily.* (Clayton, Georgia) 5 April 2004.

# CHAPTER ONE

# FIENDISH DEVICES

During the wintry first days of 1942, four British officers departed from Liverpool in a Norwegian freighter, escorting two crates of special equipment, cryptically marked "BDSE – PQ - NY." Their swift vessel, destined for New York City, went unescorted in order to avoid German "Wolfpacks" prowling the North Atlantic. After a lengthy undeclared naval war against marauding U-boats, the United States had finally entered the Second World War. Sixty years later, Thomas D. Sharman recollected an atmosphere of excitement in England after the news from Pearl Harbor: "It was obvious that America would come into the war." For the past year, Capt. Sharman had been stationed at Coventry, one of the hardest-hit cities during the London Blitz. Serving with distinction as executive officer for No. 9 Royal Engineer Bomb Disposal Company, Tom Sharman had traveled to London that December to receive his new duty assignment. He had brashly announced to his superiors: "I would like a posting to Hollywood!" Sharman later wrote: "Imagine my surprise when I was ordered to go to the U.S.A. to instruct them in Bomb Disposal." [1]

Tom Sharman already knew Maj. Geoffrey H. Yates, the Royal Engineer selected to head their secret training mission to the States. While a captain, Yates had commanded No. 2 Bomb Disposal Company in London's Balham district. Tom shared his cramped ship quarters with John Hudson, an affable scientist-turned-soldier that Sharman affectionately described as a "brilliant boffin." Capt. Hudson, who represented London's Unexploded Bomb Committee, was indeed a brilliant inventor, whose technical skills had saved the lives of many. Capt. John W. Draper rounded out this team of British bomb experts destined for the United States. They were known on both sides of "the pond" for their "outstanding records" in bomb disposal operations. On September 30, 1941, Maj. Yates and Capt. Sharman had both received the George Cross, a medal awarded for gallantry on the home front.[2]

Yates and his comrades were not only experts in their specialized field, but survivors as well. A newly commissioned lieutenant sent to command any given bomb disposal section in Great Britain had a life expectancy of perhaps ten weeks. By late 1940, Royal Engineers bomb disposal personnel had sustained 123 deaths and 67 injuries related to German bombs. Now, four members of this elite brotherhood had been sent to impart their knowledge to their newest allies, the United States Army. T/Sgt. Bob Kuehner, one of their American trainees, never forgot his British instructors, who often told stories about fallen comrades who "paid the price so that we could learn from their experience." Sergeant First Class Sam Hooper, one of the Army's first ordnance disposal historians, later hailed these Britishers as "the forefathers of EOD as we know it."[3]

For the next seven months, Yates and Sharman helped to set up both the U.S. Army's and Navy's Bomb Disposal Schools, replicating much of the success achieved at Harper Barracks. The four Royal Engineers were accompanied by three enlisted men, known in British parlance as sappers. Meanwhile, nine U.S. Army ordnancemen would receive personal instruction in England from seasoned veterans of the "London Blitz." Thereafter, as qualified instructors themselves, Maj. Thomas J. Kane and his eight colleagues would return to Maryland, supervising a new Army school responsible for training eight special ordnance companies, over two hundred bomb disposal squads, plus thousands of civilian agents supervised by the Office of Civilian Defense (OCD). With the dawning of 1942, America would shortly become a major player in the "UXB War."[4]

* * *

In a sense, Germany had commenced the "UXB War" as early as 1932, when an ambitious technical engineer, Herbert Erich Ruehlemann, brazenly patented his new ECR (Electrical Condenser Resistant) fuze designs in London. Ruehlemann's prospering corporation, Rheinmetall-Borsig, had gained some notoriety during the late 1920s for illegal weapons testing in Stalinist Russia, in violation of the Versailles Treaty. Ostensibly known for its calculators and typewriters, Rheinmetall subsequently became indispensable to the Nazi Party as a manufacturer of aerial weaponry. As the Nazi Party grew in power, Luftwaffe officers began placing greater emphasis on the development and testing of new aerial ordnance, including bombs, mines, and rockets.[5]

Despite a forced ban on German military aviation, Weimar attachés attended foreign air exhibitions, most notably England's Hendon Air Display and the Salon Aeronautique at Paris. Armed with schematics, German industrialists and military engineers secretly began to test planes and bombs in cooperation with the Stalinist government in Moscow. Gen. Paul Deichmann of Germany's II Air Corps later rationalized his nation's rearmament program as a valid response to the growth of Poland after 1926. Deichmann argued that Germany had not considered going to war against Great Britain until the latter's own rearmament after the Sudetenland Crisis of 1938. Even so, Germany's longstanding desire for revenge over the humiliating Versailles Treaty is so well-established; Deichmann's post-war justifications should be taken with a grain of salt.[6]

While the Treaty's provisions "restricted" development of offensive air weapons, the small but active German military skirted compliance through funding private corporations. Businessmen such as Herbert Ruehlemann were natural converts to the Nazi Party, in complete control by 1934. Col. Leslie E. Simon, a U.S. Army ordnance researcher, later characterized pre-war German industries like Rheinmetall as duplicitous organizations who openly manufactured peacetime goods while quietly developing munitions and fuzes for the growing Nazi war machine.[7]

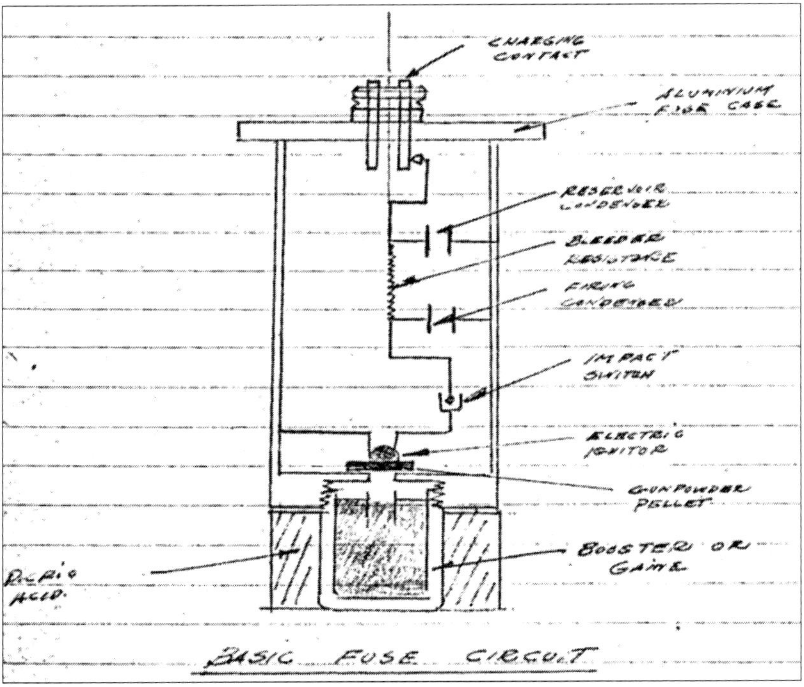


Standard German ECR bomb fuze circuit. (*Original Sketch by Walter Nass*)

During the Spanish Civil War (1936-39), Herbert Ruehlemann's technicians acted as "military advisors" to General Franco's divisions. Luftwaffe bombs incurred thousands of civilian deaths at Madrid, Guernica, and Barcelona. Germany's intervention gave Rheinmetall a chance to test their patented ECR clockwork fuze against live targets. Noting a timing malfunction in German bombs, Rheinmetall decided to exploit this ostensible mistake, refining the delayed-action principle in order to maximize panic and uncertainty. Ruehlemann's lethal discovery quickly won encouragement from none other than Hermann Göring, Hitler's chief confidante and head of the Luftwaffe. Over the years, Göring bankrolled Rheinmetall to design more unorthodox bomb fuzes.[8]

Under Nazi rule, German arms makers were subordinate to military control. Thus, Rheinmetall-Borsig fell under Göring's Head of Weapon Development; Engineer-General Ernst A. Marquard, who acted as liaison with Luftwaffe High Command. Herbert Ruehlemann enthusiastically paired his innovative fuze designs with Marquard's bomb prototypes, a partnership that would bedevil Germany's foes during the coming war. Several other German corporations also devoted their energies to fuze and bomb design, including the infamous I.G. Farben. Marquard answered directly to General Field Marshal Milch, who held dual offices as the Nazi Secretary of State and Chief of the Technical Office. Unlike his harmonious relationship with Ruehlemann, it seems Marquard frequently had clashes of opinion with the self-important Milch, a fact not lost on Marquard's colleague, Gen. Paul Deichmann.[9]

By 1939, delayed-action bomb fuzes had become a significant component of German air doctrine. While impact fuzes were initially designed for live targets, delay fuzes produced "maximum effect" against buildings. Gen. Deichmann described the overall purpose of delay fuzes: "to harass the enemy beyond the time of attack." Luftwaffe Service Regulation No. 16 went into further detail, citing "confusion and paralysis" resulting from the distribution of delay fuzes over "wide areas." Luftwaffe regulations further absolved every Luftwaffe officer, wing commander and downward, for employing such "special weapons."[10]

Deichmann also acknowledged the psychological impact of designing larger bombs, as well as more powerful bombers to deliver them. However, the most feared German bomber of 1939-40 was undoubtedly their smallest – the Ju 87 "Stuka" dive-bomber, which had special "Jericho Whistles" or "Trumpets" installed to create "infernal noises" when closing for the kill. Listed on the following page are bomb payload statistics for the Luftwaffe's chief workhorses during World War II.[11]

| German Bombers of World War II | Limited Range (1939) | Full Range (1944) | Max. Load (c. 1944) |
|---|---|---|---|
| **Dornier 17** | 2,200 lbs. | 2,200 lbs. | 4,400 lbs. |
| **Heinkel 111** | 4,400 lbs. | 4,400 lbs. | 4,400 lbs. |
| **Heinkel 177** | never used | never used | 12,000 lbs. |
| **Junkers 87 "Stuka"** | 1,100 lbs. | 3,300 lbs. | 3,960 lbs. |
| **Junkers 88** | 2,200 lbs. | 4,400 lbs. | 6,600 lbs. |

When Hitler ordered the invasion of Poland, Marquard's division possessed six standard bomb designs, weighing anywhere from 2.2 kg (4.5 lbs.) to 1800 kg (4,000 lbs.). Three types were commonly used against the West; the SC (*Spreng Cylindrisch*), SD (*Spreng Dickenwand*), and PC (*Panzerdurchschlag*) bombs. SC bombs were general purpose projectiles, built with thin steel walls for high-speed payload delivery. Early SC models suffered from poor ballistics. SD bombs were thicker-walled and streamlined for precision attacks against lightly armored and solid concrete targets. As their German descriptor implies, PC bombs were mainly directed against heavily-armored targets, such as tanks or ships. Such aerial weapons were further divided according to their tactical uses: *general-purpose* bombs against normal structures; *armor-piercing* projectiles against heavily-reinforced structures; *incendiary* charges against inflammable or combustible targets; *anti-personnel* mines and fragmentation bombs to inflict civilian casualties and to otherwise demoralize the enemy's rear-echelons.[12]

Most German bombs were painted sky blue, with different color markings to help Luftwaffe personnel identify their own ordnance. During the "UXB War," these cryptic German symbols became recognition aids to the Royal Engineers. British sappers even developed cheeky nicknames for nearly every bomb they encountered. Germany's largest general-purpose bomb, a behemoth weighing two tons, became known as a "Satan," while another 1,000 kg model was dubbed a "Herman," as it reminded some of Air Marshal Göring's corpulent profile. Semi-armor piercing bombs of comparable sizes and weights were given such code-names as "Esau" and "Fritz." After 1941, American ordnance specialists adopted the same terminology to describe German bombs, which greatly aided cooperation with Royal Engineers in the field.[13]

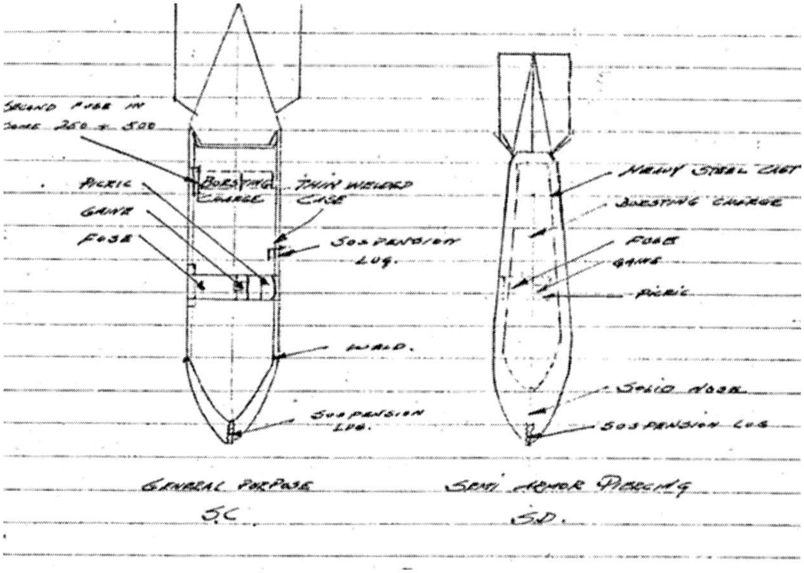


Cross-sections of two basic German bomb designs, the SC (general purpose) and SD (semi-armor piercing). (*Original Sketch by Walter Nass*)

| Color Coding of Luftwaffe Bombs[14] | Purpose or effect of Luftwaffe Bombs |
|---|---|
| **Red Ring x1** | Flash Bombs |
| **Red Ring x2** | Intensive Incendiary |
| **Red Stripe** | Fragmentation / General Purpose |
| **Yellow Stripe** | High Explosive |
| **Yellow Stripe x2** | Major Charge |
| **Blue Stripe** | Armor Piercing |

Much space has been devoted to firebombing in academic circles, predictably castigating the Allies for employing such weapons over German cities such as Dresden and Hamburg. However, few scholars have noted that, toward the end of 1918, the German Air Force had proposed an unparalleled incendiary raid on London. Such a raid would have unveiled a small yet destructive electro-incendiary bomb, the B-1(e). However, the German Army objected to the risks, citing their "militarily hopeless situation." Large stockpiles of these small bombs were destroyed after the First World War without ever being tested against an enemy city. However, Gen. Deichmann felt "certain that large fires could [have been] be started by dropping it *en masse*." By 1939, the B-1(e) was updated with a secondary explosive charge used to distribute the incendiary filling over large surfaces. Apart from spreading the flames, B-1s "endangered personnel endeavoring to extinguish the bomb." Such incendiaries were first used against Warsaw, Germany's first target of Blitzkrieg.[15]

Months before the Allies began direct bombardments over Germany, Luftwaffe Command had already planned and executed the first so-called "retaliation attacks" against weakly-defended Allied cities, such as Rotterdam. Wing headquarters sent orders describing the intended target, kinds of attacks, and types of ammunition to be utilized. Gen. Deichmann quoted German regulations governing the selection of ordnance, which stressed the "intended effect on morale as well as the types of building construction used in the cities that are to be attacked."[16]

Firebombing became an effective ploy throughout the Luftwaffe's reign of terror over Western Europe in 1940. By dropping their payloads over wooden buildings standing "close together," bombardiers could create a "sea of flames," given enough fuel and favorable winds. Ordnance makers introduced two more incendiary designs in 1940, Flam 250 and Flam 500, two forerunners of the napalm bomb. Unlike the two-pound B-1s, Flams resembled SC bombs, but contained a foul-smelling mixture designed to ignite over wide spaces. Early on, Royal Engineers let firefighters handle most incendiary bombs, but sometimes, firebombs contained time fuzes. Such variation in tactics "increased confusion and complicated the salvage, cleaning up, and fire extinguishing operations," according to Luftwaffe doctrines. Naturally, such tactics were adopted and refined by the Allies for retaliatory purposes as the war developed.[17]

* * *

During the summer of 1940, Hermann Göring's Luftwaffe launched unprecedented terror bombings against the British Isles as a precursor to

Adolf Hitler's "Sea Lion" invasion plan. Recalled as the "London Blitz," these falling German bombs presented a double threat to Great Britain. Britons emerging from their air raid shelters discovered another menace: unexploded bombs. UXBs quickly became a serious concern to Downing Street, as they directly endangered the citizenry while paralyzing vital services. In 1940, the incoming Prime Minister, Winston S. Churchill recorded his thoughts concerning "large numbers of delayed-action bombs… widely and plentifully cast" across the British Isles. Churchill saw "long stretches of railway line, important junctions, vital factories, airfields, [and] main thoroughfares, denied to us in our need." Back in 1918, Churchill had been impressed by news of the first German delayed-action fuzes discovered at Zeebrugge, Belgium. As he judged it, such bomb fuzes were "a most effective agent in warfare, on account of the prolonged uncertainty it creates. We were now to taste it ourselves."[18]

As early as November 1939, Royal Engineers had recovered their first unexploded German bombs from the Shetland Islands. Naturally, fuzes were keys to disarming any given explosive ordnance. Upon examining four Type 15 fuzes extracted from these bombs, the Ministry of Supply quickly developed a special wrench, called the Crabtree Discharger. Clamped over the fuze, it discharged its circuitry and permitted the officer to unscrew it from the fuze pocket. However, this victory proved short-lived. Swiftly, the Luftwaffe introduced a new Type 25 fuze, equipped with sensitive electric plungers designed to set off the bomb whenever touched by the Crabtree wrench. When several officers lost their lives in this fashion, the Royal Engineers assumed German spies were to blame.[19]

In fact, Ernst Marquard's initial armaments research benefited from Nazi sympathizers, or "fifth columnists." More frequently, however, well-meaning British newspapers also gave away technological details, hoping to boost morale during the "Blitz." Most likely, this explains why the Crabtree Dischargers came to Germany's notice so quickly. After the war, Marquard confessed his awareness that the "English government [had] soon realized the threat of our unexploded bombs… [so] every attempt was made to foil [their] measures." Ultimately, Germany's munitions makers introduced over thirty time-delay fuzes, implements for Marquard's self-described "guerrilla war with bombs."[20]

Marquard's colleague, Gen. Paul Deichmann, likewise extolled the psychological effects of delayed-action fuzes. Operating under loose guidelines and broader parameters, Luftwaffe armorers would set bomb fuzes at random intervals before each Blitz mission. Hence, some bombs were coupled with impact fuzes, whilst others employed clockwork delay fuzes. Deichmann underscored his branch's deliberately vague guidelines concerning ammunition and fuzes, which served to spread culpability for deliberately targeting civilians. While Air Marshal Göring might issue personal orders to use "special weapons," ordnance decisions typically rested upon lesser squadron officers who commanded the actual raids. T/Sgt. Bob Kuehner, a U.S. war veteran and researcher, later professed that the Luftwaffe enjoyed "playing mind games with the Brits."[21]

Deichmann and Marquard both articulated their policies for a postwar U.S. Air Force historical study. While Deichmann repeatedly sought to dilute the blame for deliberately targeting civilians, the clinical Marquard accepted responsibility for "research and development of all bombs for the Luftwaffe." "As a rule," Marquard explained, "all bombs were delivered through [his] supply channels fully equipped with fuses [sic]." More expensive items, such as long-delay or "nuisance" fuzes, had to be "especially requisitioned." Reich Marshal Göring repeatedly upbraided commanders for wasting these "highly valued" bombs on secondary targets, such as enemy airfields. However, the psychological impact of larger bombs remained a fixed idea, from senior officers like Deichmann all the way down to wing commanders. Delayed-action fuzes also seem to have added some spice to routine bombing missions as well.[22]

Writing to his War Secretary and the Minister of Supply in September 1940, Winston Churchill felt "rapid disposal of unexploded bombs [to be] of the highest importance." As Prime Minister, he saluted both civilians and soldiers who "pressed forward for [this] deadly game." Civilian Defence Force engineers dealt with early UXBs, but Germany's innovative but insidious fuzes required a new specialist branch to evolve within military circles. Given their demolitions skills and tunneling expertise, Royal Engineers were logical candidates to track down and unearth unexploded bombs, and twenty-five Royal Engineer Bomb Disposal (BD) companies were mobilized to counter the UXB threat.[23]

During the winter of 1940-41, many Britons distinguished themselves, from Spitfire pilots to air raid personnel, but Prime Minister Churchill fluently recalled the stoic sacrifices of bomb disposaleers, who often "ran twenty, thirty, or even forty courses, before they met their fate." Whenever the Prime Minister sallied forth from Downing Street, he observed the efforts of Royal Engineers clearing bombs from London. Noting the frequent use of certain words in the press, he opined that the adjective "grim" should be "reserved for the UXB disposal squads."[24]

Under joint civil and military authority, twelve UXB Command Centers scoured the United Kingdom for real or suspected German bombs. Answerable to a brigadier in charge of Army bomb disposal operations, Regional Commanders (RCs) set categories depending on threats to morale, production, transportation, or communications. Category A-1 required a bomb to be immediately cleared regardless of risks, while Category A-2 allowed for emergency destruction *in situ* (in place). Category B incidents were handled after 96-hour periods, allowing fuzes sufficient time to wind down. Category C reports were less crucial, sometimes taking more than a week to resolve. Bombs falling in sparsely populated regions often fell under this heading. Lastly, Category D bombs could be removed as time allowed. Lower categories were often handled by auxiliary bomb disposal (ABD) units or volunteer groups.[25]

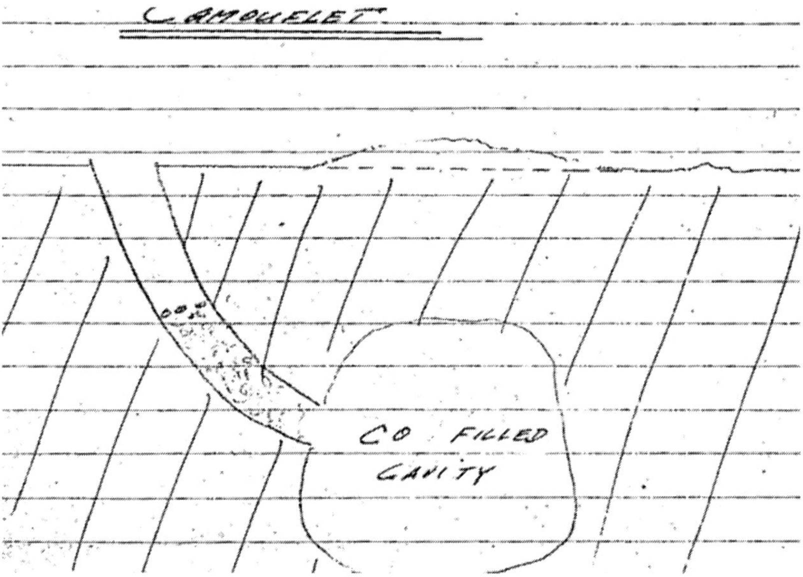


Sketch of a camouflet often filled with deadly carbon monoxide gas, the telltale sign of a subterranean bomb explosion. (*Original Sketch by Walter Nass*)

Guided by category reports, Royal Engineer Bomb Disposal companies often detached smaller field sections to resolve multiple incidents. Physical evidence, such as fin fragments, oily black deposits, and bomb craters, were important factors for determining threat levels. Air Raid Patrols (ARP) were trained to spot telltale clues, identify UXB crash sites and secure them from curiosity-seekers and souvenir hunters. ARP wardens made good reconnaissance agents, but jumpy observers sometimes called in false alarms. After receiving their assignment, enlisted Royal Engineers, known as 'sappers,' probed for UXBs. Even this preliminary task presented hazards; German bombs occasionally detonated underground, creating pockets of deadly carbon monoxide gas known as a *camouflet*. Barring such mishaps, the section's sergeant identified bomb fuzes and recommended countermeasures to the section officer, who disarmed the actual fuze.[26]

British procedures for UXB identification and disarmament produced a national defense blueprint later utilized by the Americans, but with one major exception: civilian involvement in handling explosive ordnance. Britain's demands for total mobilization required an increased level of public cooperation. Though many Royal Engineers shared the same skepticism as their American cousins, British industrialists formed voluntary Auxiliary Bomb Disposal (ABD) units to patrol London sectors. ABD units even received "A" or "B" qualifications by the British Army. "B" teams performed basic reconnaissance and excavation tasks, while "A" teams helped the Royal Engineers with the actual removal of bombs to dumpsites, known colloquially as "bomb cemeteries."[27]

"A" teams became technically proficient with UXBs, but civilian volunteers became a source of discord after calamity befell one famous group. Several writers have rightly praised the so-called "Holy Trinity," headed by the eccentric Twentieth Earl of Suffolk and Berkshire, Charles H.G. Howard. Following graduation from Edinburgh University, the youthful Earl combined his scientific gifts with a flair for espionage. In May 1940, Suffolk successfully escaped from France with many valuable documents. Shortly afterward, the Earl joined the Ministry of Supply as one of its Directors of Scientific Research, specializing in German bombs and fuzes. Suffolk's trio included his young secretary, Eileen B. Morden, and his able chauffeur, Fred W. Hards. For almost an entire year, the "Holy Trinity" tracked down UXBs with "urbane and smiling efficiency," to use Churchill's own expression. Sadly, on May 12, 1941, Suffolk's thirty-fifth mission "claimed its forfeit" in the Erith Marshes of Kent. A leftover German 250 kg specimen detonated at his bomb cemetery, killing all three "Trinity" members and several soldiers. Lord Suffolk posthumously received the George Cross.[28]

Following Charles Howard's untimely death, the Ministry of War tightened restrictions for direct handling of explosives by ABD teams. While "A" teams were still permitted to deactivate ordinary impact fuzes, they were instructed to call Royal Engineers whenever they found larger German bombs, particularly with fuzes marked with 17, 25, or 50. During the Blitz, one 1100 lb. SD-500 threatened the famous St. Paul's Cathedral. Lt. Robert Davies and his "merry men" safely disarmed it on September

12, 1940. For rescuing a historic landmark from probable destruction, Davies and one of his doughty sappers, George Wylie, received the first George Cross medals. Sadly, Davies fell from grace shortly thereafter, court-martialed and cashiered over property theft. His medal was auctioned decades later, while Wylie's medal was donated to St. Paul's.[29]

By early 1941, two more fuzes had entered bomb disposal's lexicon. Type 17 clockwork fuzes jammed upon impact, only to resume their countdowns whenever shifted or moved. Thus, while tackling a dreaded "17 fuze," bomb disposal officers could never be certain of its timing. Stevens Clock-Stoppers, huge electromagnets, were developed to disrupt the ticking fuze. Touted in newspapers as a breakthrough in the "UXB War," clock-stoppers were duly reported to Berlin by Axis spies. Quickly, Type 17 fuzes were reconfigured to detonate when touched by magnets, but the Royal Engineer developed the impact wrench. This pulley-driven invention allowed the disarmer to coax the troublesome "17" fuze from its pocket while maintaining a safe distance from the bomb.[30]

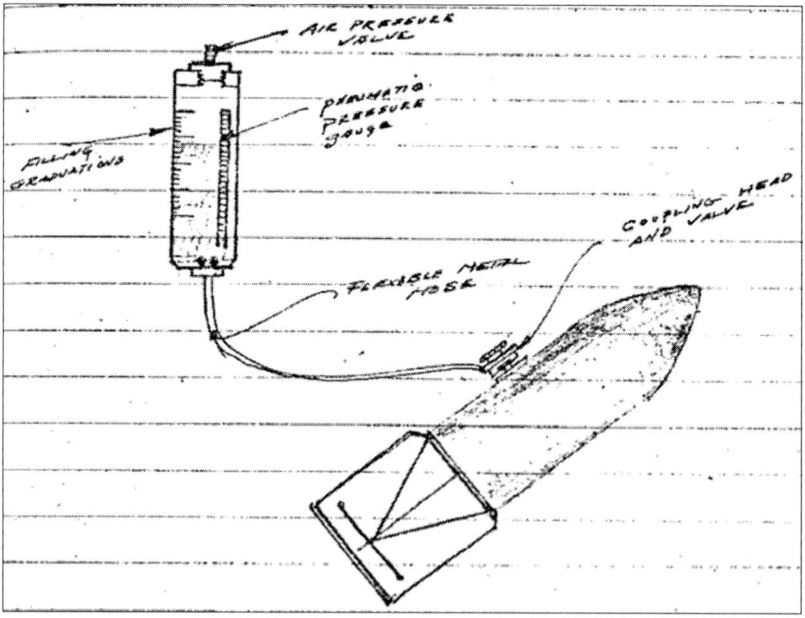


Capt. John P. Hudson designed this liquid discharger to counteract the Type 50, a bomb fuze using mercury as a highly sensitive conductor. Unwary sappers could set off the bomb by merely jostling it. (*Original Sketch by Walter Nass*)

Type 50 fuzes were capable of killing entire sections of disposaleers. UXBs often had to be rotated to allow the sergeant to identify any fuzes. But like Type 17s, such movement agitated the Type 50's components, in this case, mercury beads. Mercury, a liquid metal, is also conductive, and sudden jolts set off the fuze. Specially-angled mirrors were developed for indirect examination of all bombs. Eventually, Prof. John P. Hudson countered the "mercury tilt switch" with a liquid discharger; his life-saving invention resembled a bicycle pump with an oversized syringe.[31]

However, the most dangerous "fuze" introduced by Marquard's team actually was not a fuze, per sé. Instead, Zus-40 anti-withdrawal circuits were attached to the fuze base, or *gaine*, acting as a second detonator. Unlike British or American bombs, most German fuzes were set into the casing, rather than the nose or tail. Thus, Zus-40s could appear with any fuze design, and could not be identified until contact broke with the gaine. However, when this occurred, the whole bomb detonated instantaneously. Royal Engineers came to see Zus-40 as a personal strike against them.[32]

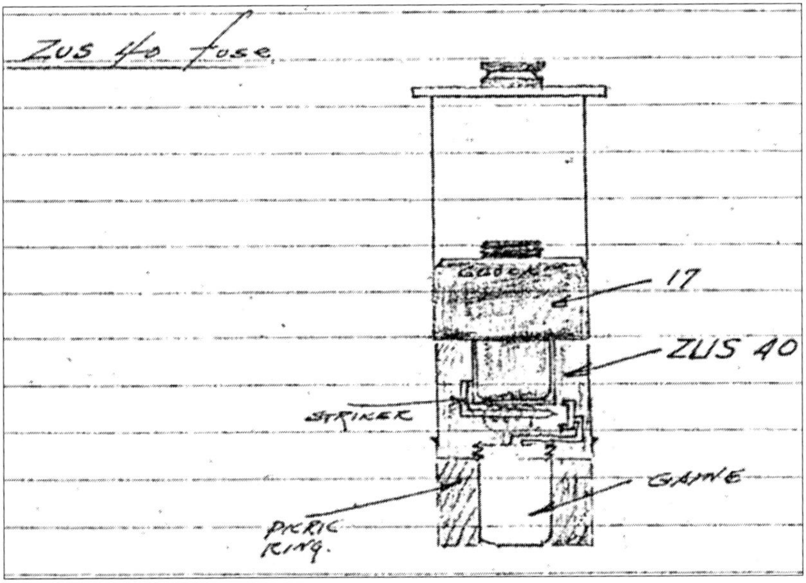


Germany's Zus-40 anti-withdrawal circuits were equipped with strikers that detonated the entire bomb when a bomb disposal officer unwittingly broke the connection. Since it was virtually impossible to detect, every UXB had to be considered armed with a Zus-40. Eventually, the Allies discovered means to sterilize the Zus-40's circuitry. (*Original Sketch by Walter Nass*)

In 1941, a number of courageous officers paid the supreme price tangling with the Rheinmetall Zus-40 circuit. UXB Committee members placed a priority on cracking the Zus-40. Scientists started by melting a suspect bomb's outer casings with acid. Then, using Capt. Hudson's steam sterilizer, they liquefied its contents. But this method worked imperfectly against Zus-40s, which began to carry secondary charges. Late in 1941, serendipity visited one Capt. Archer in South Wales. Bravely tackling a UXB near a burning oil refinery, B.S.T. Archer discovered an intact Zus-40 device, which had fallen out of its gaine. Blessing his good luck, Archer sent it to his superiors, and the UXB Committee analyzed the Luftwaffe's handiwork. Shortly before his departure for America, Prof. John Hudson had developed a bulky vacuum pump to flood Zus-40s with liquid plastic. Conquering the Zus-40 represented a great coup for the Royal Engineers.[33]

Thus, for every new fuze type introduced, the Royal Engineers developed countermeasures, some of which were superseded in turn by German technology. Gen. Paul Deichmann attributed these circumstances to a "constant developmental flux" arising between Germany's "offensive media" and Great Britain's "defensive methods." Luftwaffe doctrines warned that such "new inventions… might introduce complete changes in the combat conditions in the course of a war." Deichmann also stressed the element of surprise when employing new ordnance, warning about "disastrous consequences" when armaments research and development "cannot be kept secret." Yet, by the time John Hudson had solved the Zus-40 conundrum; British security had redoubled to the point where Marquard never learned about this success. This, perhaps, remains the most valuable lesson the British learned from their German enemies – a lesson they would shortly pass on to their American allies.[34]

When the first Americans came under British instructorship in February 1942, they were granted opportunities to learn under wartime conditions. This fact would lend an air of gravity to the proceedings. From May 1940 to September 1941, the Royal Engineers had developed a rigorous training program at RAF Melksham, Wiltshire. However, one year before the Americans arrived to study bomb disposal methodology, the Royal Engineers had permanently moved their BD school to Harper Barracks, located at Ripon, Yorkshire. Here, the Yanks would learn all the known German fuze designs, using tools heretofore exclusive to British bomb disposal services. Meanwhile, four visiting British officers would establish similar training facilities for both the U.S. Army and Navy. Through this important series of Allied exchanges, modern Explosive Ordnance Disposal servicemen can trace their professional ancestry.[35]

While U.S. President Franklin D. Roosevelt fought a public battle to overcome his nation's isolationism in 1940, his administration prepared for defense of its skies and coasts. Responding to fears of preemptive raids on New York or Washington, Roosevelt's May 20 executive order created the Office of Civilian Defense (OCD) with nine regional offices across the North American continent, corresponding with the nine Defense Commands. Integral to this joint-service network, the War Department saw increased opportunities for researching and designing new military hardware. Army and Navy reservists were activated for their respective Ordnance branches. Two national defense bills injected $1.5 billion into ordnance research, with earmarks for modern bombs and explosives.[36]

By March 1941, American sympathies had shifted perceptibly toward England, shown by Congressional approval of Lend Lease policies. Arms shipments for Great Britain's defense had doubled since the fall of France. Such material aid cloaked deeper, at times clandestine, negotiations between the two English-speaking governments, starting that previous January with the American-British Conversations (ABC). Shortly afterward, U.S. military observers began trickling into England to establish new strategic partnerships. One of these agents, Maj. Gen. James E. Chaney, had been hand-picked by the Army's brilliant Chief of Staff, George C. Marshall. Having observed the Battle of Britain in 1940, Chaney understood Britain's ordeal far better than did most Americans. However, while the United States remained officially neutral, Chaney's Special Observer Group (SPOBS) in London had to remain undercover. For their pre-war mission in England, SPOBS members wore no uniforms; yet, their presence among Germany's chief foes betrayed Washington's growing realization that their days of neutrality were numbered.[37]

Initially concerned with defending America's new outposts in the North Atlantic, Coffey's SPOBS Group paved the way for future coalition warfare. One of Chaney's staff, Lt. Col. John W. Coffey of Ordnance, reported to the U. S. War Department on technical developments within the British Ministry of Supply, including general details on the mounting "UXB War." Maj. Gen. Chaney had personally selected Coffey as his ordnance expert, sidestepping the Chief of Ordnance, Maj. Gen. Charles M. Wesson. However, Wesson offered no complaint, because Coffey, one of his trusted officers, also served the Ordnance Corps as its eyes and ears. By mid-1941, Wesson had authorized the U.S. Army's first program for a defensive war against unexploded German bombs.[38]

Based on Ordnance doctrine, air-to-surface bombs were divided into three categories: poison gas, incendiary, and high explosives. Explosive bombs and shells fell under direct control of Aberdeen Proving Ground, with instruction handled by the Ordnance Training Center (OTC), established in 1921. However, since 1940, Edgewood Arsenal had indoctrinated state policemen and fire marshals in poison gas and fire bombs at their own Chemical Warfare School (CWS). Well before their Ordnance counterparts, CWS officers had glimpsed a new military objective: ensuring national survival during a global conflict. Unexploded bombs, targeted against civilian sectors in Great Britain, might someday be utilized against the United States. Chemical Warfare officers deserve much credit for fostering a spirit of cooperation with Ordnance, avoiding unnecessary friction between two technical services.[39]

In April 1941, Ordnance and Chemical Warfare agreed to pool their resources at Edgewood Arsenal. Yet, Gen. Wesson and his staff officers registered their concerns that high explosives should remain the province of military experts. Thus, civil defense and military personnel required separate ordnance training programs at Edgewood. Even so, Chemical Warfare Service believed that uniformed bomb experts, especially officers, would be "listened to more respectfully" by civil defense agents. Maj. Gen. Wesson concurred with this opinion, as did his Chief Training Officer, Brig. Gen. Julian S. Hatcher, who selected one of his best training officers to improve Edgewood Arsenal's course on explosives safety. Thomas J. Kane, a gregarious Army major in his early forties, boasted an "extremely advantageous" background in civil engineering.[40]

* * *

Thomas Joseph Kane's formative years reveal an early burden of responsibility, spurred on by a strong dedication to his family. Born on March 31, 1900 to Irish Catholic parents in Punxsutawney, Pennsylvania, T. J. Kane grew up as an only child. His father, Thomas C. Kane, had been crippled by a paralyzing stroke in 1898, leaving his wife Catherine as the family's sole provider. As an industrious teenager, young Thomas Joseph worked for Carnegie Steel, eventually becoming a yard inspector at Homestead, site of the famous Pennsylvania strike. In September 1918, Kane registered for the Selective Service. However, as a vital war worker providing for a disabled father, Kane seems to have received an exemption from active military service. Shortly after his father's death in January 1919, T. J. Kane left Carnegie Steel to find a better-paying daytime job as a railway clerk. By 1920, Kane had begun attending regular evening classes at Carnegie Institute of Technology. His busy schedule also included a four-year commitment with the Reserve Officer Training Corps (ROTC), which helped substantially to pay for his education.[41]

Thus, when Kane graduated in 1924, he emerged as a second lieutenant. However, the isolationist Coolidge administration held very few prospects for a newly-minted Army officer with a widowed mother. While retaining his Army commission as a reservist, Kane opted to become a railway engineer; by 1930, he was yardmaster for the Buffalo, Richmond, and Pittsburgh Railroad. Entering his thirties during the Depression, Capt. Kane commanded two Civilian Conservation Corps (CCC) camps, and he oversaw the construction of a third installation. During a public gathering in 1934, sponsored by the CCC in New York, he met Margaret Goodman, and they married in the next year.[42]

Brig. Gen. Julian Hatcher (center right) at the Ordnance Training Center in January 1941. Maj. Thomas J. Kane is standing to Hatcher's left. (*Kane Collection*)

As war shadows loomed in 1940, the U.S. Army activated Thomas J. Kane's reserve commission, and his small family moved to Aberdeen Proving Ground. At age forty, Maj. Kane's towering build, intense blue eyes, and silver-blond hair distinguished him from fellow officers. Initially, Kane served as Aberdeen Proving Ground's provost marshal, vigilant for errant G.I.s who stayed out past curfew. Kane seldom raised his voice, but often left a strong impression. Toward the end of his first year at Aberdeen, Kane received a new appointment to Brig. Gen. Julian Hatcher's headquarters at the Ordnance Training Center. At the OTC, Kane gained a reputation for taking personal responsibility, upgrading defective equipment or improving training standards. As an instructor, Kane often cultivated promising officers and enlisted men. Kane also demonstrated a restless, analytical mind throughout the war.[43]

However, as a reservist serving among West Point graduates, T. J. Kane's career still languished. According to Kay Levering, her father "hated the politics of his job, but gave 150 percent to those who believed in him." One West Point officer who truly believed in Kane's potential, Brig. Gen. Hatcher, nominated the major for his first instructorship at Edgewood Arsenal. In April 1941, Kane began teaching a select group of ten officers and enlisted men, devoting seventeen course hours on high explosive bombs and practical safety countermeasures. At first, Kane's syllabus followed pre-war Ordnance manuals, G-2 reports, and bomb data gleaned by SPOBS in London. Kane and his assistant, Capt. G. B. Garrett, took steps to widen their outreach, adding six more courses at colleges in Texas, California, and Illinois. Aided by four junior officers and about twenty-five enlisted men, Kane and Garrett expanded audiences to encompass state policemen and emergency responders; ultimately, their mission reached 466 leading civil defense agents chosen from 37 states.[44]

Meanwhile, the Ordnance Department pressed for stronger military control over U.S. bomb disposal training, recognizing potential risks to national security. On September 9, 1941, Maj. Gen. Wesson proposed Edgewood Arsenal should transfer its new bomb disposal program to a permanent site at Aberdeen Proving Ground. OCD leaders opposed Wesson's proposal, under the shaky premise that, since bombs primarily created fires, they were best handled by local fire departments outside military installations. Countering the OCD's latent mistrust of the Army, Wesson shrewdly used civil defense language to buttress his own arguments versus civilians handling potentially unpredictable UXBs: "Every detail of delayed-action bomb disposal is hazardous in the extreme, and requires the utmost in skill, caution, and discipline."[45]

Maj. Gen. Wesson also believed extreme secrecy would be needed to safeguard technical information from potential German espionage – an opinion based upon sound British precedents. However, this impasse between the Army and OCD lingered for weeks, until Pearl Harbor settled the question permanently. On December 12, 1941, the War Department resolved two jurisdictional controversies: bomb disposal training and technical operations. Adjutant General Emory S. Adams granted Wesson's request, returning complete authority over unexploded bombs to Ordnance. However, as a gesture toward the Office of Civilian Defense, Adams ruled the OCD could still select its own candidates for bomb disposal courses held at Aberdeen Proving Ground, Maryland.[46]

Under the Joint Board ruling, the Army now controlled military reservations and all overseas theaters, whereas the U.S. Navy's bomb and mine specialists handled coastal regions and island outposts. The Army Corps of Engineers and Chemical Warfare Service both promised to cooperate with Ordnance. Under military supervision, the OCD held authority to locate and remove incendiaries in continental zones only.[47]

T.J. Kane at the time of his selection for training. (*Leiendecker Collection*)

During this same meeting, Maj. Gen. Adams endorsed the creation of two discrete Ordnance Bomb Disposal Schools for the Army and Navy, responsible for indoctrinating "suitable bomb disposal units" and implementing civil defense training. Asked by Maj. Gen. Wesson to recommend a suitable commandant for the Army's school, Brig. Gen. Hatcher immediately put forward Maj. Thomas Kane, based upon his effective performance as a bomb disposal instructor, as well as his proven ability to collaborate equally with military and civilian organizations. But, despite these decisions, the U. S. Army lacked experience with delayed-action bombs, and the best available instructors were across the Atlantic. Ordnance staff officers proposed a direct exchange of personnel.[48]

On December 8, even as Gen. Wesson still debated with OCD leaders before the Joint Chiefs of Staff, Lt. Col. Wingate Reed wrote to his supervisor, Col. Hugh S. Minton: "There is no question [that] the Ordnance Department will be made responsible for training both military and civilian personnel." With this certainty, Lt. Col. Reed recommended that the Ordnance Department should "jump the gun and… send a cadre of recommended personnel to London for the Bomb Disposal Course, so that a program may be established here without delay."[49]

On December 9, the British Military Attaché's office in Washington received a secure telegram from Col. Minton, requesting a joint personnel exchange – one of the early examples of a "special relationship" that subsequently emerged between the United States and Great Britain. Minton's bold proposal invited a team of Royal Engineers to design the Army and Navy ordnance disposal programs. Meanwhile, hand-picked American soldiers would travel to Ripon, Yorkshire, receiving firsthand training under the tutelage of experienced Royal Engineer instructors. Coordinating with London's Foreign and War Ministries, Pentagon officials swiftly arranged for a small contingent of four British Army officers, escorting two sets of top-secret technical equipment. One set of tools went to Aberdeen, while the other was destined for the Navy Yard.[50]

Shortly after this arrangement, the U.S. Army received a tentative agreement from London to exchange personnel with the Royal Engineers. Yet, the War Ministry would not consent to a direct exchange until Washington promised to restrict UXB intelligence to military personnel. On December 12, the same day Gen. Wesson won his arguments for full military control over bomb disposal, London formally agreed to host Kane's delegation, broken into two parties to avoid scrutiny. Both detachments were scheduled for a minimum stay of three months.[51]

Maj. Kane's upcoming training mission to Great Britain reflected a much larger commitment between the two allies, previously established by Lt.

Col. Coffey's SPOBS organization. Back in London, Coffey's group quickly established a provisional Ordnance section, and sent home for their Army uniforms. Coffey's staff began sending British manuals and lectures back to Maryland. Some difficulties arose due to their unfamiliarity with the British supply system. Unlike the Ordnance Department at Aberdeen Proving Ground, which handled all U.S. Army field equipment, British requisitions were channeled by the Ministry of Supply to individual army branches, such as Ordnance or Engineers. During this interval, a comparable Royal Engineers liaison had been set up in Washington D.C., with direct access to the Bureau of Ordnance.[52]

Just before Pearl Harbor, the Navy had contacted the British attaché concerning possible bomb disposal training. However, this proposal had nothing to do with upstaging the Army's program. Several months earlier, the Washington Navy Yard had established its first mine disposal school, so expanding into bombs made perfect sense. Moreover, one Navy Lieutenant, Draper L. Kauffman, had served a year with the Royal Navy Volunteer Reserves as a UXB disposal officer. Shortly after Kauffman's return in November 1941, Adm. William Blandy had requested his services to helm the U.S. Navy's Ordnance Bomb and Mine School.[53]

Lt. Kauffman had only lately accepted this post when Japanese bombers assailed Pearl Harbor. Scenting an opportunity to learn about Japanese naval ordnance, Kauffman traveled personally to Hawaii with special permission, arriving at the central island of Oahu on December 13. Two days later, an unexploded bomb was found near Schofield Barracks, partially buried near the wreckage of a Japanese plane. "Beautifully and carefully machined," this bomb weighed about 540 lbs., with "very simple and very efficient" fuze and bomb assemblies. This specimen proved to be a major find, because hitherto this stage, "no prior information was available on Japanese Bombs or Fuzes."[54]

While some accounts credit this early mission as Kauffman's alone, original reports indicate it was a joint service effort from start to finish. Two warrant officers from Army Ordnance dug up and removed the bomb to a "deboostering barricade." Kauffman later commended L. J. Unertle, U.S. Army, for his "coolness, courage, and common sense" while actually defuzing the bomb *in situ*. Kauffman further praised his three Navy aides for their "courage and resource," acknowledging that "any move they made might set off the bomb." Fortunately, this UXB turned out to contain only a simple delay fuze with no booby traps evident.[55]

Shortly after successfully retrieving the first American UXB, Draper Kauffman took his prize bomb back to Washington for "educational purposes." After the Army and Navy's bomb disposal schools had a glimpse at "Susabelle," it became a mascot for the Navy Bomb and Mine School. Kauffman convened the Navy's first bomb disposal class on January 14, 1942 – preempting the Army's program by just four weeks. Six months afterward, the Navy's Ordnance Bomb and Mine School relocated to American University for the war's duration.[56]

John E. Feldman. (*U.S. Army Ordnance Hall of Fame*)

Building on the existing spirit of teamwork between Army and Navy Ordnance, 1st Lt. John E. Feldman (1909-1995) helped to organize Washington Yard's Navy training facility. Feldman remained for some weeks as a guest instructor, working alongside the team of British instructors led by Maj. Yates. John Feldman would prove to be another notable personage in EOD's formative history.

John Feldman began his military career in 1933 with the Colorado National Guard. While still a civilian, he worked as an electrician through the Great Depression. Rising through the ranks in the peacetime military,

Feldman received his reserve commission as an infantry officer by December 1936. Feldman's marksmanship record was remarkably high. However, John's career stalled at this point, and he remained a second lieutenant for five long years. In late 1941, during Camp Polk's Army Maneuvers, Feldman's jury-rigged 60mm "stovepipe mortar" impressed several Army bigwigs, who promoted him to first lieutenant and sent him to Ordnance on January 29, 1942. Feldman proved a natural at bomb disposal, but arrived too late to join Kane's party.[57]

Sent to Hawaii, Lt. Feldman spent the entire summer of 1942 educating thousands of civilians and servicemen, who learned to report "potentially dangerous items." John Feldman's amiable nature and conscientious efforts impressed Army and Navy officers alike. On two occasions, Feldman became personally involved with ordnance problems. After being notified by Filipino farm-workers, the Army lieutenant personally disarmed a live Japanese depth charge, dropped prematurely in a sugarcane field. Meanwhile, Chief Gunner's Mate Robert "Ike" Eigell had recovered a Japanese "dud" from the U.S.S. *West Virginia*; a 16-inch armor-piercing bomb weighing 800 kilograms. With "Ike" Eigell's invaluable cooperation, Feldman removed the bomb's fuzes, sending the UXB back to Maryland for further examination. Feldman and Eigell's teamwork paved the way for a future Army-Navy ordnance partnership. Rising eventually to Navy commander, Robert Eigell would become an important figure in joint-service EOD training after World War II.[58]

John Feldman's four-month visit to Hawaii also provided the U.S. Army and Navy Schools with several much-needed samples of Japanese aerial ordnance. Thanks to Feldman and his Navy counterparts, U.S. bomb disposal instructors could now contribute toward an Allied victory against Imperial Japan. A brief survey of the Army Bomb Disposal School's training syllabi reveals a noticeable expansion in Japanese bomb and mine identification. Upon Feldman's return to Maryland in August 1942, the Army school's course sections on "Jap Objects from Air" expanded from three to six hours – a degree of knowledge comparable to the Ordnance Training Center's existing seven-hour block of instruction on German and Italian ordnance. This precious technical information, along with subsequent discoveries concerning Japanese weaponry, would be shared with British and Commonwealth forces engaged in the Pacific. Almost immediately after the Kane mission to England, the Americans had begun to repay their generous British comrades.[59]

U.S.S. *West Virginia's* 800 kg Japanese UXB. (*Vining Collection*)

For the upcoming Kane mission, Brig. Gen. Julian Hatcher chose eight candidates from the Ordnance Training Center to accompany the major. As Kane had already been selected as future commandant of the Army School, he presumably enjoyed some input toward the final list of four officers and four non-commissioned officers, selected from among the Army's finest engineers, technicians, and munitions experts. With Kane, these specialists comprised the original "Nine from Aberdeen."[60]

First, Kane recruited a trustworthy executive officer: Harry M. Walker (1898-1961). A stocky major with a brush-thin moustache, Walker knew Kane as a fellow Punxsutawney native. Besides his longstanding friendship with Kane, Walker was a first-rate civil engineer with real combat experience, serving first as a private in the 10th PA National Guard in the 1916 Punitive Expedition. After leaving Mexico, Cpl. Walker shipped out to France with the 103rd Combat Engineer Battalion, which saw action in three French campaigns: Meuse-Argonne, Second Marne, and St. Mihiel. Returning to college in Pennsylvania shortly after the Great War, Harry Walker gained his reserve commission in 1924.[61]

Kane also chose three reservists for other key positions in the school. 1st Lt. Frank A. Parsons (1907-1989), handpicked to serve as Kane's training director, had graduated in 1937 with his commission from Cornell University. Following his activation, Frank Parsons had relocated with his wife Dorothy to Aberdeen, becoming good friends with the Kanes. Meanwhile, 2nd Lt. Walter R. Nass (1913-2002), a 1940 honor graduate from the University of San Francisco, arrived with his young wife, Alice, early in 1941. "Wally" Nass, whose clear and precise technical notes were an asset to Kane's mission in England, had been tapped to head the new Army Bomb Disposal School's experimental section. Another senior lieutenant, William W. Prichard (1907-99), attended BD training in Great Britain, but later transferred out of the bomb disposal branch. Sometimes, BD officers became inactive, electing to transfer to other Ordnance services for better promotions. Owing to bomb disposal's specialized nature, promotions above the rank of major were extremely rare during World War II. Until recently, few EOD officers surpassed the rank of lieutenant colonel in the U.S. Army.[62]

Maj. Kane's section also included four promising ordnance sergeants. Master Sgt. Arthur E. Keller and Staff Sgt. Ronald L. Felton were selected from 40th Ordnance Training Company, owing to their munitions expertise. Richard E. Metress and Joseph C. Pilcher, both technical sergeants, were chosen from Kane's staff at the Ordnance Training Center. Each noncom who took part in the British program had already been earmarked as potential "mustangs," officer candidates promoted from enlisted ranks. In 1942, the U.S. Army had a shortage of junior officers, owing to the force's small number of professionals. Given the working-class backgrounds of most enlistees, bomb disposal offered a rare chance for such advancement. Art Keller graduated Officer Candidate School (OCS) shortly after returning from England, while Felton, Metress, and Pilcher received their commissions by 1943.[63]

Born in 1915, Richard "Dick" Metress has regrettably left behind few written traces for historians to follow. His Catholic immigrant parents, Thomas Francis and Ethel Lamoreux, were married in 1907 at St. Margaret's Church, in Pearl River, New York. Tom soon relocated his young family to Bergen County, New Jersey, where he held a machinist's position at Dexter Folder Company, a factory specializing in bookbinding machines. Over three decades, Dexter employed several Metress clan members. As a boy, Richard attended public schools in Park Ridge, Bergen County, as did his three siblings, John, Ethel, and Mary. Tom and Ethel's children also grew up in the Roman Catholic tradition.[64]

Sometime after 1920, Dick Metress lost his father to as yet undetermined causes. Exempted from wartime service in 1917, Tom last appears in census records as a skilled worker at Dexter Folder Company. However, by 1930, Ethel had remarried a Swedish immigrant, Hiram Elliott, a cab driver who fathered four more children. Dick lived briefly with his mother's new family, and remained in touch with his youngest sister, Mary Olive. Richard also maintained close ties to his father's clan at Dexter, where he worked part-time until graduating high school.[65]

Census data confirms that Metress began service prior to April 1, 1935. His first duty station, Fort DuPont, was located in Newcastle County, Delaware. In 1940, Richard was a junior non-commissioned officer based at Delaware Ordnance Depot. By early 1941, he was a tech sergeant serving with Maj. Kane at the Ordnance Training Center.[66]

Close-up from a 1941 OTC Headquarters Company group photo, left to right: T/Sgt. Joseph Pilcher, T/Sgt. Richard Metress, and a third Ordnance NCO standing next to their company commander, Maj. Thomas J. Kane. (*Pilcher Collection*)

At Aberdeen, Richard Metress befriended the quiet and reserved Joseph C. Pilcher, a fellow ordnance sergeant on Maj. Kane's OTC staff. Born November 21, 1915, Joseph Charles was the fourth of six children born to Henry and Anne Pilcher of Fabius, New York. Shortly before the Great War, both parents and their two eldest sons, George and Tom, had emigrated from Kent, England. Living in the New York countryside, Henry sometimes worked on the state highways, while his family operated a small but prosperous livestock farm. All six children pitched in, engaging in chores when not attending public school in Fabius.[67]

Joe's childhood was marred by a 1927 accident involving his older sister, Julia May. One day, as she fed hay to the livestock, Julia slipped from the scaffold and landed on a pitchfork handle. Sadly, the teenager's pelvic injuries turned septic within days, and she died in the local hospital. This traumatic event left its mark on young Joseph, who as a grown man, was not given to horseplay or rambunctious behavior. As a result, "Big Joe" also became very protective of his younger sister, Mary, and his kid brother, Jesse, who remained the closest of his six siblings.[68]

"You could say I had a case of hero worship," Jesse Pilcher recalled; "Whenever Joe made a run to Syracuse, I went with him." Joe graduated Fabius High School in 1932, but he could not afford college tuitions. Faced with unemployment, Joe signed up for the Civilian Conservation Corps in 1934. Working at Muscle Shoals, Tennessee for six months, Pilcher helped to provide for his family. Seeing another part of the country may also have inspired "Big Joe" with wanderlust; shortly after returning from Tennessee, he took off once again in his old Model A.[69]

Jesse Pilcher remembered a sad day of departure: "I thought he was just taking another ride, but Joe told me I couldn't go this time." Ranging westward, Joe worked some odd jobs in Nebraska before proceeding to California. On the West Coast, Joe found more part-time work, but he eventually had to sell his beloved Model A. In 1935, he returned to New York aboard a freight train. Returning to work in Fabius as a full-time truck farmer, Pilcher still found time enough to complete his electrician's correspondence course at the Coyne School of Chicago. While this might not have carried the same weight as a college degree, it would come in quite handy when the U.S. Army began to step up its recruitment.[70]

Like many patriotic American youths in 1939, "Big Joe" Pilcher first considered military service when Great Britain girded for war against Nazi Germany. Pilcher's English heritage may also have awakened a strong desire to fight Hitler, a sentiment that only gathered momentum as Germany's armies overran Poland and threatened his parents' former country. Over sixty years later, Jesse could still remember Joe's earnest face as they discussed the possibility of his enlistment while driving out to visit the spectacular New York World's Fair of 1939.[71]

On May 22, 1940, just one month before the French Army collapsed under Blitzkrieg, Joseph Charles Pilcher volunteered for the U.S. Army, swearing his oath in Syracuse, New York. Stationed at Mitchel Field, Pilcher completed his basic training with distinction, earning weekend pass privileges over the summer. Unlike Metress, who directly entered Ordnance after basic training, Pilcher's classification was delayed for some weeks. Consequently, he remained in garrison at New York City.[72]

Jesse recalled visiting the 1940 World Fair with his graduating class that August. On that happy occasion, Joe drove out to see him, sporting his new Army uniform. Standing at six feet, with bright red hair and piercing blue eyes, Joe Pilcher looked ruggedly handsome, perhaps even dashing. At least one New York girl certainly thought so: Edith Catherine Heim, a vivacious Long Island socialite three years Pilcher's junior. Despite their contrasting family backgrounds, Joe and Edith remained inseparable, even after his posting to Aberdeen Proving Ground that fall.[73]

At this crucial point in his new career, Joe's basic electrician's skills had opened an unexpected avenue for promotion. Faced with personnel shortages on the eve of World War II, the newly expanded Army began recruiting skilled men for the technical branches, including Ordnance. Thus, Joe Pilcher's correspondence training brought him to Aberdeen Proving Ground, where both his maturity and capability became apparent over the coming eight months. By January 1941, Joe was barely twenty-five, but had dramatically risen from private to staff sergeant.[74]

Having enlisted at an advantageous point during his nation's history, Pilcher now entered a wider professional milieu than peacetime America might have offered him. While promotions were temporary under prevalent War Department doctrines, Joe still received a higher pay grade. Moreover, Pilcher excelled as an Army electronics instructor at the OTC. On July 18, he met all requirements for promotion to technical sergeant, and transferred to OTC Headquarters, where he became a valued member of Kane's staff. One group picture dated April 1941 shows Pilcher and Metress standing to Maj. Kane's right. That same December, Kane selected both of these NCOs for special ordnance training in England.[75]

Before his departure for England, Joe Pilcher tied the knot with Edith, who would soon give birth to their first child. Married by Aberdeen Proving Ground's post chaplain, the newlyweds rented a pleasant house in nearby Havre de Grace, Maryland. T/Sgt. Richard Metress likely attended this military wedding as best man. For her part, Edith took pride in her husband's career, preserving letters, pictures, and news clippings. She also became familiar with her husband's colleagues, including Dick Metress, hosting many parties at her home. Following Joe's training in England, they would come to know yet another memorable personality, Staff Sgt. Ronald "Jobe" Felton of Pennsylvania.[76]

Staff Sergeant Ronald L. Felton. (*Frost Collection*)

Kane's youngest trainee, Ronald Lawrence Felton, was born in Warren County on January 20, 1917. Felton's parents, Roy and Dora Simmerline, were both Elk County natives. Ron Felton graduated from Sheffield High School with academic honors. He inherited the nickname, "Jobe" or "Jobey," from his parents. Like Joe Pilcher, Felton's hair was red, but his hunter's eyes were sharp grey. A lifelong reader, Felton's other avocations included listening to swing music and enjoying the outdoors. Before his May 17, 1941 induction, Felton had worked for seven years as a bridge-builder at Central Pennsylvania Lumber. As a result, he went directly into the Army's technical services; otherwise, Jobe's hunting prowess and marksmanship might have qualified him for combat arms.[77]

Private Felton completed basic training at Aberdeen Proving Ground, and proceeded to the Ordnance Department's School of Ammunition in July 1941. While stationed with 40$^{th}$ Ordnance Training Company, Felton's soldierly bearing and devotion to his new profession resulted in his promotion to staff sergeant. Felton's inclusion with Major Kane's training mission resulted from his expertise in munitions. Blessed with exuberance and good humor, Ron Felton proved a perfect counterweight to quiet, pipe-smoking "Big Joe," or "Red," as he became known at Aberdeen. Since Felton also had reddish hair, Pilcher eliminated any confusion by dubbing his wise-cracking new comrade, "Doc."[78]

* * *

With Maj. Kane's "Nine from Aberdeen" selected among the most promising Army Ordnance personnel, their departures took place on two separate dates. On the night of January 4, 1942, Kane and Walker's party departed Aberdeen Proving Ground by the main Pennsylvania Railroad. Kane's group also included Wally Nass, Art Keller, and Dick Metress. Flying aboard a chartered Pan-American clipper plane, code-named "Dixie," Kane's entourage landed early on January 6 on the British-controlled island of Bermuda. Kane subsequently reported to Bermuda Base Command Headquarters, where he discovered that all eastbound passenger flights across the Atlantic had been cancelled because of tightened security restrictions in neutral Portugal.[79]

From their temporary quarters at Castle Harbor, the major related his group's uncertain situation to Lt. Col. Reed via radiogram. "Extra time [will be] used in study [of] organization." Kane assured his superiors; "[I] believe time [will be] saved in end by [studying] British methods and experience" in Bermuda. 2$^{nd}$ Lt. Walter Nass recorded their Bermuda experiences on film, but this media has never resurfaced.[80]

Kane also suggested canceling the second group under Lt. Frank Parsons, if air travel remained an issue. He also considered sending M/Sgt. Keller to Iceland, coordinating with military personnel stationed there. But Gen. Wesson reassured Kane that proper flight clearance to Portugal would be arranged within one week. Harper Barracks also agreed to reschedule training until the diplomatic process took effect.[81]

Kane and Walker toured Castle Harbor's installations over three days. If Kane's party enjoyed the island's lovely beaches, they probably did so wearing winter jackets. For nearly two weeks, the five Yanks awaited diplomatic clearance from Lisbon. Such delays were not uncommon; Lt. Col. John Coffey, Gen. Wesson's London observer, had waited several days in Lisbon that previous May. But unlike Coffey, Kane's two detachments now traveled as representatives of a nation at war with Nazi Germany, whose agents were active in Portugal. With mounting apprehension, Kane and his fellows boarded their January 19 Pan Am flight on the clipper plane "Atlantic."[82]

Fortunately, Kane's passage through the Azores and Portugal proved uneventful. Landing in Bristol on January 21, Kane's exhausted group traveled to London by train, lodging at the Paddington Hotel. On the next day, Kane reported to the U.S. Embassy. But something must have tipped off Portuguese security, because Kane's second echelon met with unexpected difficulty. Great Britain's traditional ally, Portugal, had a troubled relationship with Spain and held deep-rooted fears of Nazi invasion. Now that America had entered the war, Portugal moved to restrict American travel across the English Channel.[83]

Frank Parsons and William Prichard, accompanied by Joseph Pilcher and Ronald Felton, departed for Lisbon on January 26. Prior to their plane's takeoff, Brig. Gen. Hatcher had instructed his four subordinates to wear civilian clothing until they reached England. Dorothy Parsons recalled watching her husband pack several Army uniforms deep within his personal baggage. Traveling in pairs to avoid being marked as U.S. servicemen, they were issued diplomatic passports by Gen. Wesson.[84]

Stopping at Bermuda, Parsons' party set off once more for Lisbon on January 28. But Portuguese security uncovered their secreted American uniforms, and promptly arrested the four Americans, pending further action. Parsons and his cohorts could be interned as potential spies, meaning they could be turned over for questioning by Nazi agents. Fortunately, all four men were released after serving a short detention in the airport; their U.S. diplomatic passports had effectively cloaked their secret military mission to England. Lt. Parsons and his men left Portugal three days later, but their narrow scrape put them even further behind.[85]

Meanwhile, as Kane waited to hear news from Lisbon, he met his official British sponsor, Philip Neill. A major in the Royal Engineers, Neill had recently concluded a visit to America. Neill recommended his new guests remain in London, observing his city's bomb disposal branch in action, while Royal Engineers rescheduled their technical course at Harper Barracks for early February. On January 25, Kane's group spent their first Sunday in England visiting blitzed areas across London. Throughout their stay, the Americans witnessed similar scenes in Birmingham, Coventry, and Belfast, Northern Ireland.[86]

On January 28, Kane's echelon visited the Hammersmith Odeon to view a bomb disposal training film. Later imported to America, *UXB* reenacted examples of possible bomb situations, with emphasis on their negative effects on civilian morale and infrastructure. Following the screening of *UXB,* Kane's party observed No. 24 Mobile Bomb Disposal Company during a training exercise at Polytechnic Stadium. To overcome maneuvering problems in heavily blitzed urban areas, the Royal Engineers designed motorized bomb disposal companies that could be temporarily broken down into smaller units to handle multiple sites.[87]

Two such companies had been developed by Lt. Col. T.H. Capron for rapid responses during the London Blitz. Unlike static Royal Engineer companies, these lighter units consisted of four detachable sections, 120 men in total. Capron had suggested to Kane that his system might best serve U.S. military needs. Kane also interviewed Major R.H. Minty, whose personal experiences in London had left him with certain misgivings about such motorized units. As a former company officer, Minty had fielded many requests for more personnel, because mobile field sections had one-third less manpower than standard platoons (22 to 31).[88]

On January 29, the Americans witnessed German UXBs "laid to rest" by detonation at Richmond Park's "bomb cemetery." Kane's group also received some preliminary training at the Royal Geological Museum, using the Royal Engineers mobile instruction van. On February 1, Lt. Parsons' group landed in Bristol. Departing King's Cross Station two days later, Kane's two parties finally reunited at Harper Barracks.[89]

* * *

When Kane's party first began training that February, they were greeted by Lt. Col. Steven H. Fisher, the Harper Barracks commandant. While Fisher confessed his unfamiliarity with the U.S. Army's Ordnance training programs, he sagely predicted that Aberdeen Proving Ground's nascent bomb disposal school should address not only German and Italian UXBs, but Japanese explosives as well. At that point, Fisher's school had obtained no specimens from the Pacific Theater, whereas the United States Navy had already retrieved the first UXB from Hawaii some weeks before. With the Japanese already victorious at Singapore and poised to conquer the Philippines, the atmosphere at Harper Barracks could have been too cheery. But these new allies shared a common purpose: victory.[90]

Maj. W.L. Andrews, the chief instructor, expressed his general views on bomb disposal training. Regardless of nation or service branch, all such units required the highest training standards. Andrews stressed the crucial roles played by section leaders. Bomb disposal officers enjoyed reputations for keen professional judgment. Even a lowly lieutenant could supersede higher ranks in matters concerning unexploded bombs. However, this authority came at a price, because incorrect fuze identification could mean a fatal mistake for all concerned.[91]

Capt. Emlyn Jones, chief safety instructor, served as Kane's escort. Jones confidently boasted that British mechanical expertise and safe handling could remove every type of German UXB. Nevertheless, Jones recommended remote demolition of unknown Axis ordnance, rather than take risks. Jones's executive officer, Lieutenant A.B. Waters, emphasized strict enforcement of safety training. For example, he required BD soldiers to wear a thick leather slicker when engaged in UXB operations. On at least one occasion, this custom averted a bomb disposal fatality.[92]

For the next six weeks, the "Nine from Aberdeen" attended a battery of lectures and demonstrations, wherein they were treated like British candidates. Both parties were greatly aided by a shared language and heritage. Metress and Pilcher were both sons of recent immigrants from England, while Kane still had an aunt living in Ulster. They all received rigorous training in bomb categories, render-safe methods, and evacuation procedures. Harper Barracks also featured a model room where trainees resolved hypothetical UXB incidents – anywhere from churchyards to railway station. Easy-to-read charts simplified the bewildering labyrinth of Axis bombs and fuzes. Kane retained a course syllabus for his records, as well as a list of available film strips and other visuals.[93]

Kane's trainees underwent 104 training hours, but only 13 hours were spent on technical briefings. Most of their learning came from practical exercises under field conditions. Joe Pilcher and Ron Felton became intimately familiar with the latest bomb disposal tools, including liquid dischargers and magnetic clock-stoppers. They also learned about bomb reconnaissance, excavation, and safe removal procedures. Following a three-hour written test, candidates were required to disarm a German UXB carrying two live fuzes, a Type 17 and Type 50. [94]

Harper Barracks instructors occasionally enlivened the classroom atmosphere with humorous anecdotes. This laid-back attitude bemused Kane, who was known for his no-nonsense attitude toward explosives. Afterward, Kane mildly criticized the English school for its "loosely drawn" teaching principles, recalling moments where the Royal Engineers had forgotten that they were dealing with relative neophytes. Nevertheless,

Kane held deep respect for his British counterparts, who were, "without exception," qualified bomb disposal experts.[95]

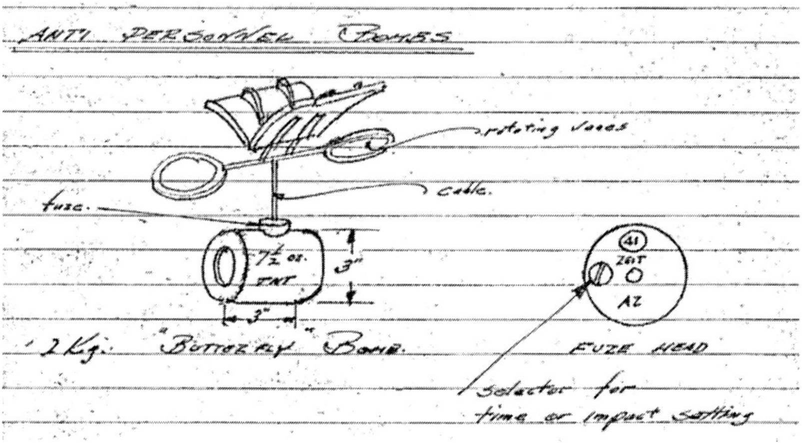


SD-2 *Splitter Bombe*, better known as the Butterfly bomb. At the lower right is a schematic for its timing mechanism and fuze. These devices were considered to be Germany's most dangerous bomb of the war. (*Original Sketch by Walter Nass*)

However, no Royal Engineer considered Germany's "Butterfly bomb" as a laughing matter. At least two of Kane's future cadre members, Felton and Pilcher, would encounter the Butterfly in its unnatural habitat. Considered the deadliest anti-personnel weapon invented during World War II, the *Splitter Bombe* and its many cousins appeared wherever the Luftwaffe prowled, whether in the Mediterranean or European Theaters.

Butterfly bombs have been considered as an example of twisted Nazi German ingenuity. By 1942, the British possessed several early samples of the SD-2, one of which appears prominently in the Nass notebook. Shortly after Kane's return, Aberdeen Proving Ground became fascinated by their design, later adopting them for military use. Yet, by the Germans' own admission, the "Butterfly" prototype came not from the Fatherland, but from occupied France, where stockpiles of two-pound fragmentation bombs had been captured after June 1940. At first, this bomb's underwhelming size failed to impress Luftwaffe High Command, particularly Field Marshal Milch, who decided to recycle an estimated one million of these items for their precious brass fittings.[96]

On the other hand, Gen. Ernst Marquard appreciated its possibilities, particularly against enemy airfields. He took some specimens back to Germany, and by October 1940, introduced the SD-2. Lacking a proper delivery method, Marquard ordered some modifications to the existing AB-50 flare container, typically slung underneath a plane's fuselage. Low-flying fighter-bombers could now scatter as many as 225 SD-2 bombs over grounded planes. However, their uses against "live targets" soon became apparent when the German 55$^{th}$ Bomber Wing first used SD-2s against the British airfield at Ipswich on October 28, 1940. Gen. Deichmann claimed this destructive raid had been executed "in contradiction to orders," but still praised the weapon's "great fragmentation effect," as well as their "time and vibration fuzes."[97]

Huetten Werke had created a sinister device, which the British soon nicknamed the "Butterfly Bomb." Sometimes classed as anti-personnel mines, Butterflies were aptly named for their distinctive twin rotating vanes. Focke-Wulf 190 escort fighters were capable of dropping half a dozen SD-2s from their undercarriages, while heavy bombers carried over two hundred bombs in metal canisters. Upon release, a Butterfly's spinning arms started a time fuze. Following impact, the timer jammed until disturbed. Whether snagged on a phone lines or lying by the roadside, a single Butterfly SD-2 could hurl lethal shrapnel at eighty feet.[98]

Initially scattered over airstrips and hangars, the Butterfly soon enjoyed a widespread reputation as a terror weapon. German pilots euphemistically referred to their SD-2 attacks as "saturation raids." Shortly before Kane's arrival in England, Germany launched a massive saturation raid against RAF Watersham, codenamed *Opera Ball*, with serious injuries among RAF ground crewmen. Worse was yet to come. On June 13, 1943, German planes flew over a seaside town, Grimsby. Within two days, multitudes of SD-2s had killed sixty-six Britons, while inflicting hundreds of serious injuries, mostly to civilians.[99]

Soldiers were likewise exposed to the murderous Butterfly bomb. Luftwaffe raiders used them against Malta in an effort to destroy fighter bases there. During the opening moves of *Barbarossa*, Russian aerodromes were also peppered with Butterfly bombs to deny their use. Gen. Marquard commissioned new models, such as the SD-2a with anti-disturbance fuze. By the time of Hitler's invasion of Russia, Luftwaffe pilots had begun to employ SD-2s to deny cover and inflict casualties on living targets. Gen. Deichmann later described their effects against Soviet infantrymen encamped in a Central Russian forest. Following a saturation raid using SD-2s, "German ground forces could enter… without encountering any resistance – the forest was truly dead."[100]

Italy's air force had played only a minor role in the "London Blitz." However, they were actively deployed against the RAF in North Africa. Early on, the Royal Engineers had determined that Italian bombs represented a lesser threat to Allied ground forces. Firstly, Italian bombs inflicted less damage than their German counterparts; their largest general purpose bomb weighed 800 kg., about one-third the size of a German "Satan." Secondly, Italy's 500 kg bombs were the only ones utilizing time delay fuzes. Having combated Mussolini's minions for two years, the British had identified almost thirty Italian bombs, torpedoes, and mines. Perhaps the most deadly Italian weapon, Manzolini aerial mines were Italy's equivalent to the "Butterfly." Weighing four kilograms apiece, and equipped with faulty anti-disturbance fuzes, Manzolinis were a menace to both sides during the various Mediterranean campaigns.[101]

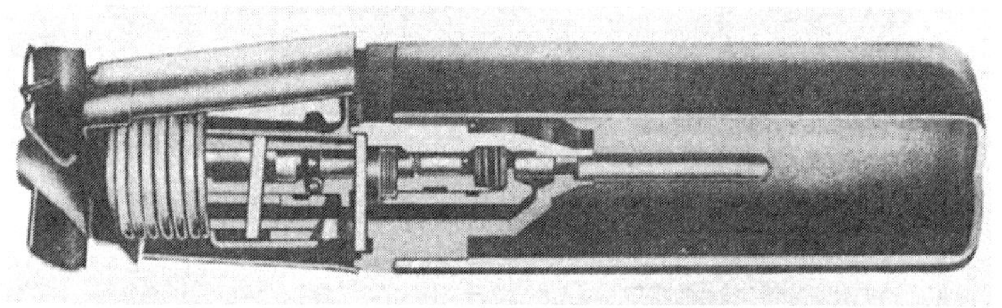

4 kg. Italian Manzolini antipersonnel bombs, also known as "thermos bombs." They were unpredictable even when dormant, and their fuzes could be set for as long as 80 hours. (*Leiendecker Collection*)

Already skilled in bomb disposal theory, Col. Kane simply had to complete a refresher course on British methods, which he achieved on February 15. Thereafter, he left his subordinates at Harper Barracks to continue his fact-finding expedition. In keeping with the British system, the eight American officers and NCOs trained jointly on many tasks, but only the officers learned to handle bomb fuzes. Nevertheless, training for non-commissioned officers proved almost as challenging. According to military records dated March 12, 1942, both Ron Felton and Joe Pilcher graduated from their enlisted Royal Engineers Bomb Disposal Courses "with distinction." All nine U.S. Army ordnancemen were also made honorary Royal Engineers, as a spirited gesture of their new Allied partnership. They were given official Royal Engineer patches – designed personally by the Queen Mother – to be worn on their sleeves.[102]

* * *

For several days in late February 1942, Maj. Kane traveled to several war-torn cities in England and Northern Ireland, meeting civil defense leaders and emergency service coordinators. On February 18, while touring Kingston-on-Hull, Kane met the Deputy Engineer, F. E. Fussey. Kane observed the Royal Navy's careful handling of several dark green cylinders. Fussey estimated that over two hundred of these "parachute mines" were responsible for fifty percent of Kingston's damaged waterfront. Only days before, German bombers had dropped over 460 tons of explosives and incendiaries over twenty square miles. Kane noted that Royal Navy, Air Force, and Army disposaleers utilized pretty much the same tools and methods. Kane's reports also underscored the shared responsibilities (and reduced frictions) between the three British services regarding explosive ordnance operations.[103]

Magnetic "parachute mines," also known as "G-Mines," were traditionally reserved for Royal Navy mine disposal officers, who normally worked with one enlisted rating. Nearly as tall as a grown man, these cylinders were released via parachute to detonate against metallic surfaces, such as a ship's deck or hull plates. Two prototypes, weighing 1,100 and 2,200 lbs., were first used in 1939. Gen. Ernst Marquard lamented that their premature use before the major raids of 1940 gave Royal Navy engineers enough time to crack their "removal locks." Tougher-to-handle fuzes, such as acoustic and remote-control models, were devised later for the Battle of Britain. Dormant "G-Mines" required careful handling with special non-metallic instruments; some later models were even outfitted with concealed photosensitive detonators, meaning technicians could only disarm a G-Mine's "magneto ignition" system under low-light conditions. Throughout the war, Army units were trained to avoid contact with "G-Mines" whenever practicable.[104]

Special bomb disposal tools, such as non-conductive instruments, would require separate provisions from Ordnance. On February 23, while visiting Snow Hill, Birmingham, Kane received useful advice from two Royal Engineers, Lieutenants T.J. Goodman and J. MacAdams. Goodman, a field officer from Gloucestershire, counseled Kane to maintain a separate equipment office, instead of relying on Army general supply services. Speaking as a maintenance officer, MacAdams stressed the delicate nature of bomb disposal tools. MacAdams found his sergeants to be integral for enforcing good practices. Both opinions were taken into consideration after Kane returned to the United States. Eventually, the U.S. Ordnance Corps approved a separate supply branch for Kane's disposaleers. Even so, supply remained a top concern as the conflict widened overseas.[105]

Leaving Kingston, Kane arrived at Coventry on February 24. Coventry was one of the worst-hit British towns since the "London Blitz" began in 1940. Kane observed No. 9 BD Company at work, and interviewed several people associated with the city. Maj. A.J. Briggs shared a mutual respect with Coventry's citizens. Briggs cited their willingness to perform bomb reconnaissance. Briggs also felt civilians, particularly ARP wardens, could contribute directly to his mission. Eight months earlier, one of his civilian aides had overlooked a 'Category A' bomb. However, upon viewing a UXB training film, this auxiliary agent discovered his error, and took Briggs to a site where a half-ton German bomb had lain all that time. Permitting more civilian involvement, Briggs argued, had the "greatest immediate benefit" of public morale.[106]

British women also played supportive roles during the London Blitz. While at Coventry, T.J. Kane interviewed Pearl M. Hyde (OBE), chief director of the Women's Welfare Services, who provided necessary food to air wardens and relief workers. She hailed Maj. Briggs and No. 9 Company as "the real heroes of the raid," whose efforts had restored confidence, enabling Coventry's people to return to a semblance of normality after the great raid of 1940.[107]

Colonel W.H.J. Gould, 16th Warwickshire Home Guard Battalion, conducted Maj. Kane through Coventry's important Daimler Works. Gould pointed out fire damage inflicted on the plant, stating that factory personnel across England had since been trained to deal with firebombs. He warned that Daimler Works might withstand high explosive or incendiary attacks, but never both. Chief Constable S.A. Hector also estimated that, during the first 1940 air raid, Coventry had suffered 70 percent fire damage within 11 hours. Another Royal Engineer, Lt. Lionel C. Maynell, put the initial damage figures closer to 80 percent, claiming that exact proof had been engulfed during the initial blaze.[108]

By February 25, Kane had returned to London. For the next few days, he previewed several training films and organized his reports from the past month. Since his profession-at-arms was very new, Kane required good evidence to convince a dubious War Department of Bomb Disposal's long-term usefulness. Ultimately, Kane's investigations would make setting up an American network much easier. Despite a few private misgivings, Kane objectively recorded and absorbed a broad cross-section of opinions. Several problems exercised the future commandant's thoughts: extent of civilian involvement with UXBs; possible tactical uses for bomb disposal units; cooperation between Army and Navy ordnance, as well as new technical developments that could assist the United States in case direct enemy bombardment occurred on the home front.[109]

During his trip, Kane repeatedly addressed civilian involvement, a decidedly touchy issue with staff officers such as Lt. Col. A.D. Childs. Childs was not only chairman of the UXB Procedure Committee, but also London's Deputy Director of UXB Operations. Childs impressed Kane with his disdain for civilian volunteers, such as Auxiliary BD Units. He even expressed his willingness to resign chairmanship of the UXB Procedure Committee if amateurs became directly involved in technical operations. In late 1941, Childs' colleagues had considered such a measure for auxiliaries operating in London's most heavily bombed industrial sectors. Childs raised the specter of a Blitzkrieg campaign in England, stating that "[Britain's] war would be won or lost before [civilian] bomb disposal work could [be] sensibly handled."[110]

Kane interviewed other skeptics on the subject of auxiliary units, ranging from Brigadier H.H. Bateman, the UXB Operations Director, who opposed any civilian involvement, to another training officer, Capt. J. Blandy, who favored marshaling air raid wardens and policemen in bomb reconnaissance. However, Capt. H.B. Patterson, military director of auxiliary operations, surprised Kane with a lack of confidence in his own people. Patterson felt Britain's civil agencies had failed the public even before German bombs actually fell on London, and he had not been very "well impressed" by civilians handling UXBs in London factories.[111]

Not every Royal Engineer shared a negative view toward ABD units. Field officers like Maj. Briggs in Coventry had already expressed kind sentiments toward civilians pitching in to clear their own neighborhoods. Maj. R.H. Rooksby likewise believed that active civilian participation served to "keep up morale" across bombed-out areas of North London. Rooksby decried the British Army's tendency to accumulate dormant bombs at its "cemeteries," and speculated that a qualified civilian might be instructed to detonate them under "strict safety precautions." Rooksby also felt that his colleagues should supervise "continuous training" for all Air Raid Personnel (ARP) responsible for locating and reporting bombs.[112]

Rooksby may have favored civilian participation owing to his exhaustive schedule in North London. Rooksby's company sections handled their own UXBs, plus high volumes at the "bomb cemeteries." They were also short of equipment, especially power-tools. Ideally, Rooksby's stores should have included at least one electric jackhammer, or power earth auger. However, power tools were limited in availability, forcing Rooksby's enlisted men to use old-fashioned shovels during excavations. UXB sections also suffered from a lack of dewatering machinery, used to drain flooded sewer tunnels. These shortages meant yet more digging and excavating for his bone-weary soldiers.[113]

Maj. Kane also surveyed British perspectives on bomb disposal combat operations. Royal Engineers had recently deployed in North Africa to contend with Axis landmines, as well as other ordnance hazards. However, the Engineers' new BD service branch had been largely confined to national defense. Kane's sponsor, Major Philip Neill, suggested that America's "greater distances" would require "considerable modification" should they be bombed or invaded by Japan. Neill also conceded that his own War Ministry had yet to determine their branch's precise combat role, beyond protecting airbases from German planes.[114]

Kane continued to quiz other Royal Engineers on this same point, but few British officers had seriously considered bomb disposal as a battle asset. Kane's direct line of questioning seldom evinced specific answers from regular Army officers or even ranking Royal Engineers. Brigadier H.H. Bateman, Director of Bomb Disposal, believed that the "highly technical character" of UXB operations could prove invaluable during a German invasion, but he could offer no further details. Lt. Col. Childs, Bateman's Deputy Director, also expressed his doubts that bomb disposal held much tactical value beyond airbases.[115]

However, Maj. Gen. K.C. Appleyard, had witnessed German bombing during the Battle of France. Appleyard believed existing BD companies required more flexibility outside the home islands, but such personnel should be included in future RAF operations. Lt. Col. E. Stanton (No. 1 BD Group - London) also enumerated two distinct tactical phases for his service branch: static operations outside military zones, and deployment with combat arms, as a motorized unit at company level.[116]

On February 27, Kane toured RAF Bomb Disposal headquarters in London. Since the U. S. Army still resisted pressures to commission a separate air force, Kane's ordnance branch also represented the U.S. Army Air Corps, with its own interests. Lt. Cdr. Dinwoodie, the principal bomb disposal officer for the Royal Air Force, had personally dealt with SD-2 Butterfly Bombs. Dinwoodie warned Kane that handling such ordnance required careful safety training, instead of reckless "experimenting" with unknown fuzes, which might cost lives. In future Allied campaigns, soldiers often paid the price for such curiosity. Even under the best circumstances, German anti-personnel weapons were risky to handle.[117]

In early March 1942, Kane's officers had an opportunity to meet scientists and technicians engaged in highly clandestine UXB research. Kane had quizzed representatives from the National Defense Research Committee, but at first, not all the Britishers were very cooperative. One scientist, F.L. Hovde, withheld UXB intelligence, perhaps for security reasons, but later admitted his error in misleading the Americans.[118]

On March 2, Kane visited London's Electrical Research Association, touring their extensive laboratory. Dr. L. Whitehead demonstrated to Kane a new short-range magnetic bomb detector, called the Mu Metal Locator. While this device showed promise, extraneous metallic objects interfered with the Mu Locator's readings. Capt. J. Meddrum, chief tester of field equipment, estimated that out of the military's catalog of 50,000 UXBs, only 20 cases required the Mu Locator's use.[119]

Capt. Meddrum further addressed the dearth of published articles concerning bomb technology. From his own experimental work, Meddrum kept personal notes with no view toward academic publication. Comprehensive papers were published under the Ministry of Supply, but the British military, practical in its outlook, left most theoretical bomb disposal problems to commercial research facilities, such as the National Physical Laboratory in Teddington. Meddrum's observations on bomb disposal technical publications were corroborated by Lt. Col. G.D. De'ath, RE, who decried a lack of UXB intelligence liaisons established between service branches, such as Royal Navy and Air Forces.[120]

Over March 3-4, Kane visited Forrest Products Research Labs at Princess Reisborough, along with the aforementioned National Physical Laboratory in Teddington. At Forrest Labs, Kane received a useful briefing on improved air raid shelter construction from Ms. R.E. Watkins, one of the few women directly involved in U.K. bomb disposal research. Dr. Binks of the NPL gave a demonstration of poisonous radon gas, useful in confirming the presence of Zus-40s or similar anti-withdrawal devices. Given the known hazards of radon gas, Binks believed this method should only be used as a last resort by specialized personnel.[121]

During his last weeks in England, Maj. Kane submitted a preliminary report to Aberdeen Proving Ground. Col. Wingate Reed responded to Kane's report with some welcome news: "Lieutenant Colonel" Kane and his immediate staff should report back to the Ordnance Training Center by March 15. Together with Maj. Walker, Lt. Nass, and M/Sgt. Keller, the newly promoted Kane traveled to Belfast, Ireland aboard the *Duke of Lancaster*, awaiting final transportation back to the United States.[122]

Kane's second detachment under Frank Parsons remained a few weeks longer for follow-up training. Having passed the Harper Barracks final examination "with distinction," Ron Felton, Dick Metress, and Joe Pilcher took a well-earned pass in London. For a few days, they lodged in Mayfair at the Park Lane Hotel, visiting the city's many attractions. Unsurprisingly, their stops included several friendly public houses. Pilcher kept an intact matchbook from the "Good Intent," where a barmaid named Kathleen wished her American patrons a "happy landing."[123]

Joseph Pilcher (right) and Dick Metress (center) sightseeing in London with another unidentified American soldier. (*Pilcher Collection*)

* * *

Despite their reversals in 1940-41, the Luftwaffe continued to bombard Great Britain, taking advantage of bad weather to attack key war industries, particularly crankshaft and aluminum factories. Following "long and exacting preparations," the best crews were sent in small formations to dive toward their targets. So-called "nuisance raids" usually involved one to three bombers, and were designed to worsen "existing bottlenecks in war production." At this time, bombers carried 550 lb. SC bombs, which comprised about 80 percent of the Luftwaffe's arsenal. Such general purpose bombs were designed for employment in large quantities, in order to concentrate "pressure waves" in a single area. However, most British plants were able to keep producing with "only a short interruption." Later on, the Germans introduced larger bombs capable of inflicting more serious damage on British industrial centers.[124]

One city, Bristol, had experienced its own fair share of nuisance raids. On March 17, Ron Felton and Joe Pilcher reported there for training with No. 7 Bomb Disposal Company. They arrived just in time to experience their first air raid. Years later, Felton recalled the unflappable courage of Bristol's inhabitants, who set their watches according to the Luftwaffe's bombing schedule. Jim Hearn, an enlisted Royal Engineer stationed at Bristol, later recalled German bombers had targeted an important brake lining factory used by the Army's motorized transportation corps. In early March, one bomber had scored a direct hit, leveling the factory's motor pool and killing a quartermaster sergeant still seated inside his lorry.[125]

Quartered at the historic Kensington House, Capt. A.V. Lucas of No. 7 Company supervised four bomb disposal sections encamped across Gloucestershire. Two teams covered the Brislington-Bath Road, where UXBs had been reported after the last raid. On Sunday, March 22, Capt. Lucas sent two Americans, Pilcher and Felton, to observe a field section probing for UXBs at The Beeches, a fashionable Brislington hotel. That Tuesday, British sappers had unearthed a genuine cast-iron killer. However, this bomb went off inside its shaft, killing Lance Sergeant Andrew H.J. Belson instantly. Standing just behind Belson, T/Sgt. Pilcher collapsed as several iron fragments pierced his abdomen. Luckily, Joe had worn his leather overcoat, which acted like a second skin, staunching his bleeding long enough to arrive at a nearby Bristol hospital ward. Felton remained steadfastly by Pilcher's side throughout his comrade's ordeal.[126]

Joseph Pilcher was the first U.S. casualty resulting from a UXB, though fortunately not the first American fatality.[127] Quickly evacuated to Belfast, he underwent emergency surgery. Doctors removed a badly hemorrhaged portion of Joe's left lung, and he recovered within two months. Edith Pilcher, expecting her first child back in Maryland, learned about her husband's injury through a misleading newspaper article describing the incident as a "German air raid." Ron Felton remained in Belfast until mid-May, looking after his comrade's personal needs. On May 28, Joe finally left Ulster, flying home to spend a few weeks of convalescent leave. Edith rejoined her husband in New York, where she gave birth to a healthy boy, named for his father.[128]

Jesse Pilcher clearly remembered his older brother's long-awaited arrival in Fabius: "Our parents had said nothing, so [my sister] Mary and I thought Joe had come home AWOL." Jesse learned the full story about his brother's injury much later. "Joe always believed that heavy British Army coat also saved his life," Jesse later recalled. "He was never as strong afterward, because the lung damage aggravated his asthma." Pilcher had lost some weight and his usual ruddy color, but he returned to active duty by June 1942. Joe rarely talked about his wounding afterward, partly because he felt remorse over the British sergeant's death.[129]

During Pilcher's absence, the U.S. Army's Ordnance Bomb Disposal School began to develop, in Lt. Col. Kane's own words, from "just an idea" into a full-fledged training facility responsible for "anticipating our enemies' fiendish devices." On February 16, 1942, the Army Bomb Disposal School officially embarked on its four years of service. Aberdeen's first scheduled bomb disposal officers' class began on February 17, but owing to a shortage of recruits, enlisted men did not begin their courses until April 8. At first, the four visiting British officers shared instructional responsibilities at both Army and Navy facilities. Maj. Geoffrey Yates and his fellow Engineers were shown the same respect as American officers. Capt. Tom Sharman remembered their ceremonious reception at Aberdeen, as some of the earliest "uniformed allies" on American soil.[130]

Until Kane's return from England, Maj. Walter C. DeBill and 1st Lt. John E. Feldman served as interim school commandant and executive officer, respectively. While Kane officially took charge on March 26, 1942, he asked Walt DeBill to stay on briefly as his deputy. John Feldman, in the meantime, realized his true calling as the "school inventor." Working closely with Wally Nass, Feldman presided over the Bomb Disposal School's Research and Development branch, where his creativity gained him a new nickname, "Kane's Brains."[131]

After Walt DeBill returned to general ordnance duty in August 1942, Lt. Col. Harry Walker left his post of Training Director to become Kane's deputy commandant. Walker and Kane remained lifelong friends, but one year later, Walker voluntarily separated from the Army Bomb Disposal branch. Rising to full colonel, Walker distinguished himself in the Italian Theater as Gen. Mark Clark's fuel administrator. However, Kane never lacked for quality officers at Aberdeen Proving Ground. He persuaded Martin J. Ehrmann to stay on as Walker's replacement, and eventually, his own successor. Walker and Ehrmann both maintained very high training standards for the U.S. Army's foundational EOD training program.[132]

One of Harry Walker's privileges as Deputy Commandant was granting awards and medals to his officers and soldiers. On December 18, 1942, he acknowledged the sacrifice and perseverance of one of his newest lieutenants: Joseph C. Pilcher. On this snowy day, as Maj. J. K. Lynch read the Army's citation, Lt. Col. Walker pinned the decoration on 2nd Lt. Pilcher's uniform. Meanwhile, five companies of Ordnance marched past in review, led by the 6th Ord. Battalion's band. Edith Pilcher proudly looked on from the sidelines as her husband received his first medal.[133]

Lt. Col. Harry Walker awards the Purple Heart medal to 2nd Lieutenant Joseph C. Pilcher for injuries suffered in England. (*Pilcher Collection*)

By early 1943, T/Sgt. Ronald Felton received his well-deserved commission, graduating from OCS on January 23. Jobe's steadfastness had earned something far more valuable than promotions or medals: lifelong friendship. On March 6, Pilcher repaid Felton's devotion by standing as his best man at the Aberdeen post chapel, with Reverend Delphine presiding. Felton's bride, Mildred "Millie" Pelava, had resided with her Ukrainian parents in Glen Lyon, Pennsylvania, before her employment at a Maryland munitions plant brought her into Aberdeen Proving Ground's orbit. Through social channels, Jobe had met Millie, whose dark hair and lustrous brown eyes were worthy of a model.[134]

Edith Pilcher, as it turned out, got along famously with Millie Felton, sometimes known as Mil. While the Feltons saved up for their own home, the Pilchers accommodated the newlyweds at Havre de Grace. Meanwhile, Lt. Dick Metress continued to lived on post until his eventual marriage and relocation to Swedesboro, New Jersey – a small town within commuting distance of Havre de Grace. These three friends, united by a common purpose at the Army Bomb Disposal School, enjoyed many weekend parties and social gatherings throughout the coming months, before the war separated them and changed their lives forever.[135]

Two newly-minted second lieutenants, Ronald Felton and Joseph Pilcher, posing with their proud wives, Millie and Edith, in early 1943. (*Pilcher Collection*)

Despite political uncertainties in Washington, logistical wrangling at Aberdeen Proving Ground, diplomatic tap-dancing with Lisbon police and one soldier's close call at Bristol, T. J. Kane's "Nine from Aberdeen" had fulfilled their training mission. One year after graduating from Harper Barracks, Kane and his men received special medals for being present during the Allied European-African-Middle Eastern Campaign of 1942. They were officially permitted to keep their colorful Royal Engineer emblems as a part of their American dress uniforms, a rare privilege that set all nine of these soldiers apart from their fellow United States Army ordnancemen.[136]

## Notes

[1] Adjutant General Emory S. Adams to Maj. Gen. Charles M. Wesson. *Disposal of Unexploded and Delayed Action Bombs.* [memorandum] 12 December 1941; London to United States War Department. [cablegram] 12 December 1941; Maj. Thomas D. Sharman, letter to author, 26 August 2003.

[2] As a lieutenant colonel, Geoffrey Yates commanded the No. 4 Royal Engineer BD Group until the war's ending. Yates, Sharman, and Hudson survived the war, but according to Sharman's account, John W. Draper later died while removing a mine toward the war's end. (*History of Bomb Disposal in the U.S.A.,* Aberdeen Proving Ground, 1942; Lt. Col. Eric Wakeling, *A Short History of Royal Engineer Bomb Disposal,* Buckinghamshire, England: B.D. Publishing, 1997, 7-9; Maj. Thomas D. Sharman, letter to author, 26 August 2003; REA Assistant Secretary Gary Woodman-Simmons, electronic mail, 24 September 2003).

[3] Lt. Col. Eric Wakeling's total statistics indicate a total of 151 officers and 339 enlistees were killed while performing bomb disposal, with wounded personnel totaling 37 and 172, respectively. Many early BD officer casualties were recent graduates from Officer Cadet Training Units. (Robert Kuehner, interview with author, 6 March 2003; A.B. Hartley, *Unexploded Bomb.*, New York: W.W. Norton Co., 1958, appendix; Hooper, 1-3; Wakeling, 20.)

[4] Col. C. Wingate Reed to Col. Hugh C. Minton, memorandum, 8 December 1941; Col. Hugh C. Minton to Secretary of General Staff, memorandum, 9 December 1941; Sharman letter, 26 August 2003.

[5] Paul Deichmann, "Luftwaffe Methods in the Selection of Offensive Weapons, Volume 1," from *USAF Historical Studies*, No. 187 (Manhattan, Kansas: MA/AH Publishing, Sunflower University Press, c. 1985), 2-12; Ernst A. Marquard, "Luftwaffe Methods in the Selection of Offensive Weapons, Volume 2," USAF *Historical Studies*, No. 187 (Manhattan, Kansas: MA/AH Publishing, Sunflower University Press. c. 1985), 39-40; Leslie E. Simon, *German Research in World War II* (London: Chapman & Hall, Limited, 1947) 51.

[6] Deichmann, 2-3, 12-13.

[7] Col. Simon also contrasted this attitude with those Americans who viewed munitions firms as unsavory enterprises, in keeping with prevalent "merchants of

death" theories circulating in the press. (Deichmann, 2-3, 12-13; Simon, 92, 188.)
[8] Melissa J. Jappy, *Danger UXB*, London: Macmillan Publishers Ltd., 2001, 34-5; Robert Kuehner, "The Deadly 88," from *UXB Volume II*, Jim Jenkinson, ed. (Sussex, England: Woodfield Publishing Co., 2001) 192-210; Simon, 51, 92, 188.
[9] Gen. Ernst Marquard (1892-1980) later contributed to post-war evaluations of Luftwaffe weapons development. (Deichmann, 78, Marquard, Appendix III).
[10] Deichmann, 11-16.
[11] Gen. Deichmann credited Gen. Udet with the invention of the Stuka's whistles. By 1941, the various models of Luftwaffe bomber planes had increased from four to fourteen. Heinkel 177 bombers were never committed because they were not ready for combat by the end of World War II. (Deichmann, 18-19).
[12] Bomb types were also defined by their percentage of explosive filler; SC bombs contained 55 percent explosive, while SD contained 35 percent. (Royal Army Bomb Disposal School, *Notes on German Bombs*, Ripon, Yorkshire: Harper Barracks, c. 1942; Walter R. Nass, *Bomb Disposal Notes*, Aberdeen Proving Ground: U.S. Army Ordnance Museum, 1942, 2-7; Marquard 31-38).
[13] Less common German bomb classifications included Z.C. (*Zement Cylindrisch*) and K.C. (*Kampfstoff Cylindrisch*), the latter designed to carry poison gas or smoke. (Marquard 31-38).
[14] Marquard, 30
[15] Deichmann, 5-9.
[16] Deichmann, 13-14.
[17] Royal Army Bomb Disposal School, *Notes on German Bombs*, Ripon, Yorkshire: Harper Barracks, c. 1942; Deichmann, 13-14; Nass, 6-7; Wakeling, 4.
[18] Winston S. Churchill, *Their Finest Hour*, Vol. 2 (Boston: Houghton-Mifflin, 1949), 360-3; David Shears, "Hitler's D-Day, from *No End Save Victory*, Robert Cowley, ed. (London: Berkley Books, 2001) 86-106.
[19] See Ernst A. Marquard, "Luftwaffe Methods in the Selection of Offensive Weapons, Volume 2," from *USAF Historical Studies*, No. 187 (Manhattan, Kansas: MA/AH Publishing, Sunflower University Press, c. 1985); Wakeling, 3.
[20] Marquard 39-40; Jappy, 34-5.
[21] Robert Kuehner, interview by author, 6 March 2003; Deichmann, 2-16.
[22] Marquard 73, Appendix XIV.
[23] Churchill, 360-3; Wakeling, 5-6.
[24] Churchill, 360-3; Hartley, 20-23; Hooper, 3.
[25] Sometimes, civil authorities could supervise a UXB Command Center; they were referred to as Regional Commissioner instead of Commanders. (Nass, 3-4, 10).
[26] Nass, 13-14.
[27] Hooper, 2.
[28] J. Frank Durham, *You Only Blow Yourself Up Once* (Lincoln, Nebraska: iUniverse Press, 2003), 125-30; Chris Ransted, *Bomb Disposal and the British Casualties of WW2* (United Kingdom: Royal Engineers Association, 2003), 122; Winston Churchill, *Their Finest Hour*, 360-3.
[29] Robert E. Leiendecker, *Bomb Disposal, The Early Years of Explosive Ordnance*

*Disposal (An Informal History)*, Charlottesville, Virginia: NATEODA Press, 2012, 1-4; Nass, 2; Wakeling, 1, 17.

[30] For nomenclature purposes, the Type 17 fuze is also known as the El A.Z. (*Electrisch Aufschlag Zunder*) Electric Impact Fuze Type 17. (Special Observer Section, European Theater of Operations, *Fuze Sterilizing Equipment for Bomb Disposal*, undated technical report, c. 1941; Wakeling, 5-6).

[31] Type 50 fuzes appeared in two major variants, the El. Z. (*Electrisch Zunder*) Electric Fuze Types 50B and 50Y. In 1942, Captain Hudson (later Major) brought his new secret discharger to the United States, where it became standard Army issue. (Special Observer Section, European Theater of Operations, *Fuze Sterilizing Equipment for Bomb Disposal*, undated technical report, c. 1941; Hartley, 20-23; Wakeling, 5-6; Hooper, 3.)

[32] Hartley, 20-23; Jappy, 49-51; Hooper, 3.

[33] Archer, decorated for his courage, eventually rose to the rank of Lieutenant Colonel in the Royal Engineers Bomb Disposal Branch. (Hartley, 20-23, 60; Wakeling, 20.)

[34] Deichmann, 17, 88.

[35] Hooper, 2-3, Wakeling, 20.

[36] OCD originally came under the federal jurisdiction of the Office of Emergency Management (OEM). First Lady Eleanor Roosevelt originally envisioned the OCD as a national civic action program akin to her husband's ambitious New Deal, but Fiorello La Guardia, the first OCD director and World War I veteran, preferred a straightforward quasi-military operation, with enforced blackouts and coastal patrols. (Stetson Conn, Rose C. Engelman, and Byron Fairchild, *Guarding the United States and its Outposts* (Washington D.C.: Office of the Chief of Military History, 1946) 68-72; Levin H. Campbell, Jr., *Industry-Ordnance Team* (New York: Whittlesey House & McGraw-Hill) 1946, 12-13, 18-20; Benjamin Franklin Cooling, "U.S. Support of Civil Defense: The Formative Years," *Military Affairs*, Vol. 35, No. 1 (Feb. 1971), 8-9).

[37] Lida Mayo, *The Ordnance Department: On Beachhead and Battlefront* (Washington D.C.: Department of Defense, 1991) 3-5; Cooling, 8-9.

[38] Major General Charles Macon Wesson (1878-1956), West Point class of 1900, commanded Aberdeen Proving Ground 1925-29 and 1934-38, before assuming overall command of Ordnance until 1942. On January 8, 1942, SPOBS ceased to exist, morphing into U.S. Army Forces in the British Isles (USAFBI), America's first European Theater headquarters. (Special Observer Section, European Theater of Operations, *Fuze Sterilizing Equipment for Bomb Disposal*, undated technical report, c. 1942; Constance M. Green, Peter C. Root, and Harry C. Thomson, *The Ordnance Department: Planning Munitions for War* (Washington D.C.: Department of the Army, 1955) 147-9; *Ordnance Corps Hall of Fame,* Aberdeen Proving Grounds, MD: 1969); www.goordnance.apg.army.mil, Accessed 23 February 2003; Mayo, 5).

[39] During the tense months of 1939-40, British home defense coordinators had anticipated a poison gas attack, based on World War I experiences, plus Fascist Italy's well-documented use of poison gas in 1936, directed against the poorly-

armed Ethiopian military. (Samuel J. Hooper, *History of U.S. Army Bomb Disposal and Explosive Ordnance Disposal (1941-1980).* [unpublished manuscript] c. 1981, 8.)

[40] Brigadier (later Major General) Julian S. Hatcher (1888-1963) served as first Commanding General of the Ordnance Training Center (1940-42) prior to promotion to Chief of Field Service in 1943. Hatcher's pistol marksmanship is still a near-legendary feat commemorated at the U.S. Army Ordnance Museum. (Thomas J. Kane to U.S. War Department, *Bomb Disposal, U. S. A.*, [unpublished report] c.1942, 1-2; U.S. Army Ordnance Corps, *Ordnance Corps Hall of Fame*, http:/ www.goordnance.apg.army.mil; Accessed 23 February 2003; Leo P. Brophy and George J. Fisher, *Chemical Warfare Service: Organizing For War*, Washington D.C., Office of the Chief of Military History, 1959, 237-8; Conn, Engelman, and Fairchild, 72; Hooper, 8.)

[41] During T. J. Kane's boyhood, his middle name may have been used in order to differentiate from his father, T. C. Kane. The elder Kane's obituary identified only one surviving son, Joseph. (Thomas C. Kane, obituary, *Punxsutawney Spirit*, 18 January 1919; Catherine G. Kane, obituary, *Punxsutawney Spirit*, 3 April 1951; Thomas J. Kane, registration card, Jefferson County Selective Service, 12 September 1918; U.S. Bureau of the Census, 1920, Jefferson County, Punxsutawney, Pennsylvania;).

[42] Kane's two daughters – Kay Levering and Mary Jo Romba – have remained in touch with veterans who served with their father. Kay Levering recalled her father as rather easy-going, often leaving the tougher parenting tasks to her mother. (Kay Levering, interview with author, 15 October 2003; Mary Jo Romba, interview with author, 15 October 2003; Bureau of the Census, 1930, Jefferson County, Punxsutawney, Pennsylvania; Hooper, E-1.)

[43] One September 1941 group photograph shows Major Thomas Kane at the head of OTC Headquarters Company. (Kay Levering, interview by author, 15 October 2003; Ed Brock, "Ordnance Group Gets New Hope," from *Clayton News Daily*, Clayton, Georgia, 5 April 2004; 15 October 2003; Mary Jo Romba, interview with author, 15 October 2003; Fred J. Puckett, interview with author, 15 February 2004; Joseph C. Pilcher, World War II Collection; Hooper, E-1.)

[44] *Bomb Disposal School History*, Aberdeen Proving Ground: U.S. Army Bomb Disposal School, 1942; *History of Bomb Disposal in the U.S.A.,* Aberdeen Proving Ground, 1942; Kane, *Bomb Disposal, U. S. A.*, 1; Green, Root and Thomson, 147-49.

[45] *History of Bomb Disposal in the U.S.A.,* Aberdeen Proving Ground, 1942; Kane, *Bomb Disposal, U. S. A.*, 1; Lt. Col. C. Wingate Reed to Col. H. C. Minton [memorandum] 8 December 1941; Green, Root, and Thomson: 147-9.

[46] Adjutant General Emory S. Adams to Maj. Gen, Charles M. Wesson, *Disposal of Unexploded and Delayed Action Bombs*. [memorandum] 12 December 1941; U.S. War Department to the Adjutant General, *Disposal of Unexploded and Delayed-Action Bombs*, 7 January 1942; Green, Root, and Thomson: 147-9; Hooper, 9.)

[47] Adjutant General Emory S. Adams to Chief of Ordnance Maj. Gen. Charles M.

Wesson. *Disposal of Unexploded and Delayed Action Bombs.* [memorandum] 12 December 1941; Guisinger to Adams. *Officers for Bomb Demolition Course.* [unpublished memorandum]; London to United States War Department. [cablegram] 12 December 1941; Green, Root, and Thomson: 147-9.

[48] London to U.S. War Department. [cablegram] 12 December 1941; C. Wingate Reed to Assistant Chief of Staff G-2. [memorandum] 17 December 1941.

[49] Col. H.C. Minton to Secretary of General Staff [memorandum] 9 December 1941; London to U.S. War Department, 12 December 1941.

[50] Adjutant General Emory S. Adams to Maj. Gen. Charles M. Wesson. *Disposal of Unexploded and Delayed Action Bombs.* [memorandum] 12 December 1941.

[51] Adjutant General Emory S. Adams to Maj. Gen. Charles M. Wesson, *Disposal of Unexploded and Delayed Action Bombs*, memorandum, 12 December 1941; London to United States War Department, cablegram, 12 December 1941.

[52] Lt. Col. B.B. McMahon to Chief of Ordnance, *Bomb Disposal Liaison,* 3 January 1942; Mayo, 88-91.

[53] J. Frank Durham, *You Only Blow Yourself Up Once* (Lincoln, Nebraska: iUniverse Press, 2003) 13-21; http://www.american.edu/arubin/wwii/bomb.htm., accessed 25 June 2003. See also Elizabeth K. Bush, *America's First Frogman: the Draper Kauffman Story* (Annapolis: Naval Academy Press, 2004).

[54] 14th Naval District to the Chief of the Bureau of Ordnance, *Report on Unexploded Japanese Bomb No. 1*, 1 January 1942; Durham, 15-16.

[55] 14th Naval District to the Chief of the Bureau of Ordnance, *Report on Unexploded Japanese Bomb No. 1*, 1 January 1942.

[56] For his efforts on Oahu, Lt. Draper Kauffman received the U.S. Navy Cross. One of Kauffman's aides, Chief Gunner's Mate Robert "Ike" Eigell, later claimed to have performed the actual fuze disarmament procedures. (14th Naval District to the Chief of the Bureau of Ordnance, *Report on Unexploded Japanese Bomb No. 1*, 1 January 1942; Durham, 15-16.)

[57] Just one month earlier, and this book might have had a slightly different title! (Maj. John E. Feldman, *Military History of John Edward Feldman*, U.S. Army Ordnance Museum).

[58] Capt. John E. Feldman eventually received a campaign medal and a commendation for his activities in Hawaii. On a more curious historical note, Lt. Feldman also recovered one naval artillery shell dating back to Captain James Cook's fatal 1778 visit to the Hawaiian Islands. (Headquarters Ordnance Bomb Disposal School, General Orders Number 1, 23 February 1943; Feldman, *Military History*; Maria Feldman, interview with author, 18 June 2003; Durham, 15-16; 133-35; Hooper, 25).

[59] Ordnance Bomb Disposal School Headquarters, Department of Training. c.1943; *Course BDC-1, Advanced Bomb Reconnaissance; BDM-1, Bomb Disposal Officer's Course; BDM-2, Bomb Reconnaissance Instructor's Course; BDM-3, Military Bomb Reconnaissance Officers and Non-Commissioned Officers Course; BDM-12 Introduction to the Bomb Disposal Problem;BDM-21 N.C.O. Bomb Disposal Course.*

[60] Robert Palmer, Bell I. Wiley, and William R. Keast, *Procurement and Training*

*of Ground Combat Troops*. Washington D.C., Center of Military History, [1948] 2003, 105-110; Earl C. Guisinger to Adjutant General Emory S. Adams, *Officers for Bomb Demolition Course*, 23 December 1941.

[61] After promotion to full colonel, Walker returned to his primary branch, the Corps of Engineers, until his retirement in 1952. Thomas Kane remained in touch with his former executive officer until Walker's death in 1961. (The *Detonator* [newsletter] (U.S. Army Bomb Disposal School: Aberdeen Proving Ground, Maryland) 17 September 1943; *Punxsutawney Spirit*. [obituaries] Punxsutawney Area Historical and Genealogical Society, Inc.; 2 March 1961.)

[62] Thomas J. Kane to U.S. War Department, *Bomb Disposal, U. S. A.*, [unpublished report] c.1942; Ordnance Bomb Disposal School Headquarters, *BD Officer Roster,* 26 November 1942; Ordnance Bomb Disposal School Headquarters, *BD Officer Roster,* 26 October 1943; Frank A. Parsons to Historical Section, Baltimore, *Report on Bomb Disposal Activities 1 July 1942 – 30 June 1943,* 9 July 1943; Alice Nass, interview by author, 14 October 2003; Dorothy Parsons, interview with author, 18 October 2003; *Firepower Magazine,* Washington D.C.: U.S. Army Signal Corps, June 1945; Social Security Death Index, available from http:// search.ancestry.com, accessed 11 September 2003, Internet; James Clifford, e-mail to author, 16 March 2011.

[63] Thomas J. Kane to U.S. War Department, *Bomb Disposal, U. S. A.*, [unpublished report] c.1942; Ordnance Bomb Disposal School Headquarters, *BD Officer Roster*, 26 November 1942; Fred J. Puckett, interview with author, 15 February 2004; Hooper, 10-11.

[64] Thomas Francis Metress appears in the 1920 Federal Census, under a misspelled heading of "Metras." Thomas and Ethel's other children included the eldest son, John (born c. 1910), Harriet (born c. 1912), and Mary (born c. 1917). Family genealogist Patrick Metress confirmed Thomas and Ethel's marriage took place at St. Margaret's Church on October 27, 1907, but could not locate further information on his New York cousins, mainly due to a church fire that destroyed the Metress children's birth and confirmation records. Metress, who also worked several summers for Dexter as a teenager, confirmed its final closure in 1982. (Patrick A. Metress, *Seven Generations of an Irish-American Family: A History of the Hayes-Hickey-Bergin Family*, 28-30, 4-1; U.S. Bureau of the Census, 1900, Bergen County, Park Ridge, New Jersey; U.S. Bureau of the Census, 1910, Bergen County, Park Ridge, New Jersey; U.S. Bureau of the Census, 1920, Bergen County, Park Ridge, New Jersey.)

[65] According to one of Mary Olive's daughters, Carole Carlo, her mother married at a relatively young age to leave her stepfather's home, but remained very close to her "Uncle Dick," who still resided in New Jersey. (Carole P. Carlo, telephone interview by author, 29 July 2011; U.S. Bureau of the Census, 1930, Bergen County, Park Ridge, New Jersey).

[66] Dick's decision to enlist in the Army might have been influenced by his uncle, John Metress, who saw action on the Western Front, and had suffered from a German gas attack. (Guisinger to Adams, *Officers for Bomb Demolition Course*; Patrick A. Metress, letter to author, 20 February 2004; Metress, *Seven*

*Generations,* 28-30; U.S. Bureau of the Census, 1940, Salem County, Oldmans Township, New Jersey; 1942 BD Officer Roster).

[67] Anne and Henry Pilcher were immigrants to the United States before the outbreak of World War I, residents of Onondaga County, New York. Henry W. Pilcher listed his year of immigration as 1911, saving his earnings so his wife, Anne, could bring their first two sons over in 1913. All four Pilcher brothers served in the U.S. Armed Forces at some point. George Pilcher went to China with the Marine Corps during the late 1920s, and later returned to service as a Marine corporal at Long Beach, California. Like his younger sibling, Tom Pilcher also served in the Army. Jesse Pilcher, youngest of the brethren, served as a Navy machinist in Hawaii. (U.S. Bureau of the Census, Department of Commerce, New York, Onondaga County, 1930; Jesse Pilcher, interview with author, 2 September 2003; Joseph C. Pilcher, *Capt. Pilcher, Bomb Demolisher, Has String of Coveted Medals*, undated newspaper article, from *World War II Scrapbook,* 1945).

[68] Jesse Pilcher, interview with author, 2 September 2003.

[69] Captain Joseph C. Pilcher, War Department Military Record, AGO Form 100, 5 December 1945; Jesse Pilcher interview.

[70] Coyne Electrician School to Joseph C. Pilcher, course diploma, dated 1936.

[71] Jesse Pilcher interview.

[72] Captain Joseph C. Pilcher, War Department Military Record, AGO Form 100, 5 December 1945.

[73] Jesse Pilcher interview; Edith H. Pilcher, obituary, Yardley, Pennsylvania, 20 January 1999; First Lieutenant Samuel C. Mitchell to Private Joseph C. Pilcher, pass card, 3 July 1940; U.S. Bureau of the Census, Department of Commerce, New York, Onondaga County, 1940.

[74] Maj. Gen. Charles M. Wesson to Private Joseph C. Pilcher, War Department AGO Form 58, 29 January 1941; Staff Sergeant Joseph C. Pilcher, *Certificate of Proficiency*, 31 January 1941; M/Sgt. Joseph C. Pilcher, War Department AGO Form 55, 27 November 1942; Captain Joseph C. Pilcher, War Department AGO Form 100, 5 December 1945; Campbell, 364.

[75] Brig. Gen. Julian S. Hatcher to Staff Sergeant Joseph C. Pilcher, War Department AGO Form 58, 18 July 1941; Wesson to Adams, letter dated 31 December 1941; Pilcher, *World War II Scrapbook,* 1945.

[76] Wesson to Adams, letter dated 31 December 1941; Joseph C. Pilcher, *Last Will and Testament*, 24 November 1943; Joseph C. Pilcher Jr., interview by author, 18 April 2003; Joseph C. Pilcher Jr., interview with author, 12 July 2003.

[77] Ronald Felton's Army records measured his raw intelligence quotient at 135, a highly superior score. (Ronald L. Felton, *Service Journal 1941-1943*; *Army Air Force Officers Qualification Record* (Form 66-2), 31 December 1944; from the Marsha Frost Collection, Springfield, Virginia).

[78] Ordnance Bomb Disposal School Headquarters. *Special Orders No. 114* [weapons qualification roster] 16 June 1943; Thomas J. Kane to 2$^{nd}$ Lieutenants Joseph C. Pilcher and Ronald L. Felton. [memorandum] 9 August 1943; Felton, *Form 66-2*; .Joseph C. Pilcher Jr. [transcript] interview by author 18 April 2003.

[79] Thomas J. Kane, unpublished travel itinerary, Aberdeen Proving Ground, Maryland, 1 December 1942 to 25 May 1943, 1.
[80] Unfortunately, this footage seems to have disappeared since the war, as no record exists of its fate. (Major Thomas J. Kane to Lt. Col. C. Wingate Reed, radiogram, 7 January 1942).
[81] Had Portugal not delayed Kane's flight, his group would have been the first U.S. servicemen to arrive in the British Isles since Pearl Harbor. On January 15, the 34th Infantry Division under Maj. Gen. Russell "Scrappy" Hartle arrived in Northern Ireland. Hartle served as temporary ETO chief until Lt. Gen. D.D. Eisenhower's arrival in early 1944. (London to the United States War Department, cablegram, 7 January 1942; Maj. Gen. Charles M. Wesson to Major Thomas J. Kane, radiogram, 13 January 1941; *Time*, 27 July 1942; *Stars and Stripes*, 3 December 1942, 1.)
[82] As noted, the Special Observation Group (SPOBS) already established a headquarters in London, and its members had passed freely through Portugal before December 1941. (Thomas J. Kane, unpublished travel itinerary, 1; Lida Mayo, 3-6.)
[83] According to historian Martin Gilbert, Hitler had considered Operation Isabella to occupy Portugal's coastline, as a direct means to intimidate Spain into full cooperation in future military operations against British-held Gibraltar. Portugal had also served as a staging group for European Jews to escape the Nazis after the fall of Western Europe in 1940. (Martin Gilbert, *The Second World War,* New York: Henry Holt & Company, 1989, 291; Kane, unpublished travel itinerary, 1.)
[84] Ronald Felton's passport, dated 31 December 1941, bears a stamp describing his "Official Business for the War Department." Sergeants Pilcher and Felton were paid one month in advance for a total of $4.00 per diem. Such arrangements were necessary, since overseas rations and quarters could not be arranged on short notice. Anticipating their lengthy stay, Ordnance Headquarters further amended baggage allowances to 77 pounds. (Thomas J. Kane, unpublished travel itinerary, 1; Brig. Gen. Julian S. Hatcher to Technical Sergeant Joseph C. Pilcher and Staff Sergeant Ronald L. Felton, Special *Orders No. 1*., unpublished draft, 1 January 1942; Dorothy Parsons, interview with author, 15 October 2003; Adjutant General (Major General Emory S. Adams) to Brig. Gen. Julian S. Hatcher, *Bomb Demolition Course*, 30 December 1941; Adjutant General to Brig. Gen. Julian S. Hatcher, *Bomb Demolition Course,* 6 January 1942; Ronald L. Felton, *Passport*, dated 31 January 1941, 5; Joseph Pilcher, *World War II Scrapbook,* unpublished memoir, 1945).
[85] (Ronald L. Felton, *Passport*, dated 31 January 1941; Dorothy Parsons, interview, 15 October 2003; Martin Gilbert, *The Second World War,* New York: Henry Holt & Company, 1989, 187-90.)
[86] Lt. Col. Thomas J. Kane, *Statements Relative to Bomb Disposal*, 4 January - 9 March 1942, 1; Kane, 1942 itinerary, 1-4.
[87] According to REA archives, Captain Thomas D. Sharman later commanded No. 24 BD Company in Chiswick. Lt. Col. Robert Leiendecker, formerly of the U.S. EOD service, has also indicated that no copy of the original instructional film,

*UXB*, exists in the Aberdeen Proving Ground or NATEODA archives. (R.M. Philips, *Visit of American Army Officers to London*, 26 January 1942; Lt. Col. Kane, *1942 itinerary*, 2; Lt. Col. Kane, *Statements*, 3-5; Gary Woodman-Simmons, email, 24 September 2003.)

[88] Major R.H. Minty, as a Royal Engineer captain, had commanded No. 11 BD Company in Edinburgh. Minty went on to lead No. 27 BD Company in Ulster. (Wakeling, 9-10, Kane, *Bomb Disposal, U. S. A.*, 3-14; Kane, *Statements*, 5, 12.)

[89] Kane, *1942 itinerary*, 3.

[90] Durham, 13-21; Kane, *Bomb Disposal, U. S. A.*, 3-14; Kane, *Statements*, 7.

[91] Kane, *Bomb Disposal, U. S. A.*, 3-14; Kane, *Statements*, 7; *1942 itinerary*, 3.

[92] Kane, *Bomb Disposal, U. S. A.*, 3-14; Kane, *Statements*, 7.

[93] *Principles of Instruction*. Ripon, Yorkshire: Harper Barracks, 1942.

[94] Civilians were trained in reconnaissance and observed practical UXB exercises, but were excluded from technical operations for security reasons. (Army Bomb Disposal School, *British Army Bomb Disposal Course Syllabus*, c. 1942; Army Bomb Disposal School, *Principles of Instruction*, Ripon, Yorkshire: Harper Barracks, 1942).

[95] Kane, *Bomb Disposal, U. S. A.*, 3-14; Army Bomb Disposal School. *Principles of Instruction*. Ripon, Yorkshire: Harper Barracks, 1942.

[96] United States armed forces later adopted the designs of German SD-series anti-personnel mines, using them in the latter stages of World War II, Korea, and Vietnam. (Royal Army BD School Notes; Deichmann, 25-26, Wakeling, 4.)

[97] Deichmann, 27-28; 32-34.

[98] Hartley, 159-60; Jappy, 155-170; Ransted, 73-79; Wakeling, 4.

[99] Deichmann, 27-28; Hartley, 159-60; Jappy, 155-170; Ransted, 73-79.

[100] Deichmann, 27-28, 32-34.

[101] German demolitionists sometimes utilized confiscated Italian and French ordnance, particularly in the Mediterranean Theater, where the Wehrmacht and Luftwaffe often contended with major supply shortages. (Army Bomb Disposal School, *Principles of Instruction*, Ripon, Yorkshire, Harper Barracks, 1942; Hooper, 1.)

[102] Royal Engineer Bomb Disposal patches were designed by Queen Mary of England, who unofficially 'adopted' the courageous bomb disposal branch. (Commandant of Army Bomb Disposal School (Lt. Col. S.H. Fisher) to Joseph C. Pilcher, certificate, 12 March 1942; Commandant of Army Bomb Disposal School (Lt. Col. S.H. Fisher) to Ronald L. Felton, [certificate] 12 March 1942; Hartley, 110.)

[103] Two models, Types C and D, ranged from six to nine feet in length, exclusive of parachutes. They were made of aluminum, and are not to be confused with "G" mines, which lacked the parachute and were made of manganese steel with plastic fins that often broke off whenever these aerial mines hit the earth. (U.S. Army Technical Manual E9-1984, *Disposal Methods for Enemy Bombs and Fuzes,* Aberdeen Proving Ground, Maryland: Chief of Ordnance, 12 November 1942; Kane, *Bomb Disposal, U. S. A.*, 5-7; Kane, *Statements*, 7-8; Kane, *1942 itinerary*, 4; Nass, 9).

[104] Later in the war, some Royal Engineer BD sections were sent to remove "friendly" mines, emplaced along the beaches and piers to discourage invasion. Casualties resulted from such home-front operations, as charges had become unstable due to exposure to elements. (Deichmann, 51-52, 91; Ransted, 43).
[105] Kane, *Bomb Disposal, U. S. A.*, 3-14; Kane, *1942 itinerary*, 4; Kane, *Statements*, 9; 14-15.
[106] Kane, *Bomb Disposal, U. S. A.*, 3-14; Kane, *Statements*, 8-9; Kane, *1942 itinerary*, 4.
[107] Kane, *Bomb Disposal, U. S. A.*, 3-14; Kane, *Statements*, 8-9.
[108] Kane, *Bomb Disposal, U. S. A.*, 3-14; Kane, *Statements*, 8-9.
[109] Kane, *Bomb Disposal, U. S. A.*, 3-14.
[110] Kane, *Bomb Disposal, U. S. A.*, 3-14; Kane, *Statements*, 5; Nass, *Bomb Disposal Notes*, 3; Hooper, 2-4.
[111] Kane, *Bomb Disposal, U. S. A.*, 3-14; Kane, *Statements*, 5-6, 10-12.
[112] EOD soldier-historian Samuel Hooper acknowledges that some auxiliary units became as proficient as Royal Engineers with disarming UXBs and extinguishing incendiaries. (Kane, *Bomb Disposal, U. S. A.*, 3-14; Kane, *Statements*, 3-5; Hooper, 7.)
[113] Kane, *Bomb Disposal, U. S. A.*, 3-14; Kane, *Statements*, 3-5; Hooper, 7.
[114] Kane, *Bomb Disposal, U. S. A.*, 3-14; Kane, *Statements*, 1.
[115] Kane, *Bomb Disposal, U. S. A.*, 3-14; Kane, *Statements*, 5-6, 12.
[116] During Operation Torch in November 1942, three Royal Engineer BD Companies, No. 8, No. 15, and No. 17, took part in the British landings at Algeria. (Kane, *Bomb Disposal, U. S. A.*, 3-14; Kane, *Statements*, 5-6, 10-12; Wakeling, 11.)
[117] Kane, *Bomb Disposal, U. S. A.*, 3-14; Kane, *Statements*, 13-14; Kane, *1942 itinerary*.
[118] Kane, *Bomb Disposal, U. S. A.*, 3-14; Kane, *Statements*, 12-13; Kane, *1942 itinerary*.
[119] Ibid.
[120] Col. G. D. De'ath succeeded Brigadier H.H. Bateman as the Director of Bomb Disposal in 1944. (Kane, *Bomb Disposal, U. S. A.*, 3-14; Kane, *Statements*, 13-14; Kane, *1942 itinerary*, Wakeling, 16.)
[121] Kane, *Bomb Disposal, U. S. A.*, 3-14; Kane, *Statements*, 13-14; Kane, *1942 itinerary*.
[122] Kane's promotion to lieutenant colonel, retroactively dated to 1 March 1942, arrived shortly before he turned forty-two. (Col. C.W. Reed to Assistant Chief of Staff G-2, memorandum, 13 March 1942; Kane, *Bomb Disposal, U. S. A.*, 3-14; Kane, *1942 itinerary*).
[123] Col. C.W. Reed to General Hatcher, memorandum, 18 March 1942; Joseph C. Pilcher, scrapbook, c. 1945; Commandant of Army Bomb Disposal School (Lt. Col. S.H. Fisher) to Joseph C. Pilcher, certificate, 12 March 1942.
[124] Deichmann, 63-64.
[125] Commandant of Army Bomb Disposal School (Lt. Col. S.H. Fisher) to Ronald L. Felton, [certificate] 12 March 1942; Sheffield Observer (Pennsylvania), 16

March 1942; Nancy Swanson, "UXB Squads: The Army's Little-Knowns," *Valley Voice of Sheffield*, 11 November 1983; Jim Hearn, letter to author, 26 April 2004; Wakeling, 9.

[126] Joseph C. Pilcher's 1942 Purple Heart citation confirms his brief attachment to No. 7 Royal Engineer BD Company in Bristol. (Lt. Gen. Brehon Somervell to Lt. Gen. Levin H. Campbell, 4 December 1942; Joseph C. Pilcher, Jr., interview with author, 12 July 2003; Jesse Pilcher, phone interview with author, 2 September 2003; Jim Hearn, letter to author, 26 April 2004; Christopher Ransted, electronic mail to author, 11 May 2004; Ransted, *Bomb Disposal*, 102).

[127] On June 11, 1942, a U.S. Navy ensign, John Howard, died while assisting Royal Navy personnel with a booby-trapped German sea mine. Howard's name is first to appear on the U.S. EOD Memorial. Pilcher and Howard's exact whereabouts in England were kept strictly quiet, consistent with Allied policy. This air of secrecy informed all foreign bomb disposal operations until 1945. (Ransted, *Bomb Disposal*, 39-40; www.eodmemorial.org).

[128] Warrant Officer Austin Unangst to T/Sgt. Joseph C. Pilcher. [certificate] 28 May 1942; Joseph C. Pilcher Jr. [transcript] interview with author 12 July 2003; Jesse Pilcher interview; *Pilcher Scrapbook*).

[129] L/Sgt. Alfred H.J. Belson is buried in Berkshire, at Earley Church of St. Peter. He was thirty-seven at the time of his death, with a widow, Violet, in Reading. (Christopher Ransted, electronic mail to author, 11 May 2004; Ransted, *Bomb Disposal*, 102; Pilcher Scrapbook*;* Jesse Pilcher interview).

[130] Captain (later Major) Tom Sharman also collaborated with U.S. Army Captain Bolick A. Saholsky to establish a joint U.S. Bomb Disposal School at the U.S. Naval College in Annapolis, paving the way for the modern EOD inter-service training program now located at Eglin AFB, Florida. Major Tom Sharman later commanded a Royal Engineers unit attached to the Canadian First Army at Normandy. (Colonel Olaf P. Winningstad to U.S. Army Ordnance School, memorandum, 19 January 1942; U.S. War Department to the Adjutant General, *Ordnance Training Center General Order #7*, 4 February 1942; *History of Bomb Disposal in the U.S.A,* Aberdeen Proving Ground, 1942, 1-3; Tom Sharman, letters to author, 8 August 2003, 26 August 2003; Kane, *Bomb Disposal School History*.)

[131] Major John E. Feldman, *Military History of John Edward Feldman*, U.S. Army Ordnance Museum, c. 1945; John E. Feldman, bomb disposal officer roster, undated; Maria Feldman, interview with author, 18 June 2003; Kay Levering, interview with author, 15 October 2003; Hooper, 9.

[132] Kay Levering recalls that Col. Kane remained very good friends with "Walker," and attended his funeral in 1961. Two other members of Kane's original school detachment also elected to leave bomb disposal service for reasons of their own. William W. Prichard's name does not appear on rosters after 26 November 1942, indicating he went to another assignment. Frank Parsons remained in bomb disposal until mid-1944. During the European campaign, Frank Parsons served with an Ordnance battalion at the Bulge, earning several medals and a battlefield promotion to lieutenant colonel. (Army Ordnance Bomb Disposal School Headquarters, *BD Officer Roster*, 26 November 1942; Ordnance Bomb Disposal

School, *Roster of all Bomb Disposal Officers*, 26 October 1943; *Bomb Disposal School History; The Detonator*, 17 September 1943; *Firepower Magazine,* Washington D.C.: U.S. Army Signal Corps, June 1945; Lt. Col. Martin J. Ehrmann to All Bomb Disposal Soldiers, *Bomb Disposal*, 11 September 1945; Dorothy Parsons, interview with author, 18 October 2003; Levering interview; Walker obituary; 1; Hooper, 11-14.)

133 Pilcher's honor guard included the 235th and 236th Ordnance BD Companies, shortly to see action in the Mediterranean Theater. Other units were the 101st and 102nd Provisional Ordnance Companies. (Lt. Gen. Brehon Somervell, *Award of Purple Heart to Joseph C. Pilcher*, 4 December 1942; William O. Benton, *Procedure for Presentation of the Order of the Purple Heart to Lt. Pilcher*, 17 December 1942; *The Flaming Bomb*. 7 January 1943, 8; Pilcher Scrapbook; Jesse Pilcher interview).

134 Lt. Col. Harry M. Walker, *General Orders Number 1,* [unpublished], 23 February 1943; Felton, *Form 66-2*; Marsha Felton Frost, email to author, 24 February 2003; Marsha Felton Frost, interview by author, 1 March 2003.

135 National Jewish Welfare Board, Bureau of War Records, 1939-45, National Archives and Records Administration. www.ancestry.com; Joseph C. Pilcher Jr., interview by author, 25 April 2003.

136 Headquarters Ordnance Bomb Disposal School, General Orders Number 1, 23 February 1943.

# CHAPTER TWO

# BOMB KILLERS

Two major bureaucratic shakeups affected the Army's Bomb Disposal branch almost from its start. To begin with, their most powerful supporter, Maj. Gen. Charles M. Wesson, planned to retire as Chief of Ordnance in May 1942. Wesson's successor, Maj. Gen. Levin H. Campbell, entered his new office with set priorities and goals. Col. Kane would have to build new rapport with his incoming supervisor. However, the second change wrought more profound changes for all the Technical Services, including the Ordnance Corps. The experts and professionals had assumed control.

Before Pearl Harbor, Wesson had enjoyed relative autonomy under the relaxed supervision of Army Services of Supply. However, this arrangement changed drastically on February 28, 1942, when Executive Order 9082 transformed Services of Supply (SOS) into Army Service Forces (ASF). Under this new supervisory board, Lt. Gen. Brehon B. Somervell consolidated all seven technical services, including the Ordnance Corps. As a leading Pentagon technocrat, Somervell even contemplated the dissolution of Army technical services, replacing them with civilian contractors. As Chief of Ordnance, Levin Campbell complied with his new superior's streamlining policies, but doggedly resisted Somervell's excessive meddling in Ordnance matters.[1]

Despite some early talk of "total mobilization" in Washington, civilians were considered very junior partners in wartime ordnance disposal. In April 1942, Maj. Gen. Dwight D. Eisenhower issued a blueprint for national emergency operations that called for increased military control over all shell and bomb disposal tasks. At that time, "Ike" had served as Gen. George C. Marshall's Deputy Chief of Staff. In keeping with Roosevelt's Executive Order 9066, Eisenhower's proposal granted broad discretionary powers to all four U.S. Defense Commands, who were responsible for defending the homeland during an actual raid. Ike's plan also authorized commanders to prescribe "military areas" wherein they reserved the powers to evacuate the civilian populace, interrupt radio broadcasts, and even segregate "enemy aliens."[2]

Since June 1942, both the U.S. College Commission and Civilian Protection Schools (CPS) had sponsored UXB reconnaissance instructors, who lectured on major campuses in Maryland, Florida, and Washington. Capt. Frank Parsons lectured on explosives at several other campuses, including Amherst, Purdue, Stanford, and Texas A&M College. During this first year, an estimated 25,000 civilians attended the 66-hour course for bomb reconnaissance agents. Additionally, over 30,000 men and women took the UXB agent correspondence course through Kane's indoctrination center; while over 125,000 others viewed instructional films synthesized from British and American training materials.[3]

Such public interest in UXBs reflected a high degree of civilian cooperation in the wake of Pearl Harbor. However, OCD agencies began squabbling with the military as well as internally. As early as July 1942, *Time* published a feature story on handling incendiaries, entitled "How to Drown a Bomb." Technicians at the University of Maryland demonstrated a method to extinguish fire-bombs, using steady streams from fire hoses. Such countermeasures were opposed by OCD and military experts, because magnesium fillings were prone to flaring, increasing risks for secondary explosions. One inspector from OCD also took Chicago firefighters to task for suggesting that live incendiary bomb might be "drowned" in a fire bucket. This spokesman further warned *Time*'s readers to avoid such "ill-advised" methods. OCD operatives believed most civilians would "lack the coolness" to perform such feats in actual raids. City leaders were sometimes accused of exaggerating threats from incendiary bombs for political ends, thereby instilling "unjustified fear."[4]

Guided by Roosevelt's "Germany First" strategy, the Pentagon initially focused on East Coast defenses. But, what were Germany's real chances for inflicting a Warsaw or Coventry? One experimental aircraft carrier, the *Graf Zeppelin*, had been constructed, but excessive gunnery limited the top-heavy *Graf*'s maneuverability. Moreover, her clumsy fighter-bombers were prone to crash-landings. In May 1942, U.S. intelligence uncovered Luftwaffe plans for token air raids, using disposable long-range bombers. One such plane, scheduled to fly from Brittany to New York, suffered from repeated technical malfunctions, and never took off. Later on, German rocketry experts speculated that a V-1 rocket might reach New York City from a special barge towed by U-boats. Vague intelligence reports later alerted the War Department to a possible "robot bombing" in November 1944. For nine days, Navy pilots fruitlessly swept the Atlantic for signs of German rockets or submarines.[5]

Without any clear direction, the national Office of Civilian Defense had foundered by late 1943. Director James Landis grew unpopular due to his mandatory blackouts. Meanwhile, Eleanor Roosevelt's conservative foes derided her program's focus on health and social welfare. Mayris Chaney, a celebrity dancer, was forced to resign as the OCD fitness director. Yet, despite such partisan wrangling, some programs were more than just "boondoggles." Throughout 1942-43, regional OCD chapters also provided invaluable relief during natural disasters, notably the Ohio River Valley Flood and West Virginia's Shinnston Tornado. Civil Air Patrol (CAP) units were incorporated into the U.S. Army in 1944 for their proven effectiveness in spotting German submarines on the coasts.[6]

* * *

As Washington prepared for chimerical Nazi raids on the East Coast, Japanese planes had already begun flying sorties over the Pacific Northwest. Toward the end of September 1942, Flight Lt. Nobuo Fujita's submarine-launched light bomber caused sporadic forest fires across Oregon and Washington. Fujita's two pinprick raids nevertheless spurred fears of an imminent West Coast invasion, already roused by an earlier July strike against Dutch Harbor, Alaska, which killed over seventy Americans and injured scores of others. Meanwhile, over the previous summer, thousands of Japanese troops had crossed over the North Pacific, establishing two sizeable footholds in the outermost Aleutian Islands, within easy air-striking distance of Alaska and British Columbia.[7]

In August 1942, Maj. Gen. Campbell sent Lt. Col. Thomas J. Kane to inspect special ordnance sections deployed at nine Service Commands, which were administered by four major Defense Commands. Never one to hide his light behind the proverbial bushel, Kane had often lobbied the War Department for an increased role for his soldiers. While some might accuse Kane of tireless self-promotion, he clearly wanted a share of wartime glory for his officers and men as well. Kane had long recognized that his ordnancemen would be invaluable to Army forces overseas. However, conservative Army officers like Somervell still tended to regard bomb disposal as a chiefly defensive asset. Recognizing this actuality, Kane published a professional article – his only one – through the Ordnance journal. Whereas "*Unexploded Bombs*" reached only a limited military readership, it elevated the hitherto unknown lieutenant colonel to a higher audience within the War Department. Kane's logical arguments impressed his superiors enough to merit Campbell's nomination.[8]

Kane, still a lieutenant colonel, stands outside the Ordnance School shortly before embarking on his stateside inspection tour in late 1942. (*Kane Collection*)

In "*Unexploded Bombs*," Kane recalled his lessons from London while invoking similar wartime visions from Nanjing, Guernica, and Warsaw. He reflected on the nature of total war, wherein "any means of affecting the war effort is considered legitimate, *at least by the Axis nations*." Kane also tactfully addressed recent clashes between military and civil authority. In essence, Kane reminded everyone: do not forget about the war. Isolation from the immediate battlefronts did not exempt the U.S. from preparedness. Citing his own observations in England, Kane recognized the destructive effects of air raids on "civil services and public morale." Kane recognized that ordinary citizens had a part to play during national emergencies. He recapitulated the OCD's wartime priorities; repairing vital establishments, caring for the injured, fighting fires caused by explosions, and evacuating civilians to shelters. Nevertheless, he firmly reserved all technical ordnance tasks for duly trained military personnel, particularly those belonging to his bomb disposal branch.[9]

Departing by plane in August 1942, Kane and Maj. B. A. Saholsky toured each stateside headquarters, save for Central Defense Command. Bolick Saholsky, formerly a liaison officer at the Navy Bomb Disposal School, served as Kane's advisor on coastal defenses. Saholsky was also one of four Army officers who had graduated from the Navy School. Over the next three months, he and Kane would determine whether the United States could survive direct bombardment on either of its coastlines.[10]

B.A. Saholsky (second row, fourth from right) graduated from Draper Kauffman's first Navy bomb disposal course in March 1942. (*Leiendecker Collection*)

Visiting the East Coast first, Kane noted its bomb disposal program coming along "slowly but surely." Kane singled out a total of three ordnance officers for deficiencies in training activities. Two offenders were based in the Northeast. In Boston, Lt. Col. W. A. Hoyle (First Service Command) drastically reduced UXB training, under the premise that German air raids were unlikely to happen. In Baltimore, Lt. Col. Murray Resnicoff (Third Service Command) had failed to recruit agents. Furthermore, Resnicoff had generated "undesirable publicity" for Kane's program. While visiting Fort Douglas, Utah, Kane found a third officer, Major Tracy Kerr (Ninth Service Command), "unsuitable" for OCD liaison work. These officers appear to have been merely reprimanded.[11]

Visiting three other landlocked Midwestern bases at Illinois, Ohio, and Nebraska, Kane detected a false sense of security, resulting in low preparedness. He also stressed a need to secure the Great Lakes canals against potential saboteurs, whether German spies or Nazi sympathizers. In particular, Kane cited the vulnerability of Sault Ste. Marie Canal, jointly patrolled by the U.S. and Canada at Michigan's border. [12]

On his final leg to the West Coast, Kane arrived shortly after Japan's incendiary raids in the Northwest. Western Defense Command had recovered some bomb debris, with assistance from the 101st Provisional Ordnance Bomb Disposal Company. Kane praised Western Command's efficient warning system, and commended these disposaleers for responding quickly. However, thanks to poor incident reporting, 1st Lt. John Drislane's field platoons had to scatter across Northern California and Oregon in order to locate the elusive bomb sites. At this juncture, Kane's school possessed limited knowledge concerning Japanese firebombs, so this incident yielded significant research data.[13]

In future emergencies, Kane declared that Service and Defense Commands should appoint at least one Army officer to every duty station. To ensure their effectiveness, such officers would require at least one week of UXB education. Kane's report urged sending cadre members from Aberdeen Proving Ground to supervise training. Later in the war, military instructors were dispatched to the West Coast. John Drislane and several of his technicians also remained for the war's duration as faculty. Using the British film, "UXB," as a springboard, these instructors lectured on emergency procedures and ordnance recognition.[14]

While military personnel remained limited in quantity, Kane cautiously endorsed more civilian participation. He profiled a "proper type" of civilian agent, suggesting that policemen, firemen, industrial managers, and municipal engineers often made the best recruits. Possessing both "education and character," he felt such men and women were more likely to remain "on the spot" during a potential bombing raid. Kane also predicted that replacement agents might be necessary in case of illness, unexpected death, or change of location.[15]

Significantly, Kane categorically included women as potential bomb reconnaissance agents. Modeled on the British system, the Office of Civilian Defense sometimes recruited female air wardens, particularly in Northern cities. During the war, the U.S. Marine Corps even trained a few females as mine and bomb disposal technicians, although they never saw combat in the Pacific Theater. While the U.S. Army did not train female bomb disposaleers, the modern EOD branch freely admits women, who have even risen to senior command positions within their specialty.[16]

One of Kane's favorite euphemisms, "housekeeping," sums up his approach toward organization. Everyone had a job to do, regardless of their position. Kane expressed disgust toward defense plant executives who felt they were above pitching in. He also criticized factory workers who cited war propaganda equating their positions with front-line soldiers. Kane had no sympathy with this mindset, which he described as "let 'George' do it; *I'm* a vital defense worker." Factory personnel were also needed to lead search parties and evacuations during raids. If this meant extra training after hours, then so be it. Kane considered this "reprehensible" attitude as a major obstacle toward war preparedness. He concluded that both defense executives and shift-workers needed to understand their specific obligations in times of national crisis.[17]

Kane urged placing "special agents... trained in UXB reconnaissance" in strategic locations where they could be reached during emergencies. Owing to poor administration at the OCD, many agents had completed their courses, but had remained unassigned to posts. OCD officials had compiled monthly surveys to keep track of graduates and their activity status, but little more progress had been made. In California, Kane heard complaints about slow civil defense response times during the Fujita raids, which left the military taking up the slack. There were also false leads and unconfirmed reports, which divided personnel. With minimal Army and Navy ordnance personnel available to a given Defense Command, UXB reports needed to be accurate and complete. Toward this goal, Navy ordnance agreed to adopt Army reporting methods to ensure uniformity.[18]

Kane's final report praised every level of civilian cooperation thus far, but he urged OCD personnel to prevent erroneous reports from circulating in the press. Kane knew the perils of undue panic created by false alarms. That December, he responded to a beached naval mine in New York City; a renegade mooring buoy, as it turned out. Kane also neutralized a real UXB when a U.S. Navy plane accidentally lost a 100-pound bomb during a practice flight over Jones Beach, New York. Both of these incidents were duly recorded in Kane's travel journals, and escaped the notice of many citizens, partly owing to poor beachcombing weather.[19]

In due course, Kane's civil defense commentaries were circulated to John M. Landis, who had just replaced the outspoken Fiorello LaGuardia as OCD's national director. However, at this juncture, Landis was more concerned about German submarine activity on the Southeastern coast. While U-boat attacks primarily affected shipping, they nevertheless prompted two requests for permanent bomb disposal sections in Atlanta and Charleston, South Carolina. For several months in 1942, stateside Army detachments patrolled these sectors, but to little purpose.[20]

After five weeks abroad, T. J. Kane returned at last to Maryland, submitting his final report to Ordnance Headquarters on October 19. Soon after, he received a promotion to "full-bird" colonel, making him eligible to compete for higher positions in Ordnance. Yet, Kane preferred to resume his school duties at Aberdeen Proving Ground. Most of his suggestions were implemented by the War Department, and the school continued to train hundreds of OCD bomb reconnaissance agents.[21]

Caricature of T.J. Kane from Aberdeen Proving Ground. (*Kane Collection*)

Col. Kane's survey created a lot of work for national defense planners. War Department officers decried a lack of "direction and coordination" between Defense Commands, whose commanders shuffled unwanted disposaleers from station to station. For a time, air raid wardens received UXB training from the Army's Field Services Division, with bomb disposal sections supervised directly by ammunition officers. Brig. Gen. Idwal H. Richards, the Assistant Chief of Staff, reminded every Service commander that the "disposition of bomb disposal troops calls for a tactical decision by one commander, not three or four."[22]

Ultimately, while each U.S. Service Command retained a detachment of BD officers for homeland defense, their roles during wartime were largely relegated to stateside reconnaissance training. However, by February 1943, even as North Africa called for increased ordnance support against the Afrika Korps, forty accredited bomb disposal officers were still billeted at Aberdeen's replacement pool. Lt. Col. Walker recommended that these lieutenants should either be given to the Bomb Disposal School as instructors, or given command over activated bomb disposal units. Kane's staff officers now realized their branch's contributions to Allied victory were extremely limited on the home front. By the end of 1942, military instruction became top priority at the Bomb Disposal School.[23]

* * *

On February 16, 1942, the Army Bomb Disposal School began training its first class of officers. During its first six months, the Army School had only 29 officers and 196 enlisted men, with ten WAACs (Women's Auxiliary Army Corps) acting as headquarters secretaries. However, with almost 90 officer candidates and 623 sergeants in training, classroom space quickly became a concern at the Ordnance Training Center. In May 1942, Kane appealed for a permanent, self-contained location, complete with barracks and mess hall. Maj. Gen. Wesson, the outgoing Chief of Ordnance, approved Kane's request for a new facility, to be located near Boothby Hill Road. Maj. Gen. Campbell seconded this motion, and this new block of buildings became officially known as the U.S. Army Bomb Disposal Center, though most ordnancemen still called it the Bomb Disposal School.[24]

At this new Bomb Disposal Center, the "Nine from Aberdeen" continued in their roles as administrators, instructors, and technicians. Col. Kane became "Director of Bomb Disposal," a unique title in EOD history. During his tenure as commandant, Kane's unique responsibilities required frequent travel to Washington as well as overseas assignments. Lt. Col. Harry Walker effectively served as school commandant until replaced by Martin Ehrmann in October 1943. Capt. Frank A. Parsons became Training Director, the third-highest position at the Army Bomb Disposal School. Parson's deputy, Capt. Art Keller, served as the Chief of Civilian Training. Lieutenants Ron Felton and Joe Pilcher trained new recruits in bombs and munitions, while Dick Metress took his place as school headquarters officer. Wally Nass, in the meantime, developed a close working relationship with John Feldman, his resident wizard in Research and Development.[25]

As the new Center's effective commandant, Lt. Col. Harry Walker safeguarded military information and handled administration. Maj. J. K. Lynch headed Walker's administrative staff, while Capt. Malcolm Antonelli's headquarters company supervised training schedules and inspections. Meanwhile, offices of Supply and Transportation fulfilled equipment requests and maintained vehicles. Finally, the school's Intelligence branch continually gathered new ordnance data, developed training aids, tested new equipment, and managed the "bomb museum."[26]

Col. Kane and his training cadre at the Army Bomb Disposal Center in early 1943. Front Row: Bolick A. Saholsky, Thomas J. Kane, and Harry M. Walker. Back Row: Stanley J. Jesatko, Clarence H. Beery, Jr., Herbert L. Karsch, and Walter R. Nass. (*Leiendecker Collection*)

Maj. Martin Ehrmann holds a disarmed Butterfly Bomb. Ehrmann eventually succeeded Col. T.J. Kane as BD school commandant. (*Vining Collection*)

Research and development required constant updating "to make its practice effective against the ingenuity and progress of the enemy." One of Col. Kane's most fortuitous recruits, Martin J. Ehrmann understood Germany's "ingenuity and progress." Fluent in both Polish and German, Martin had fled Austria for political reasons in 1923. By 1933, Ehrmann had become a naturalized U. S. citizen. As a respected gemologist and businessman, Martin specialized in rare ores and stones and often traveled aboard luxury liners such as the ill-fated *S.S. Normandie*. In 1942, Martin Ehrmann received a direct commission as a captain of Ordnance, and later attained the rank of lieutenant colonel as Kane's successor at the school.[27]

During his first year, Martin Ehrmann supervised all bomb disposal publications as well as school communications. Ehrmann got on well with his fellow training officers, especially his boss, Harry Walker, and John Feldman, now serving as head of research and development. All three were present at Baltimore's Southern Hotel, where John Feldman met his future bride, Maria Washkevich. Maria, a schoolteacher, dined regularly in the hotel restaurant with two of her companions. It seemed fitting for their two parties to mingle for a friendly evening. John and Maria hit it off, and after a patient courtship, they tied the knot in early 1944.[28]

Several of Kane's officers posing for a group photograph in the spring of 1943. Front Row: Edwin "Pappy" Trevor, William R. Bailey, and Robert E. Anderson. Back Row: James A. Westbrook, Robert P. Tobin, John E. Feldman, and Joseph K. Dana. (*Leiendecker Collection*)

Kane's earliest months as Bomb Disposal School commandant required both administrative and diplomatic skills. In mid-May, Kane lectured at the War Department, explaining the importance of his new branch of service to the heads of all Army services. On May 26, 1942, Brig. Gen. Julian S. Hatcher inspected the school, attending demonstrations of bomb disposal equipment and methods. In later months, Hatcher returned with visiting British and Royal Australian generals. That November, an unusual delegation of Russian officers watched a demonstration of the earth auger at the Ordnance School.[29]

*U.S. Navy officer observing an Army BD exercise.* (*Leiendecker Collection*)

Maj. Gen. Levin H. Campbell, Chief of Ordnance, paid at least one customary call on Kane's school in early June 1942. Campbell routinely inspected the Bomb Disposal School during his tenure. Yet another distinguished guest, Navy Lieut. Draper Kauffman, twice observed Army training methods on behalf of his burgeoning Navy program. On June 1, Kauffman attended one memorable "bomb disposal show" with a sizeable group of Navy officers and petty officers. Despite a natural degree of rivalry, Army and Navy ordnance teams shared a mutual respect that only deepened throughout the war, especially in the Pacific Theater.[30]

However, not all of Kane's visitors wore military uniforms. In mid-June, several railroad executives and inspectors from the American Association of Railroads discussed their concerns with Walker and Kane, who were themselves former railwaymen. Whether these businessmen were more worried about Axis saboteurs or labor unions remains unclear, but they were treated with the same cordiality as the armed forces.[31]

Aberdeen Proving Ground encouraged the Bomb Disposal School's efforts to instill *esprit de corps* for their officers and men. By late 1942, Col. Kane had unveiled the Army Bomb Disposal School's distinctive service badge, with crimson and yellow colors denoting Ordnance Corps affiliation. It featured a device with two armored hands breaking a bomb, creating a familiar model for later EOD badges. Kane's proposed motto, "Sweeping Along," implied his school's rapid advancement, as well as forward movements in the battlefield. School graduates were also authorized to wear black shoulder sleeve insignia; patches with red bomblets outlined in gold. Later in the war, subdued olive-drab patches were developed for battle uniforms. Sometimes, these plain insignia misled foreign civilians into blaming these ordnance men for bombing their countries, with some unintentionally amusing results.[32]

Throughout the war, Kane sought to improve his new branch's profile, without compromising the air of secrecy surrounding their mission. Initially, the Bomb Disposal School's precise location was kept secret. Photographs involving bombs or special equipment were not allowed to circulate to the press. However, by 1943, Army and Navy ordnancemen had received mention in stateside papers as well as the *Stars and Stripes*. Good publicity helped build morale, and Kane quickly realized this fact. His school's public affairs section, first headed by Martin J. Ehrmann, looked for opportunities to liaise with the general public.[33]

Kane usually resisted personal publicity, but once, in London, *Newsweek*'s Al Newman interviewed a "nameless" colonel who identified his Pennsylvania hometown as Punxsutawney. Newman vividly described this "bomb killer" as a "burly Irishman" with a thatch of graying hair, who exuded a "strange air of indestructibility," as though he could "overpower any bomb ever made." Newman quoted Kane's golden rule of ordnance: "You only make one mistake – you're either an expert or you're dead." When one considers the specialized knowledge and determination required to become a bomb disposal technician, Kane's motto hardly resembles the credo of thrill-seekers. Even today, EOD's unofficial motto, "Initial Success or Total Failure," reflects Kane's philosophy.[34]

Kane also ensured his soldiers were motivated by patriotism as well. In June 1942, Lt. Gen. Somervell's headquarters proposed reassignments to Bomb Disposal for a group of conscientious objectors. Over in Britain, hundreds of religious dissenters served in Non-Combatant Corps units on the home front. Based on this logic, Somervell convinced his Chief of Field Service, Col. H. R. Kutz, to support a similar measure. But, Kane's staff officers soon discovered these enlisted men had engaged in pro-Axis demonstrations. Bolick Saholsky wrote to Kutz in protest, emphasizing the lack of loyalty among such "undesirable personnel." Saholsky also cited past British experiences with pro-German "fifth columnists."[35]

Ultimately, the Chief of Ordnance went over Somervell's head, appealing to the War Department. Potential quislings were excluded from Bomb Disposal services, but this argument demonstrated recurring problems within the technical services, who mistakenly viewed Kane's school as a dumpsite for Ordnance Department rejects. Kane recalled hearing at least one ordnance sergeant threatening his "recalcitrant" privates with reassignment into bomb disposal units, christened by some Aberdeen wags as "suicide squads." Kane and Ehrmann discouraged using this sobriquet to identify their all-volunteer service in the press, but occasionally, there were lapses in protocol.[36]

Bomb disposal students demonstrate rigging at the Army Bomb Disposal School. Most enlisted graduates became riggers for field units. (*Kane Collection*)

Despite minor "growing pains," Lt. Col. Harry Walker confidently presided over the Army BD School's first anniversary "gala" on February 17, 1943. Ranking officers from the Ordnance Training Center were in attendance. Aberdeen Proving Ground's newspaper, *Flaming Bomb*, promoted the event, which included technical demonstrations, drill competitions, and tug-of-war challenges. Afterward, they reconvened for a relatively tame "stag party" complete with orchestra in the recently-built mess hall. Harry Walker expressed his pride in Ordnance's newest branch, which had shed its humble origins with only "a handful of men," to become a "superlative" Army training facility.[37]

With graduates leaving for combat zones, the school administrators were still understrength by early 1943. Nevertheless, the Army's Bomb Disposal Center boasted eight full classrooms, an enlisted barracks with shared mess hall for one thousand, plus a practice bombing range and technical laboratory. The school even featured its own "booby trap" obstacle course; a converted chicken coop nicknamed the "Mystery Manor." By this stage, the school's mission had diversified, as there was now a need for bomb disposal overseas, evidenced by the Center's replication in England toward year's end. In addition to "rendering safe" unexploded or delayed-action bombs "dropped by the enemy," training programs now encompassed "friendly" UXBs, along with diverse enemy projectiles and mines. Ultimately, bomb disposal specialists had to undergo further innovations in order to realize their true potential.[38]

Where did the Army Bomb Disposal School recruit its new officers? 2nd Lt. Vandel P. Kovar of New Jersey had recently graduated from Virginia Military Institute in 1939. 2nd Lt. Thomas R. Reece of Indiana, on the other hand, held a reserve commission while working as a chemist. Some officers were OCS graduates, such as George Clifford Sarauw of Maryland, who transferred as a sergeant from the 1st Infantry Division. Carl Cirocco, born into a family of Pennsylvania coal-miners, enlisted in April 1941. At age twenty, Carl progressed quickly through the ranks at Aberdeen Proving Ground, working closely with Maj. T. J. Kane, still acting provost marshal. T/Sgt. Cirocco's flair for draftsmanship and uncommon maturity impressed Kane, who sponsored him for OCS.[39]

Kane's first candidates studied under British and American instructors, using a synthesis of both schools. By November 1942, the War Department had approved the very first U.S. technical manual on UXBs, *Enemy Bombs and Fuzes* (TM E9-1984). Endorsed by Gen. George C. Marshall, this manual served both Army and Navy Bomb Disposal Schools. Periodically, this manual received new inserts with newly-discovered bombs resulting from field reports. TM E9-1984 featured detailed schematics on Axis and Allied ordnance. Wally Nass contributed many hand-drawn diagrams based on his original notes from Harper Barracks. Later on, photographs guided each stage in "render-safe procedures." Following proper identification, officers "sterilized" their fuze using recommended methods, ranging from the electric clock-stopper to thermal and liquid fuze dischargers. Afterward, the officer removed locking rings using the proper spanner. Early on, fuzes were withdrawn by hand, but the British developed the impact wrench to minimize casualties from Zus-40s. Now, a disposal officer could unscrew a fuze from its gaine at a safe distance. Unfortunately, such specialized tools were in short supply during the Bomb Disposal program's first year.[40]

Lt. Col. Harry Walker presides over the February 17, 1943 gala celebrating the Army Ordnance Bomb Disposal School's successful first year. (*Kane Collection*)

On July 9, 1942, the Army Bomb Disposal School's first graduating class of officers took their final examinations. On that sunny afternoon, two low-flying American planes each dropped a live general purpose (GP) bomb with delayed-action fuzes at the Ordnance Training Center's bombing range. Already, the Ordnance Department had foreseen the eventuality of dealing with "friendly" UXBs under battlefield conditions. For his own part, T. J. Kane frequently articulated his disapproval toward the U.S. Army Air Forces, who often created more work for his soldiers. Once asked by an unsuspecting Air Force officer to describe his organization's exact purpose, Kane replied with succinct humor: "Principally, we correct your mistakes."[41]

Capt. Wright G. Calder (standing behind the bomb) and his section graduated from the first U.S. Army Bomb Disposal course in 1942. "Scotty" later served as a bomb disposal squad commander in England and France. (*Kane Collection*)

During these July examinations, team leaders Wright G. Calder and George C. Sarauw also took the opportunity to test out a new impact wrench. However, as "Scotty" Calder recounted his tale to the author; "We only had one set of tools for two squads." Sarauw suggested a coin toss to settle the question, but instead, Scotty sportingly yielded up the impact wrench to his friend, relying on his "old plumber's wrench" to neutralize the UXB in his own freshly-dug shaft.[42]

Then, both officers entered their shafts with almost Olympic élan. Calder deftly removed his bomb fuze using basic tools, and then strode over to see his comrade's progress. Hunched inside his crater, Clifford Sarauw had just attached his impact wrench when Scotty Calder greeted him unexpectedly: "How are you doing, George?" Sarauw nearly jumped out of his skin, but recovered and made short work of his fuze. Capt.

Edwin "Pappy" Trevor, the chief training officer, credited both graduates for officially disarming UXB Number One for the school. "We had a lot of beer and whiskey that night," Calder later reminisced.[43]

Capt. George Clifford Sarauw (standing behind the bomb) later commanded the United States Army's bomb disposal company in Hawaii. (*Kane Collection*)

Initially, the Army saw its bomb disposal officers chiefly as advisors. By November 1942, at least forty Army bomb disposal officers were deployed to sixteen outposts, including U.S. bases at Iceland, Greenland, and Trinidad. Some graduates also shipped out to Allied headquarters in the Middle East, while others dispersed across the British Commonwealth. 1st Lt. Thomas Reece participated in a year-long joint training program with the Royal Canadian Army, training hundreds of Allied troops based at Newfoundland. However, save for sporadic U-boat activities, there were no direct attacks on the North Atlantic coast. When Reece finally returned to Maryland in December 1943, his sole venture against Axis ordnance had been helping the Navy with a stray German sea mine.[44]

Like their British counterparts, American bomb disposal officers coalesced into a fraternity. *Newsweek*'s war correspondent, Al Newman, met several of Kane's officers: Major Ryerson Bredin, Major Frank

Parsons, Capt. Schuyler "Sky" Larkin, and Capt. John E. Feldman. Newman described them as specialists who were "clever with their hands [and] uniformly insane." Newman also observed that they acted "clannish to a remarkable degree." Bound by secrecy, they seldom discussed their work with outsiders, even members from other technical services. However, making up for a lack of sociability, bomb disposal officers' drinking parties were "apt to be destructive." Maj. Ryerson "Rye" Bredin described his own unique cocktail, called "bomb-disposal fluid," that officers supposedly imbibed *before* physically "eating their way to the fuze." Then as now, heavy drinking was a large part of Army culture. Even Kane enjoyed a reputation as a "morning person who lived hard."[45]

Col. Kane (standing at right) cutting a special cake baked by the Bomb Disposal School mess hall. Lt. Col. Walker is seated at far right. Whether this festive occasion was a birthday party for Kane is unclear. (*Leiendecker Collection*)

Al Newman noted Kane's rapport with his junior officers, recording one instance when John Feldman accidentally set fire to Kane's office floor with a "homemade cigarette lighter." With laughing indulgence, Kane referred to Feldman as "one of my brightest boys," and sent him off to repair their broken toaster. Kay Levering fondly recalled her father's lifelong friendship with Feldman: "They were both big men, almost like twins, blessed with a wonderful sense of humor." Maria Feldman likewise affirmed her husband's long friendship with his commanding officer: "Colonel Kane treated my husband just like a son; he knew that John was never happy unless he was inventing something."[46]

By mid-1943, 159 second lieutenants had graduated the four-week BDM-1 course. At full capacity, 100 officers could train at the school, with 25 graduations per week. Moreover, 668 ordnance officers and 301 sergeants completed two-week courses in UXB reconnaissance, while 1,140 officers and 11,500 officer candidates received introductory briefings on UXBs. Nor were such classes limited to the ground forces. Still technically part of the U.S. Army, the U.S. Air Forces sent 1,435 personnel through Aberdeen Proving Ground's various UXB programs. Some Army officers later commanded the Air Force bomb disposal teams. By contrast, civilian training dropped appreciably at Aberdeen Proving Ground. Only sixteen non-military students trained at the OTC or Army Bomb Disposal Center during its first year of training.[47]

Aberdeen Proving Ground trained thousands of enlisted men under the Army's standard 13-week Mobilization Training Program. Following their combat training, enlisted ordnancemen went to specialist schools. Bomb disposal tended to accumulate men from industrialized regions. Pennsylvania's coal mining culture exerted some influence over Kane's training program. Both T. J. Kane and Harry Walker originally hailed from Punxsutawney. One of Kane's stalwarts, M/Sgt. Harry "Buck" Moore, worked for seven years as a machinist at Messmore, supervising nearly thirty employees. At twenty-eight, Buck ranked as his company's highest noncom, as well as the Bomb Disposal School's "oldest enlisted man." Lt. Carl Cirocco, also the son of a coal miner, ascribes the Bomb Disposal School's high concentration of miners to their previous backgrounds in shaft excavation and mechanical repairs.[48]

Designated "bomb salvage technicians," enlisted ordnancemen spent three weeks learning enemy and friendly bombs, shells, and fuzes. Privates scoring at least 75 percent on their proficiency tests advanced to Private First Class, and later on, Technician 5$^{th}$ Grade (T/5). After one year, T/5s were eligible for promotions to Sergeant or less frequently, Technician 4$^{th}$ Grade (T/4). Only the most dedicated men aspired to become Technical Sergeants, who were required to complete 180 hours of study in all manner of Axis and Allied bombs, mines, and projectiles.[49]

Bill Mauldin's amusing *Stars and Stripes* cartoons often portrayed soldiers with technician's stripes as "Model-T Corporals," bureaucratic oafs who made life difficult for average grunts. Latter-day Vietnam veterans might recognize this stereotype as a "REMF." Steven Spielberg's cinematic opus, *Saving Private Ryan*, has further reinforced this trope with Upham, the cowardly translator forced into battle. Yet, even Mauldin's less vulgar sobriquet, "garritrooper," still does not accurately depict the Army's original EOD soldiers – in fact, some "bomb killers" endured front-line combat as vital components of infantry divisions.[50]

While many bomb disposaleers never fired their weapons in combat, they routinely embraced danger without receiving any hazard pay. Nevertheless, ordnancemen could expect brushes with enemy forces, so nearly everyone at Aberdeen Proving Ground practiced basic marksmanship with standard Army firearms. In 1942, new .30 cal. M-1 Garand rifles were in short supply, so Kane's soldiers began their training with leftover M1903 Springfields. Most officers and noncoms preferred the Colt .45 cal. M1911A1 pistol, because they required free hands to perform technical aspects of their jobs. Some officers, like Thomas Reece, became expert shots with the .30 cal. M-2 carbine, developed by Garand in order to give field officers a sidearm with better firepower than the Colt. However, when asked to name a bomb disposal soldier's most effective weapon, Lt. Carl Cirocco instinctively replied: "ingenuity."[51]

During their advanced training, bomb disposal men were billeted apart from other technical services, living in standard two-story army barracks. Supervised by the Army BD School headquarters company, all privates and technicians were still required to serve as kitchen police and nightly fireguards. In late 1943, nightly visits to Havre de Grace's clubs were curtailed, after a series of cigarette fires placed the BD School "on the spot." Certain fireguards had covered up for "grossly negligent" buddies who enjoyed late-night smokes outside their barracks. When news reached school headquarters, Capt. Malcolm Antonelli dressed down his trainees, warning that failures to report fires would result in offenders paying hefty fines. As a disciplinary action, the school headquarters promptly instated midnight bed-checks for all junior enlisted men. Sergeants enforced a temporary ban on weeknight outings, amid many grumbles that such curfews felt like "boot camp" all over again.[52]

After stricter headcounts limited their nocturnal activity, G.I.s thirsted for escapist literature to encourage relaxation, but their barracks bookshelves lacked much in the way of novels. Arrangements were made for a bookmobile to visit every week. Disposaleers frequently re-read issues of *Ordnance Sergeant* and ever-present training manuals. S/Sgt. Bill Rock and Cpl. Teddy Cox also published *The Detonator*, a self-styled "voice of the enlisted [bomb disposal] man." Bulletins regularly announced BD unit departures and posted brief messages from overseas. Cox profiled outstanding school personnel, such as T/Sgt. Jack Hatfield

(School Services) and M/Sgt. Buck Moore (233rd Company). Cpl. Lester Rhodes and other amateur cartoonists published their own "funny page."[53]

Soldiers required provender, and the Army BD School's brand-new dining facility boasted a wide selection. Sgt. M.S. Brazil spared no effort to order dinner meats, including such delicacies as lamb and veal. Such entrées represented a surprisingly high standard of eating, especially considering wartime rationing. Brazil often berated wasteful "chow hounds" who left uneaten portions, reminding stateside "G.I.B.D.s" about their hungry comrades who were "calling for better food" overseas.[54]

Overseas deployments created problems for the school's athletics division. As participants in Aberdeen's 1942 basketball season, Capt. Rye Bredin's "formidable squad" successfully trounced their rivals from other technical services. Cpl. Teddy Cox from *The Detonator* regretted the loss of his school's winning team, as Capt. Bredin's "veterans" had since "graduated" into bomb disposal companies and later on, separate squads.[55]

* * *

In late April 1942, the Ordnance Training Center had proposed eleven or twelve "provisional" companies for stateside operations. However, after the Army Services Force took over, Lt. Gen. Brehon Somervell trimmed OTC's request down to eight companies. Somervell further gave Kane and Walker an ultimatum: they had only six weeks to organize their first company and send it to Western Defense Command. However, during this interval, enlisted disposaleers were in short supply at Aberdeen, as their first classes had not convened until April 8. Kane authorized a recruitment drive for volunteers, and sent Walker to assemble a training detachment in California, courtesy of U.S. IX Corps.[56]

While Walker and Yates engaged recruits from general ordnance and combat engineers, the Army School trained and dispatched four officers and 24 other ranks, bringing the provisional company's strength up to 203. By the summer, 1st Lt. John Drislane had assumed command over 101st Provisional Ordnance Bomb Disposal Company. On June 20, 1942, War Department officials expressed their satisfaction with this company, and authorized the 231st through 238th Ordnance Bomb Disposal Companies. Drislane's unit was henceforth designated as the 231st BD Company.[57]

Interestingly, the first Army bomb disposal organization appears to have been independently commissioned by Western Defense Command. On March 15, 1942, four Army officers had graduated from Draper Kauffman's Navy BD School. One of these graduates, 1st Lt. Robert K. Weyand, took charge of Southern California Sector's Bomb Disposal Unit based at Riverside. Weyand's volunteers comprised two platoons of 84 men, and were merged with 231st BD Company by early 1943.[58]

Officers and NCOs from the 231st Ordnance Bomb Disposal Company celebrating New Year's Day, January 1943. (*Leiendecker Collection*)

| **Unit Designation** | Date Organized | Theaters of Service | Date Disbanded |
|---|---|---|---|
| **231st Ord. BD Co.** | May 1942 | Western Defense Command | 10/1943 |
| **232nd Ord. BD Co.** | July 1942 | Central Pacific Department | 11/1943 |
| **233rd Ord. BD Co.** | Aug. 1942 | Panama Canal Zone Caribbean Theater | c. 1943 |
| **234th Ord. BD Co.** | July 1942 | Eastern Def. Comm. European Theater | 10/1944 |
| **235th Ord. BD Co.** | Aug. 1942 | Western Def. Comm. Mediterranean Theater | 6/1944 |
| **236th Ord. BD Co.** | Sept. 1942 | Eastern Def. Comm. Mediterranean Theater | 6/1944 |
| **237th Ord. BD Co.** | 1942 | Southern Pacific Department | 11/1943 |
| **238th Ord. BD Co.** | 1942 | Stateside Duty | 10/1943 |

| Bomb Disposal Company Personnel | Job Description (#) |
|---|---|
| **Captain** | Company Commander (1) |
| **First Lieutenants** | Executive Officer (1)<br>Platoon Commanders (4) |
| **Second Lieutenants** | Headquarters Officers (2) |
| **First Sergeant** | Headquarters Non-Commissioned Officer (1) |
| **Technical Sergeants** | Platoon Leaders (4)<br>General Mechanic (1) |
| **Staff Sergeants** | Assistant Platoon Leaders (4) |
| **Sergeants** | Duty Sergeants (8)<br>Mess Sergeant (1)<br>Motor Sergeant (1)<br>Supply Sergeant (1) |
| **Corporals** | Company Clerk (1)<br>Duty Corporals (8) |
| **Privates First Class** | Artificer (1)<br>Auto-Mechanic (1)<br>Blacksmith (1)<br>Bugler/Messenger (1)<br>Chauffeurs (27)<br>Cooks (4)<br>Electrician (1)<br>Mechanics (9)<br>Motorcyclists (8)<br>Operator, Air Compressor (1) |
| **Privates (unrated)** | General Duty (82) |
| **TOTALS:** | **Officers (8)**<br>**Other Ranks (165)** |

Army planners envisioned a primarily defensive role for all eight companies, four of which were allotted to four U. S. Defense Commands. Created in 1941 by executive order, the Eastern, Western, Central, and Southern Commands supervised military and civil defense. Each quadrant was further bisected into two Service Commands, headquartered at major ports of entry, such as San Francisco, New Orleans, Charleston, and New York. Theoretically, four companies went to Defense Commands, while individual officers advised Service Commands. By August 1942, however, only the 231st Company had been activated for home defense. Eventually, the 231st disbanded, with some officers heading overseas and others remaining with the Western Defense Command as advisors. Three squads culled from 231st Company, the 64th through 66th, played a key role during Japan's *Fu-Go* bombing campaign of 1944-45.[59]

Out of the eight companies of disposaleers commissioned in 1942, 238th Company (2nd Lt. Frank M. Philips, Jr.) undoubtedly had the easiest job, combing incoming U.S. ships for enemy ordnance samples. Others received orders for foreign shores. That November, Capt. Frederick H. Dillon's 235th Company reinforced the West Coast until their departure for North Africa in the spring of 1943. 233rd Company (1st Lt. Gerald E. Eddy) deployed to the Caribbean Theater and Panama Canal Zone until their recall in the summer of 1943. 234th Company (1st Lt. Fred A. Wilkie) and 236th Company (1st Lt. Francis Geisler) covered the Atlantic seaboard until their eventual reassignments to the European and Mediterranean Theaters, respectively. Two other companies, the 232nd (Capt. George C. Sarauw) and 237th (Capt. Robert G. Fisher) went directly to stations across the wide Pacific Theater. All were eventually disbanded in accordance with subsequent Army doctrines by 1944.[60]

Like all standard World War II units, the Ordnance Bomb Disposal Company was organized under a "table of basic allowances," entitling them to specific tools as well as standard Army gear. Uncle Sam paid over $275,000 to outfit a single bomb disposal company, exclusive of motor vehicle costs. T/BA 9-177 authorized one company with a headquarters plus four field platoons, led by 8 officers and staffed by 165 men. However, on paper, one can still see vestiges of an earlier Army, reminiscent of the First World War. Ordnance companies still fielded blacksmiths and personal couriers in a war that had revolutionized mechanized infantry and portable radios. Headquarters even had provisions for a bugler. Such instances of superfluity undoubtedly contributed to early impressions that bomb disposal companies wasted resources and manpower.[61]

Bomb disposal tools: one of Great Britain's greatest contributions to the UXB War, the steam sterilizer is displayed at far left. (*Kane Collection*)

Some standard bomb disposal equipment requires brief explanation. Non-metallic, extendible probes were used to gauge a bomb's depth. Power tools included gas-powered air compressors and earth augers, though bomb salvagers typically used ordinary picks and shovels to reach UXBs. Dental mirrors enabled a sergeant or officer to identify fuze types without disturbing the bomb itself. Electric stethoscopes picked up ticking sounds from most clockwork fuzes, though normal ones did in a pinch. Neutralizing fuzes required the use of special dischargers, including a liquid pump useful for flooding a fuze's circuitry. Officers also used special kits, such as the pulley-driven impact wrench or Merrilees extractor set, to ensure fuze removal at a safe distance.[62]

When special bomb disposal tools became worn out or were lost, ordinary implements such as plumber's wrenches replaced them. Special non-magnetic toolkits were devised to handle special fuzes. Ordinary blocks and tackles provided rigging in order to hoist a UXB for removal by vehicle or haulage. Every section or squad possessed sufficient demolition charges to detonate unreachable bombs. Periodically, as new tools emerged, a given unit's table of allowances required updates.[63]

Each bomb disposal unit received field training in photography, and carried portable "darkrooms" as part of their table of equipment. (*Kane Collection*)

Any given company's bomb disposal equipment counted for $210,000. Certain instruments, such as impact wrenches, were imported at first through British channels. Others were very sensitive and easily broken, such as the electric stethoscope – another key British invention. Ordnance's technical manual E9-1984 (*Disposal Methods for Enemy Bombs and Fuzes*) contained detailed instructions for proper equipment usage and maintenance. Moreover, the manual covered the possibility of enemy capture; officers and NCOs were instructed to destroy all special equipment to prevent its loss to the enemy.[64]

Early on, bomb disposal companies were prone to be misemployed. Persistent rumors about German agents and Japanese submarines convinced the War Department to dispatch the 233rd BD Company to the Panama Canal Zone for one year. Scattered across the tropical Caribbean region, 1st Lt. Eddy's soldiers often practiced night maneuvers of a different sense. One of Eddy's platoon sergeants, Staff Sgt. August Bergenthal, fondly recalled mingling with the "lovely senoritas," inhabitants of San Juan's "high class nite clubs." Less-discerning soldiers could visit "low class dives," where they liked to "go the limit for virtually nothing."[65]

233rd BD Company members training in Puerto Rico. (*Leiendecker Collection*)

As historian Karl Larew described it, Panama's Canal Zone quickly "ceased to play the all-important role cast for it" before Pearl Harbor. However, the Caribbean siphoned precious manpower, including bomb disposaleers, from more critical theaters. When the U.S. sent its first combat divisions to North Africa in late 1942, their ordnance chiefs suffered from a dearth of bomb disposal companies and squads.[66]

While staging the Army's bomb disposal units for combat support, Ordnance faced two serious hurdles. First, entire companies had to be recalled for inspection, retraining, and resupply. More importantly, War Department planners advocated a drastic reduction from companies to "squads separate." Originally, "cellular" squads consisted of nine soldiers, but later War Department rulings reduced manpower down to seven.[67]

Perhaps too much has been made concerning Col. Kane's objections to separate squads. Under Kane's direction, the Army Bomb Disposal School had already begun training seven-man units in September 1942. Kane often expressed his concerns that "separate squads" would not receive proper support in the battlefield. Yet, tempting as it may seem, Kane's image as a maverick officer is a bit misleading. One of Kane's superiors, Brig. Gen. James K. Crain, had once made a similar plea for better "housekeeping" suggesting that ordnance specialists, such as bomb disposaleers, should be grouped under general ordnance battalions.[68]

However, as future events would demonstrate, separate bomb disposal squads often fell through the Army's bureaucratic cracks in every Theater of Operations, and squad commanders, usually lieutenants, lacked sufficient authority to be taken seriously by a division or corps commander. To alleviate this problem, Kane successfully convinced Gen. Levin Campbell to increase maximum rank for squad officers to captain. By July 1943, Capt. Frank Parsons reported twenty "squads separate" had just completed training under the new T/O 9-500, with allowances for one captain, two NCOs, and four technicians. While this arrangement meant increased responsibilities for each squad member, the squad model also reinforced a sense of identity for the bomb disposal profession.[69]

Apart from manpower concerns, transportation seems to have been another concern at the War Department. Originally, bomb disposal companies were issued nineteen 1½ ton trucks and six pickups, plus eight motorcycles to serve couriers. Perceived by many as a rear-echelon unit, a bomb disposal company's nineteen trucks used too much gasoline and oil to justify their mission. Separate squads, by contrast, required just two vehicles: a three-quarter-ton pickup truck (or lorry) and one 2½ ton ammo carrier plus trailer Occasionally, squad officers in the European Theater would be issued individual motorcycles when available.[70]

Ordnance's "stripped-down" approach toward bomb disposal units might have been influenced by a successful approach by John B. Medaris. In Tunisia, Col. Medaris had resolved serious vehicle shortages by organizing his riggers, mechanics, and drivers from his ordnance battalion into self-reliant "tank recovery groups." Operating by night, close to enemy positions, these special retrieval platoons learned to sweep areas for mines and booby traps, sometimes even engaging German opponents with small arms. Writing the Army's official Ordnance history, Lida Mayo later invoked a nickname for these specialists that circulated around the Tunisian front: "Rangers of Ordnance."[71]

This sobriquet could just as easily apply to Kane's bomb disposal service, charged with the recovery of bombs, mines, and other explosives. During later campaigns, bomb squads freely roamed over recent battlegrounds, combed for booby traps, and even screened amphibious landings and armored columns. By mid-1944, celebrated war correspondent Ernie Pyle had noted two high-risk units among the otherwise "undramatic" Ordnance branches: tank "retriever" squads and seven-man bomb disposal squads. Eventually, "squads separate" won out over company formations, but they required several adjustments to their tables of organization in order to meet minimum field standards.[72]

1st Lt. Joe Pettit (holding fuze) trains with enlisted members of 67th BD Squad. Separate squads brought officers and men closer. (*Leiendecker Collection*)

Despite waning chances for a German bombing raid, the Army's new bomb disposal squads still practiced for air raids. Such drills kept the men in practice, developing camaraderie between officers and their soldiers. Squads customarily bivouacked together at public campgrounds, played touch football, went over basic Army skills, and even had frank discussions about sexual hygiene. In the words of one EOD historian, this informality between the ranks "stemmed from the small size of the [bomb disposal] unit, the similarity in training and the unique nature of their work." As the war developed, officers became reliant on their technicians to do their duty, and in nearly all cases, they demonstrated a sincere interest in the well-being of each soldier.[73]

Kane's bomb disposal branch, although initially cloaked in secrecy, presently began to take part in civil defense exercises, which sometimes doubled as public morale boosters. In November 1943, 46th BD Squad (Capt. Max H. Zimmermann) disarmed simulated "bombs" planted by OCD workers in Hazleton, Pennsylvania. Similarly, members of 43rd BD Squad excavated practice UXBs at nearby Easton. As late as the spring of 1944, 79th BD Squad (1st Lt. James M. Dobbins, Jr.) practiced driving in military convoy formations near Cooper, Maryland.[74]

1st Lt. Joseph Pilcher oversaw a remarkable joint civil defense exercise with 31st BD Squad, a unit still in training at Aberdeen Proving Ground. Recently promoted, Pilcher got on especially well with his chief noncom, T/Sgt. Sam Hobson. He was also "well-liked" by his enlisted men, who were T/5 (Sgt.) Franklin E. May, T/5 Richard W. Gilliam, T/5 Edward C. Norris, T/5 Joseph Olzewski, and T/5 Joseph E. Smith. Most of them transferred with their lieutenant to 17th BD Squad later that autumn.[75]

On October 13, 1943, Pilcher's 31st Squad attracted media notice during a Reading, Pennsylvania civil defense exercise. Two additional ordnance lieutenants, William D. Steigerwalt and Robert H. Graham, reinforced Pilcher's party for this demonstration. Lt. Graham, T. J. Kane's public affairs officer, came along ostensibly to promote the Bomb Disposal School's mission. On that Wednesday evening, Reading's citizens got a big pyrotechnics display. At 5 p.m., several thousand watched as four B-24 Liberator bombers simulated a drop of two 500-pound bombs near Albright College's stadium. Hundreds of air wardens and soldiers evacuated crowds of students to safety positions, and cordoned off the entire city block.[76]

Meanwhile, Pilcher's team responded to the city's emergency call, driving their squad truck from nearby Hamburg. With city sirens blaring, ordnance personnel arrived on the scene within the hour, working alongside the city's bomb reconnaissance team. Electric mining lamps were placed around the simulated crater. Only two officers were allowed to operate in the bomb's vicinity at one time, a measure to prevent excessive "losses." Using non-metallic probes, Joe Pilcher and Bob Graham located both "dud" UXBs, using shafts excavated by T/Sgt. Sam Hobson's team. Observing security requirements, no cameras were permitted at the "bomb site." While Graham and Steigerwalt disassembled fuzes, Joe Pilcher described the actual threats of delayed-action German bombs to journalists and interested onlookers.[77]

Joe Pilcher's expertise with German bombs made a lasting impression on the interviewing reporter. However, most local spectators quickly found "digging for bombs" a tedious pursuit, and paid more attention to some "spectacular and appealing" infantry maneuvers against a mocked-up machine-gun nest. Officers hurled small fireworks as enlisted men crawled through tall grass, firing blanks at their imaginary enemies. Wrapping up these proceedings, 1st Lt. Joseph A. Bocelato set off a vast pyrotechnical display, courtesy of the Ordnance Department. While townsfolk enjoyed an Independence Day-like atmosphere, the Reading-Berks Defense Council chairman, John S. Giles, praised the Army's "dramatic and effective" bomb disposal program.[78]

However, few outside Aberdeen Proving Ground knew about the real digging currently underway at overseas locations, with foreign names such as Gafsa, Attu, or Caltanisetta. Across the globe, Kane's ordnancemen had already participated in assault landings, delousing buildings, and combing distant beaches for mines. Moreover, several officers and men had already made the ultimate sacrifice, claimed by enemy ordnance, bullets, or ill luck. And yet, "sweeping along" World War II's storied battlefields gave Kane's pioneers the chance to prove their mettle. Otherwise, their stateside efforts might never have produced the modern Explosive Ordnance Disposal services. Today, EOD's peacetime and wartime missions are one and the same: "Defuzing Danger."

## Notes

[1] Many Ordnance documents still refer to Services of Supply until 1945. Apart from the Ordnance Corps, the other technical services included the Army Corps of Engineers, Signal Corps, Quartermaster Corps, Chemical Corps, Medical Corps, and Transportation Corps. (James E. Hewes, Jr., *From Root to McNamara: Army Organization and Administration.* Washington D.C.: Center of Military History, U.S. Army, 1975, 67-103; 129-162; Levin H. Campbell, Ordnance Department Order no. 291, *Organization of the Ordnance Department*, 8 July 1942; Levin H. Campbell, Ordnance Department Order no. 291, Change No. 1, 24 October 1942; Harry M. Walker, Ordnance Bomb Disposal School Headquarters [manpower survey] 2 February 1943.)

[2] Roosevelt's controversial presidential order was issued on February 19, 1942, in the immediate wake of Pearl Harbor. Fortunately, these unconstitutional measures were never put into general practice, save for the unfortunate wartime internments of Japanese-Americans. (Dwight D. Eisenhower to the Commanding Generals, *Defense of Continental United States*, 22 April 1942).

[3] Edgewood Arsenal's Chemical Warfare School soon terminated its own bomb disposal training program on 31 March 1942, transferring its UXB assets to the War Department's six Civilian Protection Schools. In late 1942, Texas A&M College instructors also taught 151 black civilian BD volunteers in a segregated facility at Prairie View Industrial College. (Saholsky Report; Bomb Disposal School History; Dorothy Parsons, interview with author, 18 October 2003; Brophy and Fisher, 241-5; Conn, Engelman, and Fairchild, 72.)

[4] Services of Supply, Training Memorandum No. 3, 27 July 1942 (World War II War Diaries, U.S. Army ETO, 7 December 1941 to 31 December 1945, NARA Record Group 38); "How to Drown a Bomb," *Time* (27 July 1942), 26-27.

[5] Conn, Engelman, and Fairchild, 111; for more on the *Graf Zeppelin*, see Siegfried Breyer, *The German Aircraft Carrier Graf Zeppelin* (Atglen, Pennsylvania: Schiffer Publishing Ltd. 1989).

[6] One aspect of civil defense that has been overlooked, disaster relief, actually prefigures the organization of FEMA (the U.S. Federal Emergency Management

Agency) created by the Carter Administration. However, study of World War II disaster relief is complicated by the National Archives' ill-advised 1963 decision to purge all the OCD's records except for the Western Defense Command's files. In 2005, the author had considered writing his dissertation concerning the OCD's efforts during 1942's Ohio River Valley Flood and the deadly Shinnston Tornado. While state OCD records were available, corresponding federal documents no longer existed. (Stetson Conn, Rose C. Engelman, and Byron Fairchild, *Guarding the United States and its Outposts,* Washington D.C., Office of the Chief of Military History, 1946, 72; West Virginia OCD Records 1942-43, West Virginia History Collection, West Virginia University; Bailey, 104-7.)

[7] "How to Drown a Bomb," *Time* (27 July 1942), 26-27; Ronald H. Bailey, *Home Front USA*, (Alexandria, VA: WWII Time-Life, 1977), 105; Stephen Howarth, *To Shining Sea: a History of the United States Navy, 1775-1991,* New York: Random House, 1991, 405-7.

[8] Boston, New York City, Baltimore, and Atlanta served as headquarters for First, Second, Third, and Fourth Service Commands. Fifth, Sixth, and Seventh Service Commands were located in Ft. Hayes, Ohio, Chicago, and Omaha, Nebraska, respectively. Eighth and Ninth Service Commands were situated in Dallas, Texas and Ft. Douglas, Utah. (Lt. Col. Thomas J. Kane, "Unexploded Bombs," from *Army Ordnance* Vol. 23, No. 134 (Aberdeen Proving Ground: Ordnance Department, September-October 1942), 277-88; Ordnance Bomb Disposal School, *Roster of all Bomb Disposal Officers*, 26 October 1943; *Bomb Disposal School History; The Detonator*, 17 September 1943; Hooper, 11-14; Levering interview; Kane Journal; Kane Obituary).

[9] Kane, "Unexploded Bombs," 1; Kane Journal.

[10] Central Defense Command lacked a bomb disposal officer owing to its unlikelihood of being bombed during this era before the advent of nuclear arms. (Col. Thomas J. Kane, *Report of Visit to Ordnance Activities*, 19 October 1942, 1-8; Kane Journal.)

[11] All three named individuals were still listed in March 1943 as being qualified BD officers. Kane also questioned Utah's need for its own Service Command at Fort Douglas. In Kane's estimation, Western Defense Command provided enough coverage for this region. (Kane, *Report of Ordnance Activities*; *Active Bomb Disposal Officers*.)

[12] Kane, *Report of Ordnance Activities.*

[13] (Army Ordnance Bomb Disposal School, *List of B.D. Officers Assigned to Staff and Faculty;* Aberdeen Proving Ground, Maryland, 22 March 1943; Services of Supply, Training Memorandum No. 3, 27 July 1942, NARA Record Group 38; Kane, *Report of Ordnance Activities*; Bailey, 105; Hooper, 12; *Roster of Active Bomb Disposal Officers*, November 1945.)

[14] Colonel Thomas J. Kane, *Report of Visit to Ordnance Activities*, 19 October 1942, 1-8.

[15] Kane, *Report of Ordnance Activities.*

[16] Robert Leiendecker, *World War II Statistics, Army Ordnance Bomb Disposal Squads*, Charlottesville VA; Library of National EOD Association, c. 2003.

[17] Colonel Thomas J. Kane, *Report of Visit to Ordnance Activities*, 19 October 1942, 1-8.
[18] Colonel Thomas J. Kane, *Report of Visit to Ordnance Activities*, 19 October 1942, 1-8.
[19] Thomas J. Kane, travel journal and itinerary, U.S. Ordnance Museum, Aberdeen Proving Ground, MD, 1 December 1942 – 25 May 1943, 1; Kane, "Unexploded Bombs," 1.
[20] Kane, *Report of Ordnance Activities.*
[21] Ordnance Bomb Disposal School Headquarters, *Manpower Survey*, 2 February 1943; Maj. Gen. J.A. Ulio, Adjutant General, *Delegation of Bomb Disposal Duties*, 5 February 1943.
[22] P. M. Seleen, *Delegation of Bomb Disposal Duties*, 29 April 1942; T. J. Davis to Lt. Col. Charles W. McCarthy, *Disposal of Unexploded and Delayed Action Bombs Within Continental United States*, 8 May 1942; T. J. Davis to Chief of Chemical Warfare Service, *Disposal of Unexploded and Delayed Action Bombs*, 8 May 1942; P. M. Seleen to Commanding General, Services of Supply, *The Problem of Bomb Disposal*, 25 May 1942; Levin H. Campbell, Ordnance Department Order no. 291, *Organization of the Ordnance Department*, 8 July 1942; Brig. Gen. Clarence R. Huebner, to Assistant Chief of Staff, War Department, *Unexploded Bomb Disposal*, (Adjutant General Letters 471.6), 10 August 1942 – 2 September 1942; Brig. Gen. I. H. Edwards, Assistant Chief of Staff, to the War Department, Chief of Staff, *Unexploded Bomb Disposal*, 16 August 1942; Levin H. Campbell, Ordnance Department Order no. 291, Change No. 1, 24 October 1942; A.E. O'Leary, Adjutant General's Office, War Department, *Disposal of Unexploded and Delayed Action Bombs* (Adjutant General Letters 471.6), 5 February 1943.
[23] S. R. Goodwin (Adjutant General) to Chief of Ordnance (Lt. Gen. Levin Campbell), *Officers for Bomb Disposal Duty in Foreign Stations*, 4 June 1942; Col. Thomas J. Kane, *Report of Visit to Ordnance Activities*, 19 October 1942; Harry M. Walker, *Manpower Survey*; Ordnance BD School, Aberdeen Proving Ground, Maryland, 2 February 1943; James A. Westbrook, *Organization of the Ordnance Bomb Disposal School*, 9 February 1943.
[24] Ordnance Bomb Disposal School Headquarters, *BDS History,* 1943; Bomb Disposal School History; Hooper, 11-14; Mayo, 231-2.
[25] Walter Nass eventually rose to the rank of lieutenant colonel in the peacetime U.S. Army Reserves. After the end of World War II, Maj. Art Keller worked once again with Kane, serving as intelligence officer for the EOD Office. William Prichard had left bomb disposal by November 1942. (*List of BD Officers Assigned to Staff and Faculty,* Aberdeen Proving Ground, Maryland, 22 March 1943; *List of BD Officers Assigned to Companies & Staff*, 26 October 1943; Alice Nass, interview by author, 14 October 2003.)
[26] Robert Palmer, Bell I. Wiley, and William R. Keast, *Procurement and Training of Ground Combat Troops*. Washington D.C.: Center of Military History, 1948, 377-79; James A. Westbrook, *Organization of the Ordnance Bomb Disposal*

*School*, 9 February 1943; Thomas J. Kane to U.S. War Department. *Bomb Disposal, U. S. A.*, c.1942, 13.

[27] In 1930, Martin Ehrmann identified his parents as ethnic Poles living in Kiel, Germany. His Polish parentage and Austrian origins may well have influenced his anti-Nazi views. Martin Ehrmann's citizenship took effect on December 6, 1933. During the war, Lt. Col. Ehrmann also contributed to Intelligence Services in Washington, and carried out occasional missions for the Ordnance Department. (Martin L. Ehrmann, *Declaration of Intention,* No. 2293929, 19 October 1928, U.S. Naturalization Record Indexes, 1791-1992; Martin L Ehrmann, *Certificate of Arrival.* No. 2293929, 8 August 1933, U.S. Naturalization Record Indexes, 1791-1992; U.S. Bureau of the Census, Department of Commerce, 1930, Washington, District of Columbia; George S. Switzer, "Memorial of Martin L. Ehrmann," from *American Mineralogist*, Volume 59, 1974, 414-15; *S.S. Normandie* to Immigration and Naturalization Services, List of Passengers, Southampton to New York, 27 July to 1 August 1938.)

[28] Maria Feldman interviews; Switzer, 414-15.

[29] Afterward, when Brig. Gen. Hatcher was elevated to Army Chief of Field Services, he continued to intercede on Kane's behalf at the War Department level. Hatcher's visiting Allied officers included Maj. Gen. R. H. Dewing and Brig. W. R. Blood of the British Army Staff in Washington, as well as Lt. Col. H.R. Blandy, Australian Military Mission. (*History of Bomb Disposal in the U.S.A.*, Aberdeen Proving Ground, 1942, 5-6; U.S. Army Ordnance Corps, *Ordnance Corps Hall of Fame*, http:/ www.goordnance.apg.army.mil; Accessed 23 February 2003.)

[30] Campbell's wartime history inexplicably omits Kane's name, even though it mentions several of his peers. Campbell also made scant mention of the Bomb Disposal School, suggesting his indifference toward their technical achievements. (Levin H. Campbell Jr., *The Industry-Ordnance Team*, New York: Whittlesey House & McGraw-Hill Inc., 1946, 364; *History of Bomb Disposal in the U.S.A.*, Aberdeen Proving Ground, 1942, 6-7).

[31] *History of Bomb Disposal in the U.S.A.*, Aberdeen Proving Ground, 1942, 7-8.

[32] Lt. Gen. Brehon Somervell to Quartermaster General, *Device for the Bomb Disposal School,* 29 September 1942; Col. Thomas J. Kane, *Bomb Disposal Distinctive Badge and Insignia*, 7 December 1942; Mike R. Vining, *Army Bomb Disposal & EOD Heraldry and Badges*, National EOD Association, 9 April 2011.

[33] Ehrmann was succeeded in 1943 by 1st Lt. Robert H. Graham. (Col. Thomas J. Kane to Chief of Military Training Division, Aberdeen Proving Ground, 4 August 1942; U.S. War Department, *Liaison Bulletin No. 75*, Bureau of Public Relations, Washington, D.C. 1942; 1942 BD Officer Roster; Al Newman, "Meet the Bomb Killers," from *Newsweek*, 1 May 1944, 23-24).

[34] Recently, a controversy threatened to change the EOD School motto, after U.S. Navy officers decided "Initial Success or Total Failure" was too strongly-worded and might discourage applicants. Overwhelmingly, EOD servicemen opposed this change and so far, the motto still stands. Given Col. Kane's original statement, this author is inclined to agree with the majority. (Newman, 23-24).

[35] Capt. Bolick A. Saholsky to Col. H.R. Kutz, Chief of Field Service, *Undesirable*

*Personnel for Bomb Disposal Units*, 15 June 1942.

[36] It appears this nickname originated as a badge of honor for at least one BD section operating in London in 1940. However, it is inaccurate as a descriptor of actual bomb disposal work, which seeks to ensure survival. (*Cold Springs Record*, 16 October 1940, 2; Al Newman, "Meet the Bomb Killers," from *Newsweek*, 1 May 1944, 23-24; Robert J. Kuehner, interview).

[37] "Birthday for Bomb Disposal," from the *Flaming Bomb*, 11 February 1943.

[38] Ordnance Technical Services, *ETO Bomb Disposal History* (NARA Records Group 498, 1945), 1-4; Harry M. Walker, *Manpower Survey*; Ordnance BD School, Aberdeen Proving Ground, Maryland, 2 February 1943; Capt. Schuyler V.C. Larkin to Col. Thomas J. Kane, *Bomb Disposal Training in the United Kingdom*, 1 October 1943; Robert E. Leiendecker, *Bomb Disposal, The Early Years of Explosive Ordnance Disposal (An Informal History)*, Charlottesville, Virginia: NATEODA Press, 2012, 33.

[39] Robert Palmer, Bell I. Wiley, and William R. Keast, *Procurement and Training of Ground Combat Troops*. Washington D.C.: Center of Military History, 1948, 17-18, 36, 394-400; T. Dennis Reece, *Captains of Bomb Disposal 1942-46* (Lexington, Kentucky: Xlibris Books, 2005), 15-16; Edward Dillon, interview with author, 11 April 2011; T. Dennis Reece, [transcript] interview with author, 11 June 2011, Carmel J. Cirocco, [transcript] interviews by author. 19 June 2011 and 19 June 2011; Carmel J. Cirocco, *Certificate of Service* [Form 53-98] 27 June 1945; Parsons Report.

[40] U.S. Army Technical Manual E9-1984, *Disposal Methods for Enemy Bombs and Fuzes,* Aberdeen Proving Ground, Maryland: Chief of Ordnance, 12 November 1942.

[41] Al Newman, "Meet the Bomb Killers," from *Newsweek*, 1 May 1944, 23-24; Hooper, 13-14.

[42] W.G. Calder, interview with author, 14 October 2003; Leiendecker, *Bomb Disposal*, 486-87.

[43] For decades afterward, "Scotty" Calder remained in contact with fellow veterans and their families. When interviewed in 2003, he still edited a yearly newsletter for the Bomb Disposal Reunion Club. However, their numbers have since dwindled. (Calder interview).

[44] T. Dennis Reece, *Captains of Bomb Disposal* (Lexington, Kentucky: Xlibris Press, 2005), 19-21; 1942 Officer Roster; Saholsky Report.

[45] *The Detonator*, 17 September 1943, 2; Al Newman, *Newsweek;* "Bomb Disposal," *Firepower*, Army Ordnance Association, August-September 1945, 8-9; "ETO Tells All on Bomb Removal," unsigned newspaper article,1945; "Ordnance Section Reveals Work of Bomb Disposal Squads," press release, 1945.

[46] Al Newman, "Meet the Bomb Killers," Feldman interviews; Levering interviews.

[47] One USAAF ordnance officer who trained in bomb reconnaissance at Aberdeen Proving Ground, John G. Dorondo, was wounded at Pearl Harbor. Receiving his Purple Heart in 1942, Dorondo later served in the Italian campaign. Born after World War II, Lt. Col. Dorondo's son David served as the author's thesis director

at Western Carolina University in 2003-04. (Maj. Bolick A. Saholsky, *Bomb Disposal Activities*, 21 August 1942; Frank A. Parsons, *Report on Bomb Disposal Activities*, 9 July 1943; *Course BDM-1 Bomb Disposal Officer's Course,* Department of Training, 1943; Ordnance Bomb Disposal School Headquarters, Course *BDM-2 Bomb Reconnaissance Instructor's Course,* Department of Training, 1943; Ordnance Bomb Disposal School Headquarters, *Course BDM-3 Military Bomb Reconnaissance Officers and Non-Commissioned Officers Course,* Department of Training, 1943; Ordnance Bomb Disposal School Headquarters, Course *BDC-1 Advanced Bomb Reconnaissance,* Department of Training, 1943; Ordnance Bomb Disposal School Headquarters, *Course BDM-3 Military Bomb Reconnaissance Officers and Non-Commissioned Officers Course,* Department of Training,1943; Ordnance Bomb Disposal School Headquarters, *Course BDM-12 Introduction to the Bomb Disposal Problem,* Department of Training, 1943.)

[48] Ordnance men tended to come from the upper three tiers of recruits during the 1942-43 periods, with 44.4 from Classes I and II, and another 35.3 percent from Class III. Only about 25% of Ordnance enlistees came from the lower classes (IV and V). This tendency to shunt high-scoring recruits into the technical services hampered the combat arms, who felt they were being denied quality personnel. (Robert Palmer, Bell I. Wiley, and William R. Keast, *Procurement and Training of Ground Combat Troops*. Washington D.C.: Center of Military History, 1948, 17-18; *Detonator* [newsletter], 22 October 1943; *Bomb Disposal School History*; Parsons Report.)

[49] Owing to Jim Crow regulations, black soldiers were trained only for segregated ordnance companies, but only a select few were permitted to become noncoms or officers through the Ordnance School. Only one African-American officer seems to have trained under the Army Ordnance Bomb Disposal program. (54$^{th}$ Ordnance Bomb Disposal Squad (Separate), unit history, 1943-45; 161$^{st}$ Ordnance Bomb Disposal Squad (Separate), unit history, c. 1945; Ulysses Lee, *The Employment of Negro Troops*, Washington, D.C.: Office of the Chief of Military History, 1966, 207; Hooper, C-1.)

[50] Such technician ranks were forerunners of the Vietnam-era specialist pay grades (SP-4 through SP-8), consolidated after the 1970s into the modern Army's Specialist (E-4) rank. Mauldin also took ribbings when he received his T/4 stripes as a war correspondent, and was never quite comfortable wearing the insignia, as he wished to identify with the dogfaces with whom he so often empathized. Regarding Steven Spielberg's *Saving Private Ryan*, it also comes as no surprise that T/4 Upham emerges as the most pusillanimous of the American soldiers. (Bill Mauldin, *Bill Mauldin's Up Front,* New York: Henry Holt, 1945, 138-43; 187-88).

[51] Bomb disposal units did not receive hazard pay until the Korean War. Ironically, some stateside or headquarters Bomb Disposal officers, like Wally Nass or John Feldman, ranked as rifle experts, while other officers selected for field service qualified with their firearms at lower levels of competency. (Ordnance Bomb Disposal School Headquarters, *Special Orders No. 114,* weapons qualification roster, 16 June 1943; Carmel J. Cirocco, telephone interview by author, 20 July 2011; 1942 BD Officer Roster; W. H. B. Smith, *A Basic Manual of Small Arms*,

Harrisburg, Pennsylvania: Military Publishing Company, 1943, 142-60; Louis A. Kollander, "U.S. Carbine, Cal. 30, M2," from *Ordnance Sergeant*, July 1945; Charles G. Pritchard, "Ammunition Forward: the U.S. Ordnance Corps at Kunu-Ri, Korea" from *Army Magazine*, March 2002; Reece, 27-28).

[52] *Detonator* [newsletter] (U.S. Army Bomb Disposal School: Aberdeen Proving Ground, Maryland), 22 October 1943, 4.

[53] The best ordnance cartoons, however, came from Sergeant Robert Vittur (USMC), who sketched humorous characters for the U.S. Navy BD School. Reminiscent of *Sad Sack* and later on, *Beetle Bailey*, "Mulvaney on Bomb Disposal" (1945) has become a source of mirth for all EOD services and non-military audiences alike. Vittur's strips have been published in omnibus form, and have been reprinted elsewhere. (U.S. Navy Bomb Disposal School, *"Mulvaney on Bomb Disposal," Supplement to Intelligence Bulletin No. 85.* 15 September 1945; *Detonator* [newsletter] (U.S. Army Bomb Disposal School: Aberdeen Proving Ground, Maryland) 17 September and 22 October 1943.)

[54] Most bomb disposal men appeared to have been generally satisfied with their military occupations. In general morale surveys, Ordnance troops scored well over 50 percent compared to other U.S. Army branches. (*Detonator* [newsletter] (U.S. Army Bomb Disposal School: Aberdeen Proving Ground, Maryland), 17 September 1943, 1; 22 October 1943, 4; See also Robert Palmer, Bell I. Wiley, and William R. Keast, *Procurement and Training of Ground Combat Troops.* Washington D.C.: Center of Military History, 1948).

[55] *Detonator* [newsletter] (U.S. Army Bomb Disposal School: Aberdeen Proving Ground, Maryland), 17 September 1943, 1; 22 October 1943, 4.

[56] Lt. Col. P. M. Seleen, *Activation of Bomb Disposal Companies*, 29 April 1942; Col. Walter L. Weible (Services of Supply, Training Division) to Maj. Gen. Levin H. Campbell (Chief of Ordnance), *Activation of Bomb Disposal Companies*, 8 May 1942.

[57] 1942 BD Officer Roster; Lt. Col. P. M. Seleen, *Activation of Bomb Disposal Companies*, 29 April 1942; U.S. War Department to the Adjutant General, *Constitution and Activation of the 231st Ordnance Company, Bomb Disposal*, Ordnance Department, Washington D.C., 11 May 1942; P.M. Seleen to Ordnance Officer, Western Defense Command, *Activities of the 231st Ordnance Company, Bomb Disposal*, 5 June 1942; Col. Thomas J. Kane to Brig. Gen. J. K. Crain, Chief of Field Service, *Activation of Bomb Disposal Company*, 15 June 1942; Brig. Gen. I. H. Edwards, *Activation of Bomb Disposal Companies,* 20 June 1942.

[58] Robert E. Leiendecker, *Bomb Disposal, The Early Years of Explosive Ordnance Disposal (An Informal History)*, Charlottesville, Virginia: NATEODA Press, 2012, 177-89.

[59] Two of Drislane's lieutenants, Norman L. Omodt and Sherwood B. Brockwell, Jr., were reassigned to squads bound for overseas theaters. These units included 64th through 66th BD Squads. (Colonel Thomas J. Kane, *Report of Visit to Ordnance Activities*, 19 October 1942, 1-8; Major General Emory S. Adams (Adjutant General) to Chief of Ordnance, *Disposal of Unexploded and Delayed Action Bombs*, 12 December 1941; T.J. Davis to Lt. Col. Charles W. McCarthy,

*Disposal of Unexploded and Delayed Action Bombs Within Continental United States*, 8 May 1942; Maj. Gen. J.A. Ulio (Adjutant General) to Defense Commands, *Disposal of Unexploded and Delayed Action Bombs Within the Continental Limits of the United States*, 30 May 1942; Maj. Bolick A. Saholsky, *Bomb Disposal Activities*, 21 August 1942; 1942 BD Officer Roster; 1945 BD Officer Roster; Parsons Report; Saholsky Report; Robert E. Leiendecker, *Bomb Disposal, The Early Years of Explosive Ordnance Disposal (An Informal History)*, Charlottesville, Virginia: NATEODA Press, 2012, 305-07).

[60] 238th BD Company later yielded 60th through 63rd BD Squads. (Headquarters, Ordnance Bomb Disposal School, *Active Bomb Disposal Officers within the Continental United States*, 23 March 1943; *The Detonator*, 17 September 1943; *The Detonator*, 22 October 1943; Robert E. Leiendecker, *Bomb Disposal, The Early Years of Explosive Ordnance Disposal (An Informal History)*, Charlottesville, Virginia: NATEODA Press, 2012, 304-5).

[61] Table of Organization and Equipment 9-177, U.S. Army Ordnance Bomb Disposal Company; 1942 BD Officer Roster, Parsons Report; Saholsky Report; *The Detonator*, 17 September 1943; *The Detonator*, 22 October 1943; Green, Root, and Thomson, 148-9; Hooper, B-1.

[62] Lt. Col. Thomas J. Kane, to Maj. Gen. Levin H. Campbell, *Equipment to be procured for Ordnance Bomb Disposal Companies*, 2 June 1942; Table of Organization and Equipment 9-177, U.S. Army Ordnance Bomb Disposal Company; TM E9-1984; Saholsky Report.

[63] Ibid.

[64] U.S. Army Technical Manual E9-1984, *Disposal Methods for Enemy Bombs and Fuzes,* Aberdeen Proving Ground, Maryland: Chief of Ordnance, 12 November 1942; Table of Organization and Equipment 9-177, U.S. Army Ordnance Bomb Disposal Company.

[65] Originally, the 232nd BD Company had been destined for Panama, but instead went to Hawaii. After returning in 1943, Eddy's 233rd Company disbanded into separate squads and went overseas. (*The Detonator*, 17 September 1943, 2; *Active Bomb Disposal Officers*.)

[66] Karl G. Larew, "December 7, 1941: The Day No One Bombed Panama," from *The Historian*, Summer 2004, 299; Saholsky Report.

[67] Thirteen separate squads were first organized in late 1942 under T/O & E 9-179, later updated to T/O & E 9-500. Five of these were later sent to North Africa. (Table of Organization and Equipment for U.S. Army Ordnance Bomb Disposal Squad Separate (T/O & E 9-179); Third Service Command Headquarters, *Activation of the 1st to 13th Ord. Bomb Disp. Sqd., Sep,* 4 February 1943.)

[68] During the buildup to Normandy, Kane unsuccessfully fought to retain the 234th BD Company as a headquarters for ETO removal operations. (Mayo, 112-13, 232.)

[69] Col. Thomas J. Kane, *History of the Bomb Disposal Organization in the ETO*, 1-6; Frank A. Parsons, *Report on Bomb Disposal Activities*, 9 July 1943; Table of Organization and Equipment for U.S. Army Ordnance Bomb Disposal Company (T/O & E 9-179); Kane to Chief of Ordnance, *Change to T/O & E 9-500*, 3 December 1943.

[70] Table of Organization and Equipment for U.S. Army Ordnance Bomb Disposal Company (T/O & E 9-177); Table of Organization and Equipment for U.S. Army Ordnance Bomb Disposal Squad Separate (T/O & E 9-500).
[71] Medaris, a future NASA founder, commanded 188th Ordnance Battalion under II Corps, having replaced Col. Urban Niblo in February 1943. He later played a significant role in Ordnance support planning for the Normandy Invasion. (Kane to Ordnance Officer ETOUSA, *Bomb Disposal Organization Recommended for ETOUSA*, 31 December 1942; Col. Kane to Ordnance Officer, Allied Forces Headquarters, *Bomb Disposal Organization Recommended for ETOUSA*, Aberdeen Proving Ground, 11 January 1943; Mayo, 171, 174-76.)
[72] Ernie Pyle, "Ordnance Keeps Army in Trim," from *Stars and Stripes*, 27 July 1944, 2; Mayo, 143-44, 231-32.
[73] Leiendecker, *Bomb Disposal*, 69; Reece, 27.
[74] 43rd Ordnance Bomb Disposal Squad (Separate), unit history, 11 August 1943 to 14 December 1945; 46th Ordnance Bomb Disposal Squad (Separate), unit history, 6 March 1944 to 26 May 1945; 79th Ordnance Bomb Disposal Squad (Separate), unit history, 31 May 1944 to 30 June 1944;
[75] 31st U.S. Ordnance Bomb Disposal Squad, *Squad History 1943-45.*
[76] *Reading Times*, "Realistic War Glimpse Given to City by Army," 13 October 1943, 1-4, 13; *Reading Eagle*, "Bomb Disposal Test Provides Realistic Wartime Demonstration Here," 13 October 1943, 4A-4B; War Department to 2nd Lt. Joseph C. Pilcher, *Special Orders No. 256*, 13 September 1943;
[77] Lieutenant Steigerwalt later supervised BD operations at IX Air Defense Command in the Mediterranean Theater. (*Reading Times*, 1-4, 13; *Reading Eagle*, 4A-4B; 1942 BD Officer Roster; 1945 BD Officer Roster).
[78] *Reading Times*, 1-4, 13; *Reading Eagle*, 4A-4B.

# CHAPTER THREE

# SWEEPING ALONG: NORTH AFRICA AND SICILY (1942-43)

By late 1942, U.S. Army planning officers understood that unexploded bombs and booby traps were permanent factors in a new kind of war. Ordnance officers considered the future implications of bomb disposal, even as their superiors debated the merits of an early cross-channel offensive in France. However, when the first U.S. combat divisions finally engaged the Axis Powers in November 1942, they landed in North Africa without sufficient ordnance assets, including bomb disposal units. Before long, UXBs from both sides impeded maneuvers and paralyzed supply lines. When U.S. Army officers called on the Royal Engineers to disarm bombs and mines in American zones, this added to hasty perceptions that Great Britain's new allies possessed neither the skills nor the martial spirit to hold their own against the Afrika Korps.[1]

That same October, Col. T. J. Kane had just completed his inspection tour of American defenses, when he received a new mission from the War Department. As senior bomb disposal officer, Kane would presently visit each current Allied battlefront, reporting his observations to the Ordnance and War Departments. Kane's inspection tour would last six months. Beginning with London, Kane's itinerary covered North Africa, Egypt, Saudi Arabia, and the Persian Gulf. His second leg included the troubled China-Burma-India (CBI) Theater, as well as a tentative side-trip to the Soviet Union that never materialized. Acting as a "colonel-at-large," Kane's diplomatic skills and organizational talents were put to excellent use in England, where the Americans had already begun accreting manpower and materiel for the embryonic European Theater.[2]

Maj. Gen. Dwight D. Eisenhower had just received a new command over the American Expeditionary Force in June 1942. Sponsored by Gen. George C. Marshall despite a lack of combat experience, Ike nevertheless merited his promotion based on keen logistical skills and long-term strategic vision. However, the general's outwardly genial personality masked a realistic approach toward coalition warfare. Ike forecasted needs for at least one million battle-ready Americans by April 1943. Based in England, Eisenhower's force gathered resources and men, while their commander mulled over his two cross-channel invasion plans, Operations *Roundup* and *Bolero*.[3]

Eisenhower initially grasped the critical importance of UXB removal during troop movements on foreign shores. On May 13, 1942, Eisenhower had communicated with the outgoing Chief of Ordnance, Maj. Gen. Wesson, expressing a "definite need for Bomb Disposal Units with field forces." He predicted that without such specialists, UXBs could hinder forward movements and threaten rear areas. Eisenhower further proposed that individual BD officers should serve field commanders as experts on bombs, shells, and fuzes. Pursuant to these objectives, Ike advocated training more "Static, Mobile, or Field" bomb disposal units.[4]

On July 20, Col. Henry B. Sayler became ETO Chief of Ordnance, eventually rising to major general. Sayler had replaced John W. Coffey, whose ordnance network had paved the way for the preceding six months. Sayler established his first overseas headquarters with the U.S. Army's Services of Supply based at Cheltenham. One of Sayler's first challenges was preparing Maj. Gen. Lloyd C. Fredendall's II Corps for combat.[5]

Still following the guidelines of *Roundup*, Sayler requested three bomb disposal companies to augment II Corps' three infantry divisions, clearing enemy UXBs, "duds," and unserviceable ammunition that might impede "retrograde movements." However, owing to the Army's dispersion of bomb disposal personnel to secondary theaters, Sayler's request for tactical ordnance support in North Africa went unfulfilled.[6]

By that September, Allied commanders had been forced to reassess their "second front" in France following the abortive raid on Dieppe. Operation *Roundup* was subsequently scrapped in favor of a new plan, codenamed *Torch*. By waging battle in Morocco, Algeria, and Tunisia, the Allies hoped to divert German soldiers from the Eastern Front, knock out Vichy France and Fascist Italy, and gain control over the Mediterranean. Inexperienced American soldiers would also gain valuable battlefield exposure in time for the eventual invasion of Europe.[7]

Col. Urban Niblo of II Corps also shared Sayler's favorable view toward bomb disposal units. Sayler and "Nib" crafted the first operational document concerning overseas bomb disposal, outlining jurisdictions between the Army, Navy, and Air Forces. Niblo further envisioned a mobile bomb disposal "division" for II Corps, whose three divisions might require a central headquarters to oversee bombs, munitions, and shells. Niblo anticipated some possible conflicts between two Army technical services equally skilled in removing landmines; Combat Engineers and

Ordnance. Both planning officers decided that, when not engaged with UXBs, bomb disposal outfits might be called upon to clear minefields throughout "all sectors of the theatre."[8]

Henry B. Sayler, still a lieutenant colonel just before World War II began. (Aberdeen Proving Ground Ordnance Museum).

Col. Niblo remarked a scarcity of bomb disposal officers in England. While still subscribing to a defensive posture, the War Department had sent a lion's share of bomb disposal men, including one "squad separate," to Lt. Col. Philip Schwartz, ordnance chief for 8th U.S. Army Air Force. Based in London, Schwartz's technicians and instructors still played a significant role in protecting airfields from frequent German bombings. Even so, U. S. Army's II Corps had greater need for ordnance support services, as their forces were now slated for North Africa. Col. Niblo had but one qualified bomb disposal officer, a black second lieutenant transferred to II Corps Ordnance headquarters from the segregated 63rd Ammunition Battalion. Frustratingly, Nib did not mention this exceptional officer's name in his correspondence with Col. Sayler.[9]

Col. Sayler addressed British accusations toward Yanks "hindering" domestic bomb disposal operations across England. Initially, visiting Americans were not allowed to touch German bombs, even those discovered on U.S Army or Air Force installations. Instead, Americans had to wait for appropriate British authorities, such as the R.A.F, to handle UXB incidents. Given the shortage of U.S. ordnance specialists, such a policy made sense early on. However, necessity sometimes created heroes, like Pvt. Adam A. Gross, 8th Air Force, who received a Silver Star after volunteering to drive a truckload of live UXBs to a nearby "bomb cemetery." Col. Sayler took a firm but diplomatic tone with his hosts, requesting more latitude in situations involving bombs in American sectors. He also requested more bomb disposal personnel for the ETO.[10]

Just as Operation *Torch* began in early November, Lt. Col. Schwartz proposed the creation of a unified bomb disposal agency for the unfolding North African theater. Since 8th Air Force had the advantage of an operational bomb disposal section, it seemed natural for Schwartz to suggest his own ordnance branch as a suitable headquarters. However, Col. Sayler nixed Schwartz's proposal, as he felt it would concentrate even more resources among the Air Forces. Sayler argued that the Air Force always had the "least area to cover" in terms of ground. Furthermore, he felt this arrangement would hamper front line ordnance support. Instead, Sayler decided to appoint a chief bomb disposal officer answerable only to his group ordnance headquarters. Perhaps as an olive branch to Lt. Col. Schwartz, the ETO ordnance chief suggested that Schwartz's 8th Air Force could submit a suitable candidate. However, these arrangements came far too late to have immediate impact on combat operations in North Africa.[11]

* * *

Under Maj. Gen. Mark W. Clark's overall direction, Operation *Torch* sparked on November 8. It was spearheaded by the Western Task Force (Maj. Gen. George S. Patton), which embarked directly from the United States to Morocco. Two more Anglo-American battle groups, Center Task Force (Maj. Gen Lloyd L. Fredendall) and Eastern Task Force (Maj. Gen. Charles W. Ryder), traveled from England to Algeria. One week after *Torch*'s landings, Vichy forces in Morocco and Algeria had surrendered. Oran, whose port facilities and airstrips proved integral to control over the Mediterranean, had yielded to Fredendall as early as November 10. However, the dual challenges of Tunisia's deserts and the Afrika Korps still beckoned toward the victorious Allies in 1943.[12]

According to post-operational reports from North Africa, the Army Corps of Engineers and Ordnance Services shared all bomb disposal duties. However, a lack of Ordnance specialists forced "normal" Engineer troops to become full-time bomb disposal operatives. Trained with British equipment, these volunteers were directed to remove all UXBs and anti-ship mines found on land. Likewise, the Navy would pick up all bombs and mines encountered at sea. Unfortunately, no concrete reports exist from this phase of Allied operations, but since II Corps still lacked explosive ordnance support at Algeria, Gen. Fredendall's men were forced to rely on three companies of Royal Engineers, led by Brigadier N.A. Coxwell-Rogers, Chief Engineer of the British First Army.[13]

By mid-November 1942, Maj. John Burton, 8th U.S. Air Force's executive officer, had received dismaying reports from Algeria. Over-reliance on Royal Engineers had fomented "bad relations" with the British commanders. Meeting with several Air Force and Army representatives, Burton cited two specific instances where Royal Engineers were peremptorily directed to handle UXBs within American sectors. To prevent any future "uncoordinated requisitions," Burton seconded Sayler's arguments for a London-based U.S. bomb disposal agency to supervise special equipment requests. Meanwhile, Brig. Coxwell-Rogers submitted his report, *Lessons from Operation Torch*, which made a case for service troops "in high proportion" to echelons of Allied combat troops. Bomb disposal units were among the critical needs listed by Coxwell-Rogers.[14]

In response, Lt. Col. Schwartz dispatched four BD officers to Oran, now home to the 12th U.S. Air Force. Shortly after his arrival in Algeria, 1st Lt. DeMarr Erskine recruited a few of the trained U.S. combat engineers, but at first, their activities were largely confined to Oran. While this transfer expedited the Air Force mission in North Africa, II Corps still lacked explosive ordnance support for Army ground operations. With good relations between American and British field officers at risk, diplomacy was needed. Fortunately, one man with the requisite skills and perspective was on his way to visit London by December.[15]

Shortly before Christmas, Col. Kane arrived in the United Kingdom. Kane's Pan Am flight had touched down briefly at Lisbon, Portugal on December 20, but he experienced no hassles from airport security this time. Flying over to neutral Ireland, Kane took a connecting flight to Bristol, where he caught a passenger train on the Great Western Railway. On December 22, Kane arrived in London, meeting important Army officers, including Brig. Gen. Everett C. Hughes, Ike's logistics deputy, recently arrived from Tunisia. Kane also spoke to another Eisenhower intimate, Col. Ernest "Tex" Lee, the ETO's future chief G-3 officer.[16]

In 1943, Col. Kane (at right, third from the front) traveled the globe from London to North Africa, the Middle East, India, and Western China. (*Kane Collection*)

While staying in London, Kane certainly found opportunities for socializing, but his itinerary reflected a busy schedule. The colonel also struggled with a persistent cold that had plagued him since New York. Kane conferred often with several ranking ordnance officers, including Col. Sayler and Lt. Col. Schwartz, plus their respective staff members. Kane liked Sayler's proposal for a BD headquarters, and decided to interview potential staff officers among $8^{th}$ Air Force's ordnance cadre. Maj. John Burton introduced his aide, Capt. Robert H. Savage, a graduate from Aberdeen's Bomb Disposal School. Kane enthusiastically endorsed Savage's selection, charging him with maintaining "close contacts" between Allied services. By May 1943, both Burton and Savage had permanently transferred to Sayler's staff. As Sayler's new executive, Burton rose to lieutenant colonel. Eventually, Capt. Savage was replaced as bomb disposal liaison by Schuyler V.C. Larkin, nicknamed "Sky." Capt. Larkin would energetically supervise all equipment requisitions for incoming bomb disposal units destined for France.[17]

Overcoming his seasonal illness, Kane began smoothing over recent differences with British bomb disposal officers. After New Year's Day, he visited R.A.F Wing Commander J. C. Stevens, Capt. L. H. Llewellyn, R.N., as well as the Ministry of Supply. On January 7, Kane drove up to Ripon, Yorkshire, meeting with the new school commandant, Brigadier D. Robinson. In the interim, Kane's previous bomb disposal instructor, Major W. L. Andrews, had become chief instructor at Harper Barracks. For two days, Robinson, Kane, and Andrews discussed possibilities to improve relationships between Allied bomb disposal services. Robinson and Andrews agreed to permit U.S. trainees to attend special courses at Ripon until American training facilities could be arranged in 1943.[18]

Based on reports from Algeria, plus what he had picked up from his British contacts, Kane perceived two related problems. During *Torch*, American commanders had lacked sufficient ordnance support, requiring Royal Engineers to run the extra mile. Meanwhile, back in England, there was a surfeit of Army and Air Force disposaleers, eager to help even when not required. Kane advised these soldiers to allow the Royal Engineers to perform their "necessary services." At first, Yanks were allowed to neutralize bombs only within their bases. By 1944, however, American ordnancemen were actively cooperating with their British counterparts throughout the English countryside. This arrangement reduced the British workload considerably, and it gave the Yanks practical training.[19]

Kane's meeting at Harper Barracks also produced an agreement to build a joint bomb reconnaissance school, anticipating U.S. and British ordnance activities on the Continent. As time would attest, the prompt discovery, identification, and reporting of UXBs ensured safe zones of communication during a moving campaign. Kane had previously urged the War Department to plan a standardized bomb reconnaissance program for all military branches in foreign theaters, "at the earliest opportunity." Kane persistently felt civilians in occupied regions should be cultivated for reconnaissance wherever the Allies successfully achieved a breakthrough or assault landing. This proposal eventually bore fruit by 1944.[20]

Just before departing for Tunisia, Kane observed two German raids on January 17-18. With this fresh in his mind, he recommended two bomb disposal companies should be sent to England in case of cross-channel invasions: one company to defend embarkation points and a second company to cover battlefronts. Kane also suggested establishing a bomb disposal headquarters at Army Group level in North Africa, so future units would receive proper administration. Thus, Kane proceeded to visit existing ordnance depots and headquarters across the Allied fronts to discern existing bomb disposal assets and determine future needs.[21]

* * *

Just as Kane departed Liverpool on January 23, 1943, the Allies had established a foothold in Tunisia, where Rommel posed a threat. Disembarking at Oran in early February, Kane met with Col. David J. Crawford, 12th Army Air Force. Crawford's executive officer, Lt. Col. Russell Klanderman, introduced his modest bomb disposal section, led by 1st Lt. DeMarr Erskine. Kane already knew the lieutenant as an outstanding faculty member from his school in Maryland. As noted earlier, Erskine's small party of BD officers had been hurriedly transferred from London in November 1942. Though they were still technically Air Force, they were considered the first U.S. Army bomb disposal personnel to participate in overseas military operations against Germany. By 1944, Erskine's embryonic headquarters would supervise all Air Force bomb disposal operations across the Mediterranean Theater.[22]

While visiting Oran, Col. Kane made general recommendations for defense of each Allied Forces Headquarters (AFHQ) against UXBs and other airborne ordnance. Kane's letters of instruction created a blueprint for Army Air Force disposal operations. Kane called for a senior reconnaissance officer at battalion level or higher, with ordnance sergeants handling identification at company and platoon levels. For standard Army purposes, Kane recommended one separate squad per division, two squads per corps, or three squads at group level. However, semi-permanent airbases such as at Oran or Cairo required one squad per each company (equivalent to a flight in Air Force terminology). Each Air Force headquarters would be assigned a senior BD officer with the rank of major. Kane further suggested a high-ranking ordnance officer, preferably a lieutenant colonel, be selected at each headquarters to act as liaison officer with other Allied services.[23]

In Algiers, Kane resolved lingering jurisdictional issues arising from Operation *Torch*. While overall civil and military affairs remained in British hands, U.S. forces now supervised UXB operations within their own zones. In this fashion, Kane's leadership and diplomacy skills kept the Yanks from inadvertently trampling on their British allies. Despite past friction with American officers, the Royal Engineers stationed at Algiers willingly agreed to contribute technical support until more Americans arrived. At this stage, Lt. Erskine's scant equipment consisted of four basic toolkits, plus some jury-rigged instruments. Kane promised more support for Erskine's tiny detachment in the near future.[24]

Col. Urban Niblo (at left) and two U.S. II Corps staff officers. (*Kane Collection*)

Leaving Oran, Kane flew to eastern Algeria in early February. Landing at Tebessa's damaged airfield, he visited some bomb disposal soldiers. They were engaged in fixing the former Axis facility, which had been seized by U.S. parachute infantry back in November. Tebessa also served as Gen. Lloyd Fredendall's II Corps field headquarters. Kane interviewed Fredendall's ordnance chief, Col. Urban Niblo. Possibly, Kane might have received a private earful from Niblo, who had clashed so often with his indifferent corps commander that he soon left in order to become Mark Clark's U.S. Fifth Army ordnance chief. Niblo's capable replacement, Col. John Medaris, would arrive by March.[25]

On February 13, Kane stopped briefly in Cairo, Egypt to inspect 9th U.S. Air Force's volunteer bomb disposal group. Since the RAF already covered most of the area, Kane concluded no further reinforcements were necessary. Traveling to Malta, Kane observed RAF squads removing enemy ordnance from this battered little Mediterranean island. In 1940, the Luftwaffe had ordered the first of 3,340 raids, with British interceptor bases as chief objectives. Gen. Paul Deichmann acknowledged Malta's strategic importance during the North Africa campaign. However, as stubborn British garrisons held out, German pilots scattered delayed-action bombs, anti-personnel mines, and even hand grenades over Maltese villages. Over 15,000 casualties resulted from these terror raids, forcing the survivors to dig into the rocky earth for scant cover.[26]

Disease ran rampant on beleaguered Malta, especially malaria. On February 26, Col. Kane contracted a serious malarial fever, requiring hospitalization for nearly two months. Finally discharged on April 12, Kane left Malta just before the Germans raided a subterranean British hangar, located on the island's rocky northern end. For this offensive, Luftwaffe bombers tested two experimental projectiles: a rocket-driven armor-piercing bomb weighing 2,200 lbs., and a new napalm incendiary. Both devices were successful in temporarily knocking out the hangar, but Deichmann indicated there were insufficient supplies for follow-up raids. At this point, Kane had proceeded onward to inspect Persian Gulf and Far Eastern bases, returning for his stateside debriefing in late May 1943. Meanwhile, his requests for overseas reinforcements had borne fruit. [27]

On February 23, 1943, Allied Forces Headquarters (AFHQ) at Oran, Algiers received "Casual Detachment A." Responding to multiple calls for bomb disposal support, Aberdeen Proving Ground sent five officers and thirty enlisted men who were not properly organized or equipped as separate squads under T/O 179. The five bomb disposal officers were Lieutenants Raymond J. Narwid, John A. Randall, Julian F. Reichman, Vincent J. Sibel, and Richard R. Hughes II.[28]

Capt. DeMarr Erskine, senior bomb disposal officer at AFHQ, organized these sections into five separate squads numbered one through five. However, five pre-designated units existed back at Aberdeen, so Erskine's five sections were later reclassified as the 55th through 59th BD Squads (Separate). Because several 12th Air Force documents still refer to 1st Squad, 2nd Squad, and so forth, this has naturally led to some confusion. Until October 31, 1943, these five Air Force squads retained their original designations. They also saw some action in the Mediterranean Theater that spring. In late March, Capt. Erskine thoughtfully loaned his 1st Squad to Bradley's II Corps, squaring for their final showdown in Tunisia.[29]

Shortly after Kane left the North African Theater, Maj. Gen. Fredendall had executed a desultory thrust against Erwin Rommel's Afrika Korps, but suffered a severe drubbing at Kasserine Pass on February 15. Following George S. Patton's takeover of II Corps in early March 1943, this eccentric battlefield general prepared his celebrated counterattack, which took place on March 21 at El Guettar.[30]

| AFHQ's Casual Detachment "A" | Date Reorganized | 12th U.S. Air Force's New Unit Designation |
|---|---|---|
| **1st Ord. BD Squad Sep.** | 10/31/1943 | **55th Ord. BD Squad Sep.** |
| **2nd Ord. BD Squad Sep.** | 10/31/1943 | **56th Ord. BD Squad Sep.** |
| **3rd Ord. BD Squad Sep.** | 10/31/1943 | **57th Ord. BD Squad Sep.** |
| **4th Ord. BD Squad Sep.** | 10/31/1943 | **58th Ord. BD Squad Sep.** |
| **5th Ord. BD Squad Sep.** | 10/31/1943 | **59th Ord. BD Squad Sep.** |

While Patton's forces concentrated on knocking out Rommel's Afrika Korps, Lt. Gen. Bernard L. Montgomery's Eighth Army simultaneously pressed von Armin's left at the fortified Mareth Line, just south of Bizerte. Patton's executive officer, Maj. Gen. Omar N. Bradley, took operational control of II Corps, now augmented by 1st Infantry Division, under Maj. Gen. Terry D. Allen. During this set-piece battle, Bradley's determined men crossed miles of rough terrain toward Mateur, the Afrika Korps center. Marching in Bradley's vanguard, U.S. Army Ordnance bomb disposaleers were about to witness their first battle, a fearsome contest of "drenching artillery and hidden mines and walls of machine gun fire and even of the barbaric bayonet."[31]

* * *

On April 6, 1st BD Squad began their "shakedown" mission by supporting the infantry at El Guettar. They were attached to Col. John B. Medaris' 188th Ordnance Battalion, a highly disciplined II Corps outfit. For the first ten days, Medaris directed his staff bomb disposal officer, Capt. Robert P. Tobin, to command the squad. 2nd Lt. John A. Randall thereafter assumed charge of this unit. Perhaps, Medaris felt more comfortable entrusting a more experienced officer. However, Randall soon showed much promise as an explosive ordnance officer in Tunisia.[32]

During their first month supporting II Corps, 1st BD Squad handled numerous UXBs, chiefly of Axis make, which endangered safe transit along the major roads between Sbeitla and Faid. During El Guettar, enemy planes had scattered Butterfly bombs over Allied command posts, and one full canister had failed to detonate. Randall's men made short work of these bombs, devising special tools to recover the sensitive fuzes. They also worked occasionally with the "Tommies," who sought their assistance in locating duds at Beja, where Germans had blown up a British munitions truck. On April 28, they responded to a call from Terry Allen's 1st Infantry Division to remove a 200 lb. naval mine sealed in beeswax.[33]

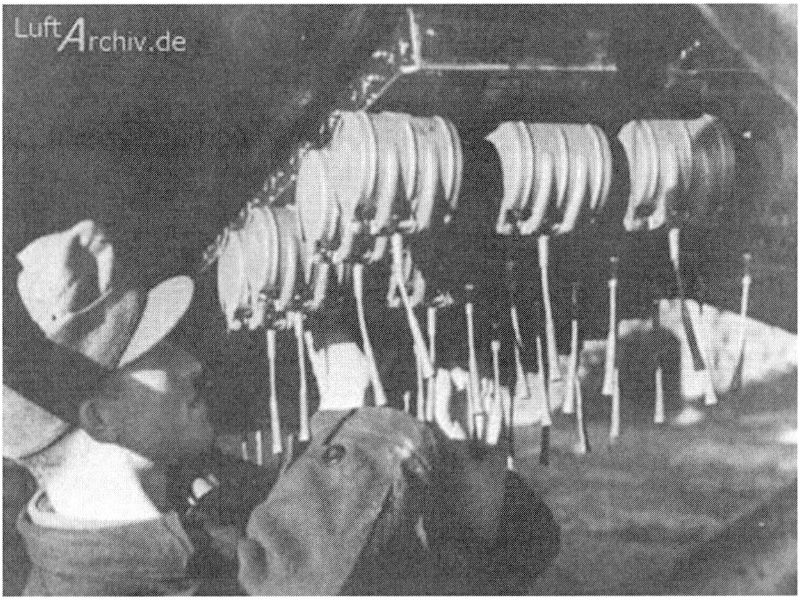


An unidentified Luftwaffe technician loads a clutch of lethal SD-2 "butterfly bombs" underneath a German plane. American bomb disposal soldiers encountered their first Butterflies in North Africa. (www.luftarchive.de)

By the first week of May, Maj. Gen. Bradley had taken Bizerte, a key Tunisian seaport infested by enemy landmines. During this breakthrough, Bradley's new ordnance chief, Col. John Medaris, had instilled his ordnancemen with remarkable courage. Medaris' deputy, Maj. William C. Farmer, shuttled back and forth in his heavily-armed jeep, personally fulfilling the infantry's ammunition requests. One observer noted that these "Ordnance boys" were "tough experienced men, front line troops."[34]

While Medaris' two ordnance battalions rendered aid to II Corps, Randall's 1st BD Squad handled all of Gen. Bradley's battlefront calls for bomb disposal. On May 3, Lt. Randall located a downed German plane near Sidi Noir and demolished two live bombs still mounted on the wreckage. En route to Bizerte on May 8, Randall braved German shellfire. Three days later, Randall defuzed 29 UXBs, and capped his day off by helping a British naval officer remove ten sea mines from Bizerte's docks. Randall even obliged his British friends by disarming at least four UXBs for them over the course of several days.[35]

During the last week of April, the 235th BD Company arrived at Oran, too late to see much action in North Africa. Their respected captain, Frederick H. Dillon, better known as "Harrison," had first entered service in February 1941. Hailing from Utica, New York, he had previously worked three years for Savage Arms, a weapons factory. Later described by one cousin as a zealous "barn-burner," Dillon had risen from lowly private to company commander within eighteen months. He had come to know his men very well during their stateside sojourn on the West Coast, watching for Japanese planes. Harrison had been offered a choice to remain stateside as a training officer, but instead, he chose to go with his original company. Hampered by an initial loss of equipment when their supply ship was intercepted, Dillon's "disposaleers" began their tour of duty near Algiers. To cover more ground, Dillon later sent his three field platoons individually to sweep for ubiquitous landmines.[36]

Two officers from 235th BD Company graduated in the 11th Class at Aberdeen Proving Ground in late 1942. Richard "Dick" Walkup is third from left, second row, wearing glasses. Steven Todorovich is standing at far right on third row. (*Leiendecker Collection*)

One of Dillon's platoon officers, 2nd Lt. Richard "Dick" Walkup, had just graduated the Army's Mine Warfare School located in Alabama. Recognizing a "serious war" in Europe, the Texan had enlisted in November 1940. Stationed with the 27th Ordnance Company, attached to the First Cavalry Division, he participated in 1941's Louisiana Maneuvers. Dick had first heard about bomb disposal through Army channels, and volunteered out of sheer curiosity. Walkup soon received his commission, completing the eleventh BD officers' course at Aberdeen Proving Ground. Walkup's impeccable qualifications made him an ideal fit for Dillon's company. Having just missed the battle in early May, Lt. Dick Walkup still believed his company "arrived at just the right time to be of service."[37]

As Dillon's company moved across Tunisia, a second company was required to continue mine removal back in Algiers. 1st Lt. Francis Geisler's 236th BD Company had embarked on May 10, 1943, bound for Oran. At the city of Fleuris, they gained a month of practical experience with German ordnance. In late June, 236th Co. joined Lt. Gen. Mark W. Clark's newly-organized U.S. Fifth Army at Tlemoen, bivouacking at a horse racing track. By September, Cpl. Edward Furey wrote to his stateside buddies, reporting that his unit felt "a lot better... than we did back in the States," because his fellow bomb disposaleers felt as though they were doing "something worthwhile" for the war effort.[38]

In June 1943, as German forces withdrew to Sicily and Italy, Randall's 1st BD Squad ranged from Mateur to Bizerte, removing many bombs, rockets, mines, and hand grenades. Randall became adept at disarming booby-traps, even locating an "ingenious specimen" inside a refrigerator. On June 9, Randall's squad detached from 188th Ordnance Battalion to pool resources with the 235th BD Company at Bizerte.[39]

Despite sharing heavy workloads at Mateur and Bizerte, moments of levity still occurred among the American disposaleers. While stationed at Mateur, Lt. Walkup befriended an injured crow he later named "Charlie." For weeks, Charlie entertained the company with his antics, roosting tamely in the officers' tent. As one might expect, Charlie coveted shiny items, such as cigarette lighters. Dick would find Charlie's plunder on his bedroll and laughingly return items to their owners. In early June, however, Lt. Walkup returned to find Charlie's neck snapped by the company dog. Evidently, the bossy bird had taunted its rival once too often. Decades later, Dick still recalled the loss of Charlie with regret.[40]

That very month, 235th BD Company and 1st BD Squad suffered their first human casualties. On June 21, two Army officers drove out to a beach outside Bizerte, where a live Italian naval mine had washed ashore. While naval ordnance theoretically belonged to the U.S. Navy, 1st Lt. William W. Farris (235th Co.) decided to disarm this item and send it back for research. Instead, the mine detonated, killing Farris instantaneously. Also killed in the blast, 2nd Lt. John A. Randall had experience dealing with sea mines in Bizerte, and was shortly due for promotion.[41]

Sent to assume temporary charge of the 1st BD Squad, Dick Walkup grimly recalled that his burial party found scarcely enough human remains to fill a single helmet. These remnants were later interred in the U.S. Army cemetery at Carthage. Farris and Randall were the first Army bomb disposal officers to perish in the Mediterranean Theater, but they were not the last. Out of twenty lieutenants and captains serving in North Africa and Sicily, seven would not live to see the war's conclusion.[42]

Shown in this 10th officer's class photo from Aberdeen are 2nd Lt. John A. Randall (1st BD Squad) and 1st Lt. William W. Farris, Jr. (235th BD Company), both killed by an Italian naval mine on June 21, 1943. Farris is second from left, first row. Randall is just visible, sixth from left, in the last row. (*Leiendecker Collection*)

EOD historians have long debated the first battle casualties among bomb disposal units serving in World War II. However, it now appears that the 2nd (later 56th) BD Squad's Pfc. Laurence Paystrup and Sgt. Ira Wiggins were killed while loading anti-tank grenades in their ordnance truck at Sbeitla. While not strictly combat-related, these two accidental deaths predate those of Randall and Farris, as well as two ordnancemen killed in action at the close of the Aleutian Islands campaign in June.[43]

In early July, Dick Walkup returned to his company, just in time to render assistance at Mateur, where a June 30 dumpsite accident had killed fourteen soldiers and destroyed over 2,000 tons of ammo earmarked for Operation *Husky* in Sicily. Over the next couple weeks, Lt. Walkup's soldiers helped to preserve ten thousand tons of serviceable ammunition, but received no credit in later Ordnance accounts. As Walkup later opined, "Few people ever knew the full scope of ordnance disposal."[44]

After the fight for Tunisia had concluded, Col. Medaris and Maj. Farmer fielded complaints from Army commanders that bomb disposal companies wasted manpower and resources. In fairness, neither Dillon's nor Geisler's companies had arrived in time to fully realize their special mission. Furthermore, both companies were often substituted for engineers or ammunition collectors. They were expected to cover desert theaters too large for even an ordnance battalion. Naturally, Medaris advocated the use of separate squads, given his successes with 1st BD Squad, now ably commanded by 1st Lt. Theodore R. Harper.[45]

During the summer of 1943, Lt. Ted Harper's squad continued to remove ordnance from various Allied command posts, thoroughfares, and airfields. Harper recorded his team's discovery of several crates containing live German 88mm artillery shells. One of the most versatile members of Hitler's arsenal, the dreaded "88" started out as an anti-aircraft gun. However, Erwin Rommel quickly realized the weapon's anti-tank capability in 1940 France, and the "88" soon became standard issue among fighting Wehrmacht and SS units. Searching recently abandoned positions full of German armaments, ordnance squads gathered samples for intelligence. One such team of specialists brought back live Butterfly bombs, while another crew dismantled a complete "88" setup for Aberdeen Proving Ground. During this period, Lt. Raymond J. Narwid of the Army BD School escorted several shipments back to Maryland.[46]

In August, Harper's 1st BD Squad teamed up with 236th BD Company, now operating as separate platoons in preparation for Italy. Despite gradual phasing-out of companies, "squads separate" had been introduced too slowly, requiring some amalgamation with company platoons. Planning for Operation *Husky*, Gen. Patton's chief ordnance officer, Col. Thomas Nixon, also suffered from chronic administration problems. Even though squads enjoyed better response times than full companies, poor communications and logistics affected both types of bomb disposal unit. Meanwhile, hazardous ordnance continued to maim and kill American troops based in Morocco, Algeria, and especially Tunisia. Col. Richard R. Arnold died June 6 as a result of a land mine at Sedjenane, leaving behind a charming Anglo-Irish fiancée, Kay Summersby.[47]

Others noticed a persistent lack of ordnance support in Tunisia. During the *Torch* campaigns, Dr. Lawrence D. Collins served with the U.S. 56th Evacuation Hospital, encamped at Bizerte's outskirts. As an Army surgeon, he had treated "many casualties from… duds, booby traps, and captured ammunition." On July 6, 1943, Collins remembered one of the Luftwaffe's last sorties over North Africa. British anti-aircraft guns made short work of German planes as they conducted a bombing raid. As this plane crashed against a nearby hillside, Collins recalled patients and medics rejoicing over a Jerry bomber's death throes as they might have done for the "fullback carrying [his] pigskin for a goal." Nevertheless, the Army doctor did not dare leave his field hospital for fears of encountering UXBs, still a threat owing to a dearth of "cleanup squads." Even though Collins did not know it yet, nearly all the II Corps bomb disposal teams were assembling at that moment for the impending Sicily landings.[48]

* * *

Launched on July 9, 1943, Operation *Husky* lasted under two months. Gela's landing zones were the first of several "bloody laboratories" wherein U.S. infantry divisions honed their amphibious warfare skills for Normandy and Southern France. Their immediate objectives were to secure Sicily's airfields and establish a lodgment for future operations on Italian soil. Following the May 1943 Trident Conference in Washington, the Combined Chiefs had ordered Gen. Eisenhower to "eliminate" Fascist Italy and "contain" all German forces on the Italian Peninsula. For six weeks, Patton's Seventh U.S. Army and Montgomery's British Eighth Army worked in uneasy tandem, owing to the unfortunate rivalry between the two generals. Lt. Gen. Harold Alexander, the overall British group commander, had a difficult task in balancing these two gigantic yet sensitive egos throughout the Sicily campaign.[49]

Landing with Bradley's U.S. II Corps, Capt. Dillon's 235th Bomb Disposal Company received their first taste of sustained warfare. Later on, their numbers were reinforced by a few separate squads from Tunisia. Sicily turned out to be the company's last hurrah as an intact group. During *Husky*, Dillon's company operated consistently at the platoon level, covering roughly two-thirds of this Fascist island stronghold. Attached to Patton's headquarters, Dillon supervised three field sections. 1st Lt. Eugene V. Struzik's First Platoon covered Seventh Army's center, traveling with the 45th Infantry Division. 1st Lt. Dick Walkup directed Second Platoon, supporting the 3rd Infantry Division along the coast to Palermo. Meanwhile, 1st Lt. Steve Todorovich's Third Platoon backed the 1st Infantry Division, which faced Germans at the dangerous Etna Line, named for the famous volcano that dominated all roads to Messina.[50]

Operation *Husky* continued the process of reshaping the military specialty of "bomb disposal." On Sicily, fewer than ten percent of Capt. Dillon's ordnance calls involved UXBs. Instead, his ordnancemen dealt with all manner of land and aerial mines. German Teller mines plagued *Husky* landings for weeks, while Italian Manzolini mines were so unstable they were destroyed *in situ*. All that summer, Lt. Dick Walkup's platoon would operate in the vicinity of Palermo, where they located and disarmed many landmines. Walkup later remembered that comparatively few German SD-2s were dropped on Sicily, although some unopened crates full of Butterfly bombs were found and destroyed.[51]

Steve Todorovich, writing one of the few surviving BD reports from Sicily, recalled his May 25 assignment to support the famous "Big Red One," under Maj. Gen. Terry Allen. After two weeks of preparation, plus a complete briefing at division headquarters, Todorovich "knew something was in the air." A native of Maryland, the twenty-six year old Todorovich was an articulate and evocative recorder of events. On *Husky*'s D-Day, July 9, Third Platoon of 235th BD Company embarked from Algiers alongside 1st Infantry Division's general ordnance company. From their landing craft, Steve's men observed the Seventh Army's short but brutal amphibious landings on the fertile coastal plains just outside Gela.[52]

Amphibious DUKW vehicles, or "Ducks," were ideal for carrying bomb disposal platoons and squads during Mediterranean assault landings. This DUKW from Fifth U.S. Army (at center) took part in the Salerno landing of September 1943.

As one 1st Infantry veteran of Gela remarked, "There were some who said that the landings… were easy, but for men who storm ashore in dawn, landings never are easy." By July 10-11, the Italians and Germans had counterattacked with all they could muster. Overlooking Seventh Army's landing zone, Gela afforded an excellent field of fire for the battle-hardened Herman Göring Panzer Division, consisting of fifty tanks. Despite a tragic friendly-fire incident that cost hundreds of paratroopers, the 82nd Airborne Division managed to link up with the "Big Red One" and Darby's U.S. Rangers. Knocking out many German tanks, Seventh Army's forward elements established a solid foothold at Gela on July 13.[53]

Like the infantry, Capt. Dillon's ordnancemen rode ashore in the new amphibious DUKW vehicles, known affectionately as "Ducks." Steve Todorovich's platoon arrived at Gela on July 16. Reporting to Ponte Olivo, they met a detachment of 1st Infantry Division combat engineers. Abandoned three days earlier by withdrawing Herman Göring panzers, Ponte Olivo was a major Sicilian airfield. However, the retreating Germans had scattered some thirty aerial mines, which turned out to be Manzolinis, primed with ticklish anti-disturbance fuzes. While lacking intrinsic knowledge about such ordnance, the Army engineers were reluctant to let Steve's platoon of disposaleers "run the works."[54]

Provincial clashes between Ordnance and the Engineers frequently occurred, such as the tussle arising from Gen. Patton's decision to transfer traditional ordnance tasks to his elite 1st Engineer Special Brigade. Patton's favoritism toward the Engineers prompted his own ordnance officer, Col. Thomas Nixon, to complain about a "black eye on Ordnance." In return, Nixon blamed the Engineers for the U.S. Seventh Army's ordnance mistakes during the Sicily mission. In the case of Ponte Olivo, since Todorovich had deployed alongside the 1st Division's combat engineers, it seems most likely that the ordnance lieutenant resolved this nettlesome situation by simply consulting his chain of command, and achieved better results through patience and tact.[55]

Whatever the case, Army engineers had granted custody of the airbase to Lt. Todorovich within twenty-four hours of his arrival. On July 17, ordnancemen began clearing Ponte Olivo for future Allied service. However, rather than taking unnecessary chances with the volatile Manzolini mines; Third Platoon practiced their rifle marksmanship, dispatching twenty of the "playthings" at a safe distance. Lt. Todorovich also ordered ten specimens detonated with shaped-charge explosives, testing his team's demolitions skill. While searching Ponte Olivo for other "thermos bombs," Third Platoon located and neutralized two semi-buried Italian UXBs, before retiring to celebrate their first day in action.[56]

Despite the Ordnance branch's efforts to distinguish bomb disposal teams from engineer sections, numerous Army battle reports have made blanket statements crediting "combat engineers." Since World War II, several respected military historians have taken such sources at face value, resulting in further obfuscation. Bomb disposal veterans later expressed disappointment regarding these frequent omissions. Rick Atkinson later credited the Engineers with the removal of thirty UXBs in the ruined Sicilian town of Adrano, located southwest of the Mount Etna. However, this location fell within Lt. Todorovich's sector, so these bombs were likely removed either by his platoon or nearby Royal Engineers.[57]

On July 18, Steve Todorovich drove forty miles southeast on Highway 115 to Vittoria, pursuing an urgent UXB report like "a retriever… after a dead duck." En route, his platoon had roped off a deserted German dumpsite to serve as their new bomb cemetery. In Vittoria, Todorovich blew up two 500 kg. German UXBs with type 25 fuzes, manually disarming a third bomb that had crashed into a house. Todorovich's convoy took this last article back for demolition, only to discover their chosen dumpsite cache housed nearly 80 free-falling G-mines, "fuzed and ready to go." Metallic items brought too close to a primed "George" mine could provoke instant detonation. Steve's men quickly improvised, commandeering a handy wooden trailer to transport their cast-iron UXB safely from their parked truck to their chosen "cemetery." Later on, they also detonated the stockpile of "Georges" at a safe distance. Todorovich decided to keep their new two-wheeled trailer for later use.[58]

Throughout 1942-43, Sicily had been subjected to destructive Allied bombing, effectively choking major roads. Seventh Army consequently charged Todorovich's platoon with supporting the "Big Red One" and the 45$^{th}$ "Thunderbirds." For almost one month, Third Platoon was on call across eastern Sicily, changing campsites four times in one day, always moving "closer toward the enemy." Bivouacking near Pietraperzia, they were strafed by marauding German fighter planes, but fortunately, Third Platoon suffered no losses. Third Platoon had been rendering safe a U.S. 500-pounder nicknamed "Peter Pan," because this shadowy UXB took three days to trace. After sending "Peter Pan" to join the other lost bombs, Steve removed another 500-pounder from Caltanisetta, a vital crossroads linking all three major Allied sectors on Sicily.[59]

Handling ordnance calls for two combat divisions kept the 235$^{th}$ BD Company hopping. Meanwhile, dormant "friendly" bombs began to outnumber German UXBs. Lt. Steve Todorovich recorded finding over 20 British duds using new T-37 anti-withdrawal fuzes. Todorovich reported his suspicions that Allied bombers had dropped these delayed-action bombs prematurely on their way to strike Catania, an occupied town on Sicily's eastern coast, about halfway to the crucial port of Messina.[60]

Montgomery's Eighth Army had grappled at Catania for weeks with the reformed Hermann Görings. Only when German forces fell back to Messina, did the town surrender to the victorious British on August 9. Patton, in the meantime, had outflanked his opponent, using amphibious maneuvers on the northern coasts, which permitted him to enter Messina ahead of Monty. Even so, two controversial "slapping incidents" in two separate field hospitals soon threatened Patton's Army career.[61]

Reaching Caltanissetta on July 23, Steve Todorovich observed that Patton's forces had "played tag" with the Germans only days before, leaving behind tons of unexploded ordnance and discarded hardware. On July 24, Todorovich left his platoon, answering an urgent call from Petralia, two hours away. Following a "reckless" drive to First Division HQ, he discovered to his horror that a 20 lb. American fragmentation bomb had landed in Gen. Terry Allen's forward command post. Fortunately, the bomb had turned out a dud, but Lt. Todorovich treated this wayward piece of ordnance with mock solemnity, earning himself a hot meal and quick shower into the bargain. On his way to rejoin Third Platoon at Caltanisetta, Steve answered a call to investigate yet another UXB on the road to Gangi. This "bomb" turned out to be a 32 cm rocket of German make, which the lieutenant shipped to his superiors.[62]

On Sicily, as in Tunisia, bomb disposal specialists served as intelligence-gathers, agents for data about new weaponry, ammunition, and vehicles. Technicians reported defects in Allied munitions, such as 1st Division's renegade U.S. fragmentation bomb. Steve Todorovich described serious faults with M103 and M106 bomb fuzes. In addition to UXBs, Army bomb salvagers were keenly interested in enemy rockets and mines. Todorovich discovered several examples of German rocketry, including 28 cm, 37 mm, and 150 mm variants. Todorovich also caught his first glimpse of Germany's huge 210 mm anti-tank rocket. All such items were sent back to North Africa for analysis. During the later Italian Theater, new German ordnance continued to surface, and bomb disposal men often risked their lives to capture new specimens.[63]

Initially, the Sicilians (and later on, Italians) were wary of American BD soldiers, driving their ordnance trucks with distinctive crimson mudguards. They also wore their field uniforms bearing red bomb insignia against an olive drab background. T/5 Al Gardner (12th BD Squad) recalled that his insignia occasionally misled civilians into blaming his fellows for the actual bombing. Eventually, Italians became cooperative after witnessing BD men in action – sometimes, *too* helpful. After responding to several false alarms in Nicosia and Cerami, Lt. Todorovich drily concluded: "*looking* for bombs is a bad policy." He soon devised a plan to meet with town mayors or police marshals every few days, collecting reports and traveling with reliable police guides. Todorovich's system allowed his platoon full coverage around Troina, arguably the scene of Sicily's fiercest combat.[64]

Often, liberated Sicilians and Italians showed tremendous kindness to American soldiers who disarmed UXBs in their farms, homes, and businesses. At Caltanisetta, Lt. Todorovich visited a "large, fashionable" hotel." Here, a U.S. bomb had landed neatly in a laundry tub down in the basement. While Steve toiled on July 23, his "cordial" hostess, one Regina, provided her gallant with "very good liquor." Todorovich hinted that more intimacy might have resulted with Regina, but as he reported, "I was busy that day." Similar offers of wine and possibly, companionship, were peculiar to Allied soldiers serving across Europe, but bomb disposal men often earned these perks by rendering direct aid to civilians. Even so, T/Sgt. Robert Kuehner tells a rather less romantic, but more enduring story of friendship with a mainland Italian family. As a noncom serving with 57th BD Squad in early 1945, Kuehner personally rescued one family's home from an unexploded bomb. After the war, Bob Kuehner met his Italian friends frequently, exchanging gifts and holiday visits.[65]

If Italian civilians showed gratitude, recognition from Army brass came more slowly. In Sicily, Lt. Col. William H. Connerat, Jr. observed the 235th BD Company in action, and his report did not greatly alter unfavorable impressions toward Ordnance's newest branch. Nevertheless, Steve Todorovich still "carried on the airs of a true B.D. officer," as he policed Nicosia's bivouac areas for discarded Italian ammunition, and disarmed 38 UXBs. Third Platoon cleared several Allied "duds" lurking in towns like Randazzo and Floresta. On August 19, their platoon leader drove seven hours to Milazzo, disarming one German bomb in the village's sole grain mill. Perhaps recognizing signs of overwork, Bradley's II Corps released Todorovich's platoon over to Patton's Seventh Army HQ in Palermo. Royal Engineers subsequently assumed charge of Allied UXB operations in East Sicily. On August 24, Third Platoon rejoined the 235th Company in Palermo, where they awaited their next mission. Todorovich's men toasted their survival with eight welcome gallons of Sicilian wine, purchased by their generous platoon leader.[66]

One of Lt. Dick Walkup's exploits, disarming a 1,100 kg German penetration bomb, took place in early August at Patton's Seventh Army Headquarters in Palermo. Walkup quickly evacuated Seventh Army staff members from their three-story building, and then disarmed this threatening "blockbuster," which had nearly penetrated to the bottom. Commandeering a landing-craft, Walkup jettisoned his dangerous cargo in the Tyrrhenian Sea. Dick remained convinced that this weapon, the only bomb dropped near Seventh Army HQ, was meant to kill Patton.[67]

By August 17, the Sicilian Campaign had been brought to a close, culminating with the Seventh Army's exultant reception at Messina. While Patton preened at Monty's expense, the principal German defenders had already fled across the Messina Straits to Southern Italy. For weeks, 235th BD Company stayed on Sicily to clear tons of leftover ordnance.[68]

While Operation *Husky* reached full tempo, Allied bases in North Africa were subjected to Luftwaffe raids launched from the heel of Italy. One night raid took place on August 7, which found 1st BD Squad responding to many calls from British positions. On August 10, Harper's men worked alongside Royal Engineers to clear a bivouac site for 342nd R.A.F. Group. When not dealing with immediate raids, they removed UXBs in the Bizerte region. 1st Lt. Ted Harper often had to split his meager resources to cover more ground. That July, he dispatched two men to Sidi Ahmed Airport to remove some British Mk. 1 fragmentation bombs reported at a nearby private residence. Sometimes, 236th BD Company lent a welcome hand to the tired boys of 1st Squad. 1st Lt. Frank E. Smith, a 236th platoon commander, helped Harper tremendously by discarding some British flare grenades erroneously tagged as Italian "Red Devils." On the lighter side, Frank Smith escorted his fellow disposaleers on a historic tour of old Carthage, serving as their "tour guide."[69]

On August 23, both Harper and Smith received an alert for Operation *Avalanche*, the U.S. Fifth Army's long-anticipated landing at Salerno. Urban Niblo, now a brigadier general under Clark, had assumed command of all Fifth Army ordnance operations, including bomb disposal. Spending a week at Oran, Algeria, Harper's team briefed other soldiers on reporting UXBs and booby-traps. Departing from Oran on September 15, Harper's men were busy disarming UXBs and shells in Salerno by the time Germans had withdrawn from Naples on October 1. On October 31, they were reclassified as the 55th BD Squad under the U.S. Fifth Army.[70]

* * *

Midway through the mounting Italian campaign, the Mediterranean Theater's two bomb disposal companies ceased to exist. Capt. Dillon's 235th Company, over-extended and under-utilized in Tunisia, had successfully covered most of Sicily without losing a single man to ordnance, strafing planes, or shellfire. Nevertheless, the War Department advanced its plans to reorganize all bomb disposal companies "at the earliest practicable date." While neither of Italy's companies formally disbanded until May 7, 1944, they never again operated as complete units. Capt. Geisler's 236th Company regrouped at Capua for the last time in October 1943, while 235th Company's platoons spent eight months divided between Sicily and Italy. When the parent ordnance companies divided into twenty-four bomb disposal "squads separate," these were evenly split between the mobile forces of U.S. Fifth Army and the static Peninsular Base Section responsible for supporting theater-wide Allied operations.[71]

| Original Army Bomb Disposal Company | Date Reorganized | New Squad Separate Designations |
|---|---|---|
| **235th Ord. BD Company (Capt. Harrison Dillon)** | 5/7/1944 | **131st to 142nd BD Squads (Peninsular Bases)** |
| **236th Ord. BD Company (Capt. Francis Geisler)** | 5/7/1944 | **143rd to 154th BD Squads (U.S. Fifth Army)** |

Col. L.M. Garner, a ranking Ordnance officer at the Peninsular Base Section, offered his explanation for why Italy's transition to separate squads took so long to effect. Garner described the two companies as having been heavily engaged in removing both Allied and Axis bombs from "an actual combat theater," specifically Naples and its satellite ports, including Salerno. Additionally, the ordnance specialists were "called upon to destroy land mines located by the Engineers *frequently*." The author has emphasized the last word. Garner further expressed his hopes for a central headquarters for these squads in the Italian Theater, suggesting that a "combination of squads could meet the situation better than several independent squads." While the Fifth Army eventually appointed a staff bomb disposal officer at Caserta to supervise its teams, the Peninsular Base Section appears not to have done so.[72]

Sadly, two 235th Company officers never made it to the Italian Theater. On October 10, 1943, Capt. Harrison Dillon and his comrade, Lt. Steve Todorovich were reported missing in action. Dick Walkup had last seen Dillon near Palermo in early October, responding to a routine UXB call. Both men were listed as "dead to non-hostile causes," but no one ever gave Walkup a straight explanation. For decades, EOD historians and family members have remained baffled to explain these two disappearances. Dillon, in particular, had been a well-regarded company commander who might have reached higher rank in the Italian Theater.[73]

Recently unearthed U.S. Air Force reports have shed new light on the fates of Dillon and Todorovich. They had both left Sicily for Algeria on undisclosed business, presumably related to their last mission on Sicily. After reporting to Algiers, Capt. Dillon and Lt. Todorovich were both scheduled as passengers aboard a B-25C Mitchell bomber plying a routine ferry route between Algeria and Tunisia. Dillon and Todorovich were scheduled to make their connecting flight from Tunis back to Naples. However, shortly after takeoff from Algiers, their flight vanished without any trace. The Air Force launched an inconclusive probe, but neither the plane's wreckage nor any human remains have ever surfaced. Both officers are still listed as missing in action, and as such, have not been formally recognized by the National EOD Memorial Foundation.[74]

# Notes

[1] Most primary documents dealing with the Mediterranean Theater date back to early preparations for the European Theater of Operations (ETO) in 1943. For my purposes, the Mediterranean Theater describes the combined Allied campaigns in North Africa and Sicily, as well as the "forgotten front" in Italy.

[2] Colonel Thomas J. Kane, travel journal and itinerary, U.S. Ordnance Museum, Aberdeen Proving Ground, Maryland, 1 December 1942 – 25 May 1943.

[3] Eisenhower's first wartime post as Marshall's chief strategist has been given thorough examinations by several American military scholars. Despite recent questions regarding its authenticity, Stephen Ambrose's two-volume biography on Eisenhower is still widely viewed as authoritative. Carlo D'Este's more recent Eisenhower study also focuses on Ike's stellar military career. (Rick Atkinson, *An Army at Dawn* (New York: Henry Holt, 2002) 11-12; See also Stephen E. Ambrose, *Eisenhower: Soldier, General of the Army, President-Elect, 1890-1952, Volume 1* (New York: Simon & Schuster, 1983), plus Carlo D'Este, *Eisenhower: A Soldier's Life*, (New York, Henry Holt, 2002).

[4] Major General Dwight Eisenhower to Chief of Ordnance, *Disposal of Unexploded and Delayed Action Bombs within Continental United States*, 13 May 1942.

[5] Colonel (later Brigadier General) Urban Niblo (1897-1957) later directed U.S. Army Ordnance in the Mediterranean Theater. Colonel (later Major General) Henry B. Sayler (1893-1970) served as General Eisenhower's ordnance chief throughout the European Campaign. (*ETO Bomb Disposal History*, NARA Records Group 498, 1945, 4-9; Mayo, 93-96, 213; Ordnance Hall of Fame website.)

[6] Colonel H. B. Sayler, *Bomb Disposal Plan for Round-up*, 9 September 1942.

[7] II Corps included the 1st Infantry Division (Terry Allen), 9th Infantry Division (M.S. Eddy), and 34th Infantry Division (Charles Ryder). (Atkinson, *An Army At Dawn,* 31-32; Williamson Murray and Allen R. Millett, *A War to be Won: Fighting the Second World* War, Cambridge, Massachusetts: Harvard University Press, 2001, 271-73).

[8] Col. Niblo to Chief Ordnance Officer ETOUSA, 13 August 1942; Col. Sayler to Col. Niblo, 27 August 1942; Col. Sayler, *Bomb Disposal Plan for Round-up*, 9 September 1942; Capt. R. W. Cary, *Proposed Bomb and Mine Disposal Policies for the U. S. Navy and U. S. Army in the Event of an Allied Invasion of Europe.* 11 January 1943.

[9] At the beginning of 1942, Aberdeen Proving Ground had trained a solitary black ordnance officer, a junior lieutenant based at Raritan Arsenal, New Jersey. This African-American officer was assigned to 63rd Ammunition Battalion, and later became Niblo's bomb disposal officer, but no further information is available. However, it is interesting to observe how this unnamed black officer's specialized ordnance skills overrode racial concerns characterizing the U.S. Army throughout World War II. For further examination of the role of black ordnance soldiers, see the U.S. Army's special study, *The Employment of Negro Troops*. (Ulysses Lee,

*The Employment of Negro Troops*, Washington, D.C.: Office of the Chief of Military History, 1966, 207; Col. Urban Niblo to Chief Ordnance Officer ETOUSA, 13 August 1942; Ordnance Technical Services; *ETO Bomb Disposal History*, NARA Records Group 498, 1945, 4-9.)

[10] Col. Niblo to Chief Ordnance Officer ETOUSA, 13 August 1942; Col. Sayler to Colonel Niblo, 27 August 1942; Colonel Sayler, *Bomb Disposal Plan for Round-up*, 9 September 1942; *Stars and Stripes*, 3 December 1942; Andrew A. Rooney, "This is the Eighth Air Force," from *Stars and Stripes*, 19 August 1943; Ordnance Technical Services; *ETO Bomb Disposal History*, NARA Records Group 498, 1945, 4-9.

[11] Ordnance Technical Services, *ETO Bomb Disposal History*, Annexes 5-7, NARA Records Group 498, 1945.

[12] Atkinson, *An Army At Dawn,* 49-57, 124-25, 148-51; Murray and Millett, 271-73; Hooper, 17; Mayo, 231.

[13] These Royal Engineer companies were Nos. 8, 15, and 17, who served throughout the Mediterranean Theater, under the 15th Allied Group Command. (U.S. Army, U.S. Forces, European Theater, Historical Division: Records, 1941-1946, Staff Section Report 547, Engineers: Chronology of Events, Monograph Schedule and Magazine Article (1941-1945); Schuyler V.C. Larkin, *Bomb Disposal since D-Day*, 52nd EOD Group Archives, Kane Hall, 2 January 1945; Eric E. Wakeling, *A Short History of Royal Engineer Bomb Disposal*, Buckinghamshire, England: B.D. Publishing, 1997, 11.)

[14] Maj. Burton to Col. Sayler, *Bomb Disposal Meeting in Ordnance Office E.T.O.*, 16 November 1942; Ordnance Technical Services, *ETO Bomb Disposal History*, Annexes 5-7, NARA Records Group 498, 1945; U.S. Army, U.S. Forces, European Theater, Historical Division: Records, 1941-1946, Staff Section Report 547, Engineers: Chronology of Events, Monograph Schedule and Magazine Article (1941-1945), N.A. Coxwell-Rogers, *Lessons from Operation Torch,*4 January 1943; Atkinson, *An Army At Dawn,* 163-67.

[15] Frank A. Parsons to Historical Section, *Report on Bomb Disposal Activities*, 1 July 1942 – 30 June 1943, 52nd EOD Group Archives, Kane Hall, 9 July 1943; Schuyler V.C. Larkin, *Bomb Disposal since D-Day*, 52nd EOD Group Archives, Kane Hall, 2 January 1945.

[16] Maj. Gen. Hughes, a West Point classmate of George S. Patton, acted as Eisenhower's eyes and ears throughout World War II, and later served as Chief of Ordnance from 1946-49. (Rick Atkinson, *An Army at Dawn*, 329; Omar N. Bradley and Clay Blair, *A General's Life* (Simon and Schuster, New York, 1983), 131*;* Martin Blumenson, *The Patton Papers* (Boston: Houghton Mifflin, 1974), 153; Carlo D'Este, *Patton: A Genius for War* (New York: Harper Collins, 1995), 451-2; Mayo, 231-2; Kane travel itinerary 1942-43).

[17] Capt. Robert Savage graduated from Army Bomb Disposal School, Class 4. (Maj. Burton to Col. Sayler, *Bomb Disposal Meeting in Ordnance Office E.T.O.*, 16 November 1942; Kane to Ordnance Office ETOUSA, *Bomb Disposal in the Communication Zone*, 11 January 1943; *ETO Bomb Disposal History*, NARA Records Group 498, 1945, 4-9; Kane travel itinerary 1942-43; Parsons report; 1942

BD Officer roster; U.S. Army, U.S. Forces, European Theater, Historical Division. Records, 1941-1946; Staff Section Reports, File 604e Ordnance Section ETO; Mayo, 231-2).

[18] Kane travel itinerary, 1942-3; Schuyler V.C. Larkin to Colonel Thomas J. Kane, *Bomb Disposal Training in the United Kingdom*, 1 October 1943; Hooper, 18-21.

[19] Captain Schuyler V.C. Larkin to Colonel Thomas J. Kane, *Bomb Disposal Training in the United Kingdom*, 1 October 1943; Kane travel itinerary, 1942-3; Hooper, 18-19, 21.

[20] By early 1944, the U.S. 234th Ordnance BD Company arrived in England, serving as bomb disposal training headquarters for American units, and as a school for French civilians thereafter. (Kane to Ordnance Office ETOUSA, *Bomb Disposal in the Communication Zone*, 11 January 1943).

[21] 235th BD Company w as activated on August 15, 1942, while 236th BD Company entered service on 15 September 1942. (Kane to Ordnance Officer ETOUSA, *Bomb Disposal Organization Recommended for ETOUSA*, 31 December 1942; *ETO Bomb Disposal History*, NARA Records Group 498, 1945, 4-9).

[22] Kane travel itinerary, 1942-3, Larkin report; Robert J. Kuehner, "The Deadly 88," from *UXB Volume II*. Sussex, England: Woodfield Publishing Co., 2001; Kuehner interviews; 1942 Bomb Disposal Officer Roster.

[23] Thomas J. Kane to Allied Forces Headquarters, *Bomb Disposal Organization*, 5 February 1943.

[24] Kane journal.

[25]Kane journal; Rick Atkinson, *An Army at Dawn*, 274; Gerard M. Devlin, *Paratrooper!* (St. Martin's Press, New York, 1979), 172; Mayo, 171, 174-76.

[26] In late 2009, a Maltese youth came across a dormant Butterfly bomb while walking in the countryside. (Thomas J. Kane to Allied Forces Headquarters, *Bomb Disposal Organization*, 5 February 1943; Kane travel itinerary, 1942-3; Paul Deichmann, "Luftwaffe Methods in the Selection of Offensive Weapons, Volume 1," from *USAF Historical Studies*, No. 187 (Manhattan, Kansas: MA/AH Publishing, Sunflower University Press, c. 1985), 25-26; Murray and Millett, 92-94; Atkinson, *An Army at Dawn,* 46-48; Kurt B. Coster, "Boy Finds Lethal WWII Bomb in Qormi Valley," from *The Malta Times*, 29 October 2009.)

[27] Col. Kane never recovered entirely from his Maltese fever, which contributed toward his untimely death in 1965. (Deichmann, 93-94; Kane travel itinerary, 1942-3; Kay Levering to author, telephone interview; 15 October 2003; Mary Jo Romba to author, telephone interview with author; 15 October 2003.)

[28] Parsons, *Report on Bomb Disposal Activities*; 9 July 1943; 1st Ordnance Bomb Disposal Squad (Separate), operation reports, April to October 1943; 55th Ordnance Bomb Disposal Squad (Separate). [unit history] 1943-45; 56th Ordnance Bomb Disposal Squad (Separate), unit history, 1943-45; 57th Ordnance Bomb Disposal Squad (Separate), unit histories, February 1943 to June 1945.

[29] Parsons, *Report on Bomb Disposal Activities*; 9 July 1943; 1st Ordnance Bomb Disposal Squad (Separate), operation reports, April to October 1943; 55th Ordnance Bomb Disposal Squad (Separate). [unit history] 1943-45; 56th Ordnance

Bomb Disposal Squad (Separate), unit history, 1943-45; 57th Ordnance Bomb Disposal Squad (Separate), unit histories, February 1943 to June 1945; Hooper, 17.
30 Atkinson, *An Army at Dawn*, 145-46, 431-529; Mayo, 139-40.
31 Stars and Stripes Press, *The First! The Story of the 1st Infantry Division,* Paris, France: Desfosses-Neogravure, 1945.
32 1st Ordnance Bomb Disposal Squad (Separate), operation reports, April to October 1943; Mayo, 171, 174-76.
33 1st Ordnance Bomb Disposal Squad (Separate), operation reports, April to October 1943.
34 Within ninety days of liberation, Bizerte had yielded more than 39,000 mines. (Peter Schrijvers, *The Crash of Ruin* (New York: New York University Press, 1998), 73-75; Mayo, 142-51.)
35 1st Ordnance Bomb Disposal Squad (Separate), operation reports, April to October 1943; Walkup manuscript, 30 March 2000;
36 Capt. Dillon's younger cousin, Maj. Edward Dillon (USAF retired), has spent years researching his relative's remarkable career in Army bomb disposal. He was in grade school during the war, but recalls his kinsman's rapid promotion through the ranks, as well as his decision to go overseas. He saw his cousin once just prior to his deployment to North Africa in April 1943. (143rd Ordnance Bomb Disposal Squad (Separate). unit history, 7 May 1944; Edward Dillon, interview with author, 11 April 2011; Robert E. Leiendecker, *Bomb Disposal, The Early Years of Explosive Ordnance Disposal (An Informal History)*, Charlottesville, Virginia, NATEODA Press, 2012, 459).
37 Lt. Col. Richard Walkup to author, telephone interview, 25 June 2010; Lt. Col. Richard W. Walkup, telephone interview, 13 November 2010; BD Officer Roster, 1945; Richard W. Walkup, [unpublished manuscript], 30 March 2000.
38 Mark W. Clark had served as Eisenhower's deputy during Operation Torch; Dick Walkup later became lifelong friends with Frank Geisler, who hailed from Laramie, Wyoming. After the war, Dick Walkup attended the University of Wyoming, and saw much of his old comrade. Unfortunately, Geisler passed away before this project began in 2003. (*The Detonator*, 17 September 1943, 6; 143rd Ordnance Bomb Disposal Squad (Separate). unit history, 7 May 1944; Lt. Col. Richard W. Walkup, telephone interview, 13 November 2010; Atkinson, *An Army at Dawn,* 271-72).
39 1st Ordnance Bomb Disposal Squad (Separate), operation reports, April to October 1943; Lt. Col. Richard Walkup to author, telephone interview, 25 June 2010.
40 Dick Walkup later became a BD squad commander, and remained on active duty with the U.S. Army after World War II, serving in Korea as an EOD officer. Dick retired in 1960 as a lieutenant colonel in the Army Ordnance Corps. (Lt. Col. Richard Walkup to author, telephone interview, 25 June 2010; Lt. Col. Richard W. Walkup, telephone interview, 13 November 2010).
41 www.wwiimemorial.com; www.eodmemorial.org/army.html; Jerome Krieger to Commander, NAVSCOLEOD, *Fact Sheet*, 5 October 1992; Robert Leiendecker, *World War II EOD Data*; National EOD Association Library, Charlottesville VA,

2003; Michael R. Vining, *Explosive Ordnance Disposal Memorial – U. S. Army,* submitted to the EOD Memorial Commission, 15 October 2011.

[42] 235th Company lost four out of seven original officers by 1943, while 236th company lost at least two of its original officers in the Italian theater. Even today, EOD groups and civil authorities still find about fifty tons of explosives per year in Tunisia. (Richard Walkup, interview with author, 25 June 2010; 1st Ordnance Bomb Disposal Squad (Separate), operation reports, April to October 1943; Atkinson, *The Day of Battle*, 533.)

[43] Also killed in the North African sector was Staff Sgt. Edwin T. Walker of 59th Squad, who was reported dead on or about June 22, 1943. (Robert E. Leiendecker, *Bomb Disposal, The Early Years of Explosive Ordnance Disposal (An Informal History)*, Charlottesville, Virginia, NATEODA Press, 2012, 193, 303).

[44] Lida Mayo's sources credited men from 188th Ordnance Battalion and the 66th Ammunition Company with extinguishing the immediate fire, but Walkup remembered the incident almost sixty years later. He also speculated the fire was caused by a vehicular accident inside the ammo dumpsite. (Lt. Col. Richard Walkup to author, telephone interview, 25 June 2010; Lt. Col. Richard W. Walkup, telephone interview, 13 November 2010; BD Officer Roster, 1945; Richard W. Walkup, [unpublished manuscript] 30 March 2000; Mayo, 159.)

[45] Kane to Chief of Ordnance, *Change to T/O & E 9-500*, 3 December 1943; Mayo, 231-32, Hooper, 18-19, Mayo, 136-38, 170-171.

[46] Using this captured German "88," the U.S. Army eventually created a 90 mm counterpart for field service. For the whole story behind Aberdeen Proving Ground's acquisition of a functioning German 88, read Lida Mayo's *On Beachhead and Battlefront.* (1st Ordnance Bomb Disposal Squad (Separate), operation reports, April to October 1943; Tom Hoge, "5 GIs Are Wizards on Nazi Arms" from *Stars and Stripes*, 25 May 1944, 2; Mayo, 24-26; Atkins, 431-35).

[47] Fueled by rumors of intimacy, many historians have speculated as to Ike's exact relationship with his driver, Kay Summersby. (1st Ordnance Bomb Disposal Squad (Separate), operation reports, April to October 1943; Mayo, 164-66; Atkinson, 329-30, 533.)

[48] Lawrence D. Collins, *The 56th Evacuation Hospital* (University of North Texas Press, 1995), 39-42.

[49] Stars and Stripes Press, *The First! The Story of the 1st Infantry Division,* Paris, France: Desfosses-Neogravure, 1945; Stars and Stripes Press, *The 45th: The Story of the 45th Infantry Division;* Paris, France: Desfosses-Neogravure, 1945; Atkinson, *The Day of Battle*, 75-175.

[50] Steve Todorovich, *American Bomb Disposal in the Sicilian Campaign*, Aberdeen Proving Ground, Maryland; Ordnance Museum Archives, September 1943; 143rd Ordnance Bomb Disposal Squad (Separate), unit history, 7 May 1944; BD Officer Roster, 1942; *Kane itinerary 1942-3*; Kane Journal, 5; Lt. Col. Richard Walkup to author, telephone interview, 25 June 2010; Mayo, 158, 231-2.

[51] Atkinson, *The Day of Battle*, 80; Hooper, 17-18; Richard Tregaskis, *Invasion Diary* (Lincoln, Nebraska: University of Nebraska, 2004), 60-61.

[52] See Devlin, 208-48 for details on airborne maneuvers and the importance of

Gela's airfields (Todorovich, 1).
[53] Stars and Stripes Press, *The First! The Story of the 1st Infantry Division*, Paris, France: Desfosses-Neogravure, 1945; Devlin, 221-48.
[54] U.S. Army Technical Manual E9-1984, *Disposal Methods for Enemy Bombs and Fuzes,* Aberdeen Proving Ground, Maryland: Chief of Ordnance, 12 November 1942; Todorovich, 1.
[55] Todorovich, 1; Mayo, 166-69.
[56] According to EOD historian Robert Leiendecker, this approach is known today as Stand-off Munitions Disruption (SMUD) , commonly used on small ordnance. (Todorovich, 1; *History of the Ordnance Bomb Disposal Division,* 5; Robert E. Leiendecker, *Bomb Disposal, The Early Years of Explosive Ordnance Disposal (An Informal History)*, Charlottesville, Virginia, NATEODA Press, 2012, 460; Atkinson, *The Day of Battle*, 111-12).
[57] Atkinson, *The Day of Battle*, 161; Hooper, 20; Todorovich, 1.
[58] U.S. Army Technical Manual E9-1984, *Disposal Methods for Enemy Bombs and Fuzes,* Aberdeen Proving Ground, Maryland: Chief of Ordnance, 12 November 1942; Todorovich, 1-2.
[59] Atkinson, *The Day of Battle*, 161; Todorovich, 1-2.
[60] Allied introduction of time delay fuzes caused some embarrassment, as the British soon discovered that Germany's tricks of the trade endangered innocent civilians in Sicily and Italy. Also in keeping with the Luftwaffe's tactics, the Allies developed and used T-41 tail fuzes equipped with anti-withdrawal mechanisms. (Technical Information Bulletin, No. 23, 1 April 1944. 58-59; Atkinson, *The Day of Battle*, 161; Todorovich, 2-3).
[61] Carlo D'Este. *Patton: a Genius for War.* New York: Harper Collins, 1995, 522-32; Atkinson, *The Day of Battle*, 142-49.
[62] Todorovich, 2.
[63] Todorovich, 1-3.
[64] Todorovich, 2-3; Al Gardner, Jr., interview with author, 6 March 2003; U.S. Army EOD Division, "A History of U.S. Bomb Disposal," Redstone Arsenal Press, NATEODA, 1969.
[65] Todorovich, 2-3; Robert J. Kuehner, interview with author.
[66] Todorovich, 3; Mayo, 170-71.
[67] Lt. Col. Richard Walkup to Lt. Col. Goodwin 52$^{nd}$ EOD Group, 30 March 2000.
[68] Patton's biographer, Carlo D'Este, argues that Patton's "race to Messina" was fueled by a rivalry with Montgomery that existed largely in his own mind. (Todorovich, 2-3; Atkinson, *The Day of Battle*, 161-70, D'Este, 522-23).
[69] 1$^{st}$ Ordnance Bomb Disposal Squad (Separate), operation reports, April to October 1943.
[70] 1$^{st}$ Ordnance Bomb Disposal Squad (Separate), operation reports, April to October 1943; 55$^{th}$ Ordnance Bomb Disposal Squad (Separate). [unit history] 1943-45.
[71] Lack of documentation has led some writers to erroneously date the two Italian Theater BD companies' official deactivation back to October 12, 1943, shortly after the liberation of Naples. Unfortunately, neither company's records have been

preserved, except for fragments retained by squad officers. Disbanded companies were expected to submit their records, time permitting, or destroy them. Incidentally, United States EOD forces have since re-adopted the company as their standard unit, following Korea. (U.S. War Department to Commanding General, North African Theater of Operations, *Constitution, Activation and Disbandment of Ordnance Bomb Disposal Units,* AG 322, 11 January 1944; Headquarters Peninsular Base Section. *General Orders No. 83.* Disbandment of 235th Ordnance Bomb Disposal Company, 6 May 1944; Headquarters Peninsular Base Section. *General Orders No. 85.* Disbandment of 235th Ordnance Bomb Disposal Company, 6 May 1944; 143rd Ordnance Bomb Disposal Squad (Separate), unit history, 7 May 1944; 87th Ordnance Ammunition Battalion, unit history, 1944-45.)

[72] U.S. Army, U.S. Forces, European Theater, Historical Division: Records, 1941-1946, Staff Section Reports 563a-6 and 598, Ordnance History; Col. L.M. Garner, PBS Ordnance Officer, *Report on Peninsular Base Section NATOUSA*, 10 February 1944.

[73] Also reported missing were the plane's essential flight crew; 1st Lt. Herbert L. Hastings (pilot), 2nd Lt. Ray B. Lobdell (co-pilot), and Staff Sergeant William D. Brezee (navigator), as well as a third passenger, Capt. Lewis T. Stoneburner III, an Army doctor assigned to the 45th General Hospital. (U.S. War Department, *U.S. Army Casualty Reports*, 1945; U.S. War Department, Missing Air Crew Report 1102, File 42-6451, 27 October 1943; Richard Walkup interview, 25 June 2010; Edward Dillon, interview with author, 11 April 2011; www.dtic.mil/dpmo/wwii; www.eodmemorial.org/army.html; Hooper, 18).

[74] No evidence suggests that Dillon and Todorovich's flight went down as a result of enemy contact, as Axis air forces were expelled from North Africa and Sicily. By early October, the Luftwaffe had just evacuated their closest remaining air bases at Foggia, Italy. Moreover, the Mitchell crew did not include any gunners or bombardiers, indicating little concern over German interception. Apart from a standard complement of seven .50 cal. machineguns, their plane carried no heavy weaponry or explosive ordnance in its manifest. One may speculate that Lt. Hastings' B-25C experienced engine trouble shortly after takeoff, crashing somewhere on the coastline, or lost in the coastal waters between Oran and Tunis. Neither Capt. Dillon nor Lt. Todorovich were included on the EOD Memorial, as their deaths were not attributed to ordnance activities. Even though their visit to North Africa remains something of a mystery, it is my contention that Harrison Dillon and Steve Todorovich should still be recognized, because they were on active duty. Tragically, Capt. Dillon's younger brother, Pvt. Daniel H. Dillon, was later killed in action during September 1944 fighting in northern Italy. Sadly, this left Harrison's parents without any sons. (Ibid.)

# CHAPTER FOUR

# NEARLY IMMORTAL: ITALY AND SOUTHERN FRANCE (1943-45)

Military scholars have debated the strategic wisdom of invading Italy, once described by Winston Churchill as Hitler's "soft underbelly." Yet, bloody encounters at Salerno and Anzio suggest otherwise. Germans escaping defeat in Sicily were subsequently redeployed across the Northern Apennines by Field Marshal Albert Kesselring. Italy swiftly became a "tough old gut," despite their last-minute defection to the Allies. In early September, the Roman government voted to depose Benito Mussolini, replacing him with the popular Field Marshal Pietro Badoglio. Just hours before the U.S. Fifth Army's landings south of Naples, the wily Badoglio agreed to a cease-fire. Enraged by Italy's separate peace, Hitler ordered the Italian military disarmed, masterminded Mussolini's rescue from captivity, and ruthlessly dispatched German reinforcements to occupy Rome. By December 1943, Italy had become a divided nation.[1]

Launched on September 9, Mark Clark's Operation *Avalanche* quickly encountered stiff German resistance on the beachhead. Meanwhile, Montgomery's 8$^{th}$ Army marched up Italy's toe and seized Foggia's vital airfields. On September 15, 82$^{nd}$ Airborne Division paratroopers rescued Clark's stalling offensive, and by October first, American forces had liberated Naples. Caserta Palace, twenty miles northeast of Naples, became Allied group headquarters for nearly an entire year.[2]

Fortunately, no U.S. Fifth Army disposaleers were killed in action during Salerno's bitter week-long struggle. During the first wave of *Avalanche*, Capt. Francis Geisler and 1$^{st}$ Lt. Frank Smith co-directed a special team culled from 236$^{th}$ Company, including one platoon specially trained for amphibious combat. While 36$^{th}$ Division infantrymen charged ashore, Geisler and Smith's taskforce helped to "cut paths through mine fields and barbed wire." However, while the 45$^{th}$ Infantry noted how Germans "exercised great skill in mine-laying and demolition," they credited only their Division's own combat engineer units for "heroically" securing the bridges and highways to Naples.[3]

At Caserta, Mark Clark's new chief of Ordnance, Brig. Gen. Urban Niblo, had to rake and scrape for disposaleers. He tapped both squads and company elements. By September 21, Ted Harper's 1st (55th) BD Squad had arrived on temporary duty, though lacking vehicles and many tools. Using their native skills, Harper's men removed anti-personnel mines from Battipaglia, Albanella, as well as Salerno's beaches. On September 25, the remaining platoons of 236th Company landed at Capua. Shortly after Salerno concluded, Capt. Francis Geisler received a promotion to major and subsequently joined Niblo's Base Section Group as Fifth Army's bomb disposal officer. By October, Geisler's former company had reverted to ammo work, supervised by 87th Ordnance Battalion. When the two Army bomb disposal companies reformed into twelve separate squads early in 1944, half came under Geisler's overall command.[4]

While the 12th U.S. Air Force had fewer bomb squads in the Mediterranean Theater, they undoubtedly fielded very effective ordnance teams. Theoretically, Air Force units were directly responsible for airfields and landing strips, but they sometimes rendered support to whichever Allied commander required their expertise. Capt. (later Maj.) DeMarr Erskine directed at least twelve squads based at aerodromes divided between the Peninsular and Northern Base Commands. For example, the 12th BD Squad served chiefly on mainland Italy, but also cleared UXBs from the Tyrrhenian island of Sardinia. 57th BD Squad, on the other hand, started the Italian campaign on Sicily, and deployed afterward to Napoleon's birthplace, Corsica. Later in the war, the 57th Squad ranged far across Southern France and Northern Italy.[5]

The Mediterranean Theater's challenges produced strong ties among the Army and Air Force's elite separate squads. They fostered a sense of community, with units routinely exchanging personnel and collaborating on tough assignments. Whenever a squad suffered losses, news traveled quickly. Usually, a given squad consisted of one officer, two sergeants, and four "Model-T corporals," but sometimes fell understrength owing to illness or death. Professional conduct was usually very high, with only minor disciplinary infractions. Personal interactions were remarkably informal, with NCOs and technicians on first-name basis. In Italy, squad officers shared many privations with their enlisted men, and tended to be more accessible than regular ordnance officers. As a corporal, Bob Kuehner remembered his 11th BD Squad officer, Robert G. Hoyt, as being an easygoing man who played cards with his squad members. Kuehner, himself a stickler for technical details, remembered working out some theoretical ordnance exercises alongside Maj. Erskine. As Bob Kuehner later remarked, "it certainly beat playing pinochle."[6]

Breaking the companies into squads also meant an increase in qualified officers. While serving as a platoon leader in Tunisia, 1st Lt. Dick Walkup had temporarily commanded 1st BD Squad after its commander's untimely demise. Walkup felt that the squad model reduced hectic schedules for bomb disposal officers. Despite ordnance regulations, some technical sergeants even became adept at removing UXBs and directing squads independently. Today's EOD sergeants execute many procedures once limited only to officers. But during this formative period, company-grade officers suffered high casualty rates from directly handling unexploded fuzes and mines. Nearly all Army and Air Force squad commanders serving in Italy eventually became captains, answerable directly to their respective Ordnance headquarters in Oran and Naples.[7]

* * *

For weeks after its liberation on October 1, Naples reeled from booby traps emplaced by retreating German saboteurs. Such insidious warfare might seem familiar to those readers accustomed to tragic headlines from Iraq and Afghanistan. Unlike the modern-day guerilla learning to make roadside bombs in makeshift terrorist camps, the German engineer (*Pionier Korps*) received his training in professional military doctrines. Nevertheless, the effects were the same. On October 7, one delayed-action bomb killed over seventy U.S. troops and Italian civilians near the city's post office. Such devices were timed to detonate within eighty hours of emplacement. On October 9, the 236th Bomb Disposal Company averted tragedy by locating a time bomb set to demolish the historic Prince of Piedmont barracks. That same day, Geisler's men secured the Parco Hotel and other buildings used by Base Section Headquarters. Unfortunately, on the following day, another German time-bomb destroyed a nearby Army barracks, killing twenty-three combat engineers.[8]

Geisler's disposaleers suffered their first casualties that same month. On October 17, 1st Lt. Frank E. Smith's platoon responded to a reported UXB just outside Naples. Inside the Poggioreale Cemetery, Smith's team discovered a British bomb of unspecified make, which abruptly detonated. Lt. Smith was reported killed in action, along with two of his enlisted men, Sgt. Carl E. Christensen and Pfc. John Gatti. Occurring just after the disappearances of Capt. Dillon and Lt. Todorovich, these tragic deaths left Clark's Fifth Army with a mere handful of bomb disposal officers. Fortunately, remaining elements of 235th Bomb Disposal Company arrived by month's end, with Capt. Eugene Struzik and 1st Lt. Dick Walkup now in charge of four experienced platoons fresh from Sicily.[9]

Meanwhile, another pressing matter required Maj. Erskine's urgent attention. Early in October, Germany's 1st Parachute Infantry Division had abandoned Foggia; a town situated one hundred miles east of Naples. Several aerodromes clustered about the city, but British patrols reported these air stations were rendered all but unusable, largely due to saboteurs. Lt. Gen. Harold Alexander, 15th Army Group commander, carefully masked his doubts about Clark's foothold at Naples. "Sufficient depth must be gained before the Foggia airfields and the port of Naples can be regarded as secure," he later informed Churchill. Alexander wisely ordered the British 8th Army to push northward in support of Clark, but could not spare many Royal Engineers to clear all Foggia's railheads and hangars. Thus, U.S. Army Air Force disposaleers were instrumental in making airfields safe for later use by James Doolittle's 15th Air Force. Yet, like their Army brethren, these units received very little credit.[10]

One of the first Air Force teams to arrive in Foggia, 11th BD Squad, secured airbases #2, # 7, and #9. Many UXBs were American, dating back to previous bombing raids to suppress Luftwaffe attacks on North Africa. On October 29, Lt. Hoyt discovered a cluster of U.S. fragmentation bombs dropped at low altitude over Foggia #2. While three had detonated, another three had insufficient time for the fuzes to work. Needless to say, these UXBs were in damaged condition, giving Hoyt's men extra incentive for caution. They also answered ordnance calls from British and South African officers based at nearby Allied airstrips.[11]

12th BD Squad encountered their full measure of danger at Foggia. Receiving their orders for Oran, Algeria in early August, they had departed by train for their staging ground at Camp Shanks, New York. Unluckily, 1st Lt. Robert J. Sheridan suffered an eye injury from some splinters that had broken loose on their decrepit boxcar. Sheridan's condition proved serious enough to delay his unit's departure, so 2nd Lt. Ronald L. Felton volunteered to replace the injured man on August 13. Promoted to first lieutenant, Felton boarded his ship one week later.[12]

On board the passenger liner *Santa Rosa*, it did not take long for T/Sgt. "Mac" McCluskey to like his commander. James K. McCluskey Jr., had entered the U.S. Army after the first national draft of March 1941. Originally from California, Mac began his military service with a mounted cavalry division at Camp Seeley, San Diego. Mac voluntarily transferred from the Quartermaster Corps to Ordnance, where his soldierly bearing and mechanical skills led him to bomb disposal. Long after his wartime service, T/Sgt. McCluskey still valued his time as "something you can never lose." Mac's fellow "Rough Riders" were not just workmates; they became "buddies for the rest of your life."[13]

12th Ordnance Bomb Disposal Squad (from left to right): Sgt. George Kramer, T/5 Al Gardner, T/5 Alan Antisdale, 1st Lt. Robert Sheridan (replaced by 1st Lt. Ronald Felton), T/5 John Thomson, Jr., T/5 Wilbur Herrig, and T/Sgt. James "Mac" McCluskey. *(Gardner Collection)*

On September 2, the 12th Squad finally disembarked at Oran. After a month of training in North Africa, Felton's unit received priority orders for Naples, dated October 11. Four days before, the first delayed-action bombs had exploded in Naples, and thoughts of German saboteurs almost certainly crossed Jobe's mind. Recent horror stories from Naples, plus their intensive training at Aberdeen, had conditioned them to expect the worst. "I'll say this for the Germans," T/Sgt. McCluskey later confided; "They made us pay with every inch of ground; they knew how to retreat." Arriving in Naples on October 12, Lt. Felton learned they were headed for Foggia instead. He signed for two vehicles; one light truck, known as a 'weapons carrier,' plus a standard Army two-ton cargo truck. While the first carried squad personnel and personal equipment, the second carried hazardous explosives to dumpsites and bomb cemeteries.[14]

For over six weeks, Felton's 12th Squad ranged across Foggia, searching several airbases for German mines and unexploded bombs. Foggia's grassy terrain presented a considerable obstacle to visual detection, as hundreds of SD-2 Butterfly bombs had been strewn by retreating Luftwaffe technicians. One careless step into the tall grass could mean instant death. T/Sgt. McCluskey dealt with partially-open mines by closing their vanes, rendering them safe for removal. Meanwhile, any mines with wings fully engaged were remotely detonated at safe distances using small arms. Felton's squad usually opted for the latter course when chasing Butterflies they could not see. One airfield alone contained 726 mines, but no injuries resulted. "Everyone remained very respectful of the ordnance," Mac recalled sixty years after; "Any time you get too familiar with explosives, you're in trouble."[15]

Even dormant, Butterfly bombs could go off quite unexpectedly. This may help explain why German fighter and bomber pilots tended to jettison their canisters as soon as possible. Yet, German cluster mines struck fear in the hearts of Allied soldiers, whether in storage or scattered across battlefields. T/5 Alfred J. Gardner, 12th Squad's youngest member, recalled traveling aboard a British LST, carrying several unopened canisters of Butterfly bombs for disposal in the Adriatic Sea. "One SD-2 container blew up just behind our craft, probably detonated by water pressure," Al Gardner later described to the author. "The English craft commander decided that *that* was enough, so we returned to shore."[16]

T/5 Gardner, a New York City native, had been an ordnance technician for just ten months. Yet, Al understood the importance of safe ammunition handling, and never forgot his bunkmate's empty cot back at Aberdeen Proving Ground. Chosen for a work detail to move unstable WWI artillery rounds, Gardner's buddy had been killed in May 1943. Throughout the Italian theater, Gardner stayed at the rank of Technician, or "Model T" corporal, but he never regretted his lack of advancement. "Promotion usually came because the man in front of you had been killed," Gardner later reasoned. Gardner credited both his sergeants and "the Captain" for getting him safely through Foggia.[17]

Hangars, sheds, and control towers were good targets for German sabotage. Gardner remembered one particular mechanic's workshop, festooned with a deadly array of primed mortar shells. Several structures in the Italian Theater were booby-trapped in this fashion. Jobe Felton's near-encyclopedic munitions knowledge identified these as French rounds. Germans routinely used foreign ordnance for demolitions. Fortunately, these shells were safely neutralized and removed to a series of old bomb craters chosen as a dumpsite by the "Rough Riders."[18]

No serious mishaps befell the 12th BD Squad at Foggia, but Gardner witnessed a narrow miss from friendly fire. Poor communications and simple curiosity were the primary causes. One day in early November, Gardner and his close friend, Sgt. Kramer, were inspecting their dumpsite. "George Kramer was an airplane enthusiast, as well as the bomb squad's photographer," Al recounted. One day, Kramer stopped to photograph incoming British fighter-bombers, not knowing that their pilots had selected these same craters for target practice. "We heard those bombers coming, and George just stopped to admire them," Gardner remembered ruefully. Fortunately, Kramer recognized his peril in time, and escaped the dumpsite before British target bombs struck home. Target bombs contained relatively small payloads for training purposes, but just one could have meant Kramer's death. Just before Thanksgiving, Kramer and Gardner returned to Naples with their unit. Six weeks of shared dangers brought the 12th Squad's members closer, and their mutual respect lasted throughout the war and beyond. For their performance at Foggia, Felton's enlisted men eventually received Bronze Star medals.[19]

Subsequently, the 12th BD Squad supervised clearance operations across Sardinia until June 1944. Securing this major Tyrrhenian isle served two strategic purposes. First, it strengthened Allied control of the seas, and second, it secured airbases for Mark Clark's long Anzio offensive. Sometimes called away for special duties on the mainland, Felton entrusted his two sergeants, McCluskey and Kramer, with increased authority. On Sardinia, Mac handled many bomb fuzes in the absence of his squad commander. In Cagliari alone, they uncovered nearly thirty U.S. bombs – one had even lodged itself beneath the city's railroad. Felton's assignment to Sardinia spared his men from experiencing Anzio's nightmarish scenes, but they were still considered as participants in the Rome-Arno campaign. Just one probing Luftwaffe raid took place on Sardinia that spring, and Felton's team quickly isolated four German UXBs. They also located and destroyed twelve armed Butterfly bombs.[20]

As a squad officer, Jobe Felton always ensured that his comrades received provisions and equipment. T/Sgt. McCluskey recalled his commander as being accessible and good-natured, becoming hard-nosed just when necessary; "Captain Felton was a man of little formality; doing our jobs was all he expected." Al Gardner recalled one grateful Italian businessman who brought them a flask of wine, just as they were digging out a UXB that had penetrated four floors into his commercial bakery. Never one to turn down such gratitude, Felton nevertheless exhorted his thirsty troops to "wait until we get the bomb out." To his disposaleers, Jobe Felton would always be known as "their Captain."[21]

Capt. Ronald "Jobe" Felton often fulfilled special assignments, such as training new bomb disposal officers for the 12th U.S. Air Force. (*Frost Collection*)

* * *

On the nearby French island of Corsica, 57th BD Squad spent many months clearing German ordnance left over from years of occupation. Serving in Tunisia under 1st Lt. Raymond J. Narwid, they had comprised part of "Casual Detachment A," sent back in March 1943 by Aberdeen Proving Ground with insufficient squad equipment. On the island of Pantellaria, and during the Sicily campaign, they operated as the 3rd BD Squad. However, just before Salerno, they were reconstituted as the 57th Squad. Their new commanding officer, 1st Lt. Richard R. Hughes II, had accompanied Capt. Erskine's original group to the 12th Air Force.[22]

When Narwid officially passed his baton to Hughes in November 1943, all squad members had become "highly trained" bomb salvagers with "very high" morale. Hughes and his men spent three months sharpening their skills in Foggia, working alongside the 11th BD Squad. On March 13, 1944, Hughes' squad received marching orders, so they bade fond farewells to all their friends. Sgt. Carmine Nicastro had practically adopted an orphaned Italian girl of eight, while T/5 Dominick Albanese had found aunts and uncles still living in the nearby Adriatic port of Bari, an Allied supply base often subjected to German bombings.[23]

Reaching the U.S. Fifth Army's headquarters at Caserta, 57th Squad received new orders for Corsica by way of Naples. Since Corsica's depots and airfields fell under Northern Base Command's jurisdiction, Hughes experienced logistical snarls that delayed his unit's departure for several days. On March 24, they finally embarked alongside a small RAF bomb disposal detachment. The weather had turned deeply unpleasant, and to worsen matters, Mount Vesuvius had just erupted in clouds of smoke and ash which reached "several thousand feet into the air." From his ship, Hughes reported that "most of the ashes were now going into the sea." Brushing past the coast of Sardinia, they crossed the Straits of Bonifacio and landed next day at the Corsican capital, Ajaccio (Ajax).[24]

At that point, Capt. Erskine had just arrived on Corsica to show Lt. Hughes the ropes. Based at Cap Corse, Hughes would be responsible for two abandoned Luftwaffe supply points located at Biguglia and Bastia. On March 28, Erskine and Hughes inspected Bastia's town cemetery, directly across the road from the German dumpsite. Explosions had destroyed most of the nearby graves and monuments, tearing vaults open and scattering coffins, much to the officers' dismay. Hughes measured the nearby dumpsite's largest crater at 30 feet wide and 80 feet deep. Both officers surmised the Germans had blown the ordnance to deny its use to the Italians. Next day, following the Germans' recent escape route, they found many SD-1 bomblets spread across a deserted strip of beach north of Bastia. After safely detonating these explosives in place, Hughes and Erskine toured Cap Corse's "very beautiful, but very wild scenery.[25]

Based at Borgo, 57th Squad's personnel bivouacked in tents while awaiting the construction of permanent living quarters. Until mid-April, they were forced to rely on "helmet baths" for hygiene. Sgt. Nicastro arranged weekly field rations from a quartermaster at the nearby 1669th Ordnance Company. Hughes exercised daily with his men, playing volleyball and other team sports. Most nights, they socialized over a "nightly game of hearts," drinking nothing else but hot cocoa or coffee. However, adventurous squad members might be found congregating at Bastia's Solforino Bar, which was "not exactly high-class, but… quite an interesting place," according to Hughes. Cpl. Frank Flash enjoyed the romantic attentions of Maria, an Italian barmaid who worked at a hillside tavern just outside Borgo.[26]

Lt. Hughes also recalled meeting Corsica's wartime denizens, an interesting kaleidoscope of French partisans, Corsican landowners, Italian laborers, plus a detachment of British military personnel. Many islanders had engaged in partisan actions against the Nazis, and were well-disposed toward the Allies. Corsicans were grateful for bomb disposal efforts, particularly as French youths were recently killed trying to recover empty ordnance crates near Bastia. Near a gunpowder works in Casemozza, Hughes met one grizzled sixty-year-old *franc-tireur*, a veteran from both world wars who claimed to have personally shot five German soldiers during the island's liberation in 1943. Not all meetings with the locals were so cordial, however; when the squad selected their first "bomb cemetery," a Corsican farmwife registered her displeasure by describing in near-perfect English how their bomb fragments kept hitting her property. They promptly relocated their cemetery by one half-mile. Over the weeks, 57th Squad also came to know their British counterparts on Corsica.[27]

On April 18, 1944, a "most disastrous" explosion at 57th Squad's storage area claimed the lives of three enlisted men: T/Sgt. John Blasko, Sgt. Carmine C. Nicastro, and T/5 Dominick Albanese. Six civilians, Yugoslav workers, were also caught in the blast. At the time, Lt. Hughes had been patrolling near Ersa, where he investigated some reported UXBs. Heartbroken, the commander returned to Bastia to mourn his fallen men: "We [were] more or less in one small family, and in spite of small troubles, were real companions." Hughes reflected sadly on Blasko, who had married his wife in Ohio just a half-hour before shipping out. Meanwhile, in New York, Nicastro's wife had just picked out a new house, while Albanese's family waited for news in Brooklyn. Capt. Erskine later concluded that one of the civilians had dropped a volatile SD-10c projectile, setting off the entire dumpsite. Presently, Hughes received two replacements, Cpl. Robert Kuehner (11th BD Squad) and Pvt. Graves (1624th Ord. Co.). About that time, 57th Squad adopted its mascot, a near-starved puppy of indeterminate breed aptly named "Grenade."[28]

* * *

During the early months of 1944, Allied divisions confronted three bristling Winter Lines, dominating all the roads leading north to Rome. On January 22, Gen. Clark's 5th U.S. Army launched Operation *Shingle* on Anzio beachhead, hoping to liberate Rome by outflanking the formidable Gustav Line. Despite being overall Allied commander, Clark obstinately refused to coordinate his landings with British-led frontal assaults against German lines to Fifth Army's east. Even worse, Clark had underestimated his German adversaries. Anzio stalled into deadlock, just as the 36th Infantry Division sought to ford the swollen Rapido River. As a result, over a thousand fighting Texans either fell to German machine-guns or were drowned in bungled crossings. Elsewhere, Allied bombers needlessly pounded Monte Cassino's historic monastery into rubble, creating a virtually impregnable position. As Churchill famously put it, Clark's gambit sputtered along for five months "like a beached whale."[29]

Bill Mauldin recalled the tenuous Allied position south of Rome as being the "only place in Europe which held an entire corps of [U.S.] infantry, a British division, all kinds of artillery and special units… without a rear echelon." 56th BD Squad (1st Lt. Robert N. Murphy) covered the beaches and docks, but more teams were required at Anzio. On February 11, Lt. John A. Morgan had arrived in charge of 236th Company's first two platoons, clearing German ordnance under "extremely difficult conditions." By May, Morgan's platoons were reformed into squads. Four were sent to 87th Ordnance Battalion, where they were responsible for sending ammunition to Clark's two corps engaged at the front. Over five months, German artillery salvos and air raids had inflicted 125 ammunition fires, costing "Ammo Joe" 2,863 tons of ordnance, plus 22 injuries and 3 fatalities.[30]

By June, bomb disposal company elements had finally disbanded. 1st Lt. John Morgan's remaining 236th Company soldiers parted ways at Cascano without much fanfare. On the other hand, Capt. Gene Struzik's 235th Company held a May 19 farewell party in Naples, enlivened by some chaperoned WACs and local Italian *signorinas.* Company trucks were reserved to give these companions a proper escort to their homes. One driver, T/5 Phillip Zore offered his services, partly to spend more time with his new girlfriend, who lived just outside Naples. Next day, a search party found the hapless T/5 Zore, floating in a nearby pond. They found no sign of his vehicle. One of Zore's buddies identified his corpse.[31]

1st Lt. Morgan (143rd BD Squad) later opined that all lieutenants who volunteered to command new squads had already shown "outstanding capabilities." However, some officers were less experienced than others. While 138th BD Squad's enlisted men boasted fourteen months in theater, 1st Lt. Rex W. Hill had just arrived via Capua's replacement depot. Yet, Hill took pride in his three self-sufficient technicians, Alex Gawarecki (driver/rigger) Frank G. Pighini (mechanic/bomb salvager) and Frank J. Radosevic, Jr. (excavator/clerk). 138th Squad also included three noncoms: Cpl. William Walls, Sgt. Carlton Moe, and S/Sgt. Edward Wiard. Despite Army quotas, sergeants transferring companies were allowed to retain their stripes. Privates were also advanced to technicians as an incentive.[32]

Dick Walkup's 136th BD Squad likewise emerged from this shakeup. Formed under Peninsular Base command in Naples, they were billeted inside a former orphanage. 136th Squad's two sergeants, T/Sgt. Raymond G. Frech and Sgt. Gaylord Krenz, supervised four technicians, as per Table 9-500. T/5 William Borchering and T/5 William Ziegler were bomb salvagers, while T/5 Michael Vlock served as squad rigger. T/5 Edward B. Fox rounded out Walkup's lineup as driver and excavator. They remained on duty in Naples until the final days of the Anzio campaign.[33]

* * *

During Salerno and Anzio, explosive ordnance squads continually found new instances of Axis weaponry and armaments. Intelligence gathered in the Mediterranean Theater had a beneficial impact on future operations in Western Europe. Most of the weaponry introduced in Italy reappeared in France and Belgium. Even so, German technical ingenuity operated faster than Washington printing presses, leaving 90 percent of U.S. infantrymen inadequately briefed on enemy landmines in early 1944. For one thing, Ordnance lacked the authority to circulate Army Corps of Engineers manuals, which were typically six months behind. April 1944 circulars from Aberdeen Proving Ground backdated the Army's most recent mine warfare doctrines to November 1943.[34]

During the Anzio campaign, landmine and booby trap casualty rates skyrocketed across Italy, as Germans used every conceivable dirty trick. "Bouncing Betty" mines hurled ball-bearings at waist-level, while a "castrator" fired a small-arms round upward, hitting a victim's groin. "Schu-mines" foiled detection with their wooden casings, blowing off a man's lower leg. Unburied corpses from both sides were sometimes hollowed out and filled with explosive charges or grenades.[35]

Mark Clark relied on intelligence from his bomb disposal units on other types of German weaponry. Lt. Robert Murphy (56th BD Squad) recovered a partial nose section from the Luftwaffe's new FX-1400, or "Fritz-X" rocket-propelled glider bomb. Controlled by radio, "Smoky Joes" were capable of breaking a warship in two. One FX-1400 weighing over 3,180 pounds had sunk an Italian battleship, *Roma*, in late 1943. Intact glider bombs were rare, as they exploded on impact, but 56th BD Squad's recovery aided research efforts, as the FX-1400 went into further production. After the war, Gen. Deichmann of the Luftwaffe hinted that a heavier prototype could have sunk a *North Carolina*-class battleship, but this glider bomb failed to go into production before the war ended.[36]

Another new weapon debuted in the Italian Theater: the "Goliath." Modeled on a captured French prototype, the Goliath (*Leichter Ladungsträger*) was a remote-controlled mini-tank carrying a 200-pound high explosive payload. Manufactured by a Bremen automobile factory, early models (Sd. Kfz. 302) were propelled by two electric motors, and were guided by a 650 meter spool of wire. German engineer companies routinely employed these devices at night or in early morning mists. Several specimens were captured at Anzio before they could be detonated underneath landing craft. When directed against reinforced positions, Goliaths also proved vulnerable to small arms or a well-aimed mortar.[37]

British soldiers stand guard over Goliaths, remote-controlled mini-tanks designed to blow up landing craft at Anzio. These devices would be encountered again at the Normandy beachheads in 1944. (*National Archives*)

Ordnance research occasionally provoked rivalry between American and British BD personnel. Working relationships generally remained positive between the cousins, but 1st Lt. Dick Walkup once had an unfortunate disagreement with a British major, after an intact Italian "circling torpedo" washed ashore on the Naples beach. Dick enjoyed good relations with his British comrades, having attended a Royal Engineers training course in North Africa. But when each officer claimed this radio-guided torpedo for their respective services, a senior British officer stepped in to arbitrate the matter. Walkup won his case, having been first officer on the scene, but the British major did not lose gracefully. "I can still remember being called a liar," Dick lamented many years afterward. In the end, the two English-speaking allies readily shared enemy weapons data across the globe. As noted, bureaucracy *within* the U.S. Army jeopardized far more Americans than perceived rivalries with the British.[38]

Evoking battlefields from the last war, Bill Mauldin recorded the "mud, rain, snow, and freezing cold weather" confronting the soldiers entrenched across Rome's rugged hill country. From the rail-mounted "Anzio Annie" to omnipresent 88s, German artillery proved the biggest killer, forcing the grunts to dig into the fetid Mussolini Canal for cover. However, at night, Allied infantry also received visits from "Popcorn Pete," who shoveled out "hundreds of butterfly bombs" to explode over their heads or bounce inside their foxholes. While *Stars and Stripes* had warned against handling SD-2s, they still inflicted numerous infantry casualties; troop morale worsened at Anzio's front lines.[39]

One incident at Fifth Army Headquarters illustrates the anxieties that Butterfly bombs had induced within the Italian Theater's high command. At Caserta, 58th BD Squad had been requested to engage in SD-2 research. Julian F. Reichman, 58th Squad's lieutenant, had won the sobriquet of "Typewriter Kid" for escaping certain death that spring. Reichman had been disassembling a Butterfly bomb when he accidentally triggered its tiny fuze. Realizing he had only seconds to act, Reichman hurled his typewriter at the mine. His typewriter absorbed most of its fragments. Reichman escaped with lacerations, but his "quick presence of mind" saved his tech sergeant's life. That summer, Reichman's unit paid a lengthy visit to Corsica. Sgt. John Shwaryk of 57th Squad reported that this unassuming ordnance hero looked "healthy and patched up."[40]

Robert Franklin, a combat medic with Fifth Army, recorded a "Butterfly" raid that took place in February 1944 along the Albano-Anzio highway, a strategic road leading straight to Rome. Bivouacked near a railroad bridge nicknamed the "Overpass," Franklin awakened to a sound much like "firecrackers" going off, somewhere to his east. As German "chandelier flares" lit up Allied infantry positions, Popcorn Pete circled overhead, dropping long canisters that split open, "whirling out foot-long personnel bombs with a propeller in the nose and noisemakers in the tail." Franklin could not count the bombs in each cluster, but recalled "there were a lot of them… screaming down and raising hell with us."[41]

Unscathed by these falling butterfly bombs, Robert Franklin watched in horror as men suffered from shrapnel and concussion. Franklin later noted "guys bleeding from their mouths, ears, and noses." Franklin bandaged one British soldier who had lost the lower half of his face to a direct blast. One of his fellow medics, a T/Sgt. Martinez, also took some "inoperable" steel fragments in his legs, and had to be evacuated. After helping his friend to safety, Franklin returned to his first aid station in Anzio. Later that same morning, however, Franklin responded to yet another Butterfly incident close to his station.[42]

That morning, one Lt. Lehman, a self-styled "expert," had found an unexploded Butterfly bomb. Sitting cross-legged on the ground, Lehman apparently had tried to determine why the mine had failed to detonate. Observers saw Lehman turning its "propeller," demonstrating its function to three enlisted men. Moments later, an explosion rocked the camp. Franklin arrived to discover that "Lehman had no arms or legs, his head was flat as a pancake, and his brains lay in a neat pile about a yard away, as if someone had scooped them out and laid them there." All three of Lehman's hapless companions were dead, too. Franklin later treated another American soldier, hit by shrapnel from thirty yards away.[43]

Even hospitals were not proof from the "popcorn man." On February 7, 1944, twenty German fighter-bombers flew sorties against both Anzio and Nettuno. Pursued by British interceptors, one German pilot jettisoned a silvery canister directly over the U.S. 95$^{th}$ Evacuation Hospital. Straight away, a 470 kg payload of deadly bomblets showered down on several tents, killing twenty-eight patients and nurses, including at least three women. Sixty-four hospital staff members received wounds, including the ranking Army physician. Based on an early design, the SD-10 was first unveiled in July 1943, but had inflicted paltry damage on thick-plated Russian tanks engaged at Kursk. However, when directed against unarmored targets, they were virtually inescapable. As the SD-10 lacked vanes to close shut, clearing them proved yet another challenge.[44]

That May, the Allies finally ended the Anzio deadlock with Operation *Diadem*. However, in this campaign, Mark Clark neglected to coordinate with his British superior, Harold Alexander, who desperately wanted to bag the German forces caught within the Allied perimeter outside Rome. Instead, Clark sent his Fifth Army divisions onward to liberate the Eternal City on June 4. This decision permitted nearly all of Gen. Heinrich von Vietinghoff's forces to withdraw northward through the Apennines, only to regroup at salients along the Po River Valley. Nevertheless, Rome was still the first Axis capital to fall during World War II.[45]

This AB-500 container, rendered safe by the British at Anzio, carried thirty-seven SD-10 bombs meant to kill rear-echelon personnel. (*National Archives*)

Several Army squads were active during the liberation of Rome. On or about June 7, Lt. Theodore M. Bye's 151st Squad volunteered to sweep Rome's government buildings. Lt. Walkup's 136th BD Squad convoyed into Rome on June 18, arriving during "a slight rain." As Dick later recalled, "Rome was supposed to be an open city," but Germans had left "quantities of ammunition and landmines," especially at Rome's vital railway stations. They pitched their tents in city parks, and selected a safe "bomb cemetery" just north of the Peninsular Base Headquarters.[46]

During the crescendo of *Diadem*, 12th BD Squad had acted as trouble-shooters near Caserta, still serving at that time as Fifth Army's headquarters. In early May, they policed ordnance in the Naples region. Shortly after Mt. Vesuvius' eruption on March 24, T/Sgt. McCluskey went armed "with a metal detector to search for explosive ordnance buried under a foot of cinder." Fortunately, the ash had cooled somewhat, but Mac could feel the heat beneath his boots. After Rome's liberation, 12th BD Squad cleared 520 tons of unstable ammo from Grazzanise's airstrips, a feat which earned them a four-day pass to the Eternal City.[47]

Despite a tight schedule clearing German mines, Dick Walkup found time to meet new friends, such as Capt. Carl Malney, a fellow Texan still recovering from a recent ordeal with the battered 36th Infantry Division. On Independence Day, Dick entertained several colonels and generals with an improvised fireworks display. Walkup was aided by Malney, who would soon be back in action during the Southern France campaign. Together, the two friends ignited piles of concussion grenades and signal flares for an unforgettable Fourth of July in Rome.[48]

Despite these jubilations, another season of misery and hardship awaited the Allies. Clark's fleeting moment of glory had become yesterday's news as Operation *Overlord* began just two days after his triumphant entrance. Germany had rallied on the brink of defeat. Meanwhile, the Allied 15th Army Group, scarred by two bloody assault landings at Salerno and Anzio, continued to face constant bombardments all along yet another demoralizing Winter Line.

* * *

As France's liberation commenced, Mediterranean commands steadily began losing manpower to Operation *Dragoon*. This series of August landings in Southern France was designed to close off German access to Marseilles and other Tyrrhenian seaports. Two crack 12th Air Force squads, the 11th and 57th, supported the 36th Infantry Division at Marseilles. In total, seven British and American bomb disposal teams, along with five Allied mine disposal teams, took part in the *Dragoon* campaign. These teams were coordinated by a Mobile Explosives Investigation Unit, which arrived at Marseilles by early September. In October, Fifth Army yielded four of its own units, 143rd through 146th Squads, which shipped out to Dijon in support of Allied ground operations against tattered German combat divisions, regrouping at their Rhineland defenses for a final stand.[49]

Weapons carriers with trailers were the mainstay for mobile bomb disposal squads. Larger than a general purpose vehicle (Jeep) but more maneuverable than a 2½ ton truck, they were still prone to breakdowns. *(Leiendecker Collection)*

Still based on "The Rock," as Corsica became known to the Yanks, 57th Squad had weathered its loss of three men. On May 13, the bomb squad experienced its first "real air raid," a probing German sortie launched from Southern France. Lt. Richard Hughes expressed his "great dislike" for being bombed, but he did not regret being on Corsica, because his team was "actually helping to win the war." Following the raid, Hughes and his technicians began clearing the first of 147 SD-10 antipersonnel bombs that had fallen on Poretta Airfield. Within six hours, Poretta airfield was classed "operational" by the Air Force.[50]

With so much Luftwaffe activity in this once-quiet sector, the 58th Squad (1st Lt. Julian F. Reichman) and 59th Squad (1st Lt. Vincent J. Sibel) were sent over to assist Hughes and his compatriots. All three officers were old friends dating back to North Africa. On May 30, the Americans were treated to a splendid night battle between Allied anti-aircraft gunners and "Photo Freddie," a German spy-plane who usually heralded bombing runs. Freddie was last seen crashing into the sea. Most likely, these May missions were meant to gauge the likelihood of assaults from Corsica, as German High Command anticipated the Allied invasion of France.[51]

Over the summer of 1944, 57th BD Squad underwent several personnel changes. On June 9, shortly after D-Day at Normandy, Richard Hughes sailed back to the States wearing a captain's bars, plus a Soldier's Medal he had won for courageous actions back at Foggia. Hughes' replacement, 2nd Lt. Howard A. Johnson, had only recently completed his bomb disposal officer's course at Aberdeen, but he quickly earned his first lieutenant's bars as *Dragoon* approached. Meanwhile, Bob Kuehner rose from corporal to staff sergeant, serving as the squad's *de facto* technical sergeant, a vacancy left by the fallen John Blasko. With Hughes back in the States, Sgt. John Shwaryk now inherited the unit chronicler's mantle.[52]

Sgt. Shwaryk recorded his team's collaboration with a British Navy mine disposal team stationed on nearby Elba. He likewise noted their performance of counterintelligence work on behalf of the 12th Air Force. Such specialized activities, plus their facility with French language, made the 57th Squad ideal candidates for the upcoming landings at Marseilles, which began on August 15, 1944. On that morning, the 36th Infantry landed as three separate regiments, claiming Red, Blue, and Green beaches within five days. Capt. DeMarr Erskine personally led a detachment consisting mainly of 11th BD Squad personnel during this operation. Erskine eventually won a major's golden clusters for his leadership.[53]

According to Navy reports, "few enemy bombs were dropped" during the assault landing. Instead, German planes concentrated on sinking LSTs with guided missiles. While naval teams handled floating mines, bomb disposaleers went after anti-personnel mines, which the enemy scattered overhead during "haphazard" dusk raids. Capt. Erskine soon required more disposaleers to help clear Marseilles and surrounding locations.[54]

On D-plus 1, 1st Lt. Johnson received orders to assemble his squad at their Corsican staging area. They bequeathed their slightly-used barracks to 58th Squad, and said farewell to their new friends on Corsica. Presumably, their mascot, Grenade, remained with 58th Squad. Unfortunately, Johnson's team was still two men short, so they scheduled a link-up with their old pals from 11th Squad on Green Beach.[55]

On the dawn of August 20, Johnson's team landed at Green Beach. Their counterparts from the R.A.F., led by Flight Lieutenant Tweedy, also arrived from Corsica. Green Beach, near St. Raphael, had just been cleared of German forces, which had left behind many nasty surprises. Capt. Erskine greeted 57th Squad and then escorted them to Toulon, where Army Engineers were already at work disassembling an elaborate demolition charge attached to a 50-kilo German UXB. Altogether, combined Allied ordnance disposal personnel had accounted for hundreds of items, including 151 sea mines, 175 land mines, 102 prepared charges,

169 assorted rockets, plus a strange "human torpedo." Only 19 UXBs were dealt with throughout the Marseilles sector. The Navy commented positively on the need for bomb and mine disposal units in shore parties.[56]

For the next few days, Johnson's squad members happily removed bombs by day and dodged MP patrols by night in order to mingle with the jubilant citizens of Marseilles. At this time, they bade farewell to 11th BD Squad, now accompanying a 36th Infantry taskforce northward to Lyon. On August 25, Erskine dispatched Lt. Johnson's squad to Dijon, about 325 miles north of Marseilles. By now, 57th Squad was experiencing vehicular problems from a faulty weapons carrier they nicknamed "the Lemon." Even so, they arrived at the outskirts of Dijon in just two days. Despite being road-weary and unshaven, Johnson and his men were comforted by clean showers and billets at a civilian hospital. French nurses showered them with grateful kisses and warm food. As it turned out, 57th BD Squad had arrived two days before the U.S. Seventh Army, making them the first Americans to "liberate" Dijon. Over the next two weeks, they stayed at a former asylum on the outskirts of town, and Lt. Johnson's two sergeants and his jeep driver entertained local girls when not on the job.[57]

Reporting to the 19th Service Group on August 18, Johnson reconnoitered two major aerodromes at Tavaux and Longevic. Tavaux, a huge German-built facility, had over 5,000 feet of pockmarked runway. At Longevic, the French had paid homage to their flying ace, Capt. Georges Guynemer with an airfield bearing his name. Both airfields demanded extensive labor to expose bombs, chiefly of American make. One mission at Tavaux also required water drainage, never a pleasant task. Even so, when ordered back to Italy, Sgt. Shwaryk expressed his team's feelings: "Hate to leave this country, it's the best deal we've had since we've left the States." On the other hand, 57th Squad had "no regrets" for leaving Corsica forever – they were headed for the city of Livorno.[58]

* * *

During the fight for Livorno, at least fourteen U.S. Army ordnance units had witnessed fierce combat with the German XIV Corps. Dick Walkup, now promoted to captain, continued to work closely with his 136th Squad. Dick missed the relatively easy duty in Rome, remembering his Fourth of July bash. Like many visiting Americans, Dick and his companions explored the fascinating Roman Catacombs. He marveled at the Swiss Guards, still keeping watch over the Vatican City despite all the chaos and destruction that had transpired across Italy.[59]

Members of the 136th BD Squad, originally an element of the 235th BD Company. These seven men were experienced veterans of Tunisia and Sicily, as well as the Italian Theater. Front row (from left to right) T/Sgt. Raymond G. Frech, 1st Lt. Richard W. Walkup, and Sgt. Gaylord W. C. Krenz. Back row (from left to right) Cpl. William Ziegler, Cpl. William Borcherding, Cpl. Edward B. Fox, and Cpl. Michael Vlock. *(Original Photograph Courtesy of Richard W, Walkup)*

In mid-June, Walkup's 136th BD Squad traveled northward to Cecina, screening the 34th Infantry's advance to Livorno. Dick recalled a "ghost city with most of its bridges demolished." His men handled more landmines and anti-personnel mines than at any previous location. One awful night, Dick was awakened by a wounded Army sergeant. Unwisely, three rear-echelon officers had commandeered the non-com's jeep to drive out and "see the front." Under blackout conditions, the sergeant had struck a mine, killing all three officers riding in his vehicle. Writing almost sixty years later, Dick tersely described recovering their mangled remains for later burial. This was not Walkup's first brush with death; back in Tunisia, he had assumed temporary command of 55th BD Squad after 2nd Lt. John Randall's untimely demise. Bomb disposal men who served closer to the front had to develop thick skin owing to the deadly nature of their work. Unsurprisingly, ordnance veterans like Walkup have experienced difficulty in articulating the most onerous wartime events.[60]

Mac McCluskey of 12th BD Squad also recognized this reticence: "Individuals with the nastiest experiences in the war will be the last to speak of them." Throughout late 1944, Mac and his comrades covered several abandoned airbases outside Rome. In August, they traveled to Cancello, where they gathered 316 tons of unstable ammo with assistance from 1920th Ord. Company. Italian civilians and soldiers furnished additional manpower to help remove this dangerous ordnance. Despite relative distance from the battlefront, there were still risks. On August 17, two men from 56th BD Squad were wounded by strafing German planes near Cecina, where Dick Walkup had just been stationed. Fortunately, T/5 Frank J. Kreil and Sgt. Cecil F. Walker were back on duty by autumn.[61]

In September, Capt. Felton requisitioned two more vehicles, an M27 cargo truck with trailer and a reconnaissance jeep. Using the trucks, Mac's team loaded 117 extra tons for destruction at Grazzanise airbase, avoiding a deadly replay of the Corsica incident. Meanwhile, Felton set out in the jeep to handle emergency UXBs. T/5 Gardner remembered his commander "often took risks on his own with bombs." Usually, Jobe took Sgt. Kramer on these short trips to act as his driver and technician.[62]

George Kramer, the squad's shutterbug, had developed a rapport with his easy-going boss. Both were Pennsylvanians; Kramer had worked for an optical factory in Pittsburgh, a natural environment to develop painstaking concentration. At eighteen, Kramer's future wife worked at the same factory as a wartime replacement. "Before the war, George's company employed only men," Dolores "Dee" Kramer recalled. "Our employers asked the unmarried girls to write servicemen; George was my choice, because of his interesting Jewish name, Yos." Mac McCluskey, a self-confessed ladies' man, ribbed his friend good-naturedly for avoiding romantic entanglements. "Thomson and I were always looking for ladies," Mac later explained; "Kramer, on the other hand, was a monk."[63]

During one of Felton's UXB missions in Central Italy, George Kramer almost did not make it back to meet his bride-to-be. Near Caserta, a German 50 kg SC bomb had penetrated a blacktop road, passing close by an Army hospital. Jobe removed the fuze quickly, but as George grasped the cylinder, it detonated, inflicting burns on his right hand. If the fuze had gone off inside the pocket, both Felton and Kramer would have undoubtedly perished. Lt. Felton felt anguish over his sergeant's injury; however, Kramer staunchly insisted he could carry on. At the hospital nearby, Jobe also found a hometown pal from Sheffield recuperating from wounds. George received outpatient treatment for his burns, and resumed light duties until fully healed. They returned to Caserta that September.[64]

With little to do on Corsica, 58th BD Squad returned in early October to Peninsular Base Command. Now led by 1st Lt. Joseph R. Eszes, they removed some unpleasant leftovers, including 82 U.S. mustard gas shells. In case the Germans decided to use gas weapons, the U.S.S. *John Harvey* carried a secret shipment of mustard gas for Allied use. However, on December 2, 1943, the *Harvey* sustained bombing damage, spilling its dangerous cargo into Bari harbor, and poisoning hundreds. 58th Squad had safely emptied and dumped all remaining gas canisters by early 1945.[65]

* * *

On September 10, 1944, the U.S. Fifth Army's North Apennines campaign opened in Tuscany, lasting until early spring of 1945. Facing pressure from Gen. Alexander's 15th Allied Army Group, German troops had disengaged from Livorno and crossed the Arno River in order to occupy Pisa to the north. Dick Walkup described three weeks of constant nighttime shelling as his men continued to secure Livorno's streets and buildings. At one point, Walkup's demolition activities convinced Fifth Army Headquarters that German V-2 rockets had been launched in Italy. Walkup described a rather amusing event at one Livorno brewery that had, in some way, managed to escape German sabotage. Having searched the entire building, Walkup's team gave way to a company of military policemen, who fought a losing battle to prevent soldiers from filling their water cans and helmets with free, high-grade beer.[66]

In early October 1944, the Allied forces entered Pisa. The roads were littered with German anti-personnel mines, including dreaded Schu-mines. Much like Livorno, Pisa's streets were largely bereft of civilians. Dick Walkup's section recovered S-Mines from municipal buildings until receiving instructions to check the famed Leaning Tower for mines. Fortunately, their investigations turned up nothing hazardous. Walkup's mission in Pisa is consistent with similar efforts in France, where bomb disposal teams helped save historic and cultural sites from UXBs.[67]

Even though the Leaning Tower of Pisa had not been booby-trapped, Dick confirmed it had been used to direct German artillery fire at Americans positioned across the Arno River. This heavy barrage had enabled Germany's XIV Corps to withdraw and reform once again. Now anchored to the west at Viareggio, this new Gothic Line tenaciously resisted Alexander and Clark's combined forces for months. Several Army and Air Force disposal teams, including the 136th and 12th Squads, contributed toward victory during this stage of the Italian campaign.[68]

Felton's 12th BD Squad had arrived in the region of Tuscany by the time Pisa had been liberated. Their bivouac point, Pontedera, had just been cleared of Germans by an offensive spearheaded by one regiment from the U.S. 92nd "Buffalo Soldiers." Covering the same battleground, Jobe focused on airstrips and hangars. His team dealt with three Italian UXBs positioned by retreating Germans to destroy the town's single runway. Nearby, Mac inspected a hangar workshop, discovering a familiar pattern of primed mortar shells, poised to topple like dominoes. Moving into Pisa, Felton's men "deloused" two abandoned factories riddled with booby traps, removing numerous S-mines emplaced along streets. Outside Pontedera, T/5 Gardner discovered a minefield populated with Model 35 Schrapnell Mines – the original "Bouncing Betties." Gardner recovered five intact specimens, modified with unusual double-headed igniters to make them more sensitive.[69]

Capt. Walkup's squad also supported the 92nd Division at Viareggio. Routinely transferred between divisions, bomb squads sometimes received inconsistent upkeep from their host unit, but for once, Walkup's team actually got a better bargain. On the beaches near Lido de Carmaiore, 136th BD Squad located a small vacant hotel. Blackening its glass windows for safety purposes, they converted this seaside inn to serve as their winter quarters. "Living in a hotel was a luxury compared to living in a tent," Walkup later commented. Covering the windows proved a wise decision; their chosen headquarters lay within range of the ever-present German artillery overlooking the American position. He cleared a safe path through a German minefield to permit access to the beach. Even so, their bathing did not always remain tranquil. While enjoying a chilly swim in early 1945, Dick and his men observed four U.S. P-47s dive-bombing and sinking an enemy ship steaming north toward La Spezia.[70]

Despite pleasant beachside accommodations, ordnance calls mounted throughout the stinging winter and muddy spring at Viareggio. German engineers had built stout fortifications on Mount Folgorito and Mt. Carchio, from whence artillery and mortar shells rained down on demoralized black troops from the 92nd Infantry Division. Maj. Gen. Edward M. Almond's infantry battalions had been unable to breach these sturdy lines, and soldiers slowly lost their resolve under "Ned" Almond's uninspiring leadership. Capt. Walkup once witnessed Maj. Gen. Almond at the battlefront, taking refuge from the German guns in a muddy roadside ditch. Walkup later opined that the general and his staff officers were "lucky" to have emerged unscathed after nine hours of continuous shelling from the Gothic Line's breastworks.[71]

Luck favored the Texas officer on at least two other occasions. Walkup's jeep often traveled along the open road leading from Pietrosante directly to the front lines, always within range of the German field guns. In daylight, just one vehicle was allowed to drive at any given interval. Open areas between the buildings offered a perfect vista for gunners and mortar crews, but Dick's jeep evaded the artillery, thanks to his fast driving and keen timing. However, on one return journey, Walkup incurred the wrath of German mortar crewmen. Having rescued two Yanks and a "Tommy" from German patrols, the captain's jeep now offered a better target. Dick nearly bought the farm, but his quick reflexes saved the day. Crossing a small creek near a blown-out bridge, Dick evacuated his three passengers just before the Germans lobbed a salvo of mortar rounds where the jeep had stood moments before.[72]

During the "Christmas Alert" of 1944, Dick Walkup received orders to prepare 92nd Division's ordnance section for emergency destruction. Maj. Gen. Almond anticipated a German winter assault on the Ligurian Coast. Given the ferocious Bulge offensive underway to their north, Almond's concerns were justifiable. Along the impregnable Gothic Line, the German 281st Infantry Regiment held "rock-ribbed" artillery positions pointed south and west. Walkup believed that, had the enemy launched a determined attack, Almond's defenses would have been quickly overrun. Fortunately, unknown to the Allies, Wehrmacht soldiers were almost as demoralized as the 92nd Division, and no winter action took place.[73]

On March 25, 1945, this Gothic Line standoff finally ended after Almond selected the best elements from his Buffalo Soldiers, and merged them into a taskforce spearheaded by the 442nd Regimental Combat Team. Newly arrived from Southern France, these elite Japanese-American fighters soon began to "crack the western anchor," despite losing troops to the well-reinforced German defenders. Watching from headquarters, Capt. Walkup recorded that this "well-coordinated team" had taken its first objective within twenty-nine minutes. By April 25, Almond's combined force had driven the enemy northward to their final holding position – Genoa, best known as the birthplace of Columbus.[74]

Meanwhile, 57th BD Squad spent these winter months in relative safety at Tarquinia. Despite grumbling over variable food and drafty living conditions, Lt. Howard Johnson's men were proud of the fact they were "indispensable" to 12th Air Force Headquarters. They responded to UXB calls as far afield as Grosseto and northern Rome. T/5 Foley offered candid remarks on the quality of their U.S.O. shows and nightly films. Except for the "Christmas Alert" coinciding with the Battle of the Bulge, they enjoyed a routine not experienced since their days on "The Rock."[75]

March 1945 marked 57th BD Squad's second full year of service with the 12th Air Force. They also received a new technical sergeant, Lyle J. Bolender, S/Sgt. Bob Kuehner having returned to Foggia. Promoted to captain, Howard Johnson handled UXBs while his men instructed airmen in safe handling of Teller mines, Butterfly bombs, and other German ordnance. In April, they demined the beaches at Marina de Grosseto, and put their cross-training on Corsica to good use by dealing with isolated sea mines. Later that spring, the 57th Squad went "chasing butterflies," gathering SD-2 mines for the Ordnance Department's ongoing armaments research. T/5 Foley described their omnipresent enemies as "most interesting and intricate, yet very dangerous if one is not familiar with them." They were busy with this mission near Florence when hostilities finally concluded in early May 1945.[76]

* * *

Northeast of Florence, the U.S. Fifth Army had launched the final blow against General-Oberst Heinrich von Vietinghoff and SS General Karl Wolff. Gen. Mark Clark's Po Valley Campaign would force all Germans in Northern Italy to surrender. Clark, recently given charge over the 15th Army Group, now waged a coalition campaign with American troops rubbing elbows with Free Italian, British, French, Brazilian, Polish, and Commonwealth soldiers. On April 23, Allied troops successfully crossed the Po River, assisted by bands of Italian partisans. Even in defeat, Germans inflicted losses on the Allied vanguard. One notable American casualty, Col. William O. Darby, suffered a mortal wound on April 30, while leading the 10th Mountain Division at Lake Garda. Meanwhile, negotiations dragged on between German and Allied commanders. On May 2, Vietinghoff and Wolff jointly surrendered their grim divisions to Clark at 15th Army Group headquarters.[77]

Although principal fighting had ceased on the peninsula, explosive ordnance remained a serious hazard for years to come, particularly in Northern Italy. American and British bomb squads were kept busy disarming and clearing munitions. On at least one occasion, post-war work proved deadly. Five days after German troops had surrendered in Northern Italy, 1st Lt. Earl M. Hamilton (55th BD Squad) was killed in Verona while engaged in operations. Officially listed as "killed in action," no further details are available concerning the nature of Hamilton's Verona mission. However, given the absence of further hostilities in Italy, his death most likely involved enemy ordnance. Earl Hamilton's name appears on the National EOD Memorial.[78]

Meanwhile, at Genoa, Dick Walkup continued to clear more mines. During this time, he witnessed "numerous bands" of Italian guerillas hunting for Fascists. Disturbed by the summary executions often meted out by these partisans, Capt. Walkup accepted the surrender of three Fascist Army officers, escorting them to nearby U.S. military police. During these tense weeks, 136th BD Squad also located carloads of booby-trapped Italian landmines. Recognizing the threat to Genoa's railroads and municipal buildings, Dick convinced the British general in charge of the railroads to let his team disarm and escort this deadly shipment post-haste outside the city limits.[79]

Capt. Walkup's last wartime mission was a scout across French Alpine territory, searching for enemy ordnance depots. Civilians on both sides of the Italo-French border reported that armed German soldiers still occupied positions. However, crossing with only his driver, Cpl. Edward Fox, Dick encountered neither enemy activity nor supply points. Walkup and Fox stayed overnight in Nice before returning to their base in Northern Italy. Walkup fondly recalled his short vacation with Fox, and they remained in touch for many years afterward. Unlike some of his fellow ordnance officers, Capt. Walkup remained in Army service for the next twenty years, participating in the Korean War as a bomb disposaleer, and eventually rising to the rank of lieutenant colonel.[80]

T/Sgt. Bolender recorded the last days of 57th BD Squad, which had endured North Africa, Sicily, Corsica, Southern France, and Northern Italy as a tightly-knit group. Most of the original "squaddies" had already departed from the Mediterranean Theater, but since "they were going in the right direction," Bolender did not begrudge them their good fortune. Ironically, a 12th Air Force mechanic had finally identified the source of the "Lemon's" continual breakdowns – a defective frame that came straight from the assembly line. 57th Squad's final operation required the disarmament of two stray hand grenades in early June. By June 15, Capt. Johnson and his remaining men had departed for home.[81]

Jobe Felton's last job on record with 12th BD Squad took place at Civitavecchia, where two lost American bombs had endangered a bridge on the Naples road in April 1945. Felton spent his final weeks in Italy teaching at the Overseas Ordnance School in Caserta, supervised by Major William A. Spence. Over the long winter, 12th BD Squad remained close to Rome, with T/Sgt. McCluskey effectively in charge. They remained busy removing faulty U.S. and British bombs, while engaging in standard ordnance tasks and light construction work.[82]

On June 15, 1945, Capt. Felton bade a fond farewell to his men, who threw him a memorable party at the southeastern port of Manfredonia. Jobe's next destination, Patterson Field, Ohio, suggested a possible redeployment to the Pacific Theater. Mac McCluskey believed that, "when they sent the Captain to Patterson Airfield, he would have probably been stationed in the Pacific." However, this transfer did not take place. McCluskey himself departed for stateside in late July, having accrued enough service points to return. Under George Kramer, now a technical sergeant, the 12th Squad received final orders on August 9 to embark for the Pacific Theater. T/5 Al Gardner recalled when their merchant marine captain received the welcome news of Japan's surrender; everyone began to cheer as their transport began to veer away from Panama, toward New York City. Al Gardner had a very personal reason to cheer; he would be seeing his home city after exactly two years.[83]

Capt. Ronald L. Felton narrowly missed being sent to the Pacific Theater after serving with distinction in the Mediterranean Theater. (*Frost Collection*)

# Notes

[1] For academic scholarship on the Italian Theater, see Martin Blumenson, *Mediterranean Theater of Operations: Salerno to Cassino*, Washington D.C.: Office of the Center for Military History, 1969; W.G.F. Jackson, *The Battle for Italy*, New York: Harper & Row, 1967; John Strawson, *The Italian Campaign*, New York: Carroll & Graf Publishers, 1988.

[2] Rick Atkinson, *The Day of Battle*, New York: Henry Holt & Son, 2007, 195-97; 202-27.

[3] 143rd Ordnance Bomb Disposal Squad (Separate), unit history, 7 May 1944; Stars and Stripes Press, *The Story of the 36th Infantry Division*, Paris, France: Desfosses-Neogravure, 1945; Stars and Stripes Press, *The 45th: The Story of the 45th Infantry Division;* Paris, France: Desfosses-Neogravure, 1945; Department of the Army Pamphlet 672-1.

[4] Reclassified as 55th BD Squad, Ted Harper's 1st BD Squad presently returned to 12th Air Force's control. (1st Ordnance Bomb Disposal Squad (Separate), operation reports, April to October 1943; 55th Ordnance Bomb Disposal Squad (Separate), unit history, 1943-45; 143rd Ordnance Bomb Disposal Squad (Separate), unit history, 7 May 1944; 87th Ordnance Ammunition Battalion, unit history, 1944-45; Headquarters Peninsular Base Section, *General Orders No. 85*, 6 May 1944; Department of the Army Pamphlet 672-1; 1943 BD Officer Roster; 1945 BD Officer Roster).

[5] Ronald L. Felton to Commanding General of XII Air Force, Special Accounts (May 1944-July 1945), unpublished documents, 1-15; 57th Ordnance Bomb Disposal Squad (Separate), unit histories, February 1943 to June 1945; Kane, *History of the Bomb Disposal Organization in the ETO*, 1-6; Hooper, 18; Mayo, 170-71; 231.

[6] Kuehner, *Deadly 88*, 192-3; Kuehner interview, 6 March 2003; Hooper, 12; ii-iv.

[7] 1st Ordnance Bomb Disposal Squad (Separate) to II Corps Ordnance. [operation reports] April to October 1943; Walkup interview, 25 June 2010; Army Pamphlet 672-1; 1945 BD Officer Roster; Mayo, 231-32.

[8] "Yanks Scoured Paris Seeking 80-Day Bombs," from *Stars and Stripes*, 15 June 1945, 4; Tregaskis, 162-66; Atkinson, *The Day of Battle*, 245-48; Robert E. Leiendecker, *Bomb Disposal, The Early Years of Explosive Ordnance Disposal (An Informal History)*, Charlottesville, Virginia, NATEODA Press, 2012, 462.

[9] Sgt. Christensen received a posthumous Purple Heart. All three soldiers have been memorialized in the Sicily-Rome American Cemetery at Nettuno. (1st Ordnance Bomb Disposal Squad (Separate) to II Corps Ordnance, operation reports, April to October 1943; Ordnance Bomb Disposal School Headquarters, *B.D. Officers assigned to U.S. Army Companies & Service Commands*, 23 March 1943; Jerome Krieger to Commander, NAVSCOLEOD, *Fact Sheet*, 5 October 1992; Robert E. Leiendecker, *Bomb Disposal, The Early Years of Explosive Ordnance Disposal (An Informal History)*, Charlottesville, Virginia, NATEODA Press, 2012, 462; Michael R. Vining, *Explosive Ordnance Disposal Memorial – U. S. Army,* submitted to the EOD Memorial Commission, 15 October 2011).

[10] Brooks, 27-37; Strawson, 136-7; Blumenson, *Mediterranean*, 170.
[11] 11th Ordnance Bomb Disposal Squad (Separate) to Headquarters, Twelfth Air Force, *Daily Journals,* October 1943 to June 1944.
[12] 1st Lt. Robert Sheridan eventually recovered and took command of 22nd BD Squad, seeing action in Western Europe in 1944-45. Sheridan was a contemporary of Joe Pilcher, graduating in the same class of bomb disposal officers. (Lt. Col. Harry M. Walker, *Special Orders Number 75*, 19 April 1943, Robert Leiendecker Collection, Charlottesville, Virginia; James K. McCluskey Jr., interview with author, 6 March 2003; Alfred J. Gardner, interview with author, 6 March 2003; Joseph C. Pilcher Jr., interview by author, 18 April 2003; Joseph C. Pilcher Jr., interview with author, 12 July 2003; Felton, Form *66-2*; 1945 BD Officer Roster, Pamphlet 672-1).
[13] Sadly, Mac McCluskey passed away in 2005. In addition to T/Sgt. James McCluskey, the 12th BD Squad included Sgt. (later T/Sgt.) George G. Kramer of Pennsylvania, T/5 Albert Gardner of New York, T/5 John Thomson, Jr. of Kentucky, T/5 Wilbur Herrig of Iowa, and T/5 (later Sergeant) Allan F. Antisdale of Wisconsin. As of this writing, only Al Gardner is still living. (McCluskey interview, 6 March 2003; *The Detonator*, 17 September 1943, 7.)
[14] Ronald L. Felton to Commanding General of XII Air Force, Special Accounts (May 1944-July 1945) [unpublished documents] 1-15, Robert Leiendecker Collection, Charlottesville, Virginia; Colonel Bowyer to 12th Bomb Disposal Squad [general transfer orders] 13 September 1943, Robert Leiendecker Collection, Charlottesville, Virginia; Army Pamphlet 672-1; 1945 BD Officer Roster; Felton, *66-2*; McCluskey interview, 6 March 2003; Gardner journal.
[15] As CSM James Clifford has noted, modern EOD teams "burn off grass and brush whenever clearing large areas." This is an absolute requirement on formal ranges. Controlled burns may cause ordnance to detonate but decrease the chances that troops will be endangered. (McCluskey interview, 6 March 2003; Walter R. Nass, *Bomb Disposal Technical Notes*, Aberdeen Proving Ground: U.S. Army Ordnance Museum, 1942; NARA Records Group 498, 1945, 10-13, 36-39; *History of the Ordnance Bomb Disposal Division,* 5; Robert E. Leiendecker, *Bomb Disposal, The Early Years of Explosive Ordnance Disposal (An Informal History)*, Charlottesville, Virginia, NATEODA Press, 2012, 215; James Clifford, e-mail to author, 16 March 2011).
[16] Gardner interview, 13 April 2003.
[17] This incident was probably the May 15 explosion at Aberdeen Proving Ground involving 2nd Lt. J. F. Donovan of 10th BD Squad and two of his privates. C. E. Mullenix was killed outright, while Donovan and D. J. Kueter were briefly hospitalized. Donovan eventually took charge of 27th BD Squad for D-Day. (Gardner journal, 1-2; Gardner interview, 6 March 2003; 10th Ordnance Bomb Disposal Squad (Separate) to Headquarters, Ninth Air Force, unit history, 15 February 1945 to 28 June 1945.)
[18] McCluskey interview, 6 March 2003; Gardner interview, 6 March 2003; Stars and Stripes Press, *Flaming Bomb: The Story of Ordnance in the ETO*, Paris, France: Desfosses-Neogravure, 1945.

---

[19] Alfred J. Gardner, interview with author, 6 March 2003; Gardner interview, 13 April 2003.

[20] 12th BD Squad, *Special Accounts*, 1 May 1944; 1 June 1944; McCluskey interview, 30 March 2003.

[21] After the war, Felton's men were encouraged to call him by his nickname, but they just as often referred to him affectionately by his former wartime rank. (McCluskey interview, 30 March 2003; 12th BD Squad, *Special Accounts*, 1 May 1944; Gardner interviews).

[22] 57th Ordnance Bomb Disposal Squad (Separate), unit histories, February 1943 to June 1945.

[23] 57th Ordnance Bomb Disposal Squad (Separate), unit histories, February 1943 to June 1945.

[24] 57th Ordnance Bomb Disposal Squad (Separate), unit histories, February 1943 to June 1945.

[25] 57th Ordnance Bomb Disposal Squad (Separate), unit histories, February 1943 to June 1945.

[26] 57th Ordnance Bomb Disposal Squad (Separate), unit histories, February 1943 to June 1945.

[27] *Franc-tireur*, or "free-shooter," is a French descriptor for irregular soldiers who waged guerilla warfare against the Germans in both World Wars. (57th Ordnance Bomb Disposal Squad (Separate), unit histories, February 1943 to June 1945).

[28] SD-10c anti-personnel bombs weighed 7 kg each, and were fitted with EAZ(66)a fuzes. Dropping one of these tubular explosives would have easily set off neighboring ordnance stockpiles. EOD records state this explosion happened at Biguglia, but 57th Squad records consistently refer to Bastia as the site in question. T/5 Albanese's body was never found, but he is memorialized at Nettuno, along with his two comrades. All three men have been further memorialized on the U.S. EOD Monument. (57th Ordnance Bomb Disposal Squad (Separate), unit histories, February 1943 to June 1945; Jerome Krieger to Commander, NAVSCOLEOD, *Fact Sheet*, 5 October 1992; Robert Leiendecker, *World War II EOD Data*; National EOD Association Library, Charlottesville VA, 2003; Michael R. Vining, *Explosive Ordnance Disposal Memorial – U. S. Army,* submitted to the EOD Memorial Commission, 15 October 2011; Kuehner, *Deadly 88*, 192-3; Kuehner interview, 6 March 2003; Hooper, 12; ii-iv).

[29] Stars and Stripes Press, *The Story of the 36th Infantry Division*, Paris, France: Desfosses-Neogravure, 1945; Stars and Stripes Press, *The 45th: The Story of the 45th Infantry Division;* Paris, France: Desfosses-Neogravure, 1945; Martin Blumenson, *Mediterranean Theater of Operations: Salerno to Cassino*, Washington D.C.: Office of the Center for Military History, 1969, 170-1; Atkinson, *The Day of Battle*, 398-442; Murray and Millett, 381-82; Hooper, 19.

[30] Morgan's squad, a "direct descendant" of the 236th BD Company, later participated in operations across Southern France, the Ardennes, and the Rhineland in 1944-45. (56th Ordnance Bomb Disposal Squad (Separate), unit history, 1944-45; 87th Ordnance Ammunition Battalion, unit history, 1944-45; 143rd Ordnance Bomb Disposal Squad (Separate), unit history, 7 May 1944; Army Pamphlet 672-

1; Mauldin, 168).

[31] T/5 Zore belonged to 142nd BD Squad at the time of his death. No records of his death or any resultant military investigations have been located as of this writing. It is the author's speculation that Phillip Zore's death might have resulted from a jealous relative or neighbor of his girlfriend, or perhaps misadventure. Since Zore's truck never turned up, he might have also been accosted and killed by black marketeers or similar criminals. (U.S. War Department to Commanding General, North African Theater of Operations, *Constitution, Activation and Disbandment of Ordnance Bomb Disposal Units,* AG 322, 11 January 1944; Headquarters Peninsular Base Section. *General Orders No. 83.* Disbandment of 235th Ordnance Bomb Disposal Company, 6 May 1944; Headquarters Peninsular Base Section. *General Orders No. 85.* Disbandment of 235th Ordnance Bomb Disposal Company, 6 May 1944; 142nd Ordnance Bomb Disposal Squad (Separate), unit history, June 1944; Mike R. Vining, *Explosive Ordnance Disposal Memorial – U. S. Army,* EOD Memorial Commission, 9 April 2011).

[32] U.S. War Department to Commanding General, North African Theater of Operations, *Constitution, Activation and Disbandment of Ordnance Bomb Disposal Units,* AG 322, 11 January 1944; Headquarters Peninsular Base Section. *General Orders No. 83.* Disbandment of 235th Ordnance Bomb Disposal Company, 6 May 1944; Headquarters Peninsular Base Section. *General Orders No. 85.* Disbandment of 235th Ordnance Bomb Disposal Company, 6 May 1944; 138th Ordnance Bomb Disposal Squad (Separate), unit history, 7 May 1944.

[33] Headquarters Peninsular Base Section, *General Orders No. 85*, 6 May 1944; 136th Ordnance Bomb Disposal Squad (Separate). [unit history] May-June 1944; 143rd Ordnance Bomb Disposal Squad (Separate), unit history, 7 May 1944; 138th Ordnance Bomb Disposal Squad (Separate), unit history, 7 May 1944; Army Pamphlet 672-1; 1945 BD Officer Roster.

[34] This specific manual, *Land Mines and Booby Traps* (FM 5-31), covered only mines from North Africa and Sicily. (Army Services Forces, *Bomb Disposal Technical Information*, No. 25, Aberdeen Proving Ground: Ordnance Bomb Disposal School, 1 April 1944; Hooper, 19; Mayo, 213-4; Schrijvers, 74-75).

[35] One may also recall that U.S. and British combatants were likewise left unprepared for the widespread use of roadside bombs and improvised explosives by enemy combatants in Iraq and Afghanistan. (Army Services Forces, Bulletin No. 25; Atkinson, *Day of Battle,* 253; Schrijvers, 74-75).

[36] Paul Deichmann, "Luftwaffe Methods in the Selection of Offensive Weapons, Volume 1," from *USAF Historical Studies*, No. 187 (Manhattan, Kansas: MA/AH Publishing, Sunflower University Press, c. 1985), 48-49; 56th Ordnance Bomb Disposal Squad (Separate), unit history, 1944-45; Army Services Forces, Bulletin No. 25; Atkinson, *Day of Battle,* 217-19; Mauldin, 164-67; Hooper, 19; Jackson, 117, 199; Army Pamphlet 672-1.

[37] Sometimes erroneously called "doodlebugs," Goliaths have been credited as a developmental step toward so-called "smart" weapons, such as guided munitions. (National World War II Museum, "Artifact Spotlight," from *V-Mail,* Vol. 12, No. 1, 12-14; Mauldin, 164-67; Mayo, 214, 247).

[38] Walkup and other BD officers in Italy contributed often to ordnance research, receiving name credit in official bulletins for their efforts. (Army Services Forces, Bulletin No. 25; Richard Walkup interview, 25 June 2010; Army Pamphlet 672-1; Hooper, 19).

[39] Bill Mauldin, *Bill Mauldin's Up Front,* New York: Henry Holt, 1945, 164-67; *Stars and Stripes*, 9 March 1943, 4; Stars and Stripes Press, *The Story of the 36th Infantry Division*, Paris, France: Desfosses-Neogravure, 1945; Stars and Stripes Press, *The 45th: The Story of the 45th Infantry Division;* Paris, France: Desfosses-Neogravure, 1945.

[40] Reichman, a Jewish serviceman, entered the Army in Newark, New Jersey as an enlisted man. He returned stateside on October 11, 1944, with two Purple Heart awards for injuries. 57th Squad's reports misspelled Reichman as being Richman, but 58th Squad's unit history recorded it properly. Reichman died in 2001. (57th Ordnance Bomb Disposal Squad (Separate), unit histories, February 1943 to June 1945; 58th Ordnance Bomb Disposal Squad (Separate), unit histories, October 1944 to April 1945; Ordnance Bomb Disposal School, roster of active BD officers, 1 December 1945; Ancestry.com. *AJHS WWII Jewish Servicemen Cards, 1942-1947* [database on-line]. Provo, Utah, USA: Ancestry.com Operations, Inc.).

[41] Robert Franklin, *Medic! How I Fought World War II with Morphine, Sulfa, and Iodine Swabs* (Omaha, University of Nebraska Press, 2008), 86-88.

[42] Franklin, 86-88.

[43] Franklin's account has been misread by others, including Flint Whitlock's memoir editor, to mean that Lt. Lehman was a bomb disposal officer. The author's comprehensive records of all serving bomb disposal officers show no one named Lehman stationed in Italy. While Franklin's own quotation mark around the word *expert* also places serious doubts on this perception held by some military writers. (Franklin, 86-88).

[44] *Anzio Beachhead*, Center of Military History, U.S. Army, Washington, D.C., 1948, 53.

[45] For more on the Italian Theater after Rome's liberation, see Thomas R. Brooks, *The War North of Rome* (New York: Sarpedon Publishers, 1996); see also Jackson, 230-246; 263-316;

[46] 136th Ordnance Bomb Disposal Squad (Separate). [unit history] May-June 1944; Robert E. Leiendecker, *Bomb Disposal, The Early Years of Explosive Ordnance Disposal (An Informal History)*, Charlottesville, Virginia, NATEODA Press, 2012, 408; Atkinson, *The Day of Battle*, 372-75.

[47] Headquarters, 1st Ordnance Regiment to 12th Ord. BD Squad, General Order 8, 4 July 1944; Felton, *Special Accounts*, 31 July 1944; Gardner journal, 2;

[48] Richard W. Walkup, unpublished manuscript, 30 March 2000; Atkinson, *The Day of Battle*, 199.

[49] U.S. Army, U.S. Forces, European Theater, Historical Division. Records, 1941-1946, War Diaries, COM 8th Fleet, *Report of the Amphibious Invasion of Southern France, 8/9/44 to 9/25/44*, Section 5.11; Headquarters Peninsular Base Section, *General Orders No. 85*, 6 May 1944; 143rd Ordnance Bomb Disposal Squad (Separate), unit history, 7 May 1944; Stars and Stripes Press, *The Story of the 36th*

*Infantry Division*, Paris, France: Desfosses-Neogravure, 1945; Stars and Stripes Press, *The 45th: The Story of the 45th Infantry Division;* Paris, France: Desfosses-Neogravure, 1945; Atkinson, *The Day of Battle*, 573-88.

[50] 57th Ordnance Bomb Disposal Squad (Separate), unit histories, February 1943 to June 1945; 58th Ordnance Bomb Disposal Squad (Separate), unit histories, October 1944 to April 1945.

[51] 57th Ordnance Bomb Disposal Squad (Separate), unit histories, February 1943 to June 1945; 58th Ordnance Bomb Disposal Squad (Separate), unit histories, October 1944 to April 1945.

[52] 57th Ordnance Bomb Disposal Squad (Separate), unit histories, February 1943 to June 1945.

[53] Unfortunately, 11th BD Squad records break off in early 1944, so no written records exist of their experiences in *Dragoon*. Bob Kuehner's memoir likewise gives very few details apart from his unit's presence in Southern France. (U.S. Army, U.S. Forces, European Theater, Historical Division, Records, 1941-1946, War Diaries, COM 8th Fleet, *Report of the Amphibious Invasion of Southern France, 8/9/44 to 9/25/44*, Section 5.11; 57th Ordnance Bomb Disposal Squad (Separate), unit histories, February 1943 to June 1945; Kuehner interview; Kuehner, *Deadly 88*).

[54] U.S. Army, U.S. Forces, European Theater, Historical Division, Records, 1941-1946, War Diaries, COM 8th Fleet, *Report of the Amphibious Invasion of Southern France, 8/9/44 to 9/25/44*, Section 5.11.

[55] One 57th squad member, Pvt. McCarnan, had been court-martialed for sleeping on duty, while T/5 Frank Flash rotated back to the States. (U.S. Army, U.S. Forces, European Theater, Historical Division. Records, 1941-1946, War Diaries, COM 8th Fleet, *Report of the Amphibious Invasion of Southern France, 8/9/44 to 9/25/44*, Section 5.11; 57th Ordnance Bomb Disposal Squad (Separate), unit histories, February 1943 to June 1945).

[56] U.S. Army, U.S. Forces, European Theater, Historical Division. Records, 1941-1946, War Diaries, COM 8th Fleet, *Report of the Amphibious Invasion of Southern France, 8/9/44 to 9/25/44*, Section 5.11; 57th Ordnance Bomb Disposal Squad (Separate), unit histories, February 1943 to June 1945.

[57] 57th Ordnance Bomb Disposal Squad (Separate), unit histories, February 1943 to June 1945; Stars and Stripes Press, *The Story of the 36th Infantry Division*, Paris, France: Desfosses-Neogravure, 1945.

[58] 57th Ordnance Bomb Disposal Squad (Separate), unit histories, February 1943 to June 1945.

[59] 34th Division belonged to the U.S. IV Corps; during this offensive, the 34th Division received support from the100th Japanese-American Battalion. (Walkup manuscript; Jackson, 258-60).

[60] For a complete listing of squads taking part in the North Apennines campaign, see the appendices. (Walkup manuscript; Army Pamphlet 672-1; Walkup manuscript; Brooks, 166-76.)

[61] McCluskey interview, 6 March 2003; 12th BD Squad, *Special Accounts*, 30 September 1944; Gardner journal, 2; 56th Squad, unit history, 1944-45; Leiendecker,

*Bomb* Disposal, 408.
[62] 12th BD Squad, *Special Accounts*, 31 July 1944; 30 September 1944; 31 October 1944.
[63] George Kramer eventually reached the rank of technical sergeant while serving in Northern Italy, and returned to marry Dee shortly after the war. (Dolores Kramer, interview with author, 16 March 2003; McCluskey interview, 30 March 2003).
[64] George Kramer received a Purple Heart for his injury in the line of duty. (Nancy Swanson, "UXB Squads: The Army's Little-Knowns," from *Valley Voice of Sheffield.*, 11 November 1983; 12th BD Squad, *Special Accounts*, 30 September 1944; Alfred J. Gardner, interview with author, 13 April 2003; Dolores Kramer, interview with author, 16 March 2003; McCluskey interview, 30 March 2003; Ancestry.com. *AJHS WWII Jewish Servicemen Cards, 1942-1947* [database on-line]. Provo, Utah, USA: Ancestry.com Operations, Inc.).
[65] Despite efforts to censor this disaster, it became common knowledge, even giving some propaganda value to the Germans, who never used gas warfare in the West. However, they did employ gas against the Red Army as well as civilians. (58th Ordnance Bomb Disposal Squad (Separate), unit histories, October 1944 to April 1945; McCluskey interview, 30 March 2003; Atkinson, *Day of Battle*, 270-78.)
[66] Walkup manuscript; Jackson, 260.
[67] Walkup manuscript.
[68] Walkup manuscript; Jackson, 258.
[69] Felton' squad supported the U.S. 370th Infantry Regiment. Alfred Gardner took many photographs at Pontedera, including some of a damaged U.S. cargo truck. (Gardner, interview with author; Gardner journal, 2; McCluskey interview, 6 March 2003; 12th BD Squad, *Special Accounts*, 30 September 1944; 31 October 1944; Brooks, 166-76.)
[70] Walkup manuscript.
[71] 92nd Infantry Division's African-American troops were dispirited at Viareggio largely due to their general's overt racism. Rick Atkinson aptly described Maj. Gen. Edward M. Almond as an "overbearing Virginian" who vehemently opposed integration until his death in 1979. Black officers were treated little better than their enlisted comrades, and a sense of despondency permeated the Buffalo Soldiers. "Ned" Almond later served as Gen. Douglas MacArthur's controversial operations officer in the Korean War, where he did not endear himself to many commanders. (David Halberstam, *The Coldest Winter: America and the Korean War* (New York: Hyperion Books, 2007), 160-64, 547-49; Walkup manuscript; Atkinson, *The Day of Battle*, 382-83).
[72] Capt. Walkup received no official recognition for this spirited act of bravery. (Orville C. Shirley, *Americans: the Story of the 442nd Combat Team* (Washington: Infantry Journal Press, 1946), 78-92; Walkup manuscript).
[73] One of the Nisei company commanders during this campaign, the late Daniel K. Inouye, became the first U.S. Congressman from Hawaii in 1959. (Walkup manuscript; Shirley, 78-92).

[74] During the 442nd Regiment's assault, landmines and other hazards were handled by the 232rd Combat Engineers. Another U.S. combat unit taking part in this offensive, the 473rd Infantry Regiment had previously served as anti-aircraft gunners. (Walkup manuscript, Jackson, 304, Shirley, 78-92).

[75] 57th Ordnance Bomb Disposal Squad (Separate), unit histories, February 1943 to June 1945.

[76] 57th Ordnance Bomb Disposal Squad (Separate), unit histories, February 1943 to June 1945.

[77] Atkinson, 585-56; Jackson, 310-16.

[78] 55th Ordnance Bomb Disposal Squad (Separate). [unit history] 1943-45; Jerome Krieger to Commander, NAVSCOLEOD, *Fact Sheet*, 5 October 1992; Michael R. Vining, *Explosive Ordnance Disposal Memorial – U. S. Army,* submitted to the EOD Memorial Commission, 15 October 2011; Leiendecker, *Bomb* Disposal, 294; Hooper, iv.

[79] Walkup manuscript.

[80] During the occupation phase, Walkup took charge of the 687th Ordnance Company, while also supervising the 13th BD Squad, both at Livorno. Capt. Walkup returned to the United States in 1946. (136th Ordnance Bomb Disposal Squad (Separate). [unit history] May-June 1944; Walkup manuscript.)

[81] 57th Ordnance Bomb Disposal Squad (Separate), unit histories, February 1943 to June 1945.

[82] Edward Roper, "Overseas Ordnance School," from *The Ordnance Sergeant*, July 1945, 44; *The Sheffield Observer* (Pennsylvania), July 1945; 12th BD Squad, *Special Accounts*, 31 January 1945; 31 March 1945; 30 April 1945; 31 May 1945; Felton, Form 66-2, 1; Gardner journal, 2.

[83] Earlier in May 1945, the Army decided to spare many Italian theater veterans from service in the Pacific Theater. Captain Ronald L. Felton's discharge papers are dated 15 December 1945. (*Stars & Stripes*. "Redeployment Vets of Italy are spared Pacific Shift." 27 May 1945; Gardner journal, 3; McCluskey interview, 30 March 2003, Felton, Form *53-9B*).

# CHAPTER FIVE

# SLEEPING BESIDE OUR FOXHOLES: FROM NORMANDY TO PARIS (1944)

While Alexander and Clark plunged their forces into the Italian crucible, the Allied planners back in England considered lessons learnt from Gela and Salerno. Since Washington's Trident Conference in May 1943, every sign had pointed toward the liberation of France. Responsible for developing a winning Allied strategy, the COSSAC headquarters soon proposed the nucleus of what became known as Operation *Overlord*. Lt. Gen. Frederick E. Morgan, author of *Overlord*, had originally called for three amphibious landings supported by a single airborne division.[1]

On November 6, the British general contacted the U.S. Army Services of Supply headquartered at Cheltenham. Morgan weighed the merits of bomb disposal squads versus companies for the upcoming campaign. Morgan requested a total of 57 U.S. bomb disposal squads to support ground forces in France. Noting cases in Sicily and Italy where "B.D. facilities have been consistently overburdened," Morgan asked his American allies to introduce three bomb disposal companies to the Communication Zone (Com Z) as soon as possible to deal with Allied UXBs. However, with the impending dissolution of full companies, Morgan's request proved impossible to fulfill.[2]

Returning from Sicily in January 1944, Gen. Dwight D. Eisenhower absorbed COSSAC into Strategic Headquarters Allied Expeditionary Forces (SHAEF). Ike retained Morgan as his Chief of Operations as a mark of favor, and at Montgomery's urging, enlarged the first *Overlord* proposal to five assault landings supported by three airborne divisions. Meanwhile, the combined navies would support the Normandy landings under Operation *Neptune*. By May of 1944, Ike would receive his fifth star as well as his appointment to Supreme Allied Command.[3]

Eisenhower had recognized the value of bomb disposal units from his previous commands in North Africa and Sicily. By 1944, Army Field Manual 9-5, *Ordnance in the Field*, had listed separate bomb disposal squads as essential personnel for a shore party or assault landing.

SHAEF's chief of ordnance, Brig. Gen. Henry B. Sayler, further advised that each Army Group or Corps headquarters should have a complement of bomb squads. However, not all of Ike's commanders were familiar with this newfangled branch, so his May 9 letter, titled *Bomb and Shell Disposal*, summarized all War Department ordinances dating to 18 April 1944. Ike delineated all phases of bomb disposal, beginning with reconnaissance and identification, followed by UXB countermeasures.[4]

As Eisenhower reminded his subordinates, "Bomb Disposal Problem is a command responsibility." When the Allies finally staged their landing, Eisenhower had already provided for a senior "Bomb Disposal Officer," responsible for determining "priorities for disposal of bombs or shells." Whereas the U.S. Navy handled all "incidents below the High Water Line," Ike now required a trustworthy officer to direct continental UXB activities among the Army and Air Forces in Western Europe.[5]

Brig. Gen. Sayler had previously employed staff BD officers, beginning with Capt. Robert H. Savage. By late 1943, the ETO Ordnance Command had relied on 1st Lt.. Schuyler V.C. Larkin, a superlative junior officer sent over from Aberdeen. But the magnitude of *Overlord* and *Neptune* required the presence of a field-grade bomb disposal officer. Only one man had the expertise and rank required for this undertaking, Col. T.J. Kane. On December 28, 1943, the colonel and eleven of his Bomb Disposal School officers received orders for London. Among these travelers were Maj. Frank Parsons, Maj. Ryerson "Rye" Bredin, and Capt. John Feldman. But, "much to [their] disgust," Kane and his companions were placed with the ETO Civil Affairs Division.[6]

Back in 1941, the Ordnance Corps had argued against Civilian Defense's takeover of bomb disposal, but the Army's Civil Affairs branch was another matter entirely. In early February 1944, Lt. Col. John Burton, Sayler's number two, discussed a possible merger with Gen. McSherry, Civil Affairs Division. While Kane subsequently made light of this bureaucratic snafu, Feldman recorded his chief's thoughts at the time.[7]

Kane had long hoped for an active wartime role, so he naturally objected to his party's unexpected relegation to the diplomatic corps. Kane told Feldman that he knew "somebody in London" who "could get us back to [Ordnance] where we belonged." Feldman observed that Kane's secret errand proved successful, although "not entirely under proper orders." However, Kane's ploy worked. Burton announced on March 12 that Kane's "highly trained" cadre would be serving as staff members for various Army and Base Section commands. On March 17, Feldman noted that Kane's unknown contact "finally got us settled" in a London apartment, working on bomb disposal problems."[8]

This author speculates that Kane's mysterious contact was none other than Brig. Gen. Sayler, shortly to become a two-star general. Lida Mayo later noted in her Ordnance history that Sayler had personally requested Kane, whom he remembered from their earlier conferences in London. Kane's many responsibilities as the new ETO Bomb Disposal Officer would include training, research, communications, and technical support.[9]

One of T.J. Kane's proposals, the Ordnance Bomb Reconnaissance School, went into effect in the fall of 1943. Their instructors passed on life-saving skills to American combat divisions destined for the "far shores" of France, Belgium, Holland, and Western Germany. (*National Archives*)

Kane's impact on the coming European campaign had already been felt in England, evidenced by the positive reception of his projected reconnaissance school. Back in September 13, 1943, the U.S. Army's Ordnance Bomb Reconnaissance School had first opened its doors. Supervised by the Army Services of Supply in Cheltenham, this facility replicated many of Kane's original principles. Staffed at first by ex-members of the 231st Bomb Disposal Company, the program attracted interest from the U.S. First Army, whose officers presently envisioned a bigger training program for Army units destined for combat.[10]

In October 1943, Capt. Schuyler Larkin witnessed this school undergoing a major expansion. Kane, who was still stateside, read Sky's favorable description of the reconnaissance school, particularly its innovative "recon exercise ground" where over seventy training bombs, ordnance fragments, and anti-personnel mines were set up as "incidents." Like its Aberdeen counterpart, this overseas school featured a mock "village" with theoretical "booby traps," as well as its own ordnance museum, full of bombs, shells, and fuzes. Thirty-five officers and noncoms attended six-day classes, and were required to score 80 percent or higher. Larkin projected that 90 percent of the U.S. ground forces would have certified instructors by the time they embarked.[11]

Studying German bombs at the ETO Reconnaissance School. (*National Archives*)

On January 14, 1944, 234$^{th}$ BD Company opened an even larger facility at Overcourt, near Almondsbury, Gloucester. Weekly enrollments among First and Third Army personnel jumped from 30 to 90 per class. Gradually, Kane's idea shaped into a superior training facility with several purposes. Starting out as a bomb recon school for Army Groups destined for France, the school also served as a replacement depot for incoming separate squads, who frequently departed from the States under-strength. Officers went to leaderless units, while spare enlisted men found berths.[12]

Bomb disposal squads also served their turns as traveling instructors, teaching ordnance recognition courses to encamped tank, artillery, and infantry units. Typically, these sessions lasted about three hours, and were nicknamed "blitz" courses by the school, owing to their rapid delivery. For example, the 54$^{th}$ BD Squad (Capt. William C. Lane) toured several English and Welsh cities, from Bristol and Liverpool to Cardiff and

Swansea. Lane brought along his portable "museum" with specimens of enemy ordnance, and showed a three-reel film to over 20,000 Americans. Thanks to similar efforts, over 7,000 U. S. combat soldiers also became qualified reconnaissance teachers who imparted these life-saving skills.[13]

Since most American squads arrived with little practical training, Royal Engineers in the Southern Base Section graciously offered "on-the-job training" to their American cousins. Even though early regulations had prohibited Yanks from handling UXBs, friendly Britishers often bucked protocol, and allowed the Yanks to disarm UXBs on their own. Undoubtedly, there were pragmatic undertones to such gestures; practical training implied that American ordnancemen would pull their own weight. Nevertheless, this amity between the English-speaking cousins proved to be genuine. Stationed at Bristol in early 1944, Capt. Wright "Scotty" Calder recalled his squad's friendly ties with the neighboring No. 7 BD Company – the same unit that had cooperated with Kane's original 1942 mission. Over several months, "Scotty" Calder's 50th BD Squad shared billets with one of Captain Lucas' sections. Scotty described both groups "operating independently by day, and enjoying pubs in the evening."[14]

Capt. Edward J. Barry studied UXBs with the Royal Engineers at London and reviewed aerial ordnance at RAF Doncaster, where he heard many horror stories about "Butterfly Bombs." Barry's 31st Squad arrived in England shortly before Christmas, having endured seasickness aboard the confines of the U.S.S. *Mexico*, a refitted cruise liner. Barry's team, together with four others (27th through 30th Squads), had arrived at the last minute, so five officers and thirty enlisted ordnancemen were forced to occupy a smelly hold near the bow. On December 15, these five bands landed at Swansea, and quickly went their own ways.[15]

Apart from their "mystifying" language and some dietary quibbles, Capt. Barry retained some good memories of his English hosts. Traveling by passenger train to Nottingham, Barry still had time to marvel at the beautiful scenery of Sherwood Forest, where his men quartered for the winter at Depot G-15. Usually, bomb disposal men resided in standard Nissen huts, but they also stayed in local hostels, private dwellings, and on at least one occasion, a historic castle. Like many other Yanks, 31st Squad suffered through the blackout conditions and air raid warnings that had characterized life in Britain for the last four years. However, U. S. bomb disposal men shared professional insights that their fellow G.I.s often lacked. 31st Squad members lectured to over 5,300 Americans concerning UXBs and mines. Later that spring, after completing his supplemental training, Barry moved his unit to a golf course near Dorchester, where they disarmed their first bomb – a 50 kg German incendiary.[16]

The earliest U.S. bomb disposal squads to arrive in the U.K., such as the 4th BD Squad, went to the 9th U.S. Army Air Force, bound for France (*Kane Collection*)

Despite improved Anglo-American relations, "confusion and inconvenience" persisted as more Americans landed in the British Isles. By December 1943, the British Air Ministry had grown frustrated with decentralized U.S. squads still volunteering to help at bomb sites. Royal Air Force officers promptly requested that their allies designate a single headquarters to manage these over-eager squads. Lt. Gen. Jacob Devers, 12th Army Group commander, implored his Ordnance officers to "improve the present situation." In early October 1943, the 234th BD Company had landed in Sherborne, Dorsetshire, ostensibly to act as a supervisory headquarters for these newcomers. However, Capt. Fred Wilkie became involved with the new recon school at Overcourt. Thus, Col. Kane's arrival in England came none too soon; 76 separate BD squads would come to England between August 1943 and the first week of June 1944.[17]

* * *

Through a combination of happenstance and initiative, Col. T. J. Kane was now a staff advisor to Gen. Eisenhower at a crucial planning stage in *Overlord*. As shown earlier, Ike's UXB policy had already incorporated many of Kane's recommendations. Kane got on well with Ike, although the colonel interacted more frequently with his immediate superior, Maj. Gen. Henry Sayler. As Ike's chief ordnance officer, Sayler supervised approximately 150,000 "Flaming Bombers," ordnance soldiers assigned to five Army groups and one Air Force headquarters. This meant that, on June 6, Ordnance would be the third-largest Army branch disembarking in France. By contrast, Kane's separate squads and service platoons comprised the ETO's smallest ordnance contingent.[18]

Kane's ETO headquarters included its own publication office, responsible for training aids, field manuals, and safety notices. (*National Archives*)

Kane's intelligence section compiled detailed files on all known explosives or bombs likely encountered in the ETO. Recognizing the fact Technical Information Bulletins (TIB) usually took weeks to circulate, Kane wanted to ensure that new information could reach everyone, whether guarding stationary airbases or marching with the armies. Capt. John Feldman proposed a stand-alone ordnance newsletter, *Fuze News*, circulated by 8th Air Force. Each month, *Fuze News* updated all known German ordnance data based on recent developments. Another publication, the *Reconnaissance Informer*, went out to UXB recon instructors based in England. Copies of both publications were also disseminated through corresponding British agencies as well.[19]

Kane credited all Allied service branches in every theater for their contributions to ETO research and development. He unstintingly praised his own school's research arm, based in Maryland, for setting the high standards under which his overseas R&D branch now operated. It also ameliorated matters that Kane's head technical researcher, Capt. John Feldman, had also served as the Army BD School's chief "inventor." Aided by a trusty sergeant named Shorling, Feldman traveled across London researching "various methods and devices to make fuzes safe." Early on, Feldman and Shorling developed an innovative "self-tapping needle," capable of "flawlessly" drilling 1/8-inch holes into any type of German fuze, jamming its time-delay mechanism.[20]

During an earlier *Newsweek* interview, Kane had boasted that his protégé's special projects would help win the war. Feldman quietly set to improving existing special tools, beginning with the "Stevens Stopper." Developed by the British back in 1940, the "Stopper" neutralized the Zus-40 and a later model, Zus-57. Both anti-withdrawal circuits were vulnerable to special liquids injected into fuze pockets. Unfortunately, the "Stopper" weighed nearly 200 pounds, making it cumbersome, and it could not be firmly attached to certain bomb types.[21]

Feldman's unpretentious five-pound "Flit Gun" resembled a simple pesticide sprayer; a grease gun pump with a rubber hose attachment. Experimenting with various substances, from powdered eggs to plaster of Paris, Feldman's team sought to find injectable substances that hardened satisfactorily without risking ignition. Feldman irreverently described the former, a staple ration for combat soldiers, as particularly unpleasant. Eventually, Feldman discovered that dental cement, when used as a two-part compound, paralyzed clockwork fuzes. This thermosetting mixture proved more effective than earlier methods using a formaldehyde resin.[22]

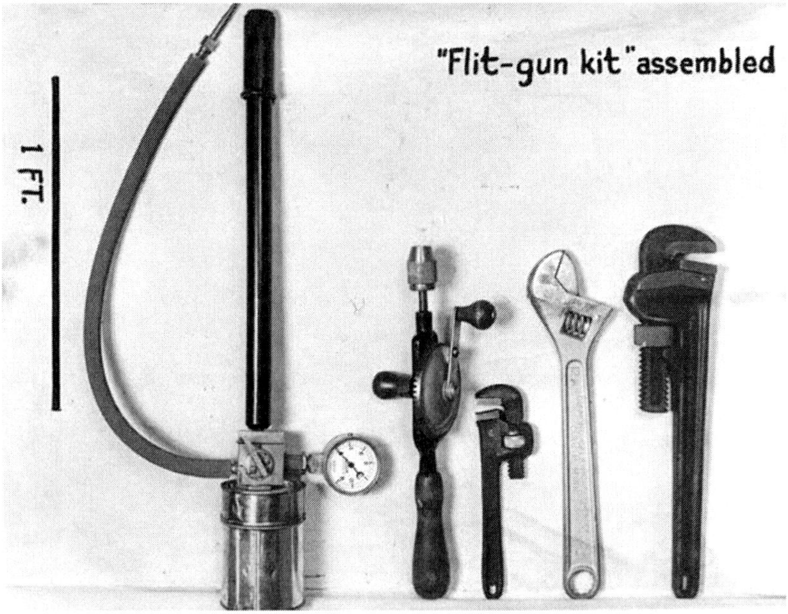


John Feldman's "Flit-Gun" fully assembled. (*National Archives*)

Shortly after D-Day, the British Home Forces bomb disposal director, Brigadier H. H. Bateman, commended the "Flit Gun" as a "most ingenious development of the Steven Stopper principle." Writing to Henry Sayler, Bateman declared it perfect for future operations, especially against Japan, "owing to its extreme portability." Requesting prototypes for practical trials, Bateman expressed his pleasure at giving "some assistance to the Ordnance Department," and acknowledged the "close co-operation" between his "Directorate" and Gen. Sayler's "Bomb Disposal Division."[23]

By August 1944, Feldman's prototype had been field-tested successfully. One U.S. Army report described the "Flit Gun" as "an effective tool, and suggested it should be "procured for units in this theater." However, according to EOD historian Robert Leiendecker, only the British Royal Engineers seem to have adopted the "Flit Gun."[24]

Aberdeen Proving Ground's Ordnance School did patent Feldman's "Self-Tapping Needle," which entered military service for years to come. Feldman also introduced a major improvement on the British impact wrench, his prized "Rocket Wrench." Instead of rotating a bomb's fuze via pulleys, Feldman's spanner used small propellant charges to torque at a considerably faster rate: 1100 foot-pounds in 1/300 of a second.[25]

John Feldman's "Flit Gun" in portable form. (*National Archives*)

Why did the American bomb disposal branch fail to implement Feldman's "Flit Guns" as part of the field service table of equipment? Kane's supply system had long experienced problems because bomb disposal tools represented "such minor size and importance in relation to the overall Ordnance supply problem." Even so, with Gen. Sayler's blessing, Capt. Sky Larkin took over the BD supply base, "almost singlehandedly" managing a sub-depot of special ordnance gear. Originally, equipment came through Services of Supply in Cheltenham, Gloucestershire. Now, Larkin's "unorthodox but practical system" placed such items under "complete control" of disposaleers, who could modify and issue new toolkits. Meanwhile, instruments could be developed, manufactured, and distributed within the ETO. Larkin's energetic coordination received numerous plaudits from Ordnance.[26]

* * *

Presently, Kane began assigning "squads separate," to Army and Air Forces destined for France. Kane believed in the squad's tactical application, but privately felt they were prone to being "kicked about as a stepchild" at Group or Division level. The first unit to arrive, 3rd BD Squad, had gone to 8th Air Force in August 1943. More squads followed, as *Overlord*'s buildup commenced, and by the eve of D-Day, 76 squads had disembarked in England. Thirty-three went to Ninth Air Force, likewise destined for France. Twenty were placed on guard at U.S. Communication Zones across England. Remaining squads were generally divided among First, Third, and Ninth Armies. For example, 17th BD Squad went to First Army, located at Swansea, Wales. They were assigned to 177th Ordnance Battalion, U.S. Army V Corps, under Maj. Gen. Leonard T. Gerow.[27]

1st Lt. Joseph C. Pilcher shortly before departure for England. (*Pilcher Collection*)

17th BD Squad, led by 1st Lt. Joseph C. Pilcher, landed in early December 1943. They had exchanged positions with 31st BD Squad owing to their high degree of readiness. During the autumn, Edith Pilcher had entertained her husband's homesick men with weekend dinner parties at their little house in Havre de Grace. After a week of squad training, Pilcher's unit gathered on October 22 for one last Friday night shindig. Following a satisfactory Saturday morning inspection, Capt. Richard Metress informed 17th BD Squad that they had been selected to leave within five weeks for England. With Ron Felton already serving in Italy, Joe Pilcher's imminent departure left Dick Metress holding the fort. Dick's signature on his friend's living will bears mute testimony to their camaraderie. Following one month of intensive training, Pilcher's men were given a week's furlough at Thanksgiving. Lt. Pilcher spent his time with Edith and little Joseph, dubbed "Skippy" by his father's troops.[28]

On December 9, 17th BD Squad left New York for Gloucester, where they joined Lt. Gen. Omar Bradley's U.S. First Army. After Christmas, Lt. Pilcher went to Grosvenor Square, London to attend a "Technical Conference on Bomb Disposal." Meanwhile, his squad left for Weston, where T/Sgt. Hobson began training the U.S. 47th Anti-Aircraft Artillery (AAA) Brigade to recognize booby traps and mines. T/5 Franklin May also distinguished himself as a keen instructor and superlative soldier.[29]

By early February 1944, Lt. Pilcher had rejoined his unit at Seven Oaks, located in his family's ancestral seat, Kent. He lectured on the various explosive hazards that anti-aircraft gunners might encounter, such as butterfly bombs. Pilcher stressed the importance of reporting hazards so that skilled personnel could remove them with minimal risk to Army personnel. Joe's "conscientious and able" efforts as a reconnaissance instructor quickly earned praise from Col. C. R. Finley, 47th AAA Brigade, who wrote a commendation to First Army on March 4, describing Pilcher's "invaluable aid." Finley's favorable letter concerning 17th Squad eventually reached Gen. Omar Bradley's headquarters. On May 24 – two weeks before D-Day – Joe Pilcher received a well-merited promotion to captain; Technician May received sergeant's stripes. Despite their different backgrounds, May and Pilcher quickly developed a keen rapport. This trust would hold their unit together through trying moments.[30]

Joe Pilcher spent that April and May at the Army Bomb Reconnaissance School, instructing other combat units, including the 440th AAA (Automatic Weapons) Battalion. Once again, anti-aircraft units could expect to be attacked frequently by Luftwaffe bombers and fighter-bombers, so reconnaissance training proved beneficial in months ahead. While teaching courses in Bristol, Joe befriended 1st Lt. Marshall T. Crow, a fellow ordnance instructor hailing from Mobile, Alabama. By early May, Crow had taken command of $16^{th}$ BD Squad, bound for the "far shores" of Normandy. In fact, Crow's team soon learned they were slated to land at Easy Red, Omaha Beach, on D-Day.[31]

One of the intrepid U.S. bomb disposal officers destined for France eyes an imposing 1000 kg "Herman" at the Reconnaissance School. (*National Archives*)

Altogether, more than 120 Army and Air Force squads were scheduled to deploy in France, following the RAF sector plan adopted by SHAEF. However, they would land without a central body of administration. Col. Kane shared his personal thoughts on administration with his successor at the Army Bomb Disposal Center, Lt. Col. Martin Ehrmann. For his part, Kane hoped to vindicate lingering prejudices against their service branch, confiding to his stateside colleague that "using Staff Officers, Platoons, and the Squads will eliminate the criticisms… as reported from North Africa and Italy." Kane expressed his private doubts that "squads separate" would receive proper field administration. Without field grade officers to oversee them, separate squads might not be "properly used or properly administrated." Kane also criticized some "younger officers" who took their roles as squad commanders too casually. He regretted that "a few months in Officer Candidate School, a few weeks at the Bomb Disposal School, and a couple of weeks training with the squad are hardly enough to give the average youngster" a sense of urgency. Kane advised Ehrmann that when it came to job accountability, "squad commanders have the same as a division commander."[32]

Kane had hoped to save the existing $234^{th}$ Bomb Disposal Company for a front-line headquarters in order "to eliminate the criticisms… made about the internal housekeeping of various squads." However, 234th Company eventually relocated to the Communication Zone in France, where it disbanded that October. Deprived of his proposed base, Kane relied increasingly on his three adjutants, Maj. Ryerson Bredin, Capt. William O. Benton and Capt. George W. Schiller. Benton and Schiller eventually became majors in their own right, as directors of bomb disposal operations at the Army Group and Communication Zone levels.[33]

Meanwhile, the U.S. Ninth Air Force planned for its D-Day landings. Gen. Elwood "Pete" Quesada's force had newly transferred from Cairo, with only a small bomb disposal section. Kane privately thought Quesada "had given little thought to Bomb Disposal" prior to his arrival in England in September 1943. However, Quesada swiftly remedied this oversight by requesting a transfer of four "squads separate" from Eighth Air Force to his own ordnance detachment, under Col. W. R. Maxwell.[34]

One such unit, $2^{nd}$ Lt. Daniel Carter's $10^{th}$ BD Squad, had arrived one month earlier in Liverpool. Carter had just replaced Jesse F. Donovan, who had been injured during a training exercise in Maryland. Like their Army compatriots, Carter's men received "practical training," courtesy of RAF bomb experts situated at Feltwell and Doncaster. Carter's efficiency impressed his new commanders at Ninth Air Force, and by April 18, he had been promoted to captain and placed in overall charge of the Ninth's bomb disposal component, which numbered 33 squads by early June. Kane observed that these Air Force squads had received their equipment directly from the RAF, and with "characteristic independence," had failed to comply with U. S. Army standards. Regardless, the Ninth's disposaleers would play their valiant part in Operation *Overlord.*[35]

* * *

During the Normandy campaign, Kane's Bomb Disposal Division finally came into its own as a specialist unit. *U.S. Army Field Manual 9-5* identified bomb disposal squads as necessary assets for assault landings. On June 6, 1944, U.S. bomb disposal squads served as "combat troops on the beaches along with the Combat Engineers, removing roadblocks, minefields, and amphibious obstacles… and supplemented the Engineers in removing and neutralizing booby traps in various buildings."[36]

This newfound understanding between Ordnance and the Engineers had started in early 1944, as Gen. Sayler's staff planned for *Overlord.* Combat engineers had proven their value in the Sicily Campaign, with Seventh Army's 1st Special Brigade performing many ordnance tasks in addition to their primary functions; "to establish, develop, and operate the beachhead beginning with the very earliest stages of the assault." However, as previously noted, Patton's over-reliance on his Engineers had inadvertently caused a jurisdictional squabble with Ordnance officers.[37]

This time around, three Engineer Special Brigades were delegated for each American sector, two for Omaha Beach and one for Utah Beach. However, in order to avoid a repeat of Seventh Army's earlier mistakes, Col. John B. Medaris "planned to place a considerable amount of Ordnance support" behind First Army's combat engineers responsible for clearing the immediate beachheads. Each special brigade would now include one ordnance battalion with requisite specialist units in tow. These units included one amphibious squad for the "first tide."[38]

Despite their high degree of technical expertise, Kane's squad officers possessed no battle experience. With the exception of 5th BD Squad, which arrived too late for *Overlord*, no unit had tasted combat. Therefore, Charles W. Stull, Joseph A. Bocelato and Jesse F. Donovan, all captains, were selected for D-Day based on rank and seniority. Stull and Bocelato were given charge over the 23rd and 26th Squads destined for Omaha Beach. Donovan, fully recovered from injuries, prepared the 27th Squad for Utah Beach. Meanwhile, five Royal Engineer bomb disposal companies – No. 5, No. 19, No. 23, No. 24, and No. 25 – supported British and Canadian landings on Gold, Juno, and Sword Beaches.[39]

Bomb disposal squads were typically among the last units "combat-loaded" aboard LSTs, which meant that these seven-man specialist teams would be among the first soldiers to disembark at Normandy's beaches. (*Reece Collection*)

Joe Bocelato, one of Kane's oldest bomb disposal officers at age forty-two, hailed from Memphis, Tennessee. He was the sole Southerner in a team that consisted mainly of Midwesterners. 26th Squad had spent some months training with RAF disposaleers. Some weeks before, Bocelato had been assisting with a Butterfly bomb when it exploded, killing the unnamed British officer standing next to him. Shaken up, he later related this awful incident to Capt. E.J. Barry of 31st Squad. However, Bocelato was still ready to face his "Short Sea Voyage" to that "far shore."[40]

Assigned to U.S. V Corps, the 5th Special Engineers Brigade participated in D-Day's dress rehearsal, Operation *Fabius I*, on April 24. Every vehicle and kitbag was "combat-loaded" for the actual landings by late May. On May 29, Brig. Gen. William M. Hoge briefed his landing party, known as "Force 'O'," that individuals could expect to use their "quick and sound judgment," in lieu of following the book. Bocelato's squad would accompany the "first tide" with 251st Ordnance Battalion. They embarked on schedule from Portland, England on June 4.[41]

SUPREME HEADQUARTERS
ALLIED EXPEDITIONARY FORCE

**Soldiers, Sailors and Airmen of the Allied Expeditionary Force!**

You are about to embark upon the Great Crusade, toward which we have striven these many months. The eyes of the world are upon you. The hopes and prayers of liberty-loving people everywhere march with you. In company with our brave Allies and brothers-in-arms on other Fronts, you will bring about the destruction of the German war machine, the elimination of Nazi tyranny over the oppressed peoples of Europe, and security for ourselves in a free world.

Your task will not be an easy one. Your enemy is well trained, well equipped and battle-hardened. He will fight savagely.

But this is the year 1944 ! Much has happened since the Nazi triumphs of 1940-41. The United Nations have inflicted upon the Germans great defeats, in open battle, man-to-man. Our air offensive has seriously reduced their strength in the air and their capacity to wage war on the ground. Our Home Fronts have given us an overwhelming superiority in weapons and munitions of war, and placed at our disposal great reserves of trained fighting men. The tide has turned ! The free men of the world are marching together to Victory !

I have full confidence in your courage, devotion to duty and skill in battle. We will accept nothing less than full Victory !

Good Luck ! And let us all beseech the blessing of Almighty God upon this great and noble undertaking.

Dwight Eisenhower

General Dwight D. Eisenhower's Normandy Address (*National Archives*)

Between D-Day and D-plus 70, a total of 32 separate squads landed on the two American beachheads. Few noted their presence among that vast armada of liberation. As Capt. Sky Larkin recorded, these specialists comprised "the smallest increment" in the Army's third largest branch. Six months later, bomb disposaleers still numbered only 245 enlisted men and 50 officers. Two weeks afterward, T. J. Kane relayed good news to Martin Ehrmann: "Informally, I understand [our Bomb Disposal Units] are turning in a very creditable performance, and so far… without casualty or loss. They have been called on to dispose of… all types of explosives ranging from anti-personnel mines to prepared demolition charges… in addition to their normal mission." Kane, however, erred on the side of optimism: some of his troops were among those hundreds of fallen heroes that day on Normandy's hallowed sands.[42]

* * *

On D-Day, Army bomb disposal squads traveled aboard U.S. Navy LSTs, which were subjected to German air raids. However, unlike the 1940 Battle of France, the Allies now had air superiority and sufficient armor support. In this photograph, a P-51 Mustang flies overhead as an LST disgorges two M-4A1 Shermans, America's mainstay tank in World War II. (*Leiendecker Collection*)

U.S. First Army's double spearhead, V Corps (Gerow) and VII Corps (Collins) tackled Omaha and Utah Beaches respectively at 6 a.m., also designated as "H-Hour." Omaha, the larger beach, cost the V Corps hundreds of casualties along a front spanning from Vierville to Colleville. One battalion commander with 5th Special Engineer Brigade, Lionel P. Smith, died within minutes of his arrival at 0700 hours. Lt. Col. Smith had just been promoted for his efficiency during the D-Day preparations. Landing at that time, Capt. Joe Bocelato (26th BD Squad) later recalled that 5th Special Brigade's sector was "covered by 88 and mortar fire." Disembarking at 0930 with the 6th Special Engineer Brigade, 27th Squad spent the morning removing "dud shells and rockets," or helping medics. That afternoon, a shell burst directly over their position, killing T/5 William "Pat" Brodish. Capt. Jesse Donovan recalled that Brodish "died instantly when a shell fragment pierced his head."[43]

While Army corps and division commanders personally directed infantry landings at Omaha and Utah, Special Brigade engineers and ordnancemen teamed up to comb Normandy's shallows and sand dunes. Over four years, the Germans had emplaced many "cruel yet ingenious obstacles" to fortify Hitler's "Festung Europa." Infantrymen encountered the usual "Bouncing Betty" and "Schu" mines, but anti-vehicular mines were also common. One favored trick involved lashing two logs together with the open "V" extended toward the sea. Landing craft striking these makeshift triggers could detonate a lethal Teller mine between the logs. Elsewhere, deep anti-tank trenches blocked access to Normandy's roads, with helpful signs that had once warned Germans: "Achtüng Minen." Brigade engineers swiftly went to work on these minefields and other obstructions, leaving their bomb disposal comrades to handle all "unexploded bombs and other enemy missiles."[44]

On Utah Beach, 23rd BD Squad averaged "five to ten calls per day." Since each call required up to eight hours of work, less important tasks were often postponed. Capt. Stull neutralized several "little Goliaths." Since Anzio, these unpredictable mini-tanks had been refitted with gasoline motors. Launched from small camouflaged bunkers, upgraded Goliaths (models 303a and 303b) were aimed at landing craft, but in most cases, their delicate wiring had been disrupted by pre-invasion volleys from the British and United States Navies. Below Utah's rocky cliffs, Capt. Stull's men also collected "mostly grenades, mines, booby-traps, and prepared charges." Sometimes, disposaleers recognized threats that the engineers tended to overlook. Once, Capt. Stull spotted a UXB some combat engineers had almost covered up with sand; it turned out to be an unexploded magnetic "G" mine, which they carefully defused.[45]

Capt. Jesse Donovan disarmed this Goliath on Omaha Beach during the early hours of D-Day. That same afternoon, while supporting the 5th Special Engineer Brigade, Donovan's 27th Bomb Disposal Squad lost an enlisted man, T/5 Pat Brodish, to German shellfire. (*Leiendecker Collection*)

Early next morning, Capt. Bocelato's squad dodged "heavy artillery fire" to render aid to 37th Combat Engineer Battalion. Searching a tunnel network intended for battalion headquarters, 26th Squad removed "fuzed grenades and mortar shells," plus several unexploded American bombs from Eighth Air Force raids over German positions. That midnight, Bocelato removed "a stick of frag bombs," thus clearing "a field through which [the] infantry would pass the following morning." Despite the loss of one soldier, Capt. Donovan's 27th Squad disposed of several unexploded rockets, found stuck in some thick hedgerows bordering their beach sector. For their deeds in Normandy's first twenty-four hours, all three bomb squads assigned to Special Engineer Brigades won the Croix de Guerre from the Free French government. After another month supporting the Allied breakout, these units were detached to other positions across the Army's developing Communications Zone.[46]

Capt. Jesse Donovan, standing at left, was exposed to German snipers, as evidenced by the bullet holes in his windshield. (*Leiendecker Collection*)

* * *

Elsewhere, ten more bomb squads were scheduled to land with infantry divisions at Omaha Beach on D-Day, but German resistance and channel storms delayed their arrivals. Only 16th BD Squad made it ashore on D-Day, albeit in two stages. From eight miles away, 1st Lt. Marshall Crow had observed the Normandy "alive with flame and smoke" at H-Hour. Lined up for Omaha at H plus 6, Crow's LST 375 had sustained a glancing hit, leaving its bow doors unable to open properly. Capt. Crow and T/Sgt. Henry leaped aboard a nearby LCT, carrying a load of vehicles. Thanks to their new "skipper," Crow and Henry arrived three hours ahead on Easy Red. Crow described this beach, "covered in American dead," and constantly "raked by enemy artillery fire." Due to their excitement, bred by a "newness to combat," Crow and Henry pushed toward the cliffs, where they exchanged shots with German snipers on the heights. After spending the afternoon looking in vain for their comrades, the two leading 16th Squad members slept in a "deep ditch among enemy dead and scattered wastage of equipment."[47]

As Crow and Henry awaited the dawn, the rest of 16th BD Squad faced "one epic night under enemy aircraft attack." At approximately 8 p.m., German planes began strafing and bombing the Allied supply lines and landing zones. Sgt. Royal A. Boyd recalled weathering "many near-misses by large bombs." Fortunately, their LST doors had been repaired, and Boyd's comrades wasted no time in driving their waterproofed squad vehicles ashore early on D plus 1. Reunited with their captain and tech sergeant, 16th BD Squad promptly got to work. Several close calls from snipers forced Crow to set up defensive perimeters, a tactic duplicated by other bomb disposal squads as they reached Normandy.[48]

While the Allied lodgment slowly widened on the Brittany coastline, the 15th BD Squad arrived two days behind schedule. For two nights, Capt. Louis D. Barbe's LST had braved "continued air raids," plus barrages from 170 mm coastal artillery. When 15th Squad landed at St. Lauren Sur Mer on June 8, they immediately contacted V Corps headquarters. Capt. Barbe reported that "many SD-1s were dropped and several casualties developed in the [rear] vicinity." On the next day, 15th Squad commenced operations in V Corps' rear echelons, removing stray SD-1s, destroying UXBs, and dismantling some German rocket launchers left on the beaches. By mid-June, they had moved further inland, operating in tandem with the 16th Squad. By posting sentries around their UXB sites, they managed to dodge enemy potshots without injury. Near La Poterie, Capt. Barbe recovered wreckage from a Fritz glider bomb and a new kind of parachute mine. Within ten days, 15th Squad had cleared out two entire French villages, Mandeville and Traviers.[49]

Joe Pilcher's 17th BD Squad, likewise scheduled to land on D plus 1, was unable to reach the far shore until June 11, owing to poor weather. On their first day, Joe's team dismantled ten "Goliath" mini-tanks, as well as three Butterfly bombs – rare specimens within Normandy's sectors. Within a few weeks, Pilcher, Crow, and Barbe became known as crack bomb disposal officers. Over the next eleven months, Joe Pilcher's squad resolved over 250 incidents, including 150 German UXBs.[50]

On June 19, Maj. Gen. Lawton "Lightning Joe" Collins (VII Corps) borrowed 16th and 17th BD Squads from V Corps, sending them to the strategic town of Carentan. There, battle-hardened 101st Airborne troopers, reinforced by the U.S. 2nd Armored Division, had just repelled furious counterattacks from the German 6th Parachute Regiment and 17th SS Panzer Grenadiers. By June 30, the entire Cherbourg Peninsula belonged to Bradley's First Army. Both squads combed Volognes and Borneville for mines before rejoining V Corps near the front on July 15. At Balleroy, "enemy strafing and artillery activities took on a new high," so just like the infantry, all bomb squad members were required to construct slit trenches or foxholes, camouflaged by logs and earth.[51]

Capt. Bernard Anderson (48th BD Squad) removes a German landmine from Normandy. Later in the campaign, Capt. Anderson was mortally injured and now rests in the U.S. military cemetery at Cambridge, U.K. (*National Archives*)

By the closing of D-Day, several Ninth Air Force squads had arrived. Working with Army engineers, Capt. Jonathan D. Stoddart's 76th BD Squad patrolled the beaches for mines. Capt. B. E. Anderson's 48th BD Squad cleared booby traps from Ninth Air Force's future headquarters at Grandcamp-le-Bain. Col. W. R. Maxwell, the Ninth's ordnance chief, eventually had over 220 disposaleers, perhaps the largest ordnance group under his direct control. Maxwell had appointed Capt. Daniel E. Carter (10th BD Squad) to serve as the Ninth's bomb disposal officer. Before long, Col. Maxwell had singled out Carter's bomb disposal squads for their material contributions toward "rapid clearing and construction of our airfields" at several crucial moments during Normandy's opening weeks.[52]

On D plus 1, Capt. Harvey W. Morgan (41st BD Squad) landed just in time to remove a 500-pound UXB from one of Ninth Air Force's designated runways in Normandy. Morgan's team also destroyed one magnetic G-mine dropped by a night-flying German plane. On June 9, Capt. Syd M. Lerner and Sgt. R. M. Carlin established a bomb disposal headquarters for Ninth Air Force. They went to work removing demolition charges and stockpiles at former German aerodromes, which were often subjected to attacks by the vengeful Luftwaffe. On June 15, both Capt. Lerner and Sgt. Carlin were hit by strafing enemy planes while dealing with UXBs. They finished their tasks despite injuries received. Two days later, Capt. James Licalzi's 30th BD Squad weathered a similar raid. Lerner and Carlin both recovered from their wounds and earned promotions from Col. Maxwell. Maj. Lerner and S/Sgt. Carlin later received Bronze Stars for their bravery under fire at Normandy.[53]

In addition to UXBs, Ninth Air Force bomb squads primarily dealt with enemy stockpiles. Many of these items were already damaged, increasing the risk factor. On July 9, 1944, a massive explosion engulfed T/Sgt. William C. Tait (6th BD Squad) just as he was preparing shells for disposal near Cretteville. On July 13, another munitions explosion occurred near St. Mere Eglise, causing a number of Army casualties and scattering tons of live ammunition and rockets. Capt. Henry E. Bezold's 35th BD Squad proceeded to remove some damaged German mini-rockets to the St. Mere Eglise railroad depot. One of these unsafe projectiles later detonated on the railway platform, killing several ammunition handlers from the U.S. 262nd Ordnance Battalion.[54]

On August 23, Maj. Lerner succeeded Capt. Carter as the Ninth's senior bomb disposal officer. Carter returned to 10th BD Squad, which he had reorganized into a command center akin to Kane's ETO division. While 10th BD Squad "proper" remained under Carter's command, Lerner presently took over a separate detachment responsible for the Ninth's remaining 32 squads. Lerner's field headquarters was staffed by three sector officers, each one corresponding with respective French, Dutch, and Belgian territories as they were gradually liberated by the Allies. Sector I became active on D plus 3 (June 9), while Sector II opened on D plus 65 (August 10) and Sector III opened on D plus 80 (August 25). However, sector positions changed hands prior to actual staging.[55]

| Ninth Air Force Sector Officers[56] | Sector | Date Appointed |
|---|---|---|
| **Capt. Daniel E. Carter** | CO | 4/18/44 |
| **Maj. Syd M. Lerner Jr.** | CO | 8/23/44 |
| **Capt. Syd M. Lerner Jr.** | I | 4/18/44 |
| **Capt. Everett E. Hughes** | I | 8/29/44 |
| **Capt. F. H. Orbison** | II | 4/18/44 |
| **Capt. Daniel E. Carter** | II | 1/7/45 |
| **Capt. Malcolm Antonelli** | III | 4/18/44 |
| **Capt. Thomas R. Reece** | III | 7/15/44 |

Capt. Thomas R. Reece (wearing garrison cap at left) acted as a sector officer with U.S. Ninth Air Force in the European Theater. (*Reece Collection*)

Capt. Thomas R. Reece arrived on August 14 – almost two weeks before Ninth Air Force began Sector III operations. However, he had received prior notice of his assignment one month earlier, while stationed at RAF Station Harwell, Berkshire. Reece and the 10th Squad lived for some days without bathing, and slept beside their foxholes, ready to take cover during night raids. Despite his senior position, Reece volunteered to handle ordnance calls. Returning from one such mission in late August,

Reece inadvertently drove his jeep over a roadside mine. Luckily, he managed to walk away from the wreckage. This close brush with death prompted Tom to write one of his rare letters home. Keeping his injuries secret, Tom quipped: "Have lost one jeep already, and am on number [two] now." Sometimes, keeping a sense of humor kept one's spirit from eroding. Before long, Reece would have need of his humor.[57]

* * *

After two long months in action, U.S. Army and Air Force bomb squads had earned sterling reputations. On July 26, *Stars and Stripes* printed the first of two favorable write-ups. "Suicide Squadrons" featured Sgt. Tony Barenbaum from Capt. Clarence H. Beery's 14th BD Squad. Barenbaum described the experience of "sweating it out," while his commander or technical sergeant disarmed all manner of explosives. This unnamed correspondent also saluted the bravery of all "Ordnance Bomb Disposal Units, who make danger their business." Ernie Pyle's July 27 newspaper column on the Ordnance Branch also received widespread syndication. It emphasized the high risks taken by bomb disposal men.[58]

By this point, Kane had crossed over at Utah Beach, establishing his new headquarters in Paris. For the next several months, Kane coordinated his squads with help from Maj. William Benton (First Army) and Maj. George Schiller (Third Army). Because squads often traveled upwards of 60 miles between calls, Eisenhower approved First Army's proposal to expedite traffic via red-painted mudguards. Ostensibly, this measure allowed "quick recognition for free passage through controlled areas and highways," but Capt. Sky Larkin observed military police halting squads to report suspected incidents. Nevertheless, Sky admitted haphazard alerts were still the "best reporting system," given that conventional "communication systems were under serious handicaps."[59]

Col. Kane reported that "Bomb Disposal… is [no longer] the primary problem," owing to "present inactivity of the German Air Force." Except for the Army's fronts, "discarded munitions" represented the most persistent threat across Western France's interior. Kane promptly requested fifteen more ammunition companies, but they never arrived. Kane also concluded that "mine and booby-trap clearance is not normally required" from bomb disposal units, except for incidental cases vital to "accomplishment of their mission." While combat engineers were best equipped to handle minefields, ordnance squads still scoured beaches, railroads, highways, and command posts for individual mines.[60]

Even though Normandy's beachheads were closed by August 1944, the rear echelons were not necessarily safe havens. Based at Bonneville, 1st Lt. Bertram Ostro's 32nd Squad had been clearing "private dwellings for reoccupation." Ostro placed nightly guards, as German snipers were still active, and reconnaissance planes came over every night to drop flares. Moreover, there were leftover mines, and not all of these were clearly marked for the benefit of German soldiers. On August 10, Bertram Ostro inadvertently drove his jeep over a hidden Teller mine.[61]

Bert Ostro died almost instantly. Meanwhile, Ostro's sole passenger, Capt. Joe Bocelato, was hurled from the vehicle into a nearby German minefield surrounded by barbwire, but miraculously escaped further injuries. Bocelato was evacuated back to England, but not before his friend, Capt. Jesse Donovan, smuggled him an entire bottle of cognac as a get-well present. Needless to say, this took place against hospital orders. The fallen Ostro received the Purple Heart award posthumously, while 1st Lt. Norman Thomas took over 32nd BD Squad. Capt. Bocelato eventually returned to duty, receiving a Purple Heart in his own turn.[62]

By late summer, Lt. Gen. Omar Bradley's Operation *Cobra* had progressed well beyond the First Army's celebrated breakout at St. Lo, which had been heavily defended by several fierce Panzer and Waffen SS divisions. While Montgomery's British and Canadian forces bore the brunt of German ferocity at Caen, U.S. First Army swung across Brittany, scattering foes west and south. Yet, thick French "bocage" offered excellent cover for withdrawing enemy divisions, who made the Allies bleed for each penetrated hedgerow. Ordnance did its best to support First Army's summer push across the "bocage." V Corps' Ordnance branch developed "Rhino" tanks with serrated blades to chop through the dense shrubbery, while 2nd Infantry Division used special demolition teams to blast an open path for tanks to roll through.[63]

Shortly after his sweep through St. Lo, Bradley received a higher command over the 12th Allied Army Group, and Lt. Gen. Courtney L. Hodge took command of First Army. With his VII and XIX Corps guarding the right and center, Hodges sent V Corps toward Vire, a fortified crossroads town ravaged by Allied bombardment and now held by an entire German battle-group. On August 5, Gen. Gerow ordered his forces to take Vire, anticipating that the British movements on his left flank would encircle Gen. Kluge's Wehrmacht. Both offensives converged at what became known as the Falaise Gap. Since 1944, generals and historians alike have debated the Allied failure to seal this "pocket" in time to entrap the entirety of German Army Group B.[64]

Three UXBs neutralized by 17th BD Squad in France. (*Pilcher Collection*)

During Hodge's drive to the Vire, Capt. Pilcher's 17th Squad swept through abandoned German command posts, hospitals, and supply depots. They usually resolved incidents "within a few hours." Capt. Pilcher reported: "It did not matter whether it was 2200 hours… or 0200 hours – if it was urgent, we went right out." Joe recorded the squad's "toughest assignments" took place "under heavy shell fire." None among his squad sustained combat injuries. However, during their August 6 bivouac, T/Sgt. Sam Hobson suffered a bad break. While brewing coffee, Hobson overheated a water-can, and its lid burst, blanketing him with scalding steam. Hobson was hospitalized for several weeks. Sgt. Franklin May served effectively as the 17th Squad's technical sergeant for the next eight months, but sadly never received his stripes.[65]

One day after losing Hobson, Pilcher's squad was dispatched to secure Pont Farey, a vital bridge spanning the Vire River. With few stone bridges capable of supporting American heavy tanks, this crossing had to be salvaged. Close by the bridge's foundations, Pilcher located a damaged 1000-pounder, his first American-made bomb. Slowly winching their sensitive cargo one hundred yards away from the bridge, Joe's unit detonated it safely. Shortly afterward, Pilcher's men located yet another "friendly" UXB, a 500-pounder with a chemical-delay fuze. Joe operated successfully on this bomb, and his men carried it off for safe disposal.[66]

Unfortunately for 17th Squad, official V Corps historians erroneously credited the Engineers for ordnance removal in conjunction with rebuilding seven destroyed bridges over the Vire River. Bomb squads were often ignored simply because risk-taking was part of their job. Needless to say, Joe Pilcher did not go out of his way for *Stars and Stripes* coverage. However, on August 14, he carried out a feat of gallantry for which he received a coveted Silver Star. Early that morning, Joe was sent to disarm a smoking German artillery shell east of Vire. Dodging mortar rounds and gunfire, Capt. Pilcher ventured alone to destroy this hazard. As a result, V Corps advanced safely along the highway to their next mark, closing in upon German forces between Argentan and Falaise.[67]

Two days later, the 17th BD Squad completed a 125-mile trek to Sees. Near Choisy-le-Roi, Pilcher secured a bridgehead over the Yonne River, about 12 km southeast of Paris. As the Americans, Canadians, and Free Poles finally closed the Falaise Pocket, Pilcher disarmed six German UXBs lurking underneath the Choisy-le-Roi viaduct. While accusations persisted over the slow progress at Falaise, the Allies still captured over 50,000 German prisoners. Ten thousand more enemies had fallen during bitter fighting along the highways and lanes. Meanwhile, George S. Patton's newly-activated Third Army pushed toward the Seine River, hotly pursuing 25,000 demoralized survivors who spread dismay among remaining German garrisons in Paris.[68]

During this stage of the war, Army bomb disposal soldiers bore witness to Nazi depredations across the French countryside. Waffen SS reprisals against the French Resistance often resulted in unwarranted massacres, such as *Das Reich*'s wholesale extermination of 642 villagers on June 10 at Oradour-sur-Glane. According to one EOD historian, a few bomb disposal men were required to testify in war crimes proceedings. Yet, it was the homeless survivors who haunted the thoughts of two compassionate bomb disposal officers. On his way toward Torigny sur Vire, Capt. Marshall Crow passed through "complete villages" shattered by German occupation. On the roads, "hungry and ragged people" were all that remained of France's "once wealthy population." Thomas Reece also lamented the "havoc" caused by Allied bombs and shells, but reassured his family that the "Yankees are winning this war." He added: "Naturally, we haven't lost our sense of humor, but my heart bleeds for the French people… they are really swell."[69]

Apart from the usual gamut of bombs, mines, and shells littering France's terrain, bomb disposal men could expect other unpleasant assignments. Occasionally, squad officers were called to field hospitals for assistance with live projectiles still lodged in the bodies of surgery patients. Medical officers routinely took laurels for successful operations, while disarming officers were merely doing their jobs. Sometimes, disposaleers received the dirtiest jobs because no other unit could perform them adequately. 88th BD Squad, from Middleton's VIII Corps, cleared damaged shells from a horse-drawn ammo train strafed by American planes. Capt. Robert H. Palmatary counted 56 dead horses "lying in the sun for about two weeks." In early August 1944, Capt. Jonathan D. Stoddart's 76th BD Squad performed a "most unusual and unappetizing task" along the Vire River. Four dead German soldiers, rigged with explosives, had been reported. "With no deodorant available," Stoddart's squad gamely deactivated this ghoulish booby trap.[70]

By mid-August, Army and Air Force disposaleers were beginning to show signs of wear and tear, after weeks of campaigning beside infantry and tank divisions. 16th BD Squad operated round-the-clock, with very little respite. Marshall Crow reported his men "in good health although rather tired – continual 'on the go' and hurried meals with below ground level sleeping soon tells on the men." Meanwhile, Tom Reece, typing at his field desk with an injured finger, confessed frankly to his wife: "You would die at the way we live." He noted a dearth of soap at his supply base, which left his group "stink[ing] like you-know-what." Tom had also not changed uniforms in several weeks, having lost "quite a few" articles of clothing in his hasty crossing to France. However, Tom reserved his chief complaints for Army field rations: "Have eaten so many C and K rations, I think the buzzards are flying [overhead] waiting for the corpse to fall over." Tom had lost his "good fat," dropping down to 145 pounds. Nevertheless, he predicted better quarters and food waiting for them in Paris, where panicked Germans had begun their withdrawal to the Rhine.[71]

On August 25, Gen. Charles de Gaulle prepared to triumphantly enter Paris at the head of his 2nd Free French Armored Division. To safely escort the future French president through the liberated city, Maj. Gen. Gerow organized 490 V Corps personnel to search for demolition charges, snipers, or other hazards. Recruited chiefly from Army technical and intelligence services, this special battalion-strength outfit was designated Task Force "T" in honor of its commander, Col. Francis P. Tompkins. Later in the war, similar "T-Forces" or "T-Sections" became standard additions to ETO Army operations, often incorporating bomb disposal units as a component. Above all, Col. Tompkins charged his officers to "preserve civil and military records, cultural treasures, and public utilities." Just as in Rome, ordnancemen were employed to protect important historical buildings in Paris from malicious acts of destruction. Nazis had no compunctions toward unleashing *Kulturkampf* on the West.[72]

Under direct orders from Adolf Hitler, two Wehrmacht *Pionier* companies had previously emplaced demolition charges on Paris bridges, mined Paris state buildings, and sabotaged Paris landmarks. Thus, Hitler's *Kulturkampf* sought to sting France like a vengeful scorpion. Fortunately, Lt. Gen. Dietrich von Choltitz, the surrendering Wehrmacht commander, feared the consequences of destroying the fabled "City of Lights," and wisely disregarded his Fuehrer's edict. He ordered Capt. Werner Ebernach to withdraw his 813th *Pionierkompanie* from Paris. Nevertheless, all forty-five Paris bridges were still rigged for destruction: a single act of Nazi fanaticism would have destroyed a great many of these strategic "arteries," not to mention historical edifices. Capt. Joseph Pilcher singlehandedly removed several explosive charges from the Pont Neuf, among the Seine River's oldest bridges. He received the Croix de Guerre, awarded personally by Gen. Charles de Gaulle himself.[73]

At this point, Col. Kane had arrived in Paris, establishing his base in Eisenhower's Communication Zone. Kane presently had all city reports sent to his headquarters, where his staff members pinpointed incidents for swift resolution – just as the British had done across London. Moreover, French labor crews were on hand to assist Kane's separate squads. On August 31, Capt. Crow's 16th Squad met the "Bomb Disposal Director" himself, spending the next five days inspecting "several large hotels and buildings for booby traps." Crow's men located several mines and removed an assortment of German bombs – one buried twenty feet deep. Some of these UXBs may have dated back to 1940, when Paris suffered from aerial bombardment. Other teams, such as 54th BD Squad, spent longer stretches in Paris. For six weeks, Lt. Glenn Miller's men occupied a nice hotel, before moving to "more undesirable quarters," a five-story garage reserved for bomb disposal units. They also inspected and stored Fort de Chatillon's considerable arsenal of explosives.[74]

With Paris safely in Allied hands, Col. Kane personally directed sustained efforts to locate suspected "80-day-clock" bombs from Paris. Recollecting intelligence reports from the 1943 Naples post office explosion, the colonel suspected similar bombs might lurk underneath Paris. Several squads plodded through the sewers, searching for suspicious containers and recently-poured concrete spots. Eighty days later, T. J. Kane canceled the search beneath Paris, but his instincts had been correct. By Thanksgiving, American troops had discovered at least three sabotaged culverts in French and Belgian towns, newly abandoned by Wehrmacht and SS divisions. Such tokens reminded the Yanks that these Rhineland defenders were prepared to face the bitter end.[75]

## Notes

[1] COSSAC is a military acronym standing for "Chief of Staff to the Supreme Allied Commander." SHAEF stands for "Strategic Headquarters, Allied Expeditionary Force." (Williamson Murray and Allen R. Millett, *A War to be Won: Fighting the Second World* War, Cambridge, Massachusetts: Harvard University Press, 2001, 302, 416).
[2] Chief of Operations to Services of Supply, letter, 6 November 1943 (U.S. Army European Theater, World War II War Diaries, 7 December 1941 to 31 December 1945, NARA Record Group 38).
[3] Dwight D. Eisenhower to R.B. Lord, *Bomb and Shell Disposal*, c. May 1944; Brig. Gen. Robert H. Dunlop, Acting Adjutant General, *Bomb Disposal Directives,* 9 May 1944; Maj. R. M. Bush to Commandant, Bomb Disposal School, *Bomb Disposal Directives,* 16 May 1944; Murray & Millett, 416; Mayo, 218.
[4] U.S. Army Field Manual 9-5, *Ordnance in the Field,* GPO, Washington D.C., 1944, 3; *Bomb Disposal Directives*; Eisenhower to Lord.
[5] *ETO Bomb Disposal History*, NARA Records Group 498, 1945, 9-10; Capt. R. W. Cary, *Proposed Bomb and Mine Disposal Policies for the U. S. Navy and U. S. Army in the Event of an Allied Invasion of Europe*, 11 January 1943; Eisenhower to Lord.
[6] Some debate has arisen from Kane's unexpected assignment, but it seems unlikely that it was motivated by personal dislike. Kay Levering, Kane's daughter, confirmed that her father, like many Reservists called to action, initially faced a certain amount of prejudice from certain quarters. However, Kane also had his share of supporters among West Pointers in Ordnance, from William C. De Bill, Julian Hatcher, Charles Wesson, Henry Sayler, all the way up to Dwight D. Eisenhower himself. More likely, this proposal was due to the Civil Affairs Division's lack of understanding of the changing role of wartime bomb disposal. (U.S. Army, U.S. Forces, European Theater, Historical Division: Records, 1941-1946, Staff Section Reports, File 483, Ordnance Journal ETOUSA Jan-Aug 1944; John E. Feldman, *Military History of John Edward Feldman*, personal data, Aberdeen Proving Ground, Maryland: U.S. Army Ordnance Museum, c. 1945; Kay Levering, telephone interview by author, 15 October 2003).
[7] The Civil Affairs Division retained some interest in bomb disposal affairs in the ETO, as evidenced by field reports from squads acting on tips from Civil Affairs. However, most ordnance calls were generated from frontline units who were in better positions to report on such matters. (U.S. Army, U.S. Forces, European Theater, Historical Division: Records, 1941-1946, Staff Section Reports, File 483, Ordnance Journal ETOUSA Jan-Aug 1944; 15th Ordnance Bomb Disposal Squad (Separate) to Adjutant General, *Action Against Enemy*, 20 July 1944).
[8] Some of Kane's officers, such as Frank Parsons, left bomb disposal service to perform general ordnance work. Though most Army commanders welcomed new staff officers, there was occasional friction. Some "old school" Ordnance officers frowned on bomb disposal's relative informality. Bomb disposaleers tended to disregard Army field manuals and regulations, because many felt their line of work

constantly rewrote the manuals. Nonetheless, Frank Parsons won a Silver Star during his service in France and Belgium, and was a credit to the Ordnance branch. (U.S. Army, U.S. Forces, European Theater, Historical Division: Records, 1941-1946, Staff Section Reports, File 483, *Ordnance Journal ETOUSA Jan-Aug* 1944; Feldman history, Maria Feldman, interview with author, 18 June 2003; Maria Feldman, interview by author, 10 August 2003; Dorothy Parsons, interview with author, 18 October 2003; Levin H. Campbell Jr., *The Industry-Ordnance Team*, New York: Whittlesey House & McGraw-Hill Inc., 1946, 364; *Firepower,* "Bomb Disposal," (Washington D.C.: Army Ordnance Association, August- September 1945.) [8]

[9] U.S. Army, U.S. Forces, European Theater, Historical Division: Records, 1941-1946, Staff Section Reports, File 483, *Ordnance Journal ETOUSA Jan-Aug* 1944; *ETO Bomb Disposal History*, NARA Records Group 498, 1945, 9-10; Feldman history; Kane to Ehrmann, 20 June 1944; Eisenhower to Lord, May 1943; Hooper 18-19; Mayo, 231-2.

[10] Ordnance Technical Services, *ETO Bomb Disposal History*, NARA Records Group 498, 1945, 16-18; Kane to Ordnance Office ETOUSA, *Bomb Disposal in the Communication Zone*, 11 January 1943; Kane travel itinerary, 1942-3.

[11] Capt. Schuyler V. C. Larkin to Col. Thomas J. Kane, *Bomb Disposal Training in the United Kingdom*, 1 October 1943.

[12] Ordnance Technical Services, *ETO Bomb Disposal History*, NARA Records Group 498, 1945, 16-18.

[13] 54th Ordnance Bomb Disposal Squad (Separate), unit history, 1943-45; Larkin to Kane, 1 October 1943; Thomas Kane to Lt. Col. Martin Ehrmann, 20 June 1944; *History of the Ordnance Bomb Disposal Division From D-Day to VE-Day in Europe* (Headquarters Communication Zone ETOUSA, 1945), 1-2; Samuel J. Hooper, *The History of U.S. Army Bomb Disposal and Explosive Ordnance Disposal (1941-1980),* c. 1981, 18-19, 21.

[14] For more on cooperation between U.S. and British bomb disposal in England, see USAFE and USSTAF records, 520.673 AFHRA 1942-45. Scotty Calder's squad served in the Communication Zones of France, and he remained active in bomb disposal veterans' affairs well into his retirement. (Captain Wright G. Calder, telephone interview with author, 14 October 2003; Ordnance Technical Services, *ETO Bomb Disposal History*, NARA Records Group 498, 1945, 16-18; John E. Feldman and Thomas J. Kane *History of the Ordnance Bomb Disposal Division From D-Day to VE-Day in Europe,* Headquarters Communication Zone ETOUSA, 1945; Reece, 31-39.)

[15] 31st Ordnance Bomb Disposal Squad (Separate), unit history, 1945; Chris Ransted, *Bomb Disposal and the British Casualties of WW2*, United Kingdom, Royal Engineers Association, 2004; T. Dennis Reece, *Captains of Bomb Disposal 1942-46* (Lexington, Kentucky: Xlibris Books, 2005) 36.

[16] 31st Ordnance Bomb Disposal Squad (Separate), unit history, 1945; Capt. Edward J. Barry, interview conducted by G. Kurt Piehler and Shaun Illingworth in New Brunswick, New Jersey, on October 23, 1998, transcript by Shaun Illingworth, Edward J. Barry and Sandra Stewart Holyoak, Rutgers Oral History

Archives of World War II.

[17] 234th U.S. Ordnance Bomb Disposal Company, unit record, NATEODA Archives, 2 October 1943- 8 February 1945; Lt. Col. Richard P. Fisk to Ordnance Officer. ETOUSA, 3 December 1943; Larkin to Kane, 1 October 1943.

[18] Kane's bomb disposal headquarters coordinated with the Ammunition Supply Branch, who sometimes exchanged personnel. Later in 1944, they organized three specialist teams, modeled on the "squad separate," to counteract German VT (variable time) artillery fuzes encountered in the European Theater. (Stars and Stripes Press, *Flaming Bomb: The Story of Ordnance in the ETO*, Paris, France: Desfosses-Neogravure, 1945; Ordnance Technical Services. *Technical Services, Ammunition Ordnance Report*, NARA Records Group 498, 1943-45, 1-10.)

[19] *ETO Bomb Disposal History*, NARA Records Group 498, 1945, 10-13; Annex 26; Kane to Ehrmann, 20 June 1944; Mayo, 231-2.

[20] *ETO Bomb Disposal History*, NARA Records Group 498, 1945, 10-13, 36-39; Kane & Feldman, *History*, Annex 11; Feldman history, Maria Feldman, interview with author, 18 June 2003; Maria Feldman, interview by author, 10 August 2003; John Feldman to Tim Tidwell, Aberdeen Proving Ground, dates unknown.

[21] Al Newman, "Meet the Bomb Killers" (Newsweek 1 May 1944) 23-24; *ETO Bomb Disposal History*, NARA Records Group 498, 1945, 10-13, 36-39; John Feldman to Tim Tidwell, Aberdeen Proving Ground, dates unknown.

[22] H.H. Bateman to Brig. Gen. Henry B. Sayler, 24 June 1944; John Feldman to Tim Tidwell, Aberdeen Proving Ground, dates unknown; Feldman history.

[23] Captain Robert E. Anderson to Commanding Officer, Ordnance Bomb Disposal Center, *Progress Report of Bomb Disposal Mission,* 29 August 1944.

[24] NARA Records Group 498, 1945, 10-13, 36-39; *History of the Ordnance Bomb Disposal Division,* 5; Robert E. Leiendecker, *Bomb Disposal, The Early Years of Explosive Ordnance Disposal (An Informal History)*, Charlottesville, Virginia, NATEODA Press, 2012, 27.

[25] NARA Records Group 498, 1945, 10-13, 36-39; *History of the Ordnance Bomb Disposal Division,* 5.

[26] NARA Records Group 498, 1945, 10-13, 36-39; *History of the Ordnance Bomb Disposal Division,* 5; Mayo, 231-32; *Firepower,* "Bomb Disposal," (Washington D.C.: Army Ordnance Association, August- September 1945).

[27] 17th U.S. Ordnance Bomb Squad (Separate) to Col. Thomas J. Kane, *Squad History 1944-1945*; 234th U.S. Ordnance BD Company record; *ETO Bomb Disposal History*, NARA Records Group 498, 1945, 10-13.

[28] Col. Thomas J. Kane, *Special Orders No. 183*, 30 September 1943; *The Detonator*, 17 September 1943, 8; 22 October 1943, 8; *BD School Roster*, 26 October 1943; Joseph C. Pilcher, *Last Will and Testament*, 24 November 1943; Joseph C. Pilcher, *Officer's Clearance Certificate.* 27 November 1943; 17th U.S. Ordnance Bomb Squad (Separate) to Col. Thomas J. Kane, *Squad History 1944-1945*, 8 June 1945; Edward J. Barry Jr., *History of the 31st U.S. Ordnance Bomb Squad*, 1945; Kane & Feldman, *History*, Annex 11; Pilcher Scrapbook.

[29] T/5 Franklin May of 17th BD Squad even christened their first squad vehicle in the toddler's honor, and sent Mrs. Pilcher and her son Christmas cards from

overseas. (1st U.S. Army Commander to First Lieutenant Joseph C. Pilcher, 20 December 1943; 84th Ordnance Battalion to Pilcher, *Special Orders No. 24*, 7 February 1944; 234th U.S. Ordnance BD Company record; Hooper, 18-21).

[30] Colonel C.R. Finley to Commanding General of First U.S. Army, 4 March 1944; Joseph C. Pilcher to Major E.F. Trevor, *Replacement of Command*, 6 April 1944; Omar N. Bradley and Clay Blair, *A General's Life* (Simon and Schuster, New York) 1983, 218; Reece, 38.

[31] 16th Ordnance Bomb Disposal Squad (Separate) to Colonel Thomas J. Kane, *Squad History Jan. 1944 to June 1945*, 8 June 1945; 234th U.S. Ordnance BD Company unit record; 440th Anti-Aircraft Artillery Weapons Battalion to Pilcher, *Rations Voucher*, 12 May 1944; Bradley & Blair, 223; Reece, 47.

[32] Thomas J. Kane to Ordnance Officer ETOUSA, *Bomb Disposal Organization Recommended for ETOUSA*, Aberdeen Proving Grounds, MD, unpublished memo, 11 January 1943; Thomas J. Kane to Headquarters ETO, United States Army, technical report, 16 January 1943; Thomas J. Kane to Ordnance Officer ETOUSA, *Bomb Disposal in the Communication Zone*, unpublished memo, 11 January 1943; Thomas J. Kane to Allied Forces Headquarters, *Bomb Disposal Organization*, unpublished memo, 5 February 1943.
Kane to Ehrmann, 20 June 1944; Eisenhower to Lord, May 1943; Mayo, 231-2.

[33] Kane to Ehrmann, 20 June 1944.

[34] Kane to Ehrmann, 20 June 1944; Maj. S. M. Lerner, Jr., Headquarters, Ninth Air Force, Office of the Bomb Disposal Officer, *Consolidated History of Bomb Disposal in the Ninth Air Force*, May 1945; Headquarters, Ninth Air Force, *Disposition of Bomb Disposal Units on the Far Shore*, memorandum, 24 May 1944; Reece, 34-5, 42.

[35] 10th Ordnance Bomb Disposal Squad (Separate) to Headquarters, Ninth Air Force. [unit history] 15 February 1945 to 28 June 1945; Maj. S. M. Lerner, Jr., Headquarters, Ninth Air Force, Office of the Bomb Disposal Officer, *Consolidated History of Bomb Disposal in the Ninth Air Force*, May 1945; Kane to Ehrmann, 20 June 194; Reece, 34-5, 42.

[36] U.S. Army Field Manual 9-5, *Ordnance in the Field* (GPO, Washington D.C.) 1944, 3; Capt. Schuyler V.C. Larkin, *Bomb Disposal since D-Day*, unpublished report, 2 January 1945; Kane to Ehrmann, 20 June 1944.

[37] Fifth Army Engineer Special Brigade, unit history, U.S. Army, U.S. Forces, European Theater, Historical Division: Records, 1941-1946, NARA Record Group 498; Mayo, 233.

[38] Fifth Army Engineer Special Brigade; Col. John B. Medaris, *Overlord Diary*, Ordnance Office, 1st U.S. Army, February 1944.

[39] Surprisingly little research has been written concerning British bomb technicians who served overseas, as most British scholarship on focuses on the home front. (5th U.S. Ordnance Bomb Disposal Squad, *History of the Fifth Ordnance Bomb Disposal Squad,* 28 February 1945; Eric E. Wakeling, *A Short History of Royal Engineer Bomb Disposal*, Buckinghamshire, England: B.D. Publishing, 1997, 11; Chris Ransted, *Bomb Disposal and the British Casualties of WW2*, 2004, 87-93; *Pamphlet 672-1: Unit Citation and Campaign Participation Credit Register*

(Washington D.C.: Government Publishing Office, 1972); Ordnance Bomb Disposal School Headquarters, *BD Officer Roster*, 26 November 1942; *Roster of all Bomb Disposal Officers*, 26 October 1943; Ordnance Bomb Disposal School, *Roster of Active BD Officers*, 1 December 1945; Kane & Feldman, *History*, 1-2).

[40] The British officer is thought by some to be Capt. Raymond Bingham of No. 14 Company, who died as a result of a Butterfly bomb on March 6, 1943. However, Bocelato's unit did not arrive in the U.K. until 1944, so his account must refer to yet another tragic victim of the SD-2. (Edward J. Barry, interview conducted by G. Kurt Piehler and Shaun Illingworth in New Brunswick, New Jersey, on October 23, 1998, transcript by Shaun Illingworth, Edward J. Barry and Sandra Stewart Holyoak, Rutgers Oral History Archives of World War II; Fifth Army Engineer Special Brigade, 55-58; *Roster of Active BD Officers*, 1 December 1945; Kane & Feldman, *History*, 1-2; Ransted, 74).

[41] Fifth Army Engineer Special Brigade, 55-58.

[42] Kane to Ehrmann, 20 June 1944; Capt. Schuyler V.C. Larkin, *Bomb Disposal since D-Day*. [unpublished report] 2 January 1945; Kane & Feldman, *History, 1*.

[43] 27th Ordnance Bomb Disposal Squad (Separate), *Squad History*, 11 June 1945; *V Corps Operations in the ETO: 6 January 1942 – 9 May 1945* (U.S. Army Historical Section: GPO, Washington D.C.), 45-52; Kane & Feldman, *History*, 1-2; Jerome Krieger to Commander, NAVSCOLEOD, *Fact Sheet*, 5 October 1992; Robert Leiendecker, *World War II EOD Data*; National EOD Association Library, Charlottesville VA, 2003; Michael R. Vining, *Explosive Ordnance Disposal Memorial – U. S. Army,* submitted to the EOD Memorial Commission, 15 October 2011; Fifth Army Engineer Special Brigade, 45, 55-58, 87.

[44] Stephen Ambrose, *Citizen Soldiers* (New York, Simon & Schuster, 1997) 142-5, 404-5; Fifth Army Engineer Special Brigade, 74-75, 117; Bradley & Blair, 223-25.)

[45] Intact gasoline-powered Goliath models (302a & 302b) were later used by the Air Force as tugs for fighter-craft, but seriously lacked durability, having been designed to blow up on contact. Goliaths were more successful when directed against poorly-armed partisan fighters in the Warsaw Uprising of 1944. German engineers used them against houses, burying their occupants under piles of rubble. (National World War II Museum, "Artifact Spotlight," from *V-Mail* (Vol. 12, No. 1) 12-14; Kane & Feldman, *History*, 1-2; *Pamphlet 672-1;* Mayo, 214, 247; U.S. Army, U.S. Forces, European Theater, Historical Division: Records, 1941-1946, Staff Section Reports, File 359, *Utah Beach*).

[46] 27th Squad, *Squad History*; Fifth Army Engineer Special Brigade, 55-58; Kane & Feldman, *History*, 1-2.

[47] 16th Ordnance Bomb Disposal Squad (Separate) to Colonel Thomas J. Kane, *Squad History Jan. 1944 to June 1945*, 8 June 1945; Hooper, 19.

[48] 16th BD Squad, *History*.

[49] Capt. Louis Barbe hailed from Lake Charles, Louisiana. (15th Ordnance Bomb Disposal Squad (Separate) to Adjutant General, *Action Against Enemy*, After Action Report, 20 July 1944; 16th BD Squad, *History*).

[50] 17th BD Squad, *History*; 16th BD Squad, *History*; Kane & Feldman, 1-2; *V*

*Corps*, 84.
[51] 17th BD Squad, *History*; Kane & Feldman, 1-2; History; *V Corps*, 84; Bradley & Blair, 223-2.
[52] Headquarters, Ninth Air Force, *Disposition of Bomb Disposal Units on the Far Shore*, memorandum, 24 May 1944; Maj. S. M. Lerner, Jr., Headquarters, Ninth Air Force, Office of the Bomb Disposal Officer, *Consolidated History of Bomb Disposal in the Ninth Air Force*, May 1945; *Monthly Ordnance Activities Reports, Headquarters, Ninth Air Force*, AFHRA File 533.804.
[53] *History of the Ordnance Bomb Disposal Division From D-Day to VE-Day in Europe* (Headquarters Communication Zone ETOUSA, 1945), 7-9; 10th Ordnance Bomb Disposal Squad (Separate) to Headquarters, Ninth Air Force. [unit history] 15 February 1945 to 28 June 1945; 30th Ordnance Bomb Disposal Squad (Separate), unit history, 1945; 41st Ordnance Bomb Disposal Squad (Separate). [unit history] May 1944.
[54] Tait was awarded posthumous Purple Heart medals. (35th Ordnance Bomb Disposal Squad (Separate), 12 June 1945; 48th Ordnance Bomb Disposal Squad (Separate), unit history, 1 June 1945 to 14 December 1945; Charles G. Pritchard, "A Yank on Bomb Disposal with the RAF," in *UXB Volume II*. Jim Jenkinson, editor, Sussex, England: Woodfield Publishing, 2001; Hooper, 20, Appendix II; Reece, 44-45; www.dtic.mil/dpmo/wwii; www.eodmemorial.org/army.html.
[55] Ninth Air Force, Office of the Bomb Disposal Officer, *Consolidated History of Bomb Disposal in the Ninth Air Force*, May 1945, 1-4.
[56] At some point after Normandy, Capt. F.H. Orbison suffered injuries in the line of duty and had to be replaced. Capt. Daniel Carter managed Sector II while commanding 87th BD Squad during the winter of 1944-45. (10th Ordnance Bomb Disposal Squad (Separate) to Headquarters, Ninth Air Force. [unit history] 15 February 1945 to 28 June 1945).
[57] According to his son, Dennis, Thomas Reece never reported his injuries, which included several lacerations and a damaged arm. Unreported injuries among disposaleers were not uncommon. (Thomas R. Reece, letter, 17 August 1944; 10th Ordnance Bomb Disposal Squad (Separate) to Headquarters, Ninth Air Force, unit history, 15 February 1945 to 28 June 1945; 80th Ordnance Bomb Disposal Squad (Separate), unit history, 29 May 1944 to 11 December 1945; T. Dennis Reece, interview with author, 11 June 2011; Reece, *Captains*, 49, 62-74).
[58] Kane's opinion toward this article, given its rather misleading title, is unknown. (*Stars & Stripes*. "Suicide Squadrons." 26 July 1944; Ernie Pyle, "Ordnance Keeps Army in Trim," *Stars and Stripes*, 27 July 1944).
[59] During the D-Day operations, Kane's divisional H.Q. had been shuttled between 1st U.S. Army Services of Supply and the Western Base Section at Weston. (R.B. Lord, *Maintenance and Operation of Motor Vehicles*, U.S. Army, U.S. Forces, European Theater, Historical Division: Records, 1941-1946, Staff Section Reports, File 236, Ordnance Vehicles, 15 June 1944; Larkin, *Bomb Disposal since D-Day*, 3; Kane & Feldman, *History of the Ordnance Bomb Disposal Division;* Reece, *Captains*, 62-74).
[60] Kane & Feldman, *History of the Ordnance Bomb Disposal Division*.

---

[61] 32nd Ordnance Bomb Disposal Squad (Separate), *Squad History*, 20 June 1945; Captain Robert E. Anderson to Commanding Officer, Ordnance Bomb Disposal Center, *Progress Report of Bomb Disposal Mission,* 29 August 1944; Martin Blumenson, *European Theater of Operations: Breakout and Pursuit.* Washington D.C.: Office of the Chief of Military History, 1961, 271.

[62] Mike R. Vining, *Explosive Ordnance Disposal Memorial – U. S. Army,* EOD Memorial Commission, 9 April 2011; www.dtic.mil/dpmo/wwii; www.eodmemorial.org/army.html; Robert E. Leiendecker, *Bomb Disposal, The Early Years of Explosive Ordnance Disposal (An Informal History)*, Charlottesville, Virginia, NATEODA Press, 2012, 267-68.

[63] Blumenson, *Breakout and Pursuit*, 205-7; Bradley & Blair, 278-83; *V Corps*, 84.

[64] Blumenson, *Breakout and Pursuit*, 290-95; 449-56; Bradley & Blair, 287-88; Murray & Millett, 432-33.

[65] T/Sgt. Hobson eventually recovered and joined 117th BD Squad. He was replaced by Pvt. Walker Stansell, who served with Pilcher's squad until given a direct commission with the Engineers in March 1945. Why Sgt. May was never duly promoted to Technical Sergeant is inexplicable, given his excellent working relationship with Capt. Pilcher. In early 1945, T/Sgt. Thomas C. Weed, a decorated hero, filled 17th BD squad's NCO vacancy until the war's conclusion. (17th BD Squad, *History*).

[66] Ibid.

[67] Captain Joseph C. Pilcher, *Citation for Silver Star*, 18 May 1945; *History of Ordnance Bomb Disposal Division*, 8; 17th BD Squad, *History*; Blumenson, *Breakout and Pursuit*, 507-27; *V Corps*, 166-7.

[68] Blumenson, *Breakout and Pursuit*, 528-58, 559-87; Bradley & Blair, 299, 308-10; *V Corps*, 172-198; 17th BD Squad, *History.*

[69] Thomas R. Reece, letter, 17 August 1944; 16th BD Squad, *History*; Antony Beevor, *D-Day: The Battle for Normandy* (London: Penguin Books, 2009), 166; Hooper, 22-24.

[70] 76th Ordnance Bomb Disposal Squad (Separate), unit history, 5 April 1944 to 17 December 1945; 88th Ordnance Bomb Disposal Squad (Separate), unit history, 23 March 1945; Kane & Feldman, 7; Hooper, 22-24.

[71] 16th BD Squad, *History*; Thomas R. Reece, letter, 17 August 1944.

[72] Larry Collins and Dominique LaPierre, *Is Paris Burning?* (New York: Simon and Schuster, 1965), 52-53; 71-73; 122-23; *V Corps,* 199-206; Hooper, 21-22.

[73] General Dietrich von Choltitz convinced he would face a war crimes tribunal for obeying Adolf Hitler's direct orders. (17th BD Squad, *History*; *V Corps*, 278-86; 328-340; Bradley & Blair, 309; Collins & LaPierre, 66-68, 210-12, 260-61.)

[74] 234th U.S. Ordnance Bomb Disposal Company, unit record, NATEODA Archives, 2 October 1943- 8 February 1945; 16th BD Squad, *History;* 54th BD Squad, *History.*

[75] Technical Information Bulletin No. 47, 1 March 1945, 73; *Stars & Stripes*, "Yanks Scoured Paris Seeking 80-Day Bombs," 15 June 1945, 4; Kane & Feldman, *History of the Ordnance Bomb Disposal Division.*

# CHAPTER SIX

# PLAYING CHECKERS WITH DEATH: FLANDERS TO BERLIN (1944-45)

During the summer of 1944, British and American commanders discussed the merits of a "single-thrust" or "broad-front" strategy against Germany. In early September, Field Marshal Bernard Montgomery persuaded Gen. Eisenhower to support his plan, Operation *Market-Garden*. Three Allied paratrooper divisions, followed by Brian Horrocks' XXX Corps, were expected to liberate Holland and penetrate Northern Germany. As matters turned out, the victorious Allies had deliberated too long, and squandered their best chance for an early end to the war. Germans were no longer in full retreat, but retrenched at their national borders. After a nine-day brawl lasting September 17-26, Germans under Gen. Model had decisively parried Monty's "full-blooded thrust" at Arnhem's bridges. When the dust cleared, over 17,000 Allied troops had been killed, wounded, or lost – at least 5,000 more casualties than D-Day.[1]

Even though Kane's Bomb Disposal Division played no active role in Montgomery's primarily airborne enterprise, Eisenhower's top ordnance officers were very concerned about one of *Market Garden*'s secondary objectives. Holland's low countryside had provided level ground for Adolf Hitler's "Vengeance Weapons," the V-1 bomb and V-2 rocket. Eisenhower particularly anticipated the Allied capture of German rocket launch sites rumored to be near the crucial city of Arnhem.[2]

Since June 11, V-1 Flying Bombs, known as "buzz bombs" or "doodlebugs," had hurtled across the English Channel at 350 miles per hour, each one carrying a ton of explosives. In late 1943, SHAEF had received the earliest V-1 intelligence reports from French resistance. In early 1944, U.S. Army and Royal Air Forces commenced Operation Crossbow, targeting suspected rocket sites across France and the Netherlands. Borrowing from contemporary language, war historian Stephen Ambrose described Hitler's "Vengeance" weapons as "terrorist devices." However, Allied fighter pilots soon learned they could knock a V-1 off course by positioning a wing underneath the bomb's stabilizing fins, and then flipping the monster. V-1s also proved vulnerable to anti-aircraft guns positions on the English coastline.[3]

Residing in London, Capt. John Feldman worked closely with the UXB Committee on the V-1 problem. By his own account, Feldman "made many trips to all parts of England to render safe reported duds, and quell falsely reported rumors." On one such mission, Feldman traveled with Royal Engineers under Brigadier H.H. Bateman to an undisclosed site where BD units had unearthed the first unexploded "flying bomb" in captivity. Pilotless V-1s often dropped short of their intended targets, leaving its three impact fuzes intact. Two electric impact fuzes (E1AZ 106 and 80A) were located in the fuselage, and one mechanical fuze (usually a 17B) rested deep inside its nose. Royal Engineers tested Feldman's self-tapping needle "with a view to immunizing some of the fuzes." Satisfied with the results, Brig. Bateman predicted that Feldman's breakthrough would revolutionize bomb disposal techniques across the board. Feldman subsequently took part in several V-1 and V-2 rocket reconstructions. Promoted to major shortly afterward, Feldman's tireless efforts won him admittance to the Order of the British Empire in 1946.[4]

1st Lt. James Patchell of 75th BD Squad (Ninth Air Force) examines a crashed V-1 "buzz bomb" near St. Trond, Belgium.

By fall 1944, Kane's ETO bomb disposal squads numbered well over seventy. They were also doing their bit to combat the V-1 menace across the Western Front. 17th BD Squad ranged across eastern France and southern Belgium, seeking V-1 launch-sites. Joe Pilcher recovered one of the first unexploded V-1s near Emerenville on September 2. During October alone, Pilcher's team disarmed five unexploded V-1 "buzz bombs," while gathering "items of intelligence value." Joe wryly referred to his busy schedule as a "bomb disposal man's picnic." By campaign's end, V Corps alone dealt with 1,091 pilotless aircraft (PACs), or "Divers," as they were codenamed by Aberdeen's Technical Information Bulletins. However, intact "Divers" were difficult to capture once launched; seven V Corps troops were killed after locating a delayed-action V-1 in Belgium.[5]

A rare glimpse inside a V-1 rocket, undressed by the Ninth Air Force.

Despite wartime security, civilian presses carried sensational reports about so-called "robot" bombs – so many articles, in fact, that Aberdeen Proving Ground ironically suggested that their bomb squads knew about as much as the average citizen. Their bulletins even borrowed V-1 pictures from *Life* and *Newsweek* magazines. However, all sarcasm aside, Ninth Air Force bomb disposal units made several key observations regarding V-1 "Buzz Bombs." 68th BD Squad (Capt. George D. Gordon) witnessed a series of V-1 attacks on Liege, Belgium in late November. Hundreds flew at low altitudes, targeting a bridge across the Meuse River in scattergun fashion. Most bombs detonated in mid-air, shattering windows but doing modest damage. Reporting from “Buzz-Bomb Alley,” Tom Reece observed the British 90mm anti-aircraft guns in action. Throughout these “Buzz Bomb” raids, most Allied soldiers were unperturbed – some even went to the movies in the evenings.[6]

German file photograph of a V-2 rocket built in 1942 at Peenemünde. V-1 and V-2 rockets remained a major Army intelligence priority throughout 1944-4. V-2s were particularly feared, as they could not be shot down or knocked off their trajectory. Bomb disposal units were instrumental in gathering data on these original weapons of mass destruction. (*German Bundesarchiv*)

On September 8, Hitler's V-2s first struck targets in Western Europe and England, and did not cease until next March. Even deadlier than "doodlebugs," V-2s were practically unstoppable by anti-aircraft guns or fighter planes. As a primitive ICBM, these weapons heralded a new kind of warfare – V-2s alone were responsible for killing over 2,700 Londoners. Over in France, Col. John Medaris of Ordnance ordered all First Army bomb disposal units to capture any V-2 hardware. Stationed in Belgium, 15th BD Squad located the first intact V-2 warhead in October 1944; however, such opportunities were exceedingly rare. Later, that December, a properly functioning rocket struck Antwerp, killing 271 theatergoers at the crowded Rex Cinema. Many of these victims were British and Canadian soldiers, who had recently fought so bravely to liberate Belgium's famous port city. For these men, and for other victims of Hitler's vengeance, there was no chance for escape.[7]

Capt. Joseph Pilcher standing next to German rocket components captured at Neustadt by 17th BD Squad in early 1945. (*Pilcher Collection*)

Meanwhile, Kane's "bomb killers" continued to "supplement the Engineers" in Paris and other newly-liberated French municipalities. They "removed and neutralized" enemy ordnance from buildings chosen for "billets, offices, and warehouses." Air Force units "operated in localities" exposed to higher degrees of bombardment, giving them a statistical edge on credited UXBs. They also discovered the Germans had used unexploded American bombs as ersatz demolition charges, especially underneath highway bridges and railway trestles. After reviewing dozens of operational reports dating back to Normandy, Col. Kane concluded that his Bomb Disposal Division's incident reporting system had been "entirely too haphazard." While Kane credited his mobile Army and Air Corps squads with resolving many bomb disposal incidents, he voiced concerns over their static counterparts in the Communication Zone.[8]

This new problem resulted from bomb disposal's ever-changing mission. While front-line squads still dealt with UXBs, "Com Z" disposaleers were kept busy clearing foreign munitions in rear echelons. In July, ETO removal efforts amounted to 344 tons of munitions vís a vís 114 tons of UXBs. Nearly 1,600 tons of ammo had been recovered from Paris between August and September. Communication Zone squads were also responsible for mounting guards over vulnerable depots to prevent German sabotage. Even though they were seldom exposed to enemy fire, "Com Z" units had their work cut out for them. Many accidents ensued because soldiers were exhausted by humdrum ammunition work.[9]

Since the colonel could not hope to be everywhere at once, he urged all his squad commanders to convey precise descriptions and tonnage, "instead of leaving the guesswork up to us." Better statistics would enable Kane's small headquarters to allocate incoming squads to actual trouble spots across France, Belgium, and Holland. While recognizing with pride that "each group of Squads [is] doing their fullest share of the work," Kane desired "a clearer picture" of each unit's "fullest share."[10]

Since Paris had regained its liberty, some of Kane's soldiers had indeed given their "fullest share." Ernie Pyle characterized general ordnance work as "more intellectual than physical," but disposaleers squared off against death on a routine basis. Several casualties resulted from mishandled ordnance. On September 22, 1st Lt. Vincent Gath's 85th BD Squad (Ninth Air Force) went to Chartres railway station, the scene of a recent skirmish with Germans. Two salvagers, charged with removing live artillery rounds, were seriously wounded when a shell toppled unexpectedly and exploded. T/5 Russell L. Byington lost both his legs, and expired on October 3. Simultaneously, friendly fire almost killed 1st Lt. Frank J. Hollenbach (37th BD Squad) while he scouted Eastern France. As T/5 Howard J. Bernart drove his CO back from an abandoned German dumpsite near Blaine, their distinctive red jeep received fire from a jittery U.S. Army anti-tank crew. Fortunately, Hollenbach and Bernart recovered fully within weeks, receiving Purple Heart medals for their troubles.[11]

"Traditional" UXB missions still took precedence for ordnance units not engaged at the front. On October 12, 1944, 1st Lt. Sherwood L. Racey (146th BD Squad) and 2nd Lt. Charles F. Hale (133rd BD Squad) responded to a German UXB near Besancon, France. Preliminary reports indicated that this bomb contained an unusual fuze – and maybe something more. No sooner had the two lieutenants removed and disassembled their fuze, when both were killed instantly. Mortally wounded in the explosion, T/5 Robert F. Chapman (146th BD Squad) lingered for nine days before succumbing. Racey, Hale, and Chapman were three more unfortunate victims in the Luftwaffe's ongoing "guerilla war" with bomb fuzes.[12]

Capt. Thomas Reece poses outside Aachen in October 1944. (*Reece Collection*)

In the fall of 1944, Germany's resistance redoubled at its borders with Belgium and Luxembourg. Capt. Floyd C. Caulfield's 20th BD Squad participated in the siege of Aachen – the historic court of Charlemagne. Besieged by elements of U.S. VII and XIX Corps, and pounded by Ninth Air Force, Aachen was the first major German city to capitulate. Caulfield's squad routinely handled ordnance calls under heavy German shellfire. During one barrage, T/5 Donald E. Bailey suffered a mortal head injury from a flying shell fragment. Bailey died in a field hospital on October 29, 1944, eight days after Aachen's surrender.[13]

By this time, Luftwaffe technicians had introduced a newly-improved Butterfly bomb. Captured enemy documents confirmed that these advanced Butterfly bombs were equipped with Type 70A delayed-action fuzes. Some time before, Tom Hoge, a *Stars and Stripes* reporter, had cautioned would-be souvenir collectors about the risks involved with disturbing a supposedly dormant SD-2: "The butterfly is known among experts as one of the most dangerous bombs in existence. Anyone who touches one of those babies signs himself a one-way ticket."[14]

Ninth Air Force's airmen often ignored these warnings. Throughout 1944, 2nd Lt. Albert J. Engel had observed numerous violations of his standing orders to leave abandoned German bomb crates undisturbed. Engle described the Butterfly bomb's unique tan container, and predicted that a "serious accident" might result if one of these still contained live projectiles. However, many Ninth Air Force scroungers emptied ordnance boxes without regard for their markings. Gen. Quesada's enlisted men found empty ordnance containers useful for makeshift furniture. Tom Reece recalled one of his 80th Squad technicians, Walter V. Smith, showing off his carpentry skills by constructing a bookcase for his unit. Since Quesada's airmen had paid small attention to a mere second lieutenant, Col. Sherman Beaty of Ninth Air Force Headquarters finally decided to put his foot down. Violations ceased before any serious tragedies took place that winter.[15]

Luftwaffe pilots continued to surprise the American with new airborne weapons. In August 1944, 1st Lt. Coolie Verner (68th BD Squad) discovered the first SD-4s on the Western Front. Introduced in 1942, these tear-shaped fragmentation munitions were designed to knock out Russian tanks. Seventy-eight bomblets were carried underneath a dive-bomber, and dispersed as the plane tilted downward for the kill. One SD-4 (H1) cluster bomb consisted of a hollow charge, and weighed 8.8 pounds. Capable of igniting fuel tanks or magazines on a near miss, they proved injurious against infantry escorts. On the Eastern Front, Gen. Paul Deichmann compared their effect to that of "concentrated shrapnel."[16]

Despite all these touted advancements, however, the Luftwaffe's ordnance manufacturers were running on borrowed time. Germany's enemies were closing on three fronts: France, Italy, and the Soviet East. As Gen. Marquard related to Deichmann, "supporting the Army in its struggle against superior enemy forces required the use of an expedient." Thus, German munitions plants began to package rejected ammunition, such as mortar shells and artillery rounds, into drop containers. Shells as large as 88mm and 105mm were dropped like fragmentation bombs, an efficacious improvisation that Marquard commended from both a "technical and military-economic viewpoint."[17]

* * *

By the year's end, T. J. Kane had identified difficulties plaguing his units, now totaling 120 squads in the ETO. Kane's "Top View" categorically blamed War Department bureaucracy for slow progress prior to 1943. Restating his earlier views on unit strengths, Kane acknowledged that individual squads were more effective at the "fluid fronts," but he maintained that full companies would have been more practical in rear echelons. Kane cited a good authority on this matter: "British experience indicated that [bomb disposal companies were] the superior organization for cities and defensive locations." Regrettably, Kane had lost his single remaining company on October 11, when the 234$^{th}$ disbanded into four Ordnance Service Platoons, each serving at the Army headquarters level. Significantly, 234$^{th}$ BD Company also yielded a training detachment that played a future role in French reconstruction.[18]

Kane openly lamented the placement of many squads at "various echelons and headquarters." Just as he had predicted, a seven-man squad was "too small a unit," generally "kicked about as a step-child by any higher unit to which they are assigned." Without a real headquarters, separate squads had trouble replacing men lost to injuries or illnesses. Furthermore, Army bomb disposal officers "doubled in brass," acting as ammunition depot officers or personnel administrators at Army or Group level. Given the magnitude of ETO ordnance activity, Kane believed that had a company-sized headquarters been granted, "existing difficulties" might have been reduced to a "negligible degree." Kane also noted the Ninth Air Force had a centralized bomb disposal organization. Despite Kane's larger-than-life bromides toward the Air Force, he willingly conceded that Maj. Syd Lerner's sector officer system had effectively coordinated 33 bomb squads over the past six months, enjoying a direct line of communications to Ninth Air Force headquarters.[19]

On October 11, 1944, the 234th Ord. Bomb Disposal Company, last of its kind, disbanded into four service platoons, plus a training headquarters at Le Mans. (*National Archives*)

By contrast, Kane's staff bomb disposal officers were often treated as peripheral figures by Army-level officers, who overlooked bomb disposal's significance. Serving with Gen. Patton's U.S. Third Army, Maj. George W. Schiller supervised fifteen squads separate, plus the 231st Ordnance Service Platoon. Nominally attached to 82nd Ordnance Group, Schiller's teams were stationed at ordinary ammo battalions – far away from their supply bases. Schiller later wrote: "For the most part, the distance between battalion to division areas made this [informal] arrangement impractical. Operationally… it got the job done, but from an administrative view, it left something to be desired. Normally, a squad is expected to be attached to a larger unit, which provides housing, mess, and administration. However, this was not the case in practice." As at Sicily, Gen. Patton demonstrated a lack of connection with Ordnance affairs.[20]

In November 1944, Lt. Col. Martin Ehrmann visited France on Ordnance business. Col. Kane met his good friend in Paris, where they discussed rotating officers and men back to Maryland for training. However, many squads with the Ninth Air Force were far too busy to take advantage of this opportunity. While touring the Third Army's developing battlefront along the Seine River, Ehrmann also observed Maj. Schiller's sixteen units clearing ordnance from Fort Chatillon. While in France, Ehrmann used his mineralogy connections to appropriate several tons of rare Madagascar tourmaline urgently needed by Ordnance for specialized pressure gauges. Maj. John Feldman accompanied the commandant back to Aberdeen on temporary assignment. He implemented the school's production of "flit-guns" before returning to the ETO in early 1945.[21]

Given a dearth of French ordnance specialists, Kane's Bomb Disposal Division increasingly relied on unskilled civilian laborers to collect, salvage, and remove immense stockpiles of inerted bombs and munitions. Kane's requests for ammunition companies had come to naught, which meant more exertion for his overworked specialists. Maj. Schiller observed that some of his troops were reluctant to handle munitions or mines, having gained the wrong impression at Aberdeen that they were "only responsible for handling bombs." Nevertheless, Schiller deplored the U.S. Third Army's lack of appreciation for his beleaguered branch. Bomb disposal squads "were given credit for having more knowledge of foreign ammunition than they possessed." Schiller felt the Third Army expected too much from "only six men and one officer, equipped with two vehicles, leading to instances of overwork and exhaustion. Schiller further noted that eight Third Army bomb disposal personnel had been killed through mishandling German or French ammunition. Others were killed by stray landmines.[22]

Recognizing the vital importance of ordnance removal to France's postwar recovery, Col. Kane resolved to alleviate his own manpower shortages by educating the best French Army officers and sergeants. However, owing to lingering British suspicions, Free French soldiers were categorically forbidden access to Royal Engineers data. To counteract unexpected intransigence, the colonel appealed to his commanding general, Eisenhower. After all, one million tons of leftover German and French ordnance presented "both a political and an economic problem." Noting the presence of German landmines, Kane observed that "not a day passes by when some adult or child meets death or is maimed for life." As recently as August 29, the 10th BD Squad had removed several S-Mines from a country lane near Chantilly, where a French child had just been killed. Yet, Kane knew that his ordnancemen could not spare further time to collect and destroy all these "weapons of death." Ike promptly concurred that such matters were now in France's hands.[23]

Few among the Free French armies were equipped with up-to-date ordnance tools, let alone educated in their use. With approval from the highest channels, Kane opened the doors of his new Ordnance, Bomb, and Mine School, situated at Le Mans. Established in October 1944 by Capt.

Joseph T. Racey, 234th BD Company, this facility taught 813 American and French students over one year. Bilingual course manuals using classified materials required translations through the Army Intelligence Services. By late 1945, Racey's school had trained 311 French graduates to become bomb disposal experts in their own right. French civilians learned to spot potential bomb sites. Maj. John Feldman speculated about the long-term benefits of American tutelage: "How many others were taught by these pioneers cannot be imagined." Since 1945, France's EOD contingent has destroyed tons of UXBs and mines unearthed by farmers.[24]

* * *

Meanwhile, as a harsh winter loomed ahead, the Allies proceeded along a broad front toward the Rhine. Belgium and Luxembourg were both liberated by early October, even though Field Marshal Montgomery did not consolidate his recapture on Antwerp until late November. Simultaneously, U.S. and Free French divisions edged toward Germany's vital Roer River dams. Gen. Omar Bradley later depicted an atmosphere of expectation in December 1944, with eight Allied armies "poised on the edge of victory." And yet, the Allies' "victory fever" had enabled Gerd von Rundstedt – widely considered Germany's best field commander – to reorganize his mauled Wehrmacht forces, which were further reinforced by fanatical SS Panzer units. That fall, two U.S. infantry divisions withdrew after a stalled offensive in Huertgen Forest, a stretch of woodland guarding access to the Roer Valley. Recalling their heady successes back in 1940, German High Command chose yet another forest – the northerly Ardennes – to stage Hitler's final gamble against the West: the Battle of the Bulge.[25]

Bastogne, a quiet Luxembourg village, would suffer the greatest brunt of Hitler's malice. Back in September, Gerow's V Corps had led the First Army's victory parade through the newly-liberated town. Riding proudly among the processions, Joe Pilcher took photographs of cheering townsfolk lining the sidewalks. 16th and 17th BD Squads looked forward to a brief respite. Marshall Crow's men billeted for some days in a "recently vacated German barracks." Joe Pilcher's men were attached to V Corps headquarters, and contributed one man to guard duty. Eventually, Gerow dispatched his bomb disposal crews to work alongside the infantry divisions positioned at the West German border. While Crow's team dodged artillery salvos in the forests of St. Vith, Pilcher's band ventured across the German frontier on V-1 scouting patrols.[26]

Sometimes, technical sergeants such as this Ninth Air Force noncom, were called on to remove bomb fuzes, usually reserved for officers. (*Reece Collection*)

While stationed in Belgium and Luxembourg, Army and Air Force NCOs often found themselves carrying almost as much clout as a captain. For example, 68th BD Squad's T/Sgt. Walter Haasis won a Presidential Unit Citation for coolness under fire at Normandy. At that time, Haasis served with the Ninth Air Force's 926th Engineer Aviation Regiment. Following the Bulge campaign, T/Sgt. Walter Haasis received a commendation from Brig. Gen. James B. Newman, Jr., drawing attention to his "superior… efficient manner" throughout the preceding months. Earlier that August, T/Sgt. Haasis had led clearance efforts at Ville Coublay airdrome, located outside Paris. He then spent two days in September combing the Duchess of Luxembourg's palace and summer home for booby traps. On November 11, he bravely disarmed an unknown explosive type discovered at Liege. Later in the war, Haasis also singlehandedly cleared an abandoned airstrip at Vogelsang, Germany.[27]

Another noncom, T/Sgt. Ralph M. Burnett, took comparable risks while serving with 90th BD Squad, attached to XX Corps, Patton's Third Army. On September 8, Burnett cleared a suspicious group of German field guns loaded on railroad flatcars near the Somme. On October 7, Burnett investigated a 36-inch entry hole near XX Corps Headquarters. Discovering a live projectile, the sergeant retrieved what turned out to be

Ordnance's first 280 mm railway gun projectile. Given the frequency of Germany railway gun barrages, Burnett's trove went to Army Intelligence for further analysis. Not to be outdone, Burnett also recovered fragments from several V-1s launched against the Third Army. For these and other heroic actions, Capt. Russell P. Althaus recommended his sergeant for a Bronze Star medal. During the Bulge campaign, 90th BD Squad rendered invaluable support to XII Corps, one of Patton's units sent to plug Gen. Gerd von Rundstedt's breach north of Luxembourg.[28]

Weeks before Rundstedt's offensive began, Liege and Antwerp had suffered from unrelenting V-1 attacks, inheriting the sobriquet of "Buzz Bomb Alley." In early October, Marshall Crow recorded "buzz bombs" taking off at twenty minute intervals: "Twenty four hours a day… one could hear a robot motor or see the plane in the sky." Based at V Corps HQ in Eupen, 16th and 17th BD Squads frequently drove out to infantry positions, demolishing V-1s only a few kilometers from Germany's borders. However, this time, both squads were fortunate to lodge indoors for a change. After work, Joe Pilcher caught up on leisure reading with his favorite pipe. Capt. Crow issued four-hour evening passes to his men, who flocked to Eupen's small cinema or frequented the local pubs.[29]

This predictable albeit busy tempo changed abruptly just before Christmas 1944. Early on December 17, Capt. Pilcher went out on his usual V-1 patrol, and witnessed the German Army jabbing southward toward Bastogne; "a push that really kept [us] busy removing bombs, shells, and 'buzz bombs'." At Eupen, V Corps headquarters underwent "heavy shelling," and both squads sent an enlisted man for guard duty. Meanwhile, after a period of relative silence, the Luftwaffe stepped up its bombing raids over Belgium and Luxembourg. Marshall Crow recalled "daily visits" from German planes at midday and just after midnight. Joe Pilcher quipped: "for each bomb neutralized," it seemed that "Jerry" came back with "half a dozen more." Pilcher and Crow's teams tackled many UXBs in the Eupen locale, sometimes operating within range of big German howitzers and troublesome 88s. As Crow quickly discovered, "the best time for concealment was early in the morning, when a haze screened our movement and observers could not see for long distances."[30]

Throughout the December and January fighting, other bomb disposal squads had memorable experiences. Capt. Gordon (68th BD Squad) spent Christmas Eve huddled in a Liege cellar during a "terrific pasting" by the Luftwaffe. Two of Gordon's men narrowly escaped death when a flaming Focke-Wulf 190 crashed forty feet from their position. Marching with III Corps to relieve Bastogne, Capt. Robert H. Palmatary's 88th BD Squad won three Purple Hearts, four Bronze Stars, and a Meritorious Service

Award for the Bulge campaign. Palmatary also recommended T/5 Leonard Bishop for a Silver Star, but he settled for a Bronze Star instead.[31]

Capt. Joseph Pilcher took this photograph in Eupen during the Belgian town's liberation by the Allies in the fall of 1944. (*Pilcher Collection*)

Rundstedt's Ardennes Forest offensive was a calculated risk, largely conceived by Hitler, a high-stakes gambler if ever there was one. Hearkening back to 1940, the Fuehrer hoped once more to divide the Allies and force them back into the English Channel. Since all major roads converged on Bastogne and St. Vith, Rundstedt quickly drove a wedge between Gerow's V Corps and Middleton's VIII Corps, whose anemic forces were quickly overrun. Only 101st Airborne Infantry Division's timely arrival saved the "battling bastards" of Bastogne from certain annihilation. Taking charge of the city's defense, Brig. Gen. Anthony C. McAuliffe, (101st Airborne) defied a German demand for VIII Corps' surrender, uttering his laconic reply: "Nuts." U.S. troops dug in at Bastogne, as Luftwaffe squadrons failed to capitalize on their short-lived air superiority. By December 22, the Americans had turned the tables on Hitler's generals. Gen. George S. Patton's U.S. Third Army entered the fray, spearheading a powerful Allied counter-offensive that forced the Germans to retreat permanently across the Rhine River.[32]

T/Sgt. Roache from 73rd BD Squad inspects another crashed V-1 rocket in Belgium. These rockets were used to soften up the U.S. Army's positions before the Battle of the Bulge commenced. (*Reece Collection*)

After Patton's sealing of the Bulge on January 22, Third Army's ordnance squads remained on the move, searching barns, hayricks, culverts, and outhouses for time-delay bombs. Wherever the Germans retreated through farmlands and crossroads, their *Pionier Korps* ruthlessly sabotaged buildings, just as they had done in Sicily and Italy. German demolitionists emplaced an average of four bombs per village. Capt. Patrick J. Hogan (5th BD Squad) informed *Stars and Stripes* that Germans particularly liked to sabotage wine cellars, for obvious reasons. Hogan's squad had prior experience dating back to the Aleutian Islands in 1943, when Japanese soldiers left behind trapped liquor containers. "Don't fool around with suspicious spots," Hogan warned. Even as reports of German sabotage increased during Patton's drive toward the Rhine, concerns were raised by officers observing their troops avidly hunting for souvenirs. Capt. Hogan sagely advised soldiers passing through Belgium and Germany that a G.I.'s "best souvenirs" were "ten fingers and two legs."[33]

* * *

Meanwhile, the U.S. First Army probed across the German center, seeking a means to take strategic dams holding back the Roer River. Largest of the seven dams, Schwammenauel was primarily an earthen structure, and if demolished, posed the greatest risk to an Allied crossing. According to 78th Infantry Division's official chronicler, "22 billion gallons of water… would be sufficient not only to submerge completely and destroy all the towns along the Roer… but to sweep away like matchsticks men and equipment in a river crossing operation."[34]

As the new V Corps commander, Lt. Gen. Clarence Huebner had to prevent the Roer River from being flooded by the German 272nd Volks Grenadiers, six thousand strong. These stout defenders had resisted Allied bombardment as well as several ground attacks. While most Volks Grenadier divisions were comprised from leftover German occupation forces, the 272nd proved a formidable adversary. Shortly before the Bulge, Maj. Gen. Edwin Parker, Jr. led the 78th Division in a costly ground assault on Schmidt, a hilltop citadel overlooking the dense Huertgen Forest. Congested with enemy pillboxes and minefields, this natural barrier chewed up several infantry regiments throughout the winter.[35]

While the "Lightning Division" had taken the town of Kesternich in early December, their progress was all but lost after the Christmas offensive in Belgium. Following the German rout in January 1945, Huebner invited Parker's 78th Infantry for a second assault on Schmidt, scheduled to commence on February 5. Parker's three infantry regiments, the 309th, 310th, and 311th, were spoiling for a rematch with the 272nd Volks Grenadiers. But Huebner, a former division commander, anticipated German reinforcements at the dam, and ordered support troops for the "Lightnings." Parker's three regiments were beefed up with British "Crocodile" flamethrower tanks, V Corps field artillery and a specialist "T-force" consisting of combat engineers and ordnancemen.[36]

Culled from V Corps' 303rd Combat Engineer Battalion, Capt. Frank Camm's "T-force" had orders to remove all demolitions and prevent sabotage to Schwammenauel Dam. Camm, a future three-star general, had been among the forces which had just retaken Kesternich on February 2. V Corps duly credited Camm's engineers, but subsequently overlooked their ordnance partners. With their experience in Paris removing demolitions, both Joseph Pilcher and Marshall Crow were natural recruits. For his taskforce, Capt. Crow selected two sergeants, William J. Henry and Royal A. Boyd, plus one technician, O. C. Lagasse. Meanwhile, Capt. Pilcher's handpicked men included two technicians; Edward C. Norris and Richard W. Gilliam, along with his trusty sergeant, Franklin May.[37]

On February 5, the "Lightnings" began their southward march along the "Monschau corridor." Pilcher slogged along with 309th Regiment, while Crow rode ahead with 311th Regiment's armored column. Periodically, the eight ordnancemen inspected bombed-out villages and deserted farms for booby-traps. Weeks before, this major road had played a part in Gen. Rundstedt's grand offensive. Now, this sector was only defended by bands of German skirmishers guarding the crossroads.[38]

By nightfall of February 6, Parker had halted on the outskirts of Schmidt. At that point, both Eisenhower and Bradley visited Parker's field tent and ordered him to seize the town of Schmidt and capture Schwammenauel Dam. Parker had two days to achieve both objectives. Following V Corps' original battle plan, 309th Regiment's battalions invested Kommerscheidt, a crossroads just northwest of Schmidt where Joe Pilcher witnessed intense fighting. Meanwhile, the 311th rode tanks toward Schmidt until forced to dismount by anti-tank fire. Marshall Crow recalled "much small arms," as well as omnipresent German artillery.[39]

Outside Schmidt, Parker's rain-soaked 310th and 311th Regiments encountered stiff German resistance, blocking their access to the dam. Bristling atop the hill opposite were pillboxes and machine-gun nests manned by reinforcements from the 85th Infantry, 9th Panzer, 3rd Parachute and 3rd Panzer-Grenadier divisions. However, the Germans had other countermeasures against the attacking "doughboys." Capt. Frank Camm was flung from his jeep after his motorized column struck Teller mines. The vehicle directly behind Camm's was completely destroyed.[40]

Capt. Joseph Pilcher is seated at center, surrounded by his 17th BD Squad cohorts. Directly to Pilcher's left stands Sgt. Franklin May. Both were active participants in 78th Infantry Division's bold seizure of Schwammenauel Dam in February 1945. (*Pilcher Collection*)

By February 8, Parker's grunts were bogged down in Schmidt, fighting the Germans house-to-house, a situation Gen. Huebner found intolerable. While Parker kept up a steady front with 310th Regiment, Huebner transferred 309th and 311th Regiments to Maj. Gen. Louis A. Craig. Huebner's new field commander promptly cleared Schwammenauel Dam's flanks of German infantry, leaving the 1st Battalion, 309th Regiment to finally mount a long-rehearsed assault on the structure at 2300 hours. Camm's "T-Force" followed closely behind, prepared to seize the dam. Joe Pilcher would never forget this "bitter cold" night as long as he lived; "It was raining," whilst enemy "shell and mortar fire were intense."[41]

Built in 1934 as a borderland defense, Schwammenauel Dam stood 188 feet high and spanned 1000 feet. Described by one 78th infantryman as a "five-tiered earthen staircase" reinforced by concrete, this impressive dam measured over 1000 feet thick at its base. According to Capt. Camm, Schwammenauel Dam had a system of maintenance tunnels with two access points; one at the dam's summit and another two hundred feet down the spillway. Camm "visualized [these tunnels] could be packed with demolitions, with the Germans waiting for the opportune moment to press the button and send [the dam] sky high."[42]

Camm divided his "T-Force" into three sections. One had orders to capture the dam's powerhouse at ground level. The second was to scale the dam's surface. Once atop the dam, a third team would enter the inspection tunnel and remove demolition charges. Camm took the powerhouse, while his executive, 1st Lt. Maurice Phelan, led the surface probe. Phelan's party included the ordnance section, which had drawn the onerous task of searching the dam's interior for explosives.[43]

Phelan's patrol faced a four-hundred-yard dash atop the dam. Halfway across, they discovered German machine-gunners blocking access to the top hatch. Warning flares illuminated the sky, marking their presence to enemy mortar crews positioned on the heights across the dam. Phelan described this scene: "It was like a ten-minute artillery barrage repeated every ten minutes; between shell explosions, we heard the burp-guns." Hurled back upon their first crossing attempt, Phelan's team recruited a squad of riflemen and made another push just after midnight. During this interval, the German mortars inflicted serious casualties. Marshall Crow took shell fragments in his left hand and left leg. After evacuating their stricken officer to the rear, T/Sgt. William Henry and Sgt. Royal Boyd led a counterattack that broke the dam's topside defenses. Using hand grenades and small arms, the bomb disposaleers claimed at least 17 slain Germans. The rest fled for the hills across from the dam.[44]

With the dam all but secure, Joe Pilcher could safely conduct his search for explosive charges within its bowels. Unluckily, topside access had been partly blocked by sabotage, so Pilcher's detachment was forced to rappel two hundred feet downward. Using the spillway opening, they climbed inside Schwammenauel Dam and made their way through its daunting interior. Despite fears of being "blown to kingdom come," demolition charges were nowhere to be found. As Capt. Pilcher later recounted to Col. Kane: "when we gained the access to the dam, the gates had already been blasted… so our troubles were all for naught."[45]

While Lt. Phelan's group struggled for possession of the dam above, Capt. Camm had fought a bitter skirmish over the powerhouse below. Germans repelled initial attempts to seize Schwammenauel's nerve center, but S/Sgt. Ed Naylor, 303rd Engineers, managed to blast the doors open with his bazooka. During the ensuing mêlée inside the pump house, Naylor fought alongside seven infantrymen and an unnamed "Bomb Disposal sergeant from the Army." However, the powerhouse garrison had fought an effective delaying action, giving the dam engineers enough time to smash the discharge valves open. On February 9, Frank Camm confirmed that "outlets had been blown and water was rushing into the valley below." This action partially flooded the Roer River Valley, delaying the Army's fording operations for several weeks. Nonetheless, as the 78th Infantry's chronicler proudly asserted, "Schwammenauel Dam no longer was a menace to the Allied forces in the north." [46]

Aerial view of Schwammenauel Dam guarding the Roer. (*National Archives*)

Capt. Marshall Crow's wounds, while serious, did not sideline him for long. Crow spent three weeks at the Army hospital in Aachen, but returned to duty by March 5. Crow's courageous efforts during the Schwammenauel Dam operation won him a Silver Star for gallantry, plus the Purple Heart medal. 16th Squad's T/Sgt. Henry and Sgt. Boyd won Bronze Stars for valor. Back at Eupen, three Bronze Stars went to 17th Squad enlisted men who took part in the operation. T/5 Richard Gilliam also received a Silver Star for his role in storming the dam.[47]

For his part, Capt. Pilcher seldom mentioned the Schwammenauel Dam operation after the war. Perhaps it had something to do with a small *Stars and Stripes* article that Joe kept in his scrapbook. It portrayed their mission as a mere "reconnaissance in force," when it was much larger than that. Ironically, Lt. Phelan and four other combat engineers took the credit for knocking out the dam's German defenders and securing the tunnel. One can sense the frustration Pilcher must have felt after taking such risks for no apparent purpose. In a letter, Ron Felton later summed up these sentiments for many disposaleers: "There were no kudos in this job, but just another day in the life of a bomb disposal man."[48]

* * *

In early 1945, Allied forces began crossing over the Rhine River, while Soviet Red Army divisions closed on Berlin. While patrolling Army sectors in Germany, ordnancemen received orders to destroy all armored vehicles, field guns, and ammo stockpiles. This directive served to prevent the reclamation or sabotage of armaments by the Germans. Such missions sometimes claimed lives, owing to the unpredictability of enemy weapons. Since their arrival shortly after D-Day, 30th BD Squad had earned accolades for coolness under fire. Capt. James LiCalzi's squad had captured an intact V-2 rocket warhead during the Ardennes campaign. However, on February 1, their fortune ran out. Near Verviers, Sgt. John H. Baxley found a live German anti-tank projectile, which detonated as he sought to render it safe. As of this writing, however, John Baxley's name has yet to be retroactively added to the National EOD Memorial.[49]

Based on their efficient performance in Paris, and their proven valor at Schwammenauel Dam, Army bomb disposaleers gradually came to the notice of division, corps, and even group commanders. 163rd BD Squad served Gen. Bradley for nearly two months as intelligence-gatherers during 12th Army Group's sweep through Cologne. If Kane's "bomb-killers" were not exactly commandoes, they showed a penchant for making level-headed decisions in tight situations. On March 6, 1945, T/Sgt. George Schuck secured vital intelligence papers from a railroad station occupied by German troops. Under heavy mortar and small-arms fire, he completed his safecracking job with little cover. On March 7, 1st Lt. William W. Hammond and T/3 Howard E. Robinson, formerly from 234th Company, extinguished a burning "rail wagon" full of 81mm mortar shells in Germany. Because their prompt actions "undoubtedly averted a serious explosion," they both received the coveted Soldier's Medal.[50]

Ninth Air Force's ordnancemen also added their weight to clearance efforts across Flanders and Holland. Capt. T.R. Reece, responsible for Sector III, had the unenviable job of sending his comrades across the Dutch border to tackle leftover bombs and landmines. One day in early February, Canadian forces situated in the Netherlands reported a dike laced with German anti-tank mines. Reece sent 77th BD Squad, commanded by Capt. George W. Collins, to assist the Canadians.[51]

Capt. George W. Collins (77th BD Squad), tragically killed while disarming a Teller mine near Steenburgen, the Netherlands. (*Reece Collection*)

"Wally" Collins and Tom Reece were old chums. Back in Maryland, Reece had stood as Collins' best man at his April 1944 wedding. Now stationed just east of Steenburgen, Holland, Wally's team began disarming a stand of Riegel 43 anti-tank mines located within a shallow dike. Riegels were capricious mines, typically outfitted with anti-disturbance fuzes. On February 16, one Riegel detonated, blasting Wally Collins fully in his face. Several anti-aircraft gun crewmen were injured during this blast, as were two of Collins' technicians. When informed of Wally's death, Capt. Reece undertook the onerous task of recovering his comrade's almost unrecognizable body for burial. Soon after the war, Tom Reece paid a brief visit to Wally's grieving young widow.[52]

By March 1945, the Luftwaffe had begun using jets, such as Messerschmitt 163 fighter-bombers, to drop payloads of Butterfly bombs. Kane's professionals tackled them to their utmost abilities. His officers and men knew that all their training could not prevent accidents, only minimize their impact. Fresh in their minds, no doubt, were rumors from other units, such as the 86th Squad, which lost Capt. Joseph Stryjewski to severe wounds in August 1944. Sometimes, entire canisters of SD-2s were "dynamited" by disposaleers, making the job somewhat easier.[53]

Stationed near Bonn in early 1945, Edward J. Barry's 31st BD Squad got rid of over five hundred specimens left behind at Hangelar Airport. "Jay" Barry had lived in dread of encountering SD-2s since departing England, having heard "horror stories" from British officers. Fortunately, his entire squad emerged unscathed from their experience. Capt. Max Zimmerman, on the other hand, did not come off quite so well. Dispatched to the Kassel-Rothwesten airfield, his veteran 46th BD Squad tackled "an abundant supply of SD-2 bombs." On April 19, a stray butterfly exploded, seriously injuring Zimmerman, and claiming his sergeant, Roland H. Engwall, who received a posthumous Purple Heart.[54]

Nearly as tragic as outright fatalities, some men lost limbs or suffered bodily disfigurement in the line of their ordnance duties. Minor injuries incurred by disposaleers in the field usually went unreported, a fact confirmed by NATEODA historian Robert Leiendecker. However, some cases were severe enough to cost bomb squads in terms of both manpower and morale. In mid-March 1945, 1st Lt. Gerald Ledford (161st BD Squad) suffered the loss of both his NCOs under disastrous circumstances while operating along the northern Rhine sector. At this point, the 161st Squad was giving technical assistance to a U.S. Army quartermaster company stationed at Satzvey, near Westphalia.[55]

T/Sgt. Victor H. Blomquist, just returned to duty after being sideswiped by a Belgian troop transport, had spotted a German UXB lying in a nearby field, and instinctively resolved to dynamite this bomb *in situ*. Pulling his wagonful of explosives, the sergeant unexpectedly felt "a sudden eruption of the ground under him." Blomquist had stumbled upon a "Schu-mine," but miraculously, it did not trigger the UXB or his dynamite cache. Nevertheless, this misstep cost Blomquist a foot, amputated six inches above his right ankle. Shortly after V-E Day, S/Sgt. Jewel Bennett, only nineteen years old, suffered massive third-degree burns across his face and shoulders after mistiming a demolition charge at the Hugo Schneider munitions plant. Despite all odds, Sergeant Bennett managed to survive his painful injuries and return to the States.[56]

Eisenhower's Chief of Ordnance, Maj. Gen. Henry B. Sayler (at left) relied on Kane's Bomb Disposal Division across the ETO. Gen. Sayler is shown here examining a Belgian mortar. He later supervised Research and Development for the Ordnance Department. (*National Archives*)

Maj. Gen. Sayler and Col. T. J. Kane kept abreast of these sad tidings and others, even as they were cheered by news of impending victory across Germany and Austria. Even President Roosevelt's passing on April 12 failed to dampen their spirits. Ultimately, Kane's ETO report disclosed 111 casualties among 972 bomb disposal officers and men serving in Western Europe. While this "human cost" meant 11 percent losses, Kane proudly underscored the fact UXBs claimed only 4 deaths and 24 injuries. Predictably, landmines and munitions were responsible for the majority, with 43 dead and 68 seriously hurt soldiers. Since D-Day, only four disposaleers had been killed and nine wounded during combat operations in the European Theater. Despite a few close calls at the "fluid front," none of Kane's squads were ever captured by the Germans.[57]

* * *

After the liberation of Paris, Maj. Eric Renner, a Grade One Luftwaffe bomb disposal officer, voluntarily surrendered to Free French officials. Renner openly claimed never to have been "in accord with the ideals of Nazism," and to show his good faith, he "expressed a desire to communicate all information in his possession." Renner's covert record for French Resistance collaboration, plus his marriage to a French woman, secured his parole in October 1944. Guarded by U.S. military police, Renner willingly interviewed Capt. John Feldman, who credited the German for rendering "great assistance to the various Bomb Disposal Squads." Feldman first interviewed Maj. Renner on October 8, with some assistance from an unnamed Army interpreter. Shortly before V-E Day, Martin Ehrmann interrogated other German technicians and scientists, convincing them to join the West in order to avoid Soviet capture.[58]

Incredibly, the Royal Engineers and Army Ordnance services did not begin researching German bomb disposal techniques until March 1944. However, the Luftwaffe's exclusive training program had commenced shortly before September 1939. Following the invasion of Poland, a projected two-year officer's course was shortened to only seven months. Training took place near Leipzig, at a school supervised by a Capt. Schweitzer. Following their graduation, *Sprengkommando* officers were graded from one to three, meaning that Maj. Renner's capture had been quite a coup. For two years, Renner had acted as the Luftwaffe's Bomb Disposal Adjutant for five airfields in the Paris region. Only five hundred officers and noncoms graduated from Schweitzer's school, but Renner estimated totals of 600 officers and 1500 men were then serving in *Sprengkommando* units. Many of these so-called "volunteers" were most likely draftees brought in to deal with the results of increased Allied bombing raids during 1943-44.[59]

*Sprengkommando* units, consisting of one officer and three men, received ample training in British and American bombs. Schweitzer moved his school to the Ruhr Valley in order to test new methods for Allied bombs. Yet, the offense-minded Luftwaffe neglected to support Schweitzer with adequate intelligence and equipment. Led by ideological Nazi Party members, the Luftwaffe's munitions wing refused to divulge many of its own trade secrets to Schweitzer's school. Perhaps, this was partly due to higher concentrations of anti-Nazis in non-combatant work. In May 1945, Bradley's 12$^{th}$ Army Group captured one German bomb disposal technician, Hanz Manderscheid, who had previously served with two Waffen SS divisions at the Russian Front. Embittered by his father's forced sterilization by the Nazis, Manderscheid willingly divulged evidence about hidden weapon caches and suspected war crimes.[60]

A German bomb disposal officer, known as a *Sprengkommando*. (*Bundesarchiv*)

However contrite Renner may have been toward his former enemies, he could not resist an opportunity to point out a few Allied mistakes. Renner asserted his country's bomb disposal teams could handle most foreign bombs, using superior German tools. He recalled early British bombs had been armed with predictable delayed-action fuzes, set for lengthy periods by the RAF to allow civilians to evacuate. Germany's *Sprengkommando* units were able to defuze these bombs before they could seriously damage targeted factories and plants. Several months passed before the British changed their configurations, and Renner surmised that it had taken their analysts some time to catch on.[61]

Renner singled out U.S. bombs for high failure rates, calculated at 10 percent – significantly higher than the British. He cited figures from June-July 1943, when close to 90 out of nearly 500 bombs failed to detonate at Le Bourget. Renner "seemed quite incensed" as he described the "gross carelessness" of Air Force bombardiers. He recalled finding Eighth Air Force bombs without fuzes, while others still had their arming wires. Such oversights made UXBs difficult to handle for all disposal teams, regardless of nationality. Combined with reports from the Mediterranean Theater, these mistakes reflected poorly on the U.S. Army Air Forces.[62]

Kane and Feldman discovered some blank areas in German ordnance intelligence. While Gen. Marquard possessed much knowledge of both British and U.S. bomb disposal networks, their security blackout seems to have worked exceedingly well. Renner freely admitted his branch's knowledge of new Allied tools and methods had been "limited" since 1942. Luftwaffe agencies did not know, for example, that the Royal Engineers had developed means to inert Zus-40s and Type 50 mercury fuzes. Moreover, Renner did not know about Feldman's revolutionary "flit gun," which, as mentioned earlier, drastically reduced over 200 pounds of ordnance equipment to a portable five-pound toolkit.[63]

On the subject of gadgetry, John Feldman was astounded to learn about Germany's "power-driven wrench," a match for his own "rocket wrench." Developed at Capt. Schweitzer's bomb disposal school lab, this device was capable of 6000 revolutions per second. Kane observed that "comparison with enemy equipment... is favorable to U.S. Ordnance equipment. With the exception of the principle of the rocket wrench, nothing has been added to U.S. equipment based on German practice." However, Maj. Renner "knew of a probe, which lighted a lamp when close to a bomb." Capt. Schweitzer had likewise developed a special bomb "trepanner" that completely removed most fuze pockets.[64]

Finally, Maj. Renner explained the lingering mystery concerning so relatively few appearances of the dangerous Butterfly bomb. Just before D-Day, Renner recalled that several FW-190 fighter-bombers had attempted to drop Butterfly bombs over the marshaling areas, but fierce anti-aircraft fire discouraged the raiders from sticking around. This fact was confirmed by U.S. Navy reports from May 1944, detailing recovery of "several" Butterfly bombs around Falmouth, Cornwall. Following *Overlord*'s success, loss of air supremacy prevented German planes from dropping SD-2s effectively. Payloads fell short, or dropped too close to German positions on the Normandy beachheads. With a few exceptions, most German planes returned to hangars with full SD-2 containers.[65]

By early 1945, Berlin had ordered all stocks of SD bomblets destroyed, but in most cases, the Allies reached these airfields before Luftwaffe technicians could carry out their final orders. Having survived the Eastern Front, Luftwaffe Gen. Paul Deichmann recorded "great shortages of 2.2 lbs. bombs in the field." He groused about superiors who failed to recognize the "great effect produced by these bombs against live targets." Russian infantrymen had proven vulnerable to smaller bombs. One might hypothesize that German High Command's orders to destroy such monstrous weapons also reflected their mounting concerns over war crimes proceedings, which proved to have substance as time went on.[66]

* * *

Hitler's final weeks were characterized by last-ditch Nazi resistance. The Allies crossed the Rhine River in late March, with Patton's Third Army taking the crucial bridge at Remagen. Shortly before, V Corps had transferred to Patton's command, along with its bomb disposal teams. Fully recovered from wounds, Marshall Crow recorded his unit's crossing "at 1000 hrs." on March 26. For the next two weeks, Crow's squad patrolled historic Leipzig. Third Army squads found themselves in the unlikely roles of captors, as Germans surrendered to Americans in droves. However, not all prisoners went so tamely. While stationed in Gottingen, Capt. Pilcher and T/5 Joseph Olszewski won Bronze Stars for "heroic achievements" on April 9. In the midst of disarming a cluster of UXBs, they were unexpectedly fired upon by two German snipers. Subduing both enemies after a brief but intense firefight, they went back to their bombs.[67]

That week, Lt. Gerald Ledford of 161st BD Squad (VIII Corps) experienced his own noteworthy German prisoner-of-war encounter. While providing technical advice to the Belgians, Ledford discovered a vacant ammo dump outside Wolfhagen on April 5. Inspecting this site, he located magazines rigged with J-Feder 504s, delay fuzes set to detonate after a 21-day period. Ledford promptly evacuated the area and removed six detonators. On April 7, Ledford received a curious morning call from VIII Corps. Interrogators had just identified one of the German saboteurs, an officer who presently guided Ledford to twelve other charges timed to go off that afternoon at 1515. With T/5 Bert Godfrey's assistance, Lt. Ledford carefully deloused these trapped bunkers. Just as they neared the last known site, however, "there was a belch of smoke." Ledford ruefully called it quits – his wristwatch showed 1515 on the dot.[68]

For most of April, V Corps swept through the Hanover region, supported by two of its bomb disposal squads. Pilcher's team demolished three to ten bombs daily. Crow boasted that his unit had destroyed nearly 1,200 tons in nearly two months, from March 15 to V-E Day. Pilcher and Crow's combined teams cleared Merseburg, the site of Germany's synthetic oil refinery and a prominent Allied target. From 14-18 April, Pilcher also supervised German factory workers at Sommerda's nearby chemical plant, where his men destroyed 150 tons of explosive primer. Joe took precautions from toxic fumes from burning mercury and chlorine fumes – one of the few times he donned a gasmask. On April 29, V Corps requested the general destruction of 600 tons of *Panzerfaust* anti-tank munitions, located at Berna. While infantrymen evacuated civilian homes, Capt. Pilcher set off what he drily reckoned as "a good explosion."[69]

Even though the Soviets and Americans had agreed to meet at the Elba River, Third Army felt the momentum of final victory, and crossed into Czech territory. On May 7, six days after Hitler's suicide, V Corps officially liberated Pilsen, Czechoslovakia. While this action created diplomatic waves in the gathering Cold War climate, Capt. Pilcher often recounted a favorite V-E Day anecdote from Pilsen. Using gunpowder charges, Joe improvised a twenty-one gun salute for the restored president of Czechoslovakia, Dr. Edvard Benes. Using a baseball bat, Pilcher tamped down the gunpowder charges, and set off each canister in quick succession. However, his contributions were forgotten after Third Army reluctantly left the Czechs to the mercies of Soviet occupation. That July, Capt. Pilcher bade his men farewell and signed over command to Capt. Edward Barry, late of 31st BD Squad. Joe demobilized and returned to his family, who were waiting for him in Havre de Grace. Pilcher's war story concluded with Col. Kane's personal praise for 17th BD Squad, which noted that each member had been decorated at least once for bravery.[70]

Capt. Joseph Pilcher, boasting his Silver and Bronze Star medals. Pilcher left Germany in July 1945 and returned to his wife and son. (*Pilcher Collection*)

Altogether, from D-Day until V-E Day, U.S. Army and Air Force squads removed 614,415 UXBs from Western Europe; nearly 600,000 were German in origin. During post-war reconstruction, hundreds more Allied UXBs were removed by German teams under American tutelage. Yet, as preceding chapters have testified, unexploded bombs represented but a fraction of Col. Kane's responsibilities. Actual bomb tonnage amounted to only 9, 387, a miniscule amount when compared to 31,504 tons of other munitions, for a total of 40, 891 tons of explosive ordnance. By 1945, Kane's branch had outgrown its old moniker, "bomb disposal."[71]

By V-E Day, 120 bomb disposal "squads separate" and four service platoons had taken part in field operations across France, Belgium, Holland, Germany, and Austria. Beginning in December 1944, and never slackening until March 1945, bomb disposal activity peaked for all these Army and Air Force squads. 787 personnel disposed of 5,187 tons, breaking down into 6.6 tons per man each month. 6,177 man hours were expended, and 1,789.7 cubic yards of earth were excavated. 18.8 percent of these missions involved hazardous materials or live explosives.[72]

To keep better track of statistics, Col. Kane and Maj. Feldman also broke down their reports to reflect three major groups involved with ETO ordnance removal – Army, Air Force, and Com Z (Communication Zone). Naturally, a vast majority of squads who were assigned to Army Groups removed about 50 percent of the total – just over 20,902 tons. Twenty squads patrolling the Com Z removed about 12, 634 tons, while thirty-three Air Corps teams were credited with clearing only 7,355 tons. However, these Air Force figures, drawn from Kane's Army report, may be slightly inaccurate, owing to inconsistent reporting methods between Ninth Air Force and Kane's Bomb Disposal Division. Kane's final report shows a paucity of Air Force ordnance data prior to October 1944.[73]

Further complicating the statistics, Ninth Air Force's chief BD officer may also have overstated his case somewhat. While Kane kept meticulous monthly data until V-E Day, Maj. Syd Lerner's brief report merely estimated ten months' worth of operations, ending April 1, 1945. Lerner's men allegedly disarmed 348,803 high explosive bombs (40,281 tons) over this timeframe. But Lerner's tonnage nearly eclipses Kane's figures, with the division's total ordnance tally at 40,891, counting *all* munitions gathered in the ETO! Given that Kane's figures encompassed all Ninth Air Force squads, Lerner's assertions become even more untenable.[74]

Fortunately, Ninth Air Force's ordnance officer, Col. W. R. Maxwell, also kept reports based on Maj. Lerner's bomb disposal activities until June. While he also lacked exact numerical data prior to November 1944, Maxwell kept reliable monthly statistics thereafter, noting ordnance tonnage and nationality. Surveying eight months' worth of reports, Maxwell judged that Lerner's bomb squads had cleared 15,523 tons of bombs, plus 782 tons of munitions. Therefore, Ninth Air Force's contributions still amount to more than twice Kane's figure of 7,355 tons. While Army and Com Z squads only dealt with bombs about 10 to 20 percent of the time, ETO Air Force squads handled an overwhelming 70 percent of UXB missions. These discrepancies also suggest that Army and Air Force bomb disposal squads cleared far more ordnance from Western Europe than Col. Kane was aware of at the time.[75]

Capt. Thomas R. Reece, handing out the mail to Ninth Air Force ordnancemen stationed in Germany. Toward the end of the war, Reece worked closely with the 82$^{nd}$ BD Squad on ordnance problems. In November 1945, Reece left the Air Force, returning home to his family in South Bend, Indiana. (*Reece Collection*)

Clearance operations in Germany would continue well into 1946, supervised by late-coming BD units who had seen relatively little action in the theater. Gradually, some longer-serving ordnance teams, such as the battle-tested 16$^{th}$ and 17$^{th}$ BD Squads, made their way back to the States, thanks in part to the War Department's point system. Despite eleven percent casualty rates during the European campaign, morale among veteran officers and enlisted men remained extremely high, with very few disciplinary actions. Maj. John Feldman spoke for many when he wrote: "Despite the trials, hazards, and fears involved, no true Bomb Disposal officer or enlisted man would willingly change his occupation while serving in this United States Army." However, at this time of jubilation, few could forget their beleaguered brethren in the Pacific Theater, still striving against Japan's potent arsenals of destruction.[76]

## Notes

[1] Market-Garden's possibilities have been obscured by decades of speculation by historians and occasional sniping from its participants. Unsurprisingly, Field Marshal Montgomery remained the plan's "unrepentant advocate," arguing that more resources should have been devoted to it. Gen. Omar Bradley felt Antwerp, not Arnhem, should have been Montgomery's objective, and suspected the British commander of trying to upstage him. Cornelius Ryan's popular history, *A Bridge Too Far,* tends to support Bradley's contention, underscoring Monty's bruised ego over Eisenhower's decision to remove him from overall command of land forces after September 1. Americans were upset to learn that Bradley's 12th U.S. Army Group took orders from Montgomery – even though Ike – an American – remained Monty's supreme commander. American historians, such as Williamson Murray and Allan R. Millet tend to fault Montgomery's operational thinking, as well as poor choice in field commanders. However, not all share this view toward his plans. Gerard M. Devlin, a respected historian of airborne operations, believed that Market-Garden may well have ended the war in 1944, if it had been implemented just two weeks earlier. (Bernard L. Montgomery, *The Memoirs of Field Marshal Montgomery* (Cleveland & New York: World Publishing Company, 1958, 258-67; Cornelius Ryan, *A Bridge Too Far* (New York: Simon & Schuster, 1974) 63-79, 599; Bradley & Blair, 326-33; Murray and Millett, 436-44).

[2] Incidentally, the U.S. Army did not begin training EOD personnel for airborne combat operations until 2012. (David Johnson, *V-1 V-2: Hitler's Vengeance on London,* New York: Stein & Day, 1981, 107-199; Lida Mayo, *The Ordnance Department: On Beachhead and Battlefront*, Washington D.C.: Department of Defense, 1991, 274-75).

[3] Historian Russell T. Weigley later proposed that these strategic raids may have delayed Hitler's missile attacks by three months, preventing their use against the Normandy landings. Gen. Paul Deichmann indicated such weapons existed prior to Normandy, but the first V-1s were not launched from Northern France until D plus 5. V-1s "doodlebugs" killed more than 8,000 victims in Great Britain, including some Americans stationed in the U.K. (Paul Deichmann, "Luftwaffe Methods in the Selection of Offensive Weapons, Volume 1," from *USAF Historical Studies*, No. 187 (Manhattan, Kansas: MA/AH Publishing, Sunflower University Press, c. 1985), 70-71; Stephen E. Ambrose, *D-Day, June 6, 1944: The Climactic Battle of World War II* (New York: Simon & Schuster, 1994), 31; B.

Franklin Cooling, "U.S. Army Support of Civil Defense: The Formative Years," from *Military Affairs*, Vol. 35, No. 1 (February 1971), 7-11; Drew Pearson, "Destruction of the Robot," from *Mt. Adams Sun*, 21 July 1944, 2; Russell T. Weigley, *Eisenhower's Lieutenants* (Bloomington: Indiana University Press, 1981), 64-5; Johnson, 107-199; 167; Mayo, 274-75; Reece, 62).

[4] Some V-1s were even equipped to carry propaganda leaflets, as Capt. Wally Collins (77th BD Squad) discovered in early 1945. His discovery initiated a line of enquiry that eventually reached the ETO's Psychological Warfare branch. (Collins, George W. to Commanding General, 50th AAA Brigade, *Propaganda Container in Divers*, 1 February 1945; *Report on New Type Warhead for V-1 Weapon*, 30 December 1944; AFHRA, Maxwell Air Force Base; Technical Information Bulletin No. 32, 15 July 1944. 209-11; Technical Information Bulletin, March 15, 1945; H.H. Bateman to Brig. Gen. Henry B. Sayler, 24 June 1944; Colonel Thomas J. Kane, *Monthly Report of Bomb Disposal Activities*, 13 November 1944; Feldman, *Military History*; Reece, 72.).

[5] *Report on New Type Warhead for V-1 Weapon*, 30 December 1944; AFHRA, Maxwell Air Force Base; Technical Information Bulletin No. 32, 15 July 1944. 209-11; 17th BD Squad, *History;* Johnson, 107-199*; History*; *V Corps*, 343-63.

[6] Technical Information Bulletin No. 32, 15 July 1944. 209-11; George D. Gordon, 68th Ordnance Bomb Disposal Squad Separate, *Report on V-1 Attack on Liege, Belgium, 21-29 November 1944*, 7 December 1944.

[7] Kane & Feldman; Johnson, 107-199; Mayo, 274-75.

[8] Col. Thomas J. Kane to Chief Ordnance Officer ETO, [unused copy] *Report on Operational Activities for October 1944*, 10 November 1944; *History of the Ordnance Bomb Disposal Division,* NARA Records Group 498, 1945, 29-30.

[9] Communication Zone Plan (World War II War Diaries, 7 December 1941 to 31 December 1945, NARA Record Group 38) 27 May 1944; Col. Thomas J. Kane to Chief Ordnance Officer ETO, [unused copy] *Report on Operational Activities for October 1944*, 10 November 1944.

[10] Ibid.

[11] Temporarily, 37th BD Squad's command went to 1st Lt. Anthony Fiala during the Bulge campaign. Dozens of other bomb disposaleers suffered lesser injuries that often went unreported. (Ernie Pyle, "Ordnance Keeps Army in Trim," from *Stars and Stripes*, 27 July 1944, 2; Stars and Stripes Press, *Flaming Bomb: The Story of Ordnance in the ETO*, Paris, France: Desfosses-Neogravure, 1945; 37th Ordnance Bomb Disposal Squad (Separate), unit history, 23 June 1945; 85th Ordnance Bomb Disposal Squad (Separate) to Headquarters, Ninth Air Force, 31 March 1945; Reece, 44-45; Hooper, Appendix III).

[12] Sometime after Lt. Racey's death, Capt. Andrew B. Nicholls took over 146th BD Squad. (Jerome Krieger to Commander, NAVSCOLEOD, *Fact Sheet*, 5 October 1992; Robert Leiendecker, *World War II EOD Data*; National EOD Association Library, Charlottesville VA, 2003; Michael R. Vining, *Explosive Ordnance Disposal Memorial – U. S. Army,* submitted to the EOD Memorial Commission, 15 October 2011; Hooper, 20, Appendix II; www.dtic.mil/dpmo/wwii; www.eodmemorial.org/army.html.)

[13] Jerome Krieger to Commander, NAVSCOLEOD, *Fact Sheet*, 5 October 1992; Robert Leiendecker, *World War II EOD Data*; National EOD Association Library, Charlottesville VA, 2003; Michael R. Vining, *Explosive Ordnance Disposal Memorial – U. S. Army,* submitted to the EOD Memorial Commission, 15 October 2011; Hooper, Appendix III.
[14] Technical Information Bulletins No. 32, 1 May 1944, 146; No. 36, 15 September 1944. 278-79; Tom Hoge, "5 GIs Are Wizards on Nazi Arms" from *Stars and Stripes*, 25 May 1944, 2.
[15] 80th Ordnance Bomb Disposal Squad (Separate), unit history, 29 May 1944 to 11 December 1945; Albert J. Engel to Ninth Air Force Headquarters, *Unexploded Enemy Ammunition*, 9 October 1944.
[16] Paul Deichmann, "Luftwaffe Methods in the Selection of Offensive Weapons, Volume 1," from *USAF Historical Studies*, No. 187 (Manhattan, Kansas: MA/AH Publishing, Sunflower University Press, c. 1985), 43-44; Stars and Stripes Press, *Flaming Bomb: The Story of Ordnance in the ETO*, Paris, France: Desfosses-Neogravure, 1945.
[17] Deichmann, 84.
[18] Colonel Thomas J. Kane, *Top View of Ordnance Bomb Disposal in ETOUSA*. c. 1945; Colonel Thomas J. Kane, *History of the Bomb Disposal Organization in the ETO*, November 1944, 1-6; Kane & Feldman, 1-2.
[19] Colonel Thomas J. Kane, *Top View of Ordnance Bomb Disposal in ETOUSA*. c. 1945; Colonel Thomas J. Kane, *History of the Bomb Disposal Organization in the ETO*, November 1944, 1-6; Headquarters, Ninth Air Force, *Disposal of UXBs*, 28 September 1944.
[20] Major George Schiller to Adjutant, 82nd Ordnance Group. [memorandum] 4 June 1945; Major George Schiller to Colonel Thomas J. Kane. [memorandum] 8 June 1945.
[21] Fort Chatillon was the future home of France's controversial nuclear research program. (George S. Switzer, "Memorial of Martin L. Ehrmann," from *American Mineralogist*, Volume 59, 1974, 414-15; United States Army Air Forces, *Passenger Manifest*, 1 December 1944; Lt. Col. H.G. Davison, *Monthly Report of Bomb Disposal Activities, No. 2*, 2 December 1944; Kane & Feldman, 35-39, Annex 19; Reece, 66).
[22] Major George Schiller to Adjutant, 82nd Ordnance Group. [memorandum] 4 June 1945; Major George Schiller to Colonel Thomas J. Kane. [memorandum] 8 June 1945.
[23] Ironically, the Royal Engineers specifically requested the U.S. Ordnance Department to restrict French access to their principles of bomb disposal – rather difficult to enforce, considering the shared instructional methods between the English-speaking allies. Despite their suspicions toward possible Nazi collaborators or Soviet agents, the American-trained French EOD servicemen trained well and performed remarkably in 1945, and their modern-day compatriots still contend with lethal unexploded ordnance from both world wars. (Lt. Col. H.G. Davison, Bomb *and Munitions School*, 4 October 1944; Kane & Feldman, *Bomb Disposal History*, 3- 4; 10th Ordnance Bomb Disposal Squad (Separate) to

Headquarters, Ninth Air Force, unit history, 15 February 1945 to 28 June 1945.)
[24] Racey's headquarters, the 3054th Ordnance Service Composite Company, served as the school directory, assisted by a mobile detachment of BD cadre. (Col. Thomas J. Kane, *History of the Bomb Disposal Organization in the ETO*, November 1944, 1-6; Captain Joseph T. Racey, *Report of Activities of Ordnance Bomb and Munitions School*, 2-11 October 1944; 234th U.S. Ordnance Bomb Disposal Company, unit record; Kane & Feldman, *Bomb Disposal History*, 3- 4.)
[25] Charles B. McDonald, *European Theater of Operations: The Siegfried Line Campaign* (Washington D.C.: Office of the Chief of Military History, 1963), 207-30, 323-74; Hugh M. Cole, *European Theater of Operations: The Ardennes: Battle of the Bulge* (Washington D.C.: Office of the Chief of Military History, 1965), 19-32; Bradley & Blair, 334-60; Reece, 67-70.
[26] 16th BD Squad, *History*; 17th BD Squad, *History*; *V Corps Operations in the ETO: 6 January 1942 – 9 May 1945* (U.S. Army Historical Section: GPO, Washington D.C., 343-63.
[27] Col. Kane also selected the 68th BD Squad for one of Ordnance's first press releases on bomb disposal, following V-E Day. Their first officer, 1st Lt. Coolie D. Verner, left for other squad commands, leaving T/Sgt. Haasis in charge for several weeks. Eventually, Capt. George D. Gordon took over squad command. (68th Ordnance Bomb Disposal Squad (Separate), unit history, 16 December 1945; James B. Newman to T/Sgt. Walter Haasis, 68th Ordnance Bomb Disposal Squad (Separate), *Commendation*, 12 June 1945; Thomas J. Kane to Commanding Officer, 68th Ordnance Bomb Disposal Squad (Separate), IX Air Force; *Bomb Disposal Publicity*, 11 July 1945; Headquarters, Ninth Air Force to Commanding Officer, 68th Ordnance Bomb Disposal Squad (Separate), *Unit Citation*, 25 November 1944.
[28] 90th Ordnance Bomb Disposal Squad (Separate), unit history, 26 March 1945; Cole, 19-32.
[29] George D. Gordon, 68th Ordnance Bomb Disposal Squad Separate, *Report on V-1 Attack on Liege, Belgium, 21-29 November 1944*, 7 December 1944; 16th BD Squad, *History*; 17th BD Squad, *History*.
[30] 16th BD Squad, *History*; 17th BD Squad, *History*.
[31] 88th Ordnance Bomb Disposal Squad (Separate), unit history, 23 March 1945; 68th BD Squad, *History*.
[32] Bradley & Blair, 334-68; Cole, 19-32, 445-81, 606-48; Gerard M. Devlin, *Paratrooper!* (St. Martin's Press, New York, 1979), 518-51
[33] Capt. Patrick J. Hogan of St. Paul, Minnesota, was misidentified as Hodges by the military newspaper. During the operation against Japan, Hogan replaced the slain commander of 5th Squad, and remained in charge of it until the war's end. (*Stars and Stripes*, "Yanks Cool Off Hot 'Welcome' Left by Enemy, 21 December 1944, 3; *History of the Fifth Ordnance Bomb Disposal Squad,* 28 February 1945.)
[34] This was part of Bradley's Operation *Lumberjack* against the Hürtgen Forest. (Stars and Stripes Press, *"Lightning: The Story of the 78th Infantry Division,"* Paris, France: Desfosses-Neogravure, 1945; Bradley & Blair, 401-4.)
[35] Charles B. McDonald, *European Theater of Operations: The Last Offensive.*

(Washington D.C.: Office of the Chief of Military History, 1973), 70-83; *"Lightning: The Story of the 78th Infantry Division;"* *V Corps*, 343-63, 378-80; 16th BD Squad, *History*; 17th BD Squad, *History*; Weigley, 603.

36 Ibid.

37 "Personal Memoirs of Lieutenant General Frank L. Camm," available from http://62vgd.de/78th/Frank_Camm/, Internet, accessed 21 January 2012; 16th BD Squad, *History*; 17th BD Squad, *History*.

38 Charles B. McDonald, *European Theater of Operations: The Last Offensive*. (Washington D.C.: Office of the Chief of Military History, 1973), 70-83; *"Lightning: The Story of the 78th Infantry Division;"* *V Corps*, 343-63, 378-80; 16th BD Squad, *History*; 17th BD Squad, *History*; Camm; Weigley, 603.

39 Ibid.

40 Charles B. McDonald, *European Theater of Operations: The Last Offensive*. (Washington D.C.: Office of the Chief of Military History, 1973), 70-83; *"Lightning: The Story of the 78th Infantry Division;"* *V Corps*, 343-63, 378-80; 16th BD Squad, *History*; 17th BD Squad, *History*; Camm; Weigley, 603.

41 Ibid.

42 Ibid.

43 Ibid.

44 Ibid.

45 161st BD Squad covered Crow's sectors until his recovery, and their report confirms his injuries at the Schwammenauel Dam. (161st Ordnance Bomb Disposal Squad (Separate), unit history, c. 1945; 16th BD Squad, *History*; 17th BD Squad, *History*; *V Corps*, 343-63, 378-80; Camm; McDonald, 81-3.)

46 It turns out Hitler had in fact ordered the Roer Dams destroyed, but fortunately, Gen. von Manteuffel did not carry out these instructions. (Ibid.)

47 16th BD Squad, *History*; 17th BD Squad, *History*.

48 "German Dam Explored by Yank Patrol," from *Stars and Stripes*, c. 1945, from Joseph C. Pilcher scrapbook; Ronald Felton to Marsha Frost, personal letter, 2 February 1987.

49 30th Ordnance Bomb Disposal Squad (Separate), unit history, c. 1945; Kane & Feldman, *History*, 7.

50 When the Allied 12th Army Group neglected to decorate Schuck after V-E Day, Capt. Alan G. Knox appealed personally to Kane for his sergeant's Bronze Star. (233rd Ordnance Bomb Disposal Platoon, unit history, April-May 1945; Ninth Army Headquarters, *General Orders 103*, 9 April 1945; Captain Alan G. Knox to Colonel Thomas J. Kane, *Recommendation for Award of Bronze Star Medal*, c. 1946; Kane & Feldman, 1-2; Hooper, 22.)

51 77th Ordnance Bomb Disposal Squad (Separate), unit history, 3 March 1945 to 15 December 1945; Reece, 73-74.

52 Reece suffered from post-traumatic experiences, partly stemming from these sad experiences. Wally Collins is still remembered gratefully by the local Dutch for his sacrifice. He was replaced by 1st Lt. Albert Engel as 77th BD Squad's leader. (Jerome Krieger to Commander, NAVSCOLEOD, *Fact Sheet*, 5 October 1992; Robert Leiendecker, *World War II EOD Data*; National EOD Association Library,

Charlottesville VA, 2003; Michael R. Vining, *Explosive Ordnance Disposal Memorial – U. S. Army,* submitted to the EOD Memorial Commission, 15 October 2011; 77th Squad, *History*; Reece, 73-74.)

[53] Paul Deichmann, "Luftwaffe Methods in the Selection of Offensive Weapons, Volume 1," from *USAF Historical Studies*, No. 187 (Manhattan, Kansas: MA/AH Publishing, Sunflower University Press, c. 1985), 22; 86th Ordnance Bomb Disposal Squad (Separate), unit history, 14 December 1945;

[54] 46th Ordnance Bomb Disposal Squad (Separate), unit history, 6 March 1944 to 26 May 1945; 31st Ordnance Bomb Disposal Squad (Separate), unit history, 1945; Chris Ransted, *Bomb Disposal and the British Casualties of WW2*, United Kingdom: self-published, 2003, 74-79; Jerome Krieger to Commander, NAVSCOLEOD, *Fact Sheet*, 5 October 1992; Robert Leiendecker, *World War II EOD Data*; National EOD Association Library, Charlottesville VA, 2003; Michael R. Vining, *Explosive Ordnance Disposal Memorial – U. S. Army,* submitted to the EOD Memorial Commission, 15 October 2011.

[55] Robert E. Leiendecker, *Bomb Disposal, The Early Years of Explosive Ordnance Disposal (An Informal History)*, Charlottesville, Virginia: NATEODA Press, 2012, 519-22; 161st Ordnance Bomb Disposal Squad (Separate), unit history, 1944-45.

[56] Additionally, two Army engineers and two members of 3275th Quartermaster Salvage Company were injured in the S-mine incident. (161st BD Squad, *History*.)

[57] *History of the Ordnance Bomb Disposal Division,* NARA Records Group 498, 1945, 39-40.

[58] Col. Thomas J. Kane, *Report of Conference with German Bomb Disposal Officer*, 8 October 1944; Switzer, 414-15.

[59] Col. Thomas J. Kane, *Report of Conference with German Bomb Disposal Officer*, 8 October 1944; Hooper, 30.

[60] Headquarters USFET MIS Center, *Final Interrogation Report No. 28*, Hanz Heinz Manderscheid, 5 September 1945; Kane, *Report of Conference.*

[61] Kane, *Report of Conference.*

[62] Kane, *Report of Conference.*

[63] Kane, *Report of Conference.*

[64] Kane, *Report of Conference.*

[65] U.S. Naval Advanced Amphibious Base Falmouth-Cornwall, *War Diaries*, 1 June 1944 (World War II War Diaries, 7 December 1941 to 31 December 1945, NARA Record Group 38); Kane, *Report of Conference.*

[66] Incidentally, John Feldman had briefly experimented with a means to detonate butterfly bombs, using a smoke projector to dislodge them on the ground. He referred to this invention as a "vortex gun," but its results were inconclusive. (Paul Deichmann, "Luftwaffe Methods in the Selection of Offensive Weapons, Volume 1," from *USAF Historical Studies*, No. 187 (Manhattan, Kansas: MA/AH Publishing, Sunflower University Press, c. 1985), 31-33; Edward J. Barry Jr., *History of the 31st U.S. Ordnance Bomb Squad*, 1945; Deichmann, 31-33; Kane, *Report of Conference*; Maria Feldman interviews; Hooper, 30).

[67] V Corps to Captain Joseph C. Pilcher and Technician Fifth Grade Joseph Olszewski, *Citations for Bronze Star*, 30 May 1945; 17th BD Squad, *History*.

---

68 161st Squad's commander received his long overdue promotion to First Lieutenant on April 21, but seems to have missed out on a medal for his exploits. On April 25, one of these concealable J-Feders probably ignited Bunker 50 at a Wulfen ammo dump, leaving behind a crater almost 75 yards across. Noting lax security at XVI Corps headquarters, 233rd Ordnance BD Platoon also discovered five similar devices in nearby Bunker 51 on April 26. (161st BD Squad, *History*; 233rd Ordnance Bomb Disposal Platoon, unit history, April-May 1945).

69 17th BD Squad, *History*; Bradley & Blair, 433-34.

70 Czechoslovakia's later fate under Communism troubled Joe deeply, partly because the Czechs were forbidden to acknowledge the role of Americans in their deliverance from National Socialism. Pilcher's scrapbook included a post-Cold War article on the Czech Republic's belated gratitude to V Corps for their freedom. (Kane & Feldman, 7; 31st BD Squad History; Joseph Pilcher Jr., interview; Jesse Pilcher, interview; Captain Joseph C. Pilcher, *Certificate of Service* [War Department AGO Form 53-98], 5 December 1945; "Captain Pilcher, Bomb Demolisher, Has String of Coveted Medals," [undated article] c. 1945, from *Pilcher Scrapbook*.)

71 Thomas J. Kane and John. E. Feldman, *History of the Ordnance Bomb Disposal Division From D-Day to VE-Day in Europe* (Headquarters Communication Zone ETOUSA, 1945), 1-8; Ordnance Technical Services, *ETO Bomb Disposal History,* NARA Records Group 498, 1945, 15.

72 Kane & Feldman, 1-8.

73 Ordnance Technical Services, *ETO Bomb Disposal History,* NARA Records Group 498, 1945; Kane & Feldman, 1-8.

74 *Consolidated History of Bomb Disposal in the Ninth Air Force*. May 1945, 1-5; Kane & Feldman, 1-8.

75 Headquarters, Ninth Air Force to Ordnance Department, *Incident Reports*, 20 September 1944; Headquarters, Ninth Air Force to Ordnance Department, *Disposal of UXBs*, 28 September 1944; Headquarters, Ninth Air Force, Office of the Ordnance Officer, *Monthly Ordnance Activities Reports* (AFHRA 533.804), August 1944 to June 1945; Ordnance Technical Services, *ETO Bomb Disposal History,* NARA Records Group 498, 1945, 33-34.

76 Kane & Feldman, 8.

# CHAPTER SEVEN

# BASTARD OUTFITS: GUADALCANAL TO V-J DAY (1942-45)

In January 1942, at the start of Japan's bid to conquer the Pacific, no bomb disposal organizations existed for Army and Navy forces located at Pearl Harbor, Oahu or Clark Field, Luzon. Save for independent visits from Draper Kauffman and John Feldman, the emerging bomb disposal schools were unable to deploy units in time to reinforce the Philippines. However, thanks to Japan's ongoing war with China, U.S. and British Imperial sources were able to identify many different armor-piercing (AP) bombs, some models weighing as much as 1000 kilograms. Japan also utilized several anti-personnel bombs, ranging from 12 to 50 kilograms.[1]

At the start, British experts were certain Japan had no anti-withdrawal circuits akin to the German Zus-40. However, Japan soon rectified this, thanks to their contacts with Nazi Germany. Since Japan's Army and Navy had separate air forces, each branch used different configurations. Special tools for exclusive use on Japanese bombs were devised by late 1942. Throughout the Pacific Theater, American disposaleers repaid their British compatriots by providing data on Japanese explosives. Yet, the lack of a Pacific equivalent to Kane's ETO division forced disposaleers to learn from trial and error, especially with naval ordnance.[2]

Col. Kane's original inspection schedule had included legs to Soviet Russia and the Pacific Theater. However, his lengthy illness in Cairo curtailed such plans, so he wrapped up his tour in China-Burma-India. Arriving in New Delhi on May 1, 1943, Kane observed that Royal Engineers and Royal Air Force teams existed in "sufficient number to cover adequately [the Allied] Bomb Disposal service in India." Kane favorably reviewed "certain India Army field units," who were using British equipment and methods. Royal Indian bomb squads also contributed discoveries to the ordnance network created by the Western alliance. One of Aberdeen's TIBs later credited a Royal Indian bomb disposal section with discovering a new Japanese anti-aircraft missile.[3]

Before leaving India, Kane held discussions with three U.S. bomb disposal officers under Brig. Gen. Benjamin Ferris (Tenth Air Force). By this stage, all three of these lieutenants had trained emergency teams to cover "certain important American installations" based in New Delhi and Bombay (Mumbai). Kane recommended that two or three separate squads should be dispatched, but the U.S. Army's limited presence in India seems to indicate no pressing need for more ordnance support.[4]

On May 7, Kane flew to Kunming, a center of Chinese Nationalist resistance against Japan. Originally, two officers from Aberdeen Proving Ground had been allotted to Northern China, but Kunming had not received them by the time of Kane's visit. Over his brief stay, Kane conferred with Brig. Gen. Edgar Glenn (Fourteenth Air Force), commander of CBI's most vulnerable sector. As future U.S. ground forces arrived in Kunming, Kane felt more "organic" units were necessary, coordinated by a qualified Ordnance officer. As with New Delhi, Kane requested at least one separate squad for each U.S. Air Force Group, primarily to train volunteers. However, as with India, the Ordnance Department did not consider Northern China a vital enough theater.[5]

Kane noted "Chinese agencies" were responsible for bomb disposal in civilian sectors, but offered no comments on their capability. Throughout the Pacific War, U. S. and British units often trained "local indigenous personnel" to recognize and sometimes remove unexploded ordnance. U.S. bomb disposal squads began examining captured Japanese weaponry for "booby traps and serviceability." Those items judged to be safe were subsequently shipped to aid the Nationalist Chinese.[6]

In June 1943, Col. Kane returned to Aberdeen Proving Ground, traveling one week by plane. Ultimately, Kane left little guidance for his Pacific-based disposaleers. Before departing the CBI Theater, Kane conceded that separate squads could perform general ordnance functions, such as ammunition handling, but only after completing primary duties.[7]

Despite Kane's absence, his spirit of amity still influenced cooperative efforts between U.S. and British Commonwealth bomb disposal men. Until 1944, Australian Royal Engineers stationed at Bonegilla instructed dozens of U.S. Army and Navy technicians in UXBs and other ordnance. Later on, U.S. "mobile bomb disposal schools" had taken over this duty, providing refresher courses for their own engineers and ordnance men. Aberdeen Proving Ground continued to circulate Technical Information Bulletins (TIBs) across the Pacific departments, even as their units scattered to different commands, thus rendering secure channels all but impossible during this pre-digital era. Lacking an actual training center, disposaleers in the Pacific Theater became increasingly self-reliant.[8]

By the time Kane returned stateside in mid-1943, Aberdeen Proving Ground had sent out Army disposaleers to all three Pacific Theater departments: Central Pacific (Hawaii), South Pacific (New Guinea & Philippines), and North Pacific (Alaska). Over the course of one year, two U.S. Army bomb disposal companies arrived, alongside two U.S. Marine bomb disposal companies and several Navy mine disposal teams. Navy teams usually consisted of one officer and a rating, and thus, were limited in number and operational range. As the Marines lost their UXB specialists to attrition, they trained combat engineers in many bomb disposal tasks. They cooperated frequently with Army units, experiencing many of the same hazards. Eventually, "squads separate" replaced Army companies in the Pacific Theater. As with other theaters, Kane's worst predictions came true, as Army squads were occasionally misused by infantry division commanders, who employed them as general ordnancemen, combat engineers, or even cavalry scouts.[9]

Having crushed the Japanese fleet's offensive capabilities at Midway and secured Australia from further attacks, Adm. Chester Nimitz and Gen. Douglas MacArthur subsequently joined forces in their "Twin Drive" strategy aimed at liberating the Philippines and conquering the Japanese home islands. Nimitz and MacArthur received one Army bomb disposal company each, in addition to Marine and Navy elements. The first one, 232$^{nd}$ BD Company, arrived at Honolulu in August 1942. MacArthur did not receive 237$^{th}$ BD Company until that November, just in time to participate in the closing stages of Guadalcanal. Meanwhile, two smaller units, the 5$^{th}$ and 7$^{th}$ BD Squads, were shipped over to Alaska to contend with Japan's designs against America's northern outposts. Each band of ordnancemen would experience the ferocity of war firsthand.[10]

* * *

Based at Schofield Barracks, Hawaii, Capt. George Clifford Sarauw supervised 232$^{nd}$ BD Company, responsible for the Central Pacific. Clifford, a former infantry sergeant, had an almost cherubic face that offset his bullish stature and determined chin. Just before departure, he bade farewell to his young wife, Margaret, in San Francisco. Popular with his enlisted men, Clifford kept them active with routine ordnance tasks. One such assignment involved clearing a warehouse full of jerry-built mines stored in case of invasion. They also continued to find Japanese UXBs from the Pearl Harbor raid. By June 1943, Clifford's efficient style won an appointment to Lt. Gen. R. C. Richardson's staff. 1$^{st}$ Lt. Harry Miller, a well-liked OCS graduate, took over Sarauw's former company for its remaining term of service. On November 10, 232nd Company reorganized into eight separate squads, and five days afterward, 237th Company followed suit in the South Pacific.[11]

Early on, Army disposaleers stationed in Hawaii were sent out on routine calls to pick up leftover Japanese ordnance from the Pearl Harbor raids, such as the "dud" aircraft bomb shown in this picture. (*Vining Collection*)

| Original Bomb Disposal Company | Date Reorganized | New Squad Separate Designations |
|---|---|---|
| **232nd Ord. BD Company (Capt. Clifford Sarauw)** | 11/10/1943 | **92nd to 100th BD Squads (Central Pacific)** |
| **237th Ord. BD Company (Capt. Robert G. Fisher)** | 11/15/1943 | **101st to 109th BD Squads (South Pacific)** |

Clifford Sarauw could have remained as a staff officer in Honolulu, with the likelihood of promotion to major. Instead, he elected to take an active field command. By mid-November 1943, Clifford had assumed charge of 92nd BD Squad, now attached to Maj. Gen. Ralph C. Smith's 27th Infantry, a National Guard division notorious for its lack of discipline.

During the Gilbert Islands campaign, Smith's infantrymen had suffered criticism by the U.S. Marines for perceived slowness on Makin Island. While the Marines carried out the majority of the Pacific island landings, the Army deployed alongside them. Oftentimes, the two services shared their resources and specialists. Marine divisions or amphibious corps typically included one bomb disposal company, supervised by combat engineer battalions. Meanwhile, Pacific-based Army divisions usually carried one or two separate squads, administrated by an ordnance company whenever practicable.[12]

For 27th Division's impending landing on Pitt Island, Clifford Sarauw's 92nd BD Squad deployed with the 727th Ordnance Company, a light maintenance unit responsible for supporting the entire division. Sarauw's unit was comprised of seven men handpicked from his disbanded company. Enlisted technicians were supervised by T/Sgt. Arthur J. Zellmer of Lone Wolf, Oklahoma, who had won the Army's Soldier Medal for "singlehandedly preventing a demolition and bomb storage site from exploding." Sarauw's team also included two "buck" sergeants, Eldon Conley and Francis H. Zurn, At age thirty-seven, Zurn was the oldest squad member in 1943. Four ordnance technicians; Harry L. Babbin, Charles M. Grove, Raymond J. Rondeau, and T/5 Elmer J. Craddock rounded out Sarauw's enlisted personnel.[13]

On November 20, 1943, Capt. Sarauw's team landed with the 27th Infantry on Pitt Island, sometimes known as Butaritari. Pitt Island, deserted by its erstwhile Japanese defenders, contained an airstrip connecting the Marshall Islands to distant supply bases. Patrolling this island's lightly reinforced positions, Capt. Sarauw confirmed that they were "not mined, nor were any booby traps found." However, Clifford observed "carelessness on the part of troops during the initial operations." According to Sarauw's report, the infantry's lax behavior during this maneuver might have caused "a great number of casualties… in the event that traps had been set" on the beachhead.

Over the Christmas holidays, Clifford's ordnancemen had ample opportunities to practice their trades: no fewer than five Japanese Navy bomber squadrons paid visits to lonely Pitt Island. Sarauw personally disarmed over twenty "Jap" UXBs left behind by these persistent raiders. While based at Makin Atoll, Capt. Sarauw's team carried out similar bomb disposal assignments across the Gilbert, Marshall, and Marianas Islands. During the coming months, the 92nd Bomb Disposal Squad gained a theater-wide reputation for its professionalism and efficiency.[14]

Sgt. George Clifford Sarauw, 1st Infantry Division. (*Sarauw Collection*)

One joint operation, *Flintlock*, required Marines from the Fifth Amphibious Force (PHIBFOR) to link up with the 7th Infantry Division. Departing from Hawaii on January 22, 1944, U.S. forces converged on Kwajalein Atoll, not knowing its Japanese captors had recently evacuated. Landing with 7th Infantry Division's "special troops," 1st Lt. J.D. Campbell's 93rd BD Squad encountered Japanese mines and booby-traps. In early February, Capt. Sarauw received classified orders by radio to assist Campbell with his workload. This arduous job lasted several weeks, and in May, Clifford's men were granted three months on Oahu.[15]

After recuperating at Hawaii, 92nd Squad proceeded to their new host: Maj. Gen. A. D. Bruce's 77th Infantry Division, U.S. Army XIV Corps. On July 23, the 77th Division joined U.S. Marines for the liberation of Guam, a much tougher landing than Kwajalein. Disposaleers from Army and Marine units were kept busy patrolling for beachside mines and evacuating civilians, in addition to their "normal duties." Fortunately, booby trapping was "not extensive and was often crude." On one grisly occasion, a "yardstick mine" had been wired to a dead Japanese soldier.[16]

All through the U.S. landings at Gazelle Harbor, mobile Japanese gun crews shelled the 111st Amphibious Corps. They were hard to trace, owing to their rapid escape from Motupena Point. As a parting shot, Japanese gunners fired on two U.S. Navy torpedo boats, sinking PT-251. Later that morning, Capt. Sarauw's "bomb disposal experts" responded to a call to remove a live 57mm round from one of PT-252's portside torpedoes. Incredibly, a Japanese armor-piercing shell had struck a torpedo warhead, but failed to go off. Sarauw removed it safely.[17]

Following the successful wrap-up at Guam, each 92nd BD Squad member received a Bronze Star; T/Sgt. Arthur J. Zellmer's third overall. 92nd Squad's top noncom soon received a rare battlefield commission to second lieutenant. Under rather exceptional circumstances, 92nd Squad was permitted to retain both its officers, while Sgt. Francis Zum was duly advanced to technical sergeant. For the remainder of its Pacific service, Sarauw's team would consist of eight personnel instead of seven.[18]

Still attached to 77th Infantry Division, Sarauw's men were placed on routine ordnance duty at Guam. Even with natives helping with manual labor, 92nd Squad routinely suffered from overwork. In December 1944, Capt. Sarauw politely directed his divisional commander to review the proper functions of ordnance disposal squads. "The requirements of [77th] Division… [have] to date been in excess of the capabilities of this unit." Once again, the presence of a central administration might have ameliorated their situation. Until 1945, one of the Army's best squads had been temporarily sidelined by red tape and poor administration.[19]

* * *

Detached by Aberdeen Proving Ground to the South Pacific Department, the 237th BD Company had arrived on Guadalcanal back in October 1942. Their commander, Capt. Robert G. Fisher, hailed from Fresno, California. Fisher's unit had deployed midway through America's crucial struggle for air bases in the Southern Pacific. For six grueling months, Marines and later on, Army divisions dug in tenaciously, defending Guadalcanal's precious Henderson Field, until they declared victory on February 9, 1943. After the Marines were relieved that previous December, Capt. Fisher's bomb disposal company took over from the Navy detachment already based at Henderson Field.[20]

Following Guadalcanal, the South Pacific's "island-hopping" strategy required more ordnance support than Gen. MacArthur possessed. Until the closing months of 1943, most newly-organized separate squads were still being sent to the Mediterranean and European Theaters. However, MacArthur's chief of ordnance, Col. Jonathan L. Holman, compensated for the Army's shortages by training "organic" mine-disposal sections, usually with help from the Royal Australian Engineers. Usually, such "unofficial" disposaleers were led by qualified Ordnance School graduates. During Operation *Cartwheel*, a seven-man ordnance squad culled from ammo handlers with the 158th Regimental Combat Team's oversaw successful mine and UXB removals during MacArthur's bid to liberate New Guinea and Papua from their Japanese occupiers.[21]

On June 1, 1943, Capt. Fisher's 167 officers and men began operating as four separate platoons. For five months, they carried out ordnance assignments in the New Hebrides, an archipelago jointly under British and Free French jurisdiction. Ernie Neeper, then a private first class serving with 237th Co., recalled his platoon's arduous ocean-going schedule: "We spent 110 days traveling between different Pacific islands… on LCIs, LSTs, and Liberty Ships." He recollected the Liberty Ships were the least uncomfortable mode of transportation, but he still got seasick. Neeper also described lugging his platoon's heavy steam-sterilizer from place to place, seeking out Japanese UXBs among the New Hebrides.[22]

In July 1943, one of Capt. Fisher's officers, 1st Lt. Delafield H. Wyckoff, received new orders for the Central Solomons, New Georgia. At this time, the 37th Infantry Division required a disposal officer for their planned assault on Munda Island. On July 17, Wyckoff departed Guadalcanal aboard LST-342, a cargo transport helmed by Cdr. Paul Slawson. Just before 1:30 a.m. on July 18, Slawson's unescorted LST fatefully crossed paths with a Japanese submarine. One deadly torpedo shivered through the water, shattering the vulnerable craft in two.[23]

According to the Navy's chief eyewitness, First Officer T. B. Montgomery, there were no secondary explosions, only a clean break amidships. Montgomery observed LST 342's stern section sinking quickly off the coast of Ghavutu, carrying a majority of the ship's passengers below the depths of Purvis Bay. Montgomery noted that the weather was rainy, and most of his crew and passengers were sleeping below-decks. Had they slept topside, fewer casualties might have resulted. Incredibly, LST-342's bow section was able to right itself, and after several tense hours, the survivors were located by friendly vessels that towed their wreck to nearby Florida Island. Ultimately, 121 Americans were killed by the torpedo's blast or drowned aboard the stern section. Sadly, Lt. Delafield Wyckoff was not among LST-342's 158 survivors.[24]

By autumn 1943, the First Marine Amphibious Corps had landed on the island of Bougainville, with the Army's 37th Infantry Division in tow. Marines lacked ordnance support, so the 37th Division made its services available, courtesy of the 737th Ordnance Company (Light Maintenance), which arrived with its bomb disposal complement on November 5, 1943. 102nd and 103rd BD Squads handled nearly all Bougainville UXB calls, supervised by 1st Lt. William E. Comstock. Comstock soon located a couple of Japanese 63 kilogram bombs with "hitherto unknown" fuze designs. On November 11, Comstock and two of his men recovered a live torpedo from a downed Japanese bomber. Comstock sent these items stateside through 737th Ordnance Company's intelligence section.[25]

On November 15, 1943, Capt. Fisher's 237th BD Company permanently disbanded into squads, pursuant to War Department policy. Even before that point, Fisher's company had broken into separate elements to join incoming Army divisions. Combined with units derived from Sarauw's old company, this adjustment yielded eighteen "squads separate" to the Pacific Theater, divided evenly between the Central and South Pacific departments. Capt. Fisher's section spent the winter attached to the First Island Command in New Caledonia, where they engaged in camp activities and waited for reinforcements.[26]

* * *

In early 1944, Gen. MacArthur's began receiving much-needed reinforcements at New Guinea. In the past, he had relied largely on Australian engineers or U.S. Marines to cover his South Pacific amphibious landings. However, the activation of Gen. Walter Krueger's

U.S. Sixth Army in Brisbane, Australia soon brought infusions of new blood, including ordnance specialists. Krueger's capable ordnance chief, Col. Philip G. Blackmore, quickly organized his own bomb disposal section, consisting of three officers and eight enlisted men, culled from the 21st Medium Maintenance Ordnance Company.[27]

One of these officers, Capt. Vandel "Bud" Kovar, acted as Sixth Army's top bomb disposal officer until 1945. Kovar, an athletic VMI graduate, had been one of Kane's earliest bomb disposal school students, completing the second class offered at Aberdeen. Regrettably, Kovar suffered from a perennial shortage of qualified officers, owing to ETO priorities as well as rampant tropical illness. 1st Lt. James S. Brown remembered being a mere lieutenant "rubbing elbows with lieutenant colonels and upward" within the Sixth Army hierarchy. Responsible for all ordnance removal across the developing Southwest Pacific Department, "Bud" Kovar eventually received a major's clusters for his service.[28]

MacArthur's first acquisition, the 100th BD Squad, had previously earned Bronze Stars for supporting Army operations across the Northern Solomon Islands. With 1st Lt. Sidney F. Smith in charge, the squad had arrived at Sixth Army's new headquarters: Munda Island, New Georgia. Col. Blackmore's requests for more ordnance support had resulted in Smith's operational transfer to Munda. Starting in mid-December 1943, Smith's men located and disarmed thousands of Japanese explosives. Within their first two weeks alone, 100th Squad had discovered a new Japanese fuze design as well as their "anti-parked" improvised bomb. During this period, Sidney Smith's men often bivouacked and collaborated with their friendly counterparts in the Royal Australian Air Force.[29]

Also present on Munda, Maj. Robert G. Fisher had supervised training and organization for several squads commissioned from his original 237th BD Company. They were mostly experienced ordnancemen, hardened by the South Pacific climate. For the time being, the 109th BD Squad remained attached to Army Service Command at Guadalcanal. However, the 107th BD Squad's captain, Alberto Gavaldon, won a Bronze Star in this period for repeatedly showing "great personal courage" as he dodged small arms fire to remove duds, booby traps, and mines. Meanwhile, the 108th BD Squad, under 1st Lt. Leonard J. Stuart, had performed exceedingly well in the Bismarck Archipelago. All three of these teams, plus Sidney Smith's 100th Squad, would be required for the second stage of MacArthur's New Guinea-Papua campaign in spring 1944.[30]

Despite MacArthur's successes on New Guinea that previous year, pockets of Japanese invaders still resisted Allied efforts to dislodge them. On April 22, 1944, the Allies launched dual operations, *Reckless* and *Persecution*, designed to knock out Japanese supply bases at Hollandia and Aitape. The latter village, situated on the northern coast of New Guinea, fell to the Allies within a day. Aitape yielded up its valuable airstrips. With the still-potent Japanese 18th Army isolated on nearby Wewak, MacArthur's long-awaited path to the Philippines now lay open.[31]

1st Lt. Carmel J. Cirocco rose from the enlisted ranks to become an Army bomb disposal officer based solely on his leadership potential and technical skills, like many others who joined Kane's all-volunteer organization. (*Cirocco Collection*)

Just before the kick-off, 1st Lt. Carmel J. Cirocco had arrived on Guadalcanal to assume command over 109th BD Squad. Formerly an enlisted man, T/Sgt. Cirocco had graduated from OCS and transferred to bomb disposal at Col. Kane's urging. After an uneventful year at Panama with the 233rd BD Company, Carl had returned by October 1943 to await reassignment to an available squad. Since Maj. Robert Fisher's recent elevation to staff officer, 109th Squad now lacked its own commander. Cirocco accepted this new duty station, and by June 1944, his personnel had joined forces with Smith's 100th Squad, also bound for New Guinea. After an entire week aboard the U.S.S. *Serpens*, all fourteen disposaleers disembarked at New Zealand, where they were assigned to 743rd Ordnance Light Maintenance Company, 43rd Infantry Division.[32]

That July, 43rd Infantry finally arrived at Aitape, now a staging ground for Sixth Army's impending Philippines campaign. 109th BD Squad ranged across New Guinea's interior, where Australian units were still engaged with Japanese stragglers. On August 25, they patrolled by a recently destroyed enemy position, only to discover some scorched Japanese artillery shells. Recognizing a hazard to marching infantry, Lt. Cirocco and his men began clearing damaged 12.7 inch rounds. Suddenly, one of the shells hissed in Lt. Cirocco's hands. Thinking quickly, Carl threw the projectile far away enough to save his life, but he nonetheless took shell fragments across his left arm and upper chest. One splinter came dangerously close to Carl's heart. On September 13, T/Sgt. Frank O'Leary reported his CO "evacuated and dropped from the rolls," indicating doubts as to Lt. Cirocco's future. Later that month, 2nd Lt. Walter D. Garland took over 109th Squad, at least for the present.[33]

Throughout 1944, a combination of Army ordnancemen, Navy mine disposal teams, and Marine combat engineers scoured South and Central Pacific islands, bearing such famous names as Peleliu, Tinian, and Saipan. During February, 97th BD Squad operated in the Eastern Mandates, where they cleared the Kwajalein Atoll. Serving in the Marshall Islands, 93rd BD Squad's commander, 1st Lt. James D. Campbell, was seriously wounded on 11 March 1944. 106th BD Squad (1st Lt. Albert Wheeler) contributed to the successful Northern Solomons campaign. On June 17, T/5 Clarence W. Bobrowski was injured while disarming a Japanese Type 88 artillery fuze. That same month, both 94th and 95th Squads supported the 27th Infantry Division's troubled assault landing on Saipan. 97th BD Squad operated across the Eastern Mandates and cleared the Kwajalein Atoll. Thanks to combined efforts of American ordnance units across the Gilbert, Marshall, and Mariana island chains, these former enemy outposts were quickly transformed into stepping stones toward Japan.[34]

* * *

In 1943, United States and Canadian forces had just driven Imperial Japanese forces from their dangerous lodgments in the Alaska Territory. Often ignored in the annals of World War II, the Aleutian Islands campaign was admittedly secondary to the Central and South Pacific. Nevertheless, Japan's deliberate invasion of sovereign territory erupted into one of the conflict's bloodiest encounters. Gone unchecked, Japan might have utilized these Alaskan islands as important staging areas for a major invasion of the Northwest. At minimum, Attu and Kiska provided airbases to launch raids against the vulnerable coastlines.

Despite their avowed purpose of "co-prosperity," Japanese forces were responsible for the brutal subjugation of peoples in Malaysia, Burma, and elsewhere. Native Americans also felt the iron claw of oppression. When the Emperor's forces landed on Attu and Kiska in early 1942, more than two hundred indigenous Aleut Indians were also displaced and imprisoned by Japanese captors. In 1943, hundreds of American servicemen were to die regaining these barren rocks from their hard-bitten Japanese foes. Furthermore, Attu set the stage for future Pacific island engagements, such as Guam and Tinian, where few enemy soldiers were captured alive.[35]

Adm. Isoroku Yamamoto's decision to invade the Alaskan territory coincided with his ambitious Midway campaign. On June 3, Japanese planes commenced their raid on Dutch Harbor, a bold yet vain diversionary strike. Carriers used against Alaska might have been better utilized at Midway Island, where U.S. Navy intelligence predicted the main Japanese fleet would strike. Despite the astounding American victory on June 4, Yamamoto mulled over ways to avenge his losses and save face. Between June and September 1942, Tokyo sent thousands of men to secure the two outermost Aleutians. Dodging a naval dragnet, Japanese subs continually supplied the twin garrisons over the winter months. By April 1943, over 1,500 Japanese soldiers and sailors controlled Attu, while 5,300 others held the larger island, Kiska.[36]

Coupled with abortive coastal raids over Oregon, full-blown invasion fears heightened for a time. Fearing interceptions, Lend Lease traffic across the Bering Straits even halted temporarily. But Japan's Fifth Pacific Fleet did not exploit their footholds sufficiently, giving Washington time to reinforce Alaska. Both islands were then subjected to intense bombardment. U.S. and Canadian planes were responsible for leveling Attu's one village in order to deny shelter to Japanese invaders.[37]

Before the North Pacific buildup in late 1942, Maj. Gen. Simon B. Buckner had received three bomb disposal officers at Ft. Richardson:

Capt. Clair A. Hill and two first lieutenants, George C. Heim and George F. Switzer. At the headquarters level, Capt. Hill trained *ad hoc* ordnance teams, including Sgt. R. M. "Dix" Fetzer and his fellow "Nuts," who later provided combat support to infantry or engineers, "whoever needed our services." Fetzer recalled his team's informal yet hectic work schedule throughout the Alaska campaign: "Whoever had gotten the most sleep responded and took care of the problem."[38]

In early 1943, overall U.S. forces at Fairbanks, Alaska swelled from 21,500 to 40,424. These reinforcements included another provisional ordnance team, recruited from 1741st Ordnance Maintenance Company (Aviation) and attached temporarily to 7th U.S. Infantry Division. Originally destined for North Africa, Maj. Gen. Albert Brown's entire division received a last-minute transfer from the Mojave Desert. T/5 Clarence Fulcher of 1741st Co., a Virginian, once worked for Fieldcrest Mill as a supply manager. After basic training at Camp Lee, Clarence went to the Ordnance School, where "he had it made working with machinery." Sent to bomb disposal school, Clarence ended up in general ordnance, but over in Alaska, explosives technicians were in short supply. "We learned a little bit at Aberdeen, but we learned a lot more in the field," Fulcher later said about his service in the Aleutian Islands.[39]

On May 11, 1943, 7th Infantry Division's grunts spearheaded Operation *Sandcrab*, one of the Army's costliest battles in the Pacific. Seventy-one Americans were killed or wounded to one hundred Japanese, a staggering ratio second only to Iwo Jima. Yet, such sacrifices removed a psychological threat to continental security, as well as freeing up Army forces for later campaigns in the Central Pacific. Above and beyond, their efforts discouraged Japan from possibly building forward launch stations for their *Fu-Go* balloon bombs, unveiled late in the coming year.[40]

Weather conditions and dense fog hindered visibility and delayed *Sandcrab*'s two landings at Holtz Bay and Massacre Bay. On May 11th, Maj. Gen. Albert Brown ordered the 7th Infantry into action. While supporting the infantry on May 25, Sgt. Dix Fetzer took shrapnel from a Japanese grenade. Unbeknownst to Gen. Brown, preceding bombardments had convinced Japan to sacrifice Attu's garrison in order to buy time for Kiska's evacuation. Col. Yosuya Yamakazi's defenders fought tenaciously for over three weeks, often committing suicide with grenades. Only 29 Japanese soldiers were taken alive, while 2,351 of their fellows were killed in action. For their part, Americans suffered 549 deaths, 1,100 battle wounds, and more than 2,200 cases of trench-foot or frostbite.[41]

Most official Army histories declare May 30 as the last day of hostilities. Certainly, principal resistance ended when Col. Yamakazi led over 800 screaming *bushi* in a desperate charge to capture Engineer Hill and destroy American supply bases. Yamakazi and his men were slain shortly after their early-morning suicidal charge, but for weeks afterward, isolated Japanese bands prowled Attu's rocky interior, harrying American troops. Navy communiqués recorded several instances of Japanese soldiers killed or captured over the following weeks.[42]

Late on June 8, T/5 Clarence Fulcher's ordnance company landed at Attu's Cape Khlebnikov. During the night, Clarence observed an armored D-8 bulldozer crushing enemy machinegun nests, using its blades to deflect bullets. Official naval reports later confirmed that sixty-six Japanese lost their lives during this mopping-up exercise on June 8.[43]

Fulcher carried away other grim memories from his first days on Attu, including the grisly sight of perhaps a dozen Japanese dressed in full uniform and lying dead amid the snow on Engineer Hill. "I could see where the officer [had fallen] on his sword, and the others [had] shot themselves with sidearms," Clarence recounted. Sometime later, Fulcher stood in the mess line waiting for chow. He watched in horror as a Chinese cook grabbed a large knife and stabbed who seemed to be a GI standing in line. As it turned out, the cook had noticed something odd about this soldier, who appeared Chinese but could or would not answer his greetings. The mortally wounded man proved to be a Japanese impostor wearing a stolen American uniform.[44]

Fulcher's team cleared the Japanese docks of several crude booby traps, ducking every so often as Zeroes continued to strafe their beach. They also searched vacant buildings, searching for what the Army later called "sucker traps;" trapped sake bottles, souvenir items, and so forth. Soldiers were also told to watch for abandoned telephones, radios, or phonograph players, which might detonate with the click of a switch. Such traps were set mainly for the purpose of lowering enemy morale, affecting living quarters, abandoned equipment, and corpses. Sometimes, Japanese saboteurs left warning signs to keep their comrades from stumbling across booby traps. Owing to their good fortune, Fulcher's section took no major injuries from enemy ordnance on Attu.[45]

By June 1943, Aberdeen Proving Ground had sent two of its newest separate squads to aid the taskforce on Attu. 5$^{th}$ BD Squad arrived first, led by 2$^{nd}$ Lt. Robert B. Rodger. Born in 1911, Rodger had left his native Scotland shortly after finishing school. Rodger resided in Westchester, New York, where he earned sufficient wages to sail back to visit Glasgow periodically. Rodger appears to have been married, but this union had ended in divorce sometime before the outbreak of war. By this point, Rodger had decided to become a permanent American citizen. Despite his draft-exempt status as a resident non-citizen, Rodger went so far as to volunteer, enlisting with the U.S. Army in April 1942 at Governor's Island, New York. Rodger's induction profile reveals he had a practical background in chemistry, making him a good candidate for the Army's technical services. Rodger's citizenship papers were approved by Baltimore's district courts on October 6, 1942. Rodger subsequently earned a second lieutenant's commission, and qualified as a bomb disposal officer in early 1943.[46]

Robert B. Rodger (third from left, second row) was an expatriate British subject who volunteered for Army service while awaiting formal U.S. citizenship. Sadly, he died after one year in the service of his new nation. (*Leiendecker Collection*)

On June 3, Rodger's 5th BD Squad departed Seattle, steaming for Alaska. On June 12, they commenced patrolling the shores and hillsides of Attu, where Japanese engineers had erected several gun emplacements. Rodger's men secured ammunition dumps and searched for booby traps. On June 21, 2nd Lt. Rodger and T/Sgt. Harry F. Rapp were reportedly "killed in action;" which usually implies contact with the enemy. Attu's rocky terrain had been sown with "dud artillery shells," "large numbers of unexploded bombs," and numerous booby traps. However, the possibility of attack by Japanese snipers cannot be entirely ruled out. Only three days after Rodger's death, Army patrols reported killing fifteen Japanese soldiers who had resisted capture on Attu. Finally, the last holdouts were rounded up in early July. Regardless of their cause of death, Rapp and Rodger were among the first EOD men killed in action. Capt. George C. Heim assumed temporary command until relieved by Patrick Hogan in August. Harry Rapp's short-term replacement, T/Sgt. Fred M. Walden, had incidentally worked in Alaska as a gold miner and fur trapper.[47]

Clarence Fulcher's ten-man squad included members of Native American and Latino descent. When not clearing the docks, they built runways, repaired weapons, and even did a few spots of carpentry. 1741st Ord. Company's band of bomb disposaleers also survived on the Aleutian beaches without much shelter. During the summer, Attu and Kiska were buffeted by windstorms, known as *williwaws*, adding to discomforts already caused by slushy *muskeg*. Clarence recalled at least one forced march across Attu's rough interior, lasting three days. Such feats bear witness to the ordnanceman's resiliency, and yet, Fulcher always recalled "infantry had the worst job." Later on, two 5th BD Squad members were deemed unfit for overseas duty after another tour on nearby Kiska.[48]

On August 15, 1943, Maj. Gen. Charles H. Corlett inaugurated Operation *Cottage* at Kiska. For two months, United States and Royal Canadian ships and planes had lobbed 1,500 tons of shells and bombs at Kiska's elusive defenders. Ultimately, *Cottage* turned out to be a costly training exercise. Panicky Yanks and Canadians fired on each other, inflicting dozens of "friendly fire" casualties. Shortly thereafter, Corlett's officers ascertained that the Japanese had evacuated the island two weeks previously. When Pfc. Fulcher's team stole ashore to blow up an ammo depot a couple days before *Cottage*, they observed no signs of the enemy. Despite numerous setbacks, many Kiska participants, such as the elite First Special Service Force, gained invaluable amphibious training. Two separate squads later used their Kiska experiences to great advantage in the European Theater. 5th BD Squad, now led by Patrick Hogan, landed with Corlett's main force. 7th BD Squad joined them later from Adak.[49]

Hogan, selected from Western Defense Command to replace the fallen Rodger, reported a "lack of knowledge on the danger of bombs and projectiles" on Kiska. He observed one American foolishly using a U.S. fragmentation bomb as a tent-peg hammer, while another had killed himself and several others after blithely tapping the base of an unexploded shell with his weapon. Canadians too, suffered from a lack of training in observing booby-traps. Four Royal Canadian soldiers were killed, and four others took serious wounds from shrapnel.[50]

For several months, ordnance specialists cleared traps from abandoned Japanese encampments and gun emplacements. Sgt. Dix Fetzer recalled deactivating booby traps in Kiska's abandoned caves, hidden beneath several Sake containers. Having recovered from his shrapnel wounds, Fetzer suffered a second unlucky break in late August. Injured seriously in one leg, Fetzer underwent one of the first knee replacement operations. Dix spent the rest of his war recovering in Adak Island's hospital.[51]

In January 1944, 5th BD Squad departed for Maryland, anticipating their "long dreamed-of furlough." Gen. Corlett sent a unit commendation to Aberdeen Proving Ground. By contrast, the 1741st Ordnance Company remained on station, braving miserable weather and dodging occasional Japanese planes. Eventually, the Aleutian Islands came to play a marginal role, but occasionally, action flared up. Pfc. Clarence Fulcher took shrapnel wounds from a strafing Zero on Amchitka, a major airbase for bomber squadrons targeting the Japanese Kuriles. Pfc. Fulcher entered the hospital in early February 1944, after nearly losing his right arm. Clarence spent a year in convalescence, while some of his buddies were later reassigned to Buckner's Tenth Army just in time for Okinawa.[52]

* * *

Allied technicians grappling with Japanese armaments required some knowledge of Chinese ideographs as well as both Japanese alphabets. They were as familiar with their respective enemy's manufacturers as their ETO counterparts. But unlike Nazi Germany, with its semblance of "free enterprise," Japan's military leaders took direct control over their nation's ordnance plants – five arsenals for their fleets, plus two for their armies. Moreover, each Japanese service branch had its own separate air force, with separate markings usually found on packing cases, wrappings, or labels fixed to the explosive charge. One U.S. Army manual on Japanese ordnance advised "care in handling all [such] explosives," because "sensitive [gaines] on Japanese fuzes, grenades, and mines have caused scores of injuries to personnel in all Pacific campaigns."[53]

One tragic reminder took place on December 22, 1943, when Sgt. Alfred F. Sanders (105th BD Squad) tinkered with a variety of bombs on Espiritu Santo, New Hebrides. Since the Army forbade taking "souvenirs," it seems more likely Sgt. Sanders had been engaged in ordnance research, encouraged by the Bomb Disposal Center. As one-time school commandant, Kane left instructions that any new "intelligence information" should be relayed "directly" to Aberdeen. However, in this same publication, he also stressed caution when handing Axis fuze types, whether familiar or unknown: "The enemy is able, with only slight variations… in his bombs, to force us to completely change all of our present methods." Whatever the case, Sgt. Sanders perished when an unidentified Japanese item triggered a fatal ordnance explosion.[54]

In particular, Japanese Army bombs were something of a puzzle, as many "known" types had not yet been captured. Soldiers had to use their instincts and past experience to discern their contents and purpose. Most commonly, picric acids or TNT were used for a bomb's payload. Sometimes, picric acid fillers boiled over in tropical weather, creating "cook offs." Direct exposure to bomb fillings themselves presented hazards, as toxic fumes caused dermatitis when detonated or burned. Army Type 88 "Karitto" explosives also proved risky to incinerate. Japanese bombs also employed TNT/RDX, a volatile aluminum-based compound liable to detonate when exposed to heat. Japanese chemical fuzes were also considered too hazardous for usual demolition methods.[55]

Japanese munitions and fuzes showed undeniable German influences by late 1943. German intelligence funneled tidbits to Tokyo, and Japan soon had a Zus-40 equivalent: the E-1 (a) anti-withdrawal fuze. Unlike the Zus-40, these booby-traps were built into the actual fuze, making them difficult to sterilize. Japanese pilots also began dropping cluster bombs, sometimes known as "anarchists." Similar in size to the German "Butterfly" bombs, these fire-bombs each weighed one kilogram, and came in sticks of forty. Lt. William E. Comstock's 102nd BD Squad recovered several bomblets from Bougainville, and when these were tested at a bomb cemetery, their arming mechanisms never "failed to function."[56]

U.S. Army and Navy units encountered some extraordinary Japanese war machines. Back in 1942, Wally Nass had recorded British rumors concerning Japanese "glider bombs" under development. In this case, Royal Engineers had been correctly informed, as Japanese Navy bombers began launching *Oka* flying bombs in 1944. These piloted suicide rockets, nicknamed *Baka* ("idiot") by Americans, were launched underneath "Betty" bombers to smash into Allied vessels at 500 miles per hour. Japanese flying bombs had little in common with V-1s, but bore similarities to the German "Fritz X" used in the Mediterranean.[57]

On Tinian and other Japanese-held islands, Army ordnancemen and Marine engineers dealt with beachheads peppered with horn-type mines, tape mines, yard-stick mines, and other booby-traps. Japanese defenders also used anti-boat mines and depth charges. Underwater Demolition Teams, Draper Kauffman's brainchild, were developed to handle these obstacles. But these Navy SEAL forerunners were fewer in number than bomb disposaleers, who suffered casualties when they encountered naval mines and depth charges, armaments beyond their usual ken.[58]

To remedy this oversight, Navy instructors in Honolulu trained a handful of Army squads in underwater demolitions and sea mine disposal. Lt. James Brown recalled the Navy training that later saved his life in the Philippines. However, not all Army personnel were able to receive such opportunities. While inter-service ordnance training came too late to make much impact, joint Army-Navy efforts would pay off at a future date.[59]

Japanese Army units developed a knack for adapting aerial bombs, grenades, or shells into makeshift mines. On Guam, U.S. Marines first reported "normal bombs" being used as beachside mines, with specimens as large as 250 kilograms. 21-inch torpedoes were also utilized in this fashion. All such items were "cleverly camouflaged" by driftwood or palm fronds. Japanese prisoners were interrogated for their knowledge of existing UXB sites, and one captive helpfully pointed out five of them to the Marine technicians. As time went on, Ernie Neeper (109th BD Squad) encountered many U.S. bombs camouflaged deep within the sand with only their detonators exposed, waiting for an unlucky landing craft.[60]

As Japanese ground troops faced their last year of bitter jungle warfare, they left ever more ingenious booby traps for the unwary. Improvised bombs, triggered by springs, often lurked beneath docks and floorboards. Ordnance bulletins circulated full details about common Japanese sabotage techniques, with Pacific-based officers and NCOs contributing regularly to these reports. Based in the Northern Solomons, Lt. Albert E. Wheeler (106th Squad) analyzed one "crudely constructed" device, consisting of twelve blocks aluminum RDX explosive, with a Japanese hand grenade serving as a detonator. Lt. Wheeler predicted a scenario wherein these contraptions might be used as anti-personnel or anti-tank mines, which led him to conclude that the enemy had run short of conventional landmines. Given Japan's general disparity in anti-tank weaponry, the Ordnance Department foretold that "mining and suicide attacks" would receive more emphasis, as combined U.S. forces reached for the "heart of Japan's empire." [61]

* * *

By the summer of 1944, almost thirty new "squads separate" had filtered into the Pacific Theater, just in time for Gen. MacArthur's two historic landings at Leyte Gulf and Southern Luzon. MacArthur faced a resolute Japanese opponent, no less than Gen. Tomoyuki Yamashita, the "Tiger of Malaya" who had humbled the British lion at Singapore in 1942. Since MacArthur had fled Corregidor under presidential orders, he had sought to keep his famous vow to liberate his beloved Philippines. For three years of Japanese occupation, the largely Catholic Filipinos had suffered violence, exploitation, and sexual slavery. Now, faced with an American armada bearing down on him, Yamashita marshaled 381,000 soldiers. Two-thirds of his resolute 35th Army fighters would perish during the coming battles on Leyte, Luzon, and Mindanao.[62]

Despite Japan's ostensible crusade to eliminate Western racial hierarchy from the Pacific, their own soldiers had conducted themselves with oppression and brutality throughout Asia and the Pacific Rim. Despite past tensions with the United States, the Filipinos greeted

MacArthur and his men undeniably as liberators. After the Philippine Islands received their independence in 1946, sixteen Army bomb squads were honored by the first Filipino president, Sergio Osmena. Unfortunately, a number of these Americans did not survive to receive their well-merited decorations. During this perilous last gauntlet of World War II, Japanese sabotage efforts increased along with their desperation, just as predicted by the Ordnance Department. In addition to booby-traps, mines, and depth charges, the Japanese Army and Navy unleashed one of the most unorthodox weapons of the war. For a brief period, North American skies bore witness to hundreds of odd balloons…[63]

* * *

During MacArthur's and Nimitz's preparations for the Philippines, 178th BD Squad arrived from the West Coast to assist Krueger's Sixth Army. Commanded by James S. Brown III from Santa Clara, California, they were fresh from Aberdeen Proving Ground. Only twenty-one, Brown had interrupted his college education in order to enlist in May 1943. Lt. Brown's team served all across the Philippines, and was present during MacArthur's landing at Leyte Island on October 20, 1944. Sixty years on, Brown fluently recalled Sixth Army's landing at San Fernando la Union: "We were dead center of the formation, where kamikazes kept hitting our LSTs. If anybody tells you it was easy, they're wrong."[64]

On the first day of Leyte, Brown's 178th BD Squad saw "little action," but by October 21, "the Japanese were there." Brown remembered fighting alongside the 33rd Infantry Division: "You have no choice, once they start charging down the hill at you." Wrongly anticipating MacArthur's blows to land on Luzon, Yamashita quickly saw his danger, and dispatched thousands of Japanese warriors to Leyte. During the next week, Brown's men also managed to remove several Japanese UXBs from Leyte's Tacloban Field. At this low elevation point, the water table measured only four feet, so their bomb shafts "kept taking sea water."[65]

Also landing on Leyte's D-Day, 109th BD Squad helped render Tacloban Field safe for later use. Still operating under 1st Lt. Walt Garland, 109th Squad covered MacArthur's famous wade ashore, four hours after the Sixth Army's landing on Palo Beach. T/5 Ernie Neeper enjoyed a fine vantage point for MacArthur's historic moment, as they "cleaned up" Palo Beach "to make sure nothing could harm him." However, despite long service to MacArthur, dating to New Guinea and Papua, the general never recognized their contribution to his victory.[66]

Meanwhile, the principal naval action at Leyte Gulf took place October 23-26, resulting in the virtual destruction of Japan's last fleet, including their super-battleship *Musashi.* Now, the U.S. Navy could interdict Yamashita's supply lines to the Philippines. Nevertheless, MacArthur's air and ground forces were beset by Japanese forces. U.S. planes based on Tacloban Field suffered appalling damage from Japanese Army bombers. Around this time, *kamikaze* and *baka* attacks stepped up their frequency, with devastating psychological effect.[67]

However, the pivotal struggle ensued with Krueger's Sixth Army facing a hard uphill slog against Yamashita's 35th Army. Despite spirited attacks on both sides, stalemate resulted after three weeks. At one point, Yamashita even ordered a paratrooper commando raid against Krueger's rear. Despite this tactical stroke, Krueger gathered forces to outflank the Japanese near the crucial Leyte port of Ormoc in early December.[68]

Spearheaded by 77th Infantry Division, this taskforce included Capt. Sarauw's 92nd BD Squad, all recipients of the Bronze Star medal for "meritorious service" during the retaking of Guam that summer. Toughened by over two years in the tropics, Clifford and his gallant crew were ready for another challenge. T/Sgt. Arthur Zellmer, now bucking for his commission, had just earned a Soldier's Medal for preventing an explosion on Guam. On Halloween, 77th Infantry departed from Guam, receiving new orders on November 15 to join with Sixth Army at Leyte.[69]

On November 23, Clifford Sarauw arrived on Leyte with advance elements of 77th Infantry. On December 6, his team received its assignment: Tarragona Beach, near the Yamashita Line's southern end. They were tasked to support 77th Infantry's amphibious landing and resulting envelopment. On December 7, 92nd Squad disembarked at Ipil, four hours after the first wave. They engaged in the "destruction of enemy ammunition dumps." Initially, Clifford's team made no efforts to "salvage any enemy material," because they had to cover a lot of ground quickly, and could not permit the Japanese a chance to resupply. In this fashion, 92nd Squad swept along the Ormoc-Valencia road, destroying over thirty ordnance dumps and forty Japanese landing barges. In total, they denied 2,800 tons of munitions to the 35th Japanese Army. Over the coming weeks, they found and neutralized hundreds of improvised booby traps and charges. Clifford also found time to field-test some jury-rigged Japanese mortars, plus anti-aircraft guns and anti-tank rifles.[70]

Meanwhile, Sixth Army launched a northward pincer toward Ormoc Bay. While they geared up, 109th BD Squad received some welcome news. Despite taking shrapnel wounds close to his heart, 1st Lt. Carl Cirocco had made a strenuous recovery, and now obtained leave to go back to his team. At this time, Sixth Army had placed his squad on loan to U.S. XIV Corps. On November 28, 109th BD Squad joined 11th Airborne Division's westward trek to Ormoc Bay. Leading the way, Col. Orin "Rock" Haugen's 511th Parachute Regiment crested the Ormoc and Mahonag mountain ranges.[71]

Lt. Cirocco recalled eerie nights when Japanese troops hurled flares and other small explosives from their mountaintop positions. Carl's ordnance team searched underground bunkers thought to be abandoned. Ernie Neeper remembered some caves were filled with uncooperative Japanese soldiers who exchanged fire. Completing their jungle trek to Ormoc, Maj. Gen. Joseph Swing's 11th Division had thwarted all enemy resistance across central Leyte within one month. Carl's veteran squad could take pride in weathering this arduous journey just as well as if they had been hardened paratroopers.[72]

By late December 1944, Krueger's two pincers met at Ormoc Bay, leaving only isolated pockets of Japanese on Leyte. Clifford Sarauw's group remained on Leyte Island for the next three months or so, lending a hand during Sixth Army's mopping up. In January's first week alone, 92nd Squad cleared Japanese ordnance within an eight-mile radius of Valencia and Palompon. They gathered "technical intelligence," particularly "Chemical Warfare" items. At Valencia, 92nd Squad discovered four immense storage caves, similar to those described by 109th Squad. All told, they held five hundred 250 kilo Japanese bombs, plus 50,000 gallons of aviation gasoline. Clifford received orders from the XXIV Corps to blow these dumps up; they were taking no chances on booby-traps.[73]

* * *

By January 1945, Axis forces worldwide were reeling from defeat. Patton's counterattack had hurled the Germans across the Rhine, while MacArthur now cast his eye toward Luzon, largest of the Philippine isles. On January 9, Sixth Army secured Lingayen Gulf's valuable airfields as a precursor to Luzon operations. Anticipating his enemy's desire to liberate Manila, Yamashita had arrayed a defensive perimeter across West Luzon, known as the Genko Line. Late in January, Sixth Army Headquarters gave a risky assignment to 178th BD Squad: secure a landing zone for MacArthur's famous "March on Manila." After a quick skydiving refresher, Lt. Jim Brown and his two sergeants parachuted over Nasugbu Point, a pleasant resort town otherwise untouched by the war. As MacArthur's intelligence had correctly divined, the beach itself had few defenses other than a minefield, which Brown's team cleared in the early hours of January 30. As Brown recounted sixty years later, "there were no engineers in the area, so we volunteered to handle these mines."[74]

On January 30, 109th BD Squad covered Swing's 11th Airborne at Nasugbu Point. Landing in barges, Swing's troopers trudged along Route 17, a paved thoroughfare flanked by defensible hills on either side. While two airborne regiments cleared the imposing Tagatay Ridge to their right flank, Swing's remaining elements followed a densely forested highway, frequently harried by Japanese ambuscades. Swing's objective, Nichols Field, formed the Genko Line's hardened center. For nearly three years, Japanese engineers had reinforced this American-built airfield with salvaged 5-inch naval guns, capable of raining havoc among MacArthur's liberators. Swing's formidable siege train also boasted a Sixth Army tank column to deal with Nichols Field's heavy guns.[75]

On February 8, Lt. Carl Cirocco and T/5 George Wassil were driving ahead of Swing's vanguard, while T/Sgt. Frank O'Leary swept for mines. They reported two well-camouflaged checkpoints flanking their path. As Ernie Neeper recollected, his officer and tech sergeant were ordered to guide tanks to these blockades, exposing themselves to mortar shells. Carl knew his men were being employed as glorified cavalry scouts, specialist ratings aside. As Carl stoically observed, many bomb disposal squads were treated like "bastard outfits… [but] we had to do whatever the mission required." During this skirmish, Carl's jeep was attacked by a "small band" of Japanese firing small arms and hurling grenades. Cirocco received extensive shrapnel injuries and a fractured right arm. T/5 Wassil reacted quickly, turning his jeep around with his fallen officer still inside. O'Leary fled into the jungle to evade the Japanese patrol. Meanwhile, Gen. Swing's column knocked out the barricades. Swing finally arrived at Nichols Field, where remaining 109th Squad members went back to work. Their mine-clearing efforts greatly reduced Swing's casualties.[76]

By February 15, 11th Airborne had penetrated the Genko Line, reaching the streets of Manila, now set aflame by vengeful Japanese. Col. Rock Haugen suffered a mortal wound during the street-fighting. However, 109th BD Squad "never entered Manila," according to T/5 Neeper. Instead, they were relieved from 11th Airborne, and dispatched to Bicol Peninsula. By this point, T/5 Wassil had safely driven his injured lieutenant to a field hospital, where a quick-thinking and skillful Filipino doctor saved Lt. Cirocco's right arm from amputation. This time, Carl's injuries would prove too severe for his return to active service. Cirocco's dauntless efforts outside Luzon and Nichols Field earned a Bronze Star medal, plus a second Purple Heart. Alas, Carl's medical discharge later that June precluded him from a well-merited promotion.[77]

Capt. Vendel P. Kovar, Sixth Army's senior bomb disposal officer, investigated 109th Squad's unlucky incident to the best of his ability. Responding to Sgt. McNeese's report on February 15, Kovar queried about O'Leary's status. Fortunately, partisans rescued a starving O'Leary on that very day. Ernie Neeper described his squad leader emerging "as thin as a rail," but T/Sgt. O'Leary soon recovered. Kovar particularly inquired whether O'Leary had lost any special equipment in his flight. Facing capture, bomb squads were required to demolish their special equipment and burn documents. Sgt. McNeese did not confirm the captain's fears, so it appears no sensitive data fell into enemy hands. Kovar directed Capt. Elmo A. Lane to assume command over 109th Squad, now with the 158th Regimental Combat Team. Lane supervised the squad until war's end, and commended each member for a Bronze Star award.[78]

* * *

During mid-February 1945, MacArthur's forces continued to free Luzon, regaining Bataan, site of the infamous "Death March." Shortly before arriving on Bataan, 174th BD Squad had narrowly escaped death on Corregidor after their quarters, dubbed "Hotseat Hall," blew up after some ordnance caught fire on October 6, 1944. 175th BD Squad supported Army operations on tiny Caballo Island in late March, just as Maj. Gen. William Arnold's veteran Americal Division (23rd Infantry) began its reconquest of Cebu, with the experienced 184th BD Squad in support.[79]

Capt. James M. Tucker's 184th Squad cooperated well with the U.S. Navy's ordnance network, and was the unit responsible for singlehandedly clearing UXBs from Negros and Panay Islands. However, when Arnold's Americal Division landed at Talisay on March 26, his grunts ran into serious trouble. Eight LVTs had struck improvised landmines on Cebu's beaches, while four more were crippled at nearby Mactan Island. Japanese sappers had systematically buried "yardstick" bombs at three-yard intervals, with only the fuzes exposed to detonate against metallic hulls. Dividing into two teams, 184th BD Squad cleared the heavily mined beaches, aided by 57th Engineer Combat Battalion's officers. After one crucial hour, the Americal's Cebu landings resumed, but this experience boded ill for future amphibious assaults.[80]

For the next few months, Manila offered practical experience to incoming Army bomb squads. During the last days, Manila had suffered profuse shelling. Tons of unexploded ammunition were left behind by Yamashita's retreating men. Capt. Robert L. Starr's 176th BD Squad arrived from Finschaven, New Zealand in mid-March. Based on Luzon,

Starr's team cut their teeth on "Jap munitions," serving as a "ready operations group" to handle problems in Manila. Unexploded ordnance and booby traps posed a threat to civilians, especially Filipino children, who were likely to pick up anything to sell for scrap metal or as war souvenirs to American soldiers. Capt. Starr later received a Bronze Star.[81]

Jim Brown encountered multitudes of eight-inch "parachute pencil" bombs scattered across Luzon. Generally referred to as "para-frags," these deadly little Japanese pests were designed to kill unsuspecting souvenir hunters. "Filipino kids loved to pick them up… pull the parachutes... and then they would get killed," Brown remembered with evident regret. Brown expressed amazement at the "ignorance" demonstrated by many Americans, who seemed to have had "no training at all" in bomb reconnaissance. Once, the 178th Squad had to cross a small lake outside Manila in order to remove a Japanese frag-bomb from a position held by the 33rd U.S. Infantry. As Lt. Brown's DUKW vehicle approached the bomb, he could hear Japanese soldiers taking pot-shots at them. Brown recollected that the grunts were "scared of the bomb; we were scared of the Japs." Fortunately, 178th BD Squad emerged unscathed from this lake incident, with one more UXB to their credit.[82]

Reclassified for a time as 178th Ordnance Service Detachment, Brown's team proceeded to remove hazards over the spring months, occasionally aided by fellow ordnance soldiers or Filipino natives. Searching across San Fernando, 178th Detachment located and destroyed a variety of bombs, plus two enemy torpedoes. One "fish" lurked beneath nine feet of water, close by the 31st General Hospital on the north side. Elsewhere, they found crates of Japanese ammunition buried underneath the rubble of a trade school.[83]

Around mid-June, Lt. Brown received a call to handle a traditional UXB, buried seven feet below the Northern Luzon Academy. Later on, his team inerted 250 or so Japanese mines, a mix of "Pottery Mines" and "Tape Measure Mines." Pottery Mines were Type 4 ceramic-encased grenades often used with booby traps. Type 93 "Tape Measure Mines" were frequently emplaced in clusters for added damage. Type 93 mines also could be set for anti-tank or anti-personnel purposes, and they were occasionally equipped with anti-lifting devices. Undoubtedly, the selfless actions of Jim Brown and his team made San Fernando a safer place for its liberated Filipino inhabitants.[84]

178th Detachment's tech sergeant, George A. Bruce, led a vital operation at Davis Ordnance Ammunition Depot, a "bombed-out" Army installation at Rabon. For most of April and early May, Bruce supervised a group of natives and soldiers as they dumped phosphorous artillery shells and hand grenades. At one point, several civilians were slightly injured by shrapnel when unstable hand grenades detonated. By May 9, 178th Squad had cleared an estimated 2,500 tons from Rabon. On June 26, T/Sgt. Bruce returned with T/5 Lovit Hines to finish clearing Davis Depot's most dangerous section, mainly consisting of "Bangalore [torpedoes] and land mines." Lt. Brown praised his sergeant and technicians for acting quickly to minimize casualties and for overcoming numerous adversities during their month-long ordeal.[85]

Given intense jungle conditions, Army squads unsurprisingly suffered from tropical diseases, heat exhaustion, and poor field sanitation. Promoted to first lieutenant in July, Jim Brown attributes his relative seniority in bomb disposal due largely to "attrition from diseases." Brown's soldiers learned hunting tricks from neighboring Filipino guerillas, who had survived in Luzon's jungles for years hiding from Japanese patrols. By setting booby traps outside their bivouac points, Brown's men supplemented their flavorless K-rations with caribou meat. By July, ordnance calls had slackened on Luzon, permitting Brown's squad to erect better quarters at the 226th Ordnance Base Depot.[86]

* * *

By April 1945, only Mindanao, southernmost of the Philippines awaited liberation: a sparsely populated, "mountainous, primitive island." Indeed, though a vast island, Mindanao had but one major town, Davao. Mindanao had no strategic value, but its liberation went far toward winning the Filipino government's goodwill. During recent months, guerilla bands had forced the Japanese into the interior hill country. Two U.S. infantry divisions (24th and 31st) entered the Mindanao sector at Llana Bay on April 17. Jungle paths were then patrolled for improvised mines by two BD units, the 181st Squad (1st Lt. Summers J. Gostin) and 182nd Squad (1st Lt. Charles H. Commons, Jr.). When these fourteen men proved too few for the workload, three new separate squads were flown across from Luzon during the first half of May.[87]

Among these recent arrivals, the 209th BD Squad had a distinguished commanding officer, Capt. Richard E. Metress. For nearly three years, Dick had worked to build the Army Bomb Disposal School into a facility respected by the War Department and the Ordnance Department. However, almost everyone he had known at the school had gone overseas. Back in autumn 1943, Dick had said farewell to his close friends, Ron Felton and Joe Pilcher. By early 1944, Capt. Malcolm Antonelli, his company officer, had also departed for England. Promoted to captain, Metress subsequently took over the Bomb Disposal Center headquarters.[88]

About this time, Dick married a Jewish girl, Anita, but they evidently chose to keep their wedding low-profile. Two of Dick's nieces recalled hearing news of a marriage, but never met his new wife. Every weekend, Dick commuted to and from nearby Swedesboro, New Jersey, driving on the same turnpike that passed through Havre de Grace and led to Aberdeen, where he enjoyed a tranquil stateside post.[89]

By late 1944, the Ordnance Department had recognized that the ETO required no more squads, so the Bomb Disposal School scheduled over thirty squads for deployment to the Pacific. The author speculates that Metress may have volunteered for combat duty. However, unlike his two friends at Aberdeen, Dick left no records of his thoughts on deployment overseas. Nevertheless, on October 30, Dick took over 209th BD Squad, one of the last activated. His new unit included T/Sgt. Howard A. Leith, Sgt. Robert C. Ryan, and four technicians: William J. Hackett, Anthony Piergrossi, Raymond W. Johnson, and William F. Seik.[90]

On March 24, 1945, Capt. Metress and his unit reached Luzon, now firmly in U.S. hands. Disembarking from S.S. *Sea Snipe*, the 209th BD Squad crossed Manila Bay to Yacht Basin, where they temporarily liaised with the 580th Ordnance Ammunition Co., a part of the U.S. Eighth Army. Metress' team later pitched their pup tents at Parañaque, a town south of Manila. On March 28, they began clearance operations, hauling away Japanese explosives from Manila's war-torn City Hall and its surrounding rubble-choked streets. Metress also neutralized a Japanese anti-boat mine lurking beneath downtown Manila's Astrada Bridge.[91]

Richard Metress reported fair weather and excellent morale during his first weeks on Luzon. At Manila, 209th BD Squad received two "Duck" vehicles to dump loads in northern Manila Harbor. Many squad officers, for expediency, chose to dump their hazardous cargoes among its many harbors and straits, with unforeseen environmental consequences in the future. Carl Cirocco, for one, later voiced his regrets about this necessary but potentially harmful wartime practice. Metress and his team spent five days clearing out 70 tons of 155 mm artillery shells from a Japanese ammo supply point at nearby Baranka. 209th Squad's strenuous physical efforts were greatly alleviated by several Filipino day laborers.[92]

209th Squad transferred on April 1 to Las Piñas, where they segregated and stored "serviceable boxed Japanese ammunition," presumably for Nationalist Chinese soldiers. Metress' team discarded bad rounds, dud shells, and unstable explosives. On one occasion, their convoy drove 17 bumpy miles down toward Cavite, where soldiers detonated a cargo of depth charges and UXBs. With aid from native laborers, the 209th Squad managed to destroy about 10 tons of ordnance per day. However, this routine broke abruptly on May 15. Capt. Metress received urgent orders to report to the 24th Infantry Division, under the U.S. X Corps stationed on Mindanao. Attached to the 724th Ordnance Company, 209th Squad disarmed a multitude of "enemy bombs, depth charges, and anti-boat mines." On May 23, 209th Squad once more departed, this time headed for Mandog Hill, a scene of bloody guerilla warfare.[93]

Six weeks earlier, Lt. Gen. Robert Eichelberger had tasked I Corps with dislodging the Japanese 100th Army Division (Lt. Gen. Jiro Harada) from Mandog Hill. American commanders viewed Mandog as Harada's "strongest last-stand defense." Eichelberger's three infantry divisions, reinforced by grim Filipino and Moro partisan groups, had managed to press Harada's flanks. Japanese breastworks spanned across ten miles of hillside earthworks, between Wangan and Mandog Hills. By the time I Corps finally cleared Mandog Hill on June 10, 3,700 Americans lay slain or wounded across Eastern Mindanao. 24th Division incurred the worst losses, at 350 fatalities and 1,615 injuries. 21,100 Japanese died, and Harada's remaining 34,000 troops did not surrender until August.[94]

* * *

On May 29, patrolling U.S. infantrymen from the 19th Regiment discovered a "large explosive item" west of Mandog Hill. Similar reports reached divisional headquarters, confirming that Harada's engineers were now using naval depth charges as mines to deter possible frontal assaults. Set up with "pull-wires," these semi-buried obstacles were hard to spot, and could be easily detonated by any "Jap in a nearby dugout." Moreover, these canisters might be rolled downhill, toward unsuspecting victims.[95]

Contemporary ordnance intelligence identified these devices as Japanese Type 2s, virtually copied from captured British models. Such canisters saw recent use in the Philippines as payloads for Japanese "suicide boats," plywood speedboats designed to ram into larger vessels. However, these depth charges had been adapted for land use. Some used camouflaged wooden "pressure plates," which served to trigger the depth charge's "pistol," or starter, setting off the improvised mine. Another specimen might function after a broken tripwire dropped a weight onto the "plate." Finally, such booby traps could be primed with electrical wiring, going off as a single blast, or multiple "controlled charges."[96]

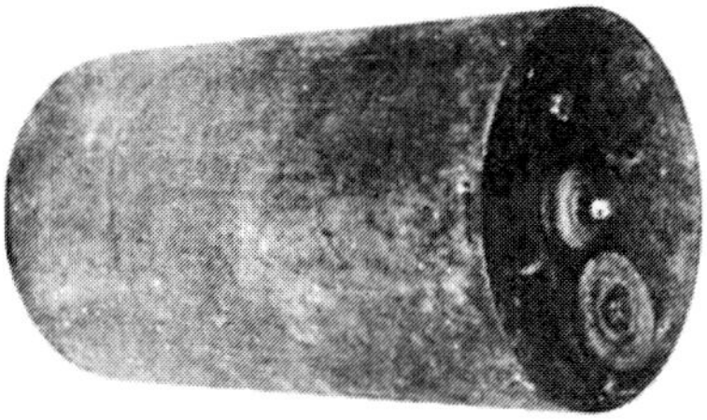

Type 2 Japanese Depth Charge, often used as a landmine. (*Leiendecker Collection*)

In 1945, few ordnance specialists outside the Navy could handle depth charges. One technical manual warned American divers "unfamiliar with… depth charge operation" should leave well alone, as "Mine Disposal personnel" would be on hand to deal with them. However, at this late point in the Philippines campaign, no Navy or Marine teams were to be found on Mindanao, so Richard Metress and his Army squad voluntarily undertook this perilous job. They had to clear all depth charges from Mandog Hill before the Allied attack could commence.[97]

Leaving Sgt. Robert Ryan and T/5 Raymond Johnson at base camp, Capt. Metress and his remaining squad members formed an advance party to sweep 19th Regiment's jungle path. For nearly two weeks, they successfully combed the hillside for suspicious humps in the undergrowth, sometimes coming into small arms range. Metress and his teammates were spared enemy bullets, but, on June 8, they suffered a far worse fate. As they removed one particular depth charge, it went off suddenly, killing Dick Metress, along with T/Sgt. Howard Leith, and two specialists, William Hackett and Tony Piergrossi. T/5 William Seik miraculously survived the blast, albeit with serious injuries. Only two days afterward, Gen. Eichelberger's forces drove the Japanese from Mandog Hill.[98]

For his unsung bravery, Capt. Richard E. Metress received a posthumous Purple Heart and Navy Commendation. Memorialized at Fort Bonifacio, Manila, Metress and his slain comrades have also been honored by the EOD Memorial. 209th Squad's remaining members, Sgt. Ryan and T/5 Johnson, remained inactive until mid-July, when 1st Lt. Morris E. Tarleton arrived to take over 209th Squad. Despite two new enlisted men. Tarleton's ensuing operations were "seriously handicapped by a lack of special tools, vehicles, and personnel." However, the new squad officer did secure at least one sample of the E-1(a) fuze for Aberdeen Proving Ground. During the final week of July 1945, the five squad members completed several missions across the Davao City area, eventually receiving the Philippines Presidential Unit Citation for their efforts.[99]

* * *

As MacArthur engaged in his triumphant campaign to the south, U.S. Tenth Army forces stabbed northeast under Lt. Gen. Simon B. Buckner Jr., angling toward Japan's home islands. In March 1945, two Marine Corps divisions triumphed over Iwo Jima's 21,000 defenders, led by Gen. Tadamichi Kuribayashi. During the battle, Capt. Thomas Keane's 156th BD Squad handled cluster bombs dropped over the American beachhead. Afterward, they removed a daily average of twelve tons from this blood-drenched island. Keane described the scene north of Mount Suribachi, where the Japanese made their final stand: Here, 156th BD Squad "found every type of mine imaginable." Keane also noted other "methods used to slow up American advances." One of the squad's "biggest and messiest jobs," removing 237 grenades from dead Japanese, took place several days after Kuribayashi's final *banzai* on March 24. Considering the burning sun on Iwo Jima's volcanic surface, this amounts to one of the worst jobs ever undertaken by a bomb disposal squad. Nevertheless, Capt. Keane's 156th Squad was greatly honored with an unusual U.S. Navy Unit Citation for their support role in Iwo Jima.[100]

Afterward, a second bomb disposal officer coordinated with Navy demolitions teams to clear dangerous explosives from Iwo Jima. 1st Lt. Lewis Tyree had a background in ordnance, prior to commanding the 2881st and 2882nd Engineer Detachments. Searching through the warrens, Tyree's party had discovered huge revetments containing 600 tons of high explosive. One Japanese prisoner, a major, hinted that these explosives had been emplaced to "sink" the entire island. However, Tyree indicated that these stockpiles were detonated without noticeable effects.[101]

On April 16, 1945, a final battle took place between conventional forces in the Central Pacific, centering on the Ryukyu's largest island, Okinawa. Under Lt. Gen. Buckner's Tenth Army, each division carried its own bomb squad or detachment. 7th Infantry, doughty veterans from the Aleutians, received the 206th BD Squad, while 77th Infantry regained 92nd Squad's invaluable services. 9 6th Infantry took along the 204th BD Squad, while the 27th Infantry had its own team from the 61st Ordnance Company. Meanwhile, 1st and 6th Marine Divisions shared one BD company.[102]

At Okinawa, Gen. Mitsuru Ushijima's 32nd Army fielded close to 100,000 combat troops, augmented by a Japanese suicide fleet, *kamikaze* planes, and remote-controlled *baka* bombs. Tenth Army's protracted three-month struggle in the Ryukyus incurred 65,000 Army and Marine casualties, over a quarter of Buckner's effectives, further reinforcing predictions that Japan would be another costly endeavor.[103]

Five days before "Landing-Day" at Okinawa, 92nd BD Squad arrived to bolster Maj. Gen. Bruce's under-strength 77th Division. At this point, this division was earmarked for a secondary landing on Ie Shima (sometimes called Ie Jima), a neighboring island dominated by a single pinnacle, Mt. Iegusugu. Bruce's main objectives were Ie Shima's airstrips. On April 16, Bruce's two regimental combat teams (the 305th and 306th) embarked for Red and Green Beaches respectively. Despite rocket and mortar support, Red's four sectors proved the toughest landings, because they fell within range of Japanese pillboxes, part of a defensive network ringing the pinnacle. Thousand of improvised mines, often using unexploded aerial bombs, cluttered the island's shoreline. While the Navy's escort carriers and destroyers were responsible for softening up the beaches, they could not reach all of the mines. Capt. Sarauw's team members had their work cut out for them.[104]

After two days of slow combat, Bruce sent in his reserves, the 307th RCT, unaware that several Japanese detachments were still concealed behind American lines. One of these isolated pillboxes cut down correspondent Ernie Pyle, on his way to "Bloody Ridge" on April 18. That same day, five members of 92nd Squad were killed instantly when their landing craft struck a mine. Records are unclear as to the precise nature of the mine, but Capt. George C. Sarauw, former company commander and one-time staff officer, was among the fallen. 92nd Squad had been sent to patrol southwest of Ie Shima, where mines had discouraged the Navy's supply craft from landing. For his extreme devotion to duty, Clifford Sarauw received a posthumous Legion of Merit, one of America's highest decorations for meritorious wartime service.[105]

Shortly before the Ryukyu Islands campaign opened, the Central Pacific had received the 6th Provisional Bomb Disposal Group, dispatched from Island Command, in Hawaii. However, no other records exist, beyond a single mention in the U.S. Army's war campaign credit roster. Who might have led such a headquarters detachment? One good candidate might be Maj. Robert G. Fisher, who resurfaced with U.S. occupation forces in Nagoya, Japan. However, Capt. G. C. Sarauw is also a good possibility, a hypothesis based on several premises.[106]

Capt. George Clifford Sarauw's grave marker, courtesy of Mike R. Vining.

Like Fisher, Capt. Sarauw had two years of company-grade experience. Secondly, Sarauw had administrative experience as Hawaii's senior bomb disposal officer. Furthermore, Clifford's old command, the 92nd BD Squad, had recently gained a new commander, 2nd Lt. Arthur Zellmer – formerly its tech sergeant. Two officers seldom worked within the same bomb disposal squad; therefore, Capt. Sarauw's presence within the 92nd Squad suggests he might have remained with his unit for administrative purposes. This corresponds with Maj. Syd Lerner's relationship with the 10th Squad in France. Given 92nd Squad's virtual annihilation, it might go some way to explain 6th Bomb Disposal Group's missing records.[107]

Okinawa and its neighbors fell at last to American forces on July 2, yet this final engagement inflicted terrible losses. Lt. Gen. Buckner died on June 18, the highest-ranking U.S. officer lost during the entire war. Following the principal action, Robert Starr's 176th BD Squad, (308th Bomber Wing) removed ordnance from Motubu's airstrips, which later played a role in the controversial fire-bombing of Tokyo. Despite horrific consequences from napalm and incendiary bombs, the Japanese government showed no signs of surrender, and even mobilized school children as a last-ditch force. Faced with the possibility of widespread casualties, the incoming U.S. President, Harry S. Truman, approved the use of atomic bombs, averting the long-feared invasion of Japan.[108]

Following Japan's surrender on August 15, U.S. bomb disposal forces arrived to clear leftover arsenals and coastal forts. 178th Squad had been slated to join MacArthur's planned initial assault, Operation *Olympic*. When V-J Day arrived, they were in the midst of support operations with the 24th Infantry on Mindanao. By October, T/Sgt. George Bruce had received new orders for Shikoku, the smallest of Japan's four home islands. Boarding the U.S.S. *Griggs*, Bruce's team landed at the port city of Matsuyama on October 23. They were assigned to 724th Ordnance Company, stationed at the West Airstrip. Within five days, they had cleared several U.S. fragmentation bombs from the installation.[109]

Delayed by a couple weeks in hospital, 1st Lt. James Brown arrived in Matsuyama on October 31, 1945. Before long, Brown became captain, and supervised all removal work on Shikoku. Brown's teammates also served as "advisors or consultants in disposing of enemy explosive materiel." They dismantled guns, destroyed fortifications, and closed hidden cave arsenals. Capt. Brown surveyed Matsuyama's "very impressive coastal positions," and concluded that President Truman's atomic bomb decision had saved his entire squad.[110]

* * *

Shortly after Gen. MacArthur's occupation began, the U.S. Navy's technical mission gathered information concerning Japanese bomb disposal methods. Primarily, the War Department required technical data on the effectiveness of American ordnance, such as bomb fuzes. However, the Navy's report also aided post-war bomb removal efforts, as Japanese technicians discovered new means of defuzing U. S. bombs. Furthermore, Lt. Kikuo Nishida's narrative on bomb disposal provided posterity with a rare and honest glimpse of Japanese society under fire.[111]

Initially, the Japanese government believed their nation invulnerable to bombardment. In April 1942, following Lt. Col. Jimmy Doolittle's B-25 Tokyo raid, Imperial High Command approved bomb and shell disposal training programs at Yokosuka Naval Base, a major ordnance center. However, Japanese Army and Navy commanders took no further preparatory steps until early 1943, after staggering setbacks at Midway and Guadalcanal. Lt. Kikuo Nishida, a naval ordnance officer at Kure, recalled the loss of Guadalcanal as a turning point in Japan's morale. Even though technicians gathered some Allied ordnance samples in 1942, they did little more than research into fuzes. Lt. Nishida conceded that their research and development section lacked central organization, and that Japan failed to incorporate Allied innovations into their arsenal.[112]

Coastal defense units (*bobitai*) were selected for Japan's first ordnance removal squads; ten soldiers led by an officer. Yokosuka's school played no further role in training their graduates, who were thereafter assigned to coastal artillery and anti-aircraft bases. Their primary role was defensive, but *bobitai* also conducted rudimentary UXB research. Earlier in the war, German sources contributed three volumes of data on Allied fuzes and bombs, with occasional data fed to the Japanese embassy in Berlin. Later on, translated manuals were circulated through Kanazawa's First Air Technical Arsenal Branch, located forty miles north of Yokosuka.[113]

Poor organization and inconsistent training hampered bomb removal across Japan's gradually shrinking empire. For one thing, the Japanese High Command waited two years too long to shift toward a defensive contingency against air raids. Also, they lacked a bomb disposal center with its own research and development arm, as the Allies had developed at Aberdeen Proving Ground or at Harper Barracks. Inter-service rivalry also interfered with operations, as the Japanese Navy sometimes withheld ordnance intelligence from their Army counterparts. By contrast, both United States and United Kingdom forces usually overcame such pointless competition over weapons data. Given the Imperial Army's unequal treatment, no wonder Nishida could boast to his interrogators that Japan's best *bobitai* squads belonged to the Imperial Navy! As the Allies had discovered with tragic consequences, the Japanese Army typically solved its UXB problems by converting enemy bombs into landmines and booby-traps. So, even without the Imperial Navy's aid, Army sappers and demolitionists were deadly enough adversaries on their own accounts.[114]

Back on Japanese soil, Lt. Nishida and his compatriots relied on primitive methods for excavating and transporting American UXBs. Nishida frequently used the expression "blind" to denote unexploded ordnance. Sappers used picks and shovels to gain access to "blind" aerial bombs, which typically left a small crater but did little impact damage. Japan's bomb squads preferred to detonate UXBs *in situ*, largely because U.S. time-delay fuzes were considered dangerous for up to 100 hours. When bombs were transported at all, crews employed handcarts instead of motor vehicles, adding to the risk factor. *Bobitai* commanders extracted bomb fuzes only when deemed safe or vital for intelligence purposes. Nishida became familiar with many fuzes, and field-tested an "incendiary tube" for burning out fuze pockets. However, this risky method still meant exploding the bomb, potentially causing structural damage. Nishida had recently heard rumors of Japanese Army technicians steaming out some bombs at the Imperial Castle, but had no further information. Evidently, the Japanese Army's bomb squads were not sharing, either.[115]

Usually, general purpose (G.P.) high explosive bombs were most commonly encountered on Japan. When ammunition shortages threatened Japanese factories, UXBs were often recycled for their explosive fillers. *Bobitai* grew to respect the larger U.S. incendiary bomb, weighing 100 pounds, primarily because it could readily ignite civilian dwellings. However, the Japanese also discovered a flaw in the Navy's smaller napalm bomblets. Sometimes, these six-pound projectiles only smoldered, and could be extinguished quickly. *Bobitai* went from district to district, showing civilians how to counteract these fire-bombs. Sometimes, their napalm fillings were even recycled for automobile fuel. Nishida took pride in these morale-building efforts, but felt he only "succeeded to diminish somewhat the instinctive horror of citizens." Toward the end, untrained city-dwellers were also pressed into volunteer cleanup groups.[116]

As Japanese UXB crews toiled to remove American bombs, they could take cold comfort in their own nation's effort to demoralize North America. *Fu-Go* balloon bombs had been a source of panic across the West Coast for nearly a year. While civilian and military patrols scoped in vain for V-1s on the East Coast, a U.S. Navy vessel plying the Pacific waters found an odd Japanese balloon floating near San Pedro, California on November 4, 1944. This specimen proved to be the first of about 9,300 *Fu-Go* bombs launched against North America. Originally tested during their Chinese offensives in 1937-39, explosive-bearing *Fu-Go* balloons received increased priority as Japan's new instrument of vengeance after the successful Doolittle Raids of 1942.[117]

Even though Robert Mikesh's 1973 study underscored the *Fu-Go* balloon's unrealized potential for biological or chemical strikes, other Americans dismissed Japan's balloon raids as "pathetic, last-ditch" efforts. *Fu-Go* weapons were approximately 33.5 ft. in diameter, constructed in makeshift factories using child labor. Teenage girls were usually preferred for sewing the balloons. Japanese Army balloons (Type A) used lacquered rice paper, while Japanese Navy balloons (Type B) used rubberized silk. Army balloons were launched from Honshu, northernmost of Japan's home islands. Japanese Navy balloons were delivered by submarines or surface vessels, rendering them rather more dangerous. Bungee shock cords suspended the unmanned balloon's payload: a combination of three explosive or thermite bombs, tilted downward, with delayed-action fuzes. Early *Fu-Go* models also carried a flash-bomb that destroyed the balloon before dropping its cargo. Some were equipped with anti-personnel bombs to prevent tampering. Later *Fu-Go* balloon models included a clever descent-control mechanism triggered by atmospheric pressure.[118]

Only a fraction of these *Fu-Go* weapons, perhaps three hundred, actually reached North America, peaking in March 1945. Some *Fu-Go* reached as far east as Michigan and Canada, prompting a cooperative patrol system between United States and Royal Canadian Air Forces to spot and dismantle these bombs before they caused forest fires. U.S. government officials took the *Fu-Go* menace seriously, but wished to avoid panic. Thus, American citizens were not sufficiently warned about touching these balloons, although some local newspapers did carry warnings. Most survivors from the lengthy Pacific crossing landed across the sparsely-populated Northwest, where they inflicted relatively little damage, except for one fatal incident near Bly, Oregon.[119]

One Sunday afternoon, on May 5, 1945, Reverend Archie Mitchell and his pretty, dark-haired wife, Elsie, had taken five children for a picnic at Mount Gearhart, Oregon. While the young minister parked his car, Elsie Mitchell escorted her young charges to their predetermined campsite. On their way, Elsie's group encountered a balloon heaped near a tree trunk. One of the boys began prodding the mysterious pile of wreckage with a stick. Just as Mitchell approached the scene, the fragmentation bomb discharged, instantly killing his pregnant wife and all five children.[120]

Reverend Mitchell had heard vague rumors concerning enemy balloons, but had never thought to encounter a live bomb during his church picnic. Speaking to police shortly after the tragedy, Mitchell recalled finding a sizeable crater surrounded by the six sprawled victims. Their clothes were still burning when he arrived at the blast site. Today, the Mitchell Recreation Area contains a stone monument dedicated to the sole Americans killed by direct enemy bombardment in the continental United States during World War II. Had the bombs been staged earlier, doubtless there would have been more victims in North America.[121]

Ultimately, Japan's *Fu-Go* weapons were a tactical failure, due to their faulty ballast controls and their relatively late introduction in World War II. Yet, for a brief time, "balloon bombs" instilled fear across the West Coast. Only the cooperation of news agencies kept the Japanese from exploiting the psychological effects of their balloons. Apart from Mount Gearhart, *Fu-Go* weapons succeeded in igniting several forest fires across Washington and Oregon. One bomb severed power lines to a secret atomic research facility at Hanford, Washington, nearly causing a nuclear meltdown. Such problems were considered serious enough to devote military resources to contain them. At Ft. Douglas, Utah, 9$^{th}$ Service Command launched "Operation Firefly," airdropping "Smokejumpers" to combat blazes erupting across the Pacific Northwest. John F. Cleeves, a recent Ordnance School graduate, oversaw bomb disposal training.[122]

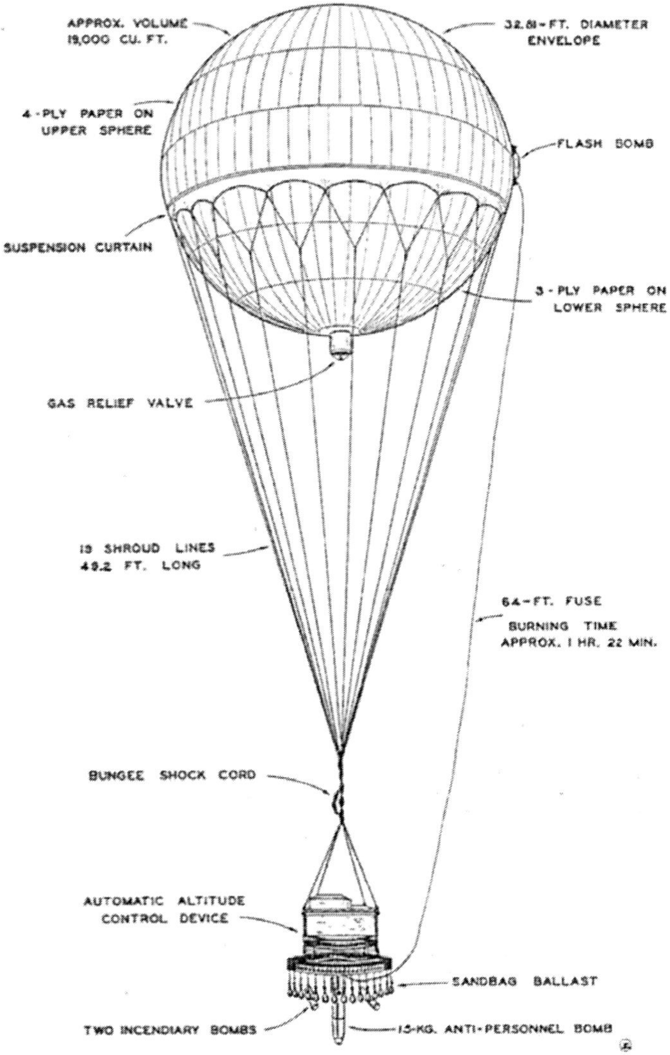


Standard design for Japanese *Fu-Go* balloon, armed with two incendiary charges and a single anti-personnel bomb to prevent disarmament. One of these bombs killed six Americans on the West Coast, the only civilians killed by enemy action on the U.S. mainland. (Illustration by Robert C. Mikesh)

More than 2,700 U.S. Army servicemen, including the all-black 555th Parachute Infantry Battalion took part in "Operation Firefly." Commanded by Lt. Col. Bradley Biggs, the "Triple Nickels" were first activated in Fort Bragg, North Carolina, addressing concerns that black Americans were barred from serving in the combat arms. However, despite being commissioned on 30 December 1943, the 555th never saw action in Europe for political reasons. Instead, the "Triple Nickels" were kept on indefinite training status until the summer of 1945.[123]

Shortly after the Bly incident, members of the 555th Battalion were mobilized for special training in the Northwest. Even so, John Cannon, a second lieutenant at the time, recalled that only a portion of the 555th became actual "Smokejumpers." Even a state of national emergency could not fully eliminate the outmoded policies of Jim Crow. However, the Triple Nickels were eventually integrated with Ft. Bragg's existing airborne regiments at Lt. Gen. James B. Gavin's personal request.[124]

On June 8, 1945, Army bomb disposal officers from Ninth Service Command began training the first "Smokejumpers" in UXB reconnaissance and disarming tasks. John Cleeves and other ordnance soldiers worked with this team of paratroopers, rangers, and firefighters. Though not ordnance soldiers, Lt. Col. Biggs and his "Triple Nickels" were among the first documented black soldiers to perform EOD tasks under wartime conditions. Some incendiary charges were still undetonated, making their jobs hazardous. Yet, Biggs recalled that his parachutists suffered only one death, due to a jumping accident.[125]

"Operation Firefly" proved successful largely because an actual (albeit short-lived) national crisis brought military forces and civilian emergency workers together to combat a menace to national security. Furthermore, black troops were given a chance to shine, instead of being relegated to passive roles. U.S. Army Ordnance personnel, although given very little credit for their role in this affair, proved a catalyst in resolving America's largest "homeland security" crisis during World War II.

## Notes

[1] *Notes on German Bombs* [Army Bomb Disposal School], 1942; *Italian Aircraft Bombs* [Army Bomb Disposal School], 1942; *Course Syllabus* [Army Bomb Disposal School] from *Thomas J. Kane Travel Itinerary* [4 January - 9 March 1942], Aberdeen Proving Ground, MD, 1942; Walter R. Nass, *Bomb Disposal Notes*, Aberdeen Proving Ground: U.S. Army Ordnance Museum, 1942.

[2] War Department Technical Manual E9-1984, *Disposal Methods for Enemy Bombs and Fuzes,* Aberdeen Proving Ground, Maryland: Chief of Ordnance, 12

November 1942; 1st Lt. Carl Super and 1st Lt. David E. Stuart, "Japanese Artillery," from *Ordnance Sergeant* (July 1945); U.S. Explosive Ordnance Disposal Technical Manual 60A, *Japanese Explosive Ordnance,* 15 August 1945 (Naval Explosive Ordnance Disposal Technology Division, Indian Head, Maryland, 1978); Office of the Chief of Military History, *The War Against Japan*, Washington D.C.: Chief of Military History, 2001, 402.

[3] Army Services Forces Ordnance Department, *Bomb Disposal Technical Information* (Bulletin No. 25) Aberdeen Proving Ground, M.D.: Ordnance Bomb Disposal School, 1 April 1944, F-18; Col. Thomas J. Kane, unpublished travel itinerary, Aberdeen Proving Ground, MD, 1 December 1942 – 25 May 1943.

[4] Kane met several individual officers in the CBI sectors. Lieutenants Joseph A. Arnold and Robert F. Guilfoy were sent to India, while Paul J. Gebelein Jr. served in Chungking, China. (Col. Thomas J. Kane to Chief of U.S. Army Ordnance. *Report on Bomb Disposal Activities in Various Theatres of Operation*, Aberdeen Proving Grounds, MD, 29 May 1943; Ordnance Bomb Disposal School, BD officer roster, 26 November 1942; Kane itinerary.)

[5] Lt. Col. Paul M. Seleen, *Officers for Bomb Disposal Duty in Foreign Stations*, 25 May 1942; Col. Thomas J. Kane to 10th U.S. Army Air Force, New Delhi, India, 3 May 1943; Kane, *1943 Itinerary*; *Report on Bomb Disposal Activities in Various Theatres of Operation*; Charles F. Romanus and Riley Sunderland, *Time Runs Out in CBI* (Washington D.C.: Center For Military History, 1985, 248-9.)

[6] Aberdeen Proving Ground's BD School trained one Chinese Army officer, Tsao The-Chuan, stationed at the Nationalist Chinese Embassy in Washington. Tsao is listed as a graduate of Class 39 from Aberdeen Proving Ground, and may have been a member of Alpha Division, elite Chinese personnel trained to defend against Communist sabotage efforts. (Col. Thomas J. Kane to 14th U.S. Air Force, Kunming, China, 7 May 1943; Col. Thomas J. Kane to Commanding General, U.S.A.F. in China-Burma-India, 12 May 1943; Lt. Col. Paul M. Seleen, *Officers for Bomb Disposal Duty in Foreign Stations*, 25 May 1942.)

[7] Even though Kane passed through Hawaii, he did not record whether he ever contacted the 232nd BD Company stationed in Honolulu. (Col. Thomas J. Kane, unpublished travel itinerary, Aberdeen Proving Ground, MD, 1 December 1942 – 25 May 1943; Thomas J. Kane to 14th U.S. Air Force, Kunming, China, 7 May 1943; Mayo, 232.)

[8] Australian Royal Engineers and their Kiwi counterparts had their own manuals and training methods, which they freely shared with their allies. (*Engineer-in-Chief, Bomb Disposal Instructions*, Headquarters, Australian Military Forces, 11 March 1944; *Demolitions and Explosives,* Australian Engineer-in-Chief, Intelligence Summary, May 1944; Headquarters Communication Zone ETOUSA. *History of the Ordnance Bomb Disposal Division From D-Day to VE-Day in Europe.* c. 1945. Karl C. Dod, *The Corps of Engineers*. Washington D.C.: Center for Military History, 1966, 271, 560-1; Mayo, 231-2, Hooper, 27.)

[9] As recently as 1981, EOD researcher Samuel Hooper noted a dearth of primary sources relative to Pacific-based units. However, unit histories and EOD Memorial researchers indicate that nine Navy technicians and three Marines were

killed disarming mines or UXBs; nearly all of these died in the Pacific Theater. Army BD deaths in the Pacific were slightly higher, hovering at twenty official names, while others are still awaiting confirmation by the EOD Foundation. (Marines, 1st Amphibious Corps, *Report on Bougainville Operations*, 3 November – 15 December 1943, World War II War Diaries, 7 December 1941 to 31 December 1945, NARA Records Group 38; Samuel J. Hooper, *History of U.S. Army Bomb Disposal and Explosive Ordnance Disposal (1941-1980),* 1981, 25; Department of the Army, *Pamphlet 672-1: Unit Citation and Campaign Participation Credit Register.* Washington D.C.: Government Publishing Office, 1972; Mike R. Vining, *Explosive Ordnance Disposal Memorial – U. S. Army*, EOD Memorial Commission, 9 April 2011).

[10] 92nd Ordnance Bomb Disposal Squad (Separate), unit history, November 1943 to February 1945; 109th Ordnance Bomb Disposal Squad (Separate), unit history, November 1943 to October 1945; Hooper, 13-14, 25-26; Williamson Murray and Allen R. Millett, *A War to be Won: Fighting the Second World* War, Cambridge, Massachusetts: Harvard University Press, 2001, 200.

[11] 92nd Ordnance Bomb Disposal Squad (Separate), unit history, November 1943 to February 1945; J. A. Ulio to Margaret E. Sarauw, telegram, 14 June 1945; *Detonator* [newsletter] U.S. Army Bomb Disposal School: Aberdeen Proving Ground, Maryland, 17 September 1943; *List of B.D. officers Assigned to Companies*; 26 October 1943;

[12] 92nd Ordnance Bomb Disposal Squad (Separate), unit history, November 1943 to February 1945; Hooper, 25; Murray and Millett, 346.

[13] 92nd Ordnance Bomb Disposal Squad (Separate), unit history, November 1943 to February 1945.

[14] 92nd U.S. Ordnance Bomb Disposal Squad to Commandant, Ordnance Bomb Disposal School, operation report, 1 February 1944.

[15] 92nd Ordnance Bomb Disposal Squad (Separate), unit history, November 1943 to February 1945; Commander, 5th Amphibious Force, *Report of Amphibious Ops for the Capture of Marshall Islands*, 25 February 1944 (World War II War Diaries, 7 December 1941 to 31 December 1945, NARA Records Group 38).

[16] 111st Amphibious Corps, *Report of Operations for the Capture and Occupation of Guam Island, Marianas*, 21 July – 10 August 1944 (World War II War Diaries, 7 December 1941 to 31 December 1945, NARA Records Group 38); 92nd Ordnance Bomb Disposal Squad (Separate), unit history, November 1943 to February 1945.

[17] Navy records credit the XIV Army Corps' bomb disposal experts, which could only have been the 92nd BD Squad, assigned to 77th Infantry Division – the sole XIV Corps unit to participate in the Guam campaign. (111st Amphibious Corps, *Report of Operations for the Capture and Occupation of Guam Island, Marianas*, 21 July – 10 August 1944, World War II War Diaries, 7 December 1941 to 31 December 1945, NARA Records Group 38)

[18] 92nd Ordnance Bomb Disposal Squad (Separate), unit history, November 1943 to February 1945; 92nd U.S. Ordnance Bomb Disposal Squad to Commandant, Ordnance Bomb Disposal School, operation report, 1 February 1944.

[19] 92nd Ordnance Bomb Disposal Squad (Separate), unit history, November 1943 to February 1945.

[20] One major problem with U.S. Navy bomb disposal sections lay with their smaller size – just one officer plus a noncom or enlisted rating. (*List of B.D. officers Assigned to Companies*; 26 October 1943; Ordnance Bomb Disposal School Headquarters, 26 November 1942; Ernest Neeper, [transcript] interview by author, 14 February 2004; J. Frank Durham, *You Only Blow Yourself Up Once: Confessions of a World War Two Bomb Disposaleer*, Lincoln, Nebraska: iUniverse, 2003, 36-50; 1945 BD Officer Roster; see also Samuel E. Morison, "The Struggle for Guadalcanal, August 1942 – February 1943," Vol. 5 of *The History of United States Naval Operations in World War II*, Boston: Little, Brown and Company, 1958; Samuel B. Griffith, *The Battle for Guadalcanal*, Champaign, Illinois: University of Illinois Press, 1963.)

[21] Ordnance BD squads with credit for New Guinea include the 100th, 107th 108th, 171st, 172nd, 173rd, and 174th. In late 1942, MacArthur also had four ordnance bomb disposal officers at his disposal. Aberdeen Proving Ground sent three first lieutenants to Australia: Landy B. Altman, and John R. Cordell, Jr. and Vandel P. Kovar. Meanwhile, 1st Lt. Herrin E. McInnis went to Auckland, New Zealand by November 1942. By December 1945, all except Kovar had either left military service, or had transferred to other duties. U.S. Marines also provided bomb disposal personnel, breaking their two companies into detachments. (Technical Information Bulletins, AFHRA 173.8 through 173.11, Maxwell Air Force Base, 15 March 1945, 283; 1942 Officer Roster; 1945 Officer Roster; Army Pamphlet 672-1; Mayo, 48-53; 353-86).

[22] Ernest Neeper, interview by author, 14 February 2004.

[23] T. B. Montgomery to U.S. Pacific Fleet Commander, *Report of Torpedoing U.S.S. L.S.T. 342 – 0130 LOVE July 18, 1943*, 28 July 1943; 1942 Officer Roster.

[24] LST-342 belonged to Boat Pool 8, based in the Solomon Islands. Submarine RO-106 took credit for the sinking at Lat. 09.03 South; Long. 158.11 East. After a brief investigation, Navy officials commended LST 342's crewmen for evacuating survivors, and absolved the Navy Group commander from blame in the sinking, as the Navy had a shortage of escort craft. 1st Lt. Wyckoff is listed as killed-in-action at sea and a posthumous recipient of the Purple Heart Medal. (T. B. Montgomery to U.S. Pacific Fleet Commander, *Report of Torpedoing U.S.S. L.S.T. 342 – 0130 LOVE July 18, 1943*, 28 July 1943; Jerome Krieger to Commander, NAVSCOLEOD, *Fact Sheet*, 5 October 1992; Robert Leiendecker, *World War II EOD Data*; National EOD Association Library, Charlottesville VA, 2003; Michael R. Vining, *Explosive Ordnance Disposal Memorial – U. S. Army,* submitted to the EOD Memorial Commission, 15 October 2011; Karl C. Dod, *The Corps of Engineers: The War Against Japan*, Washington D.C.: Center for Military History, 1966, 249-51.)

[25] Marines, 1st Amphibious Corps, *Report on Bougainville Operations*, 3 November – 15 December 1943, World War II War Diaries, 7 December 1941 to 31 December 1945, NARA Records Group 38); 1942 Officer Roster; *Pamphlet 672-1*.

[26] 109th Ordnance Bomb Disposal Squad (Separate), unit history, November 1943 to October 1945; U. S. War Department, *Table of Organization No. 9: Bomb Disposal Company*, Ordnance Department, Washington D.C., 1942; *Detonator* [newsletter] U.S. Army Bomb Disposal School: Aberdeen Proving Ground, Maryland, 22 October 1943; Ernest Neeper, interview by author, 14 February 2004; Hooper, 12-14, 25-26.
[27] Donald L. Miller, *D-Days in the Pacific* (New York City, New York: Simon & Schuster, 2005), 183-85; See also Philip A. Crowl, *Campaign in the Marianas* (Washington D.C.: Chief of Military History, 1960).
[28] James S. Brown III, Telephone interview by author, 28 June 2003; Dod, 476-516; Mayo, 353-57; 1945 Officer Roster.
[29] 100th BD Squad participated in every South Pacific and Philippines campaign. Unfortunately, their narrative records at the National Archives (like many other separate squads) are incomplete. (100th Ordnance Bomb Disposal Squad (Separate), unit history, 1944-45.)
[30] Capt. Alberto Gavaldon, a Mexican-American, hailed from El Paso, Texas. Unfortunately, no rosters or histories exist for the 107th and 108th Squads, according to National EOD Association records. (100th Ordnance Bomb Disposal Squad (Separate), unit history, 1944-45; Technical Information Bulletins, AFHRA 173.8 through 173.11, Maxwell Air Force Base, 15 March 1945, 283; 1945 Officer Roster; Mayo, 170-1; Murray & Millett, 196-215).
[31] Robert Smith Ross, *The Approach to the Philippines* (Washington: United States Center for Military History) 1953, 113; Howarth, 447-49; Murray & Millett, 492-93; Miller, 129, 158.
[32] 109th Ordnance Bomb Disposal Squad (Separate), unit history, November 1943 to October 1945; Carmel J. Cirocco, transcript, interview by author, 19 June 2011.
[33] 109th Ordnance Bomb Disposal Squad (Separate), unit history, November 1943 to October 1945; Carmel J. Cirocco, transcript, interview by author, 19 June 2011; Ernest Neeper, interview by author, 14 February 2004;.
[34] Robert E. Leiendecker, *Bomb Disposal, The Early Years of Explosive Ordnance Disposal (An Informal History)*, Charlottesville, Virginia: NATEODA Press, 2012, 343-50; Technical Information Bulletins, AFHRA 173.8 through 173.11, Maxwell Air Force Base, 15 March 1945, 283; Dod, 381-85; *Pamphlet 671-1*.
[35] Williamson Murray and Allen R. Millett, *A War to be Won: Fighting the Second World* War, Cambridge, Massachusetts: Harvard University Press, 2001, 143-68, 169-95, 197; Ronald H. Bailey, *Home Front USA*, (Alexandria, VA: WWII Time-Life, 1977), 105; Stephen Howarth, *To Shining Sea: a History of the United States Navy, 1775-1991,* New York: Random House, 1991, 405-07.
[36] Besides Adm. Yamamoto's defeat at Midway, Japan also had a score to settle over Lt. Col. Jimmy Doolittle's audacious bombing raid earlier that spring. (Stetson Conn, Rose C. Engleman, and Byron Fairchild, *Guarding the United States and its Outposts*, Washington D.C.: Chief of Military History, 1946, 259; 268-70; Hisashi Takahashi, "The Japanese Campaign in Alaska as Seen from the Strategic Perspective," from *Alaska at War 1941-1945: The Forgotten War Remembered*, Fern Chandonnet, ed., Fairbanks: University of Alaska Press, 2008,

33-38; Alvin D. Coox, "Reflecting on the Alaska Theater in Pacific War Operations," from *Alaska at War 1941-1945: The Forgotten War Remembered*, Fern Chandonnet, ed., Fairbanks: University of Alaska Press, 2008, 39-42; Teruo Nishijima, "Recalling the Battle of Attu," from *Alaska at War 1941-1945: The Forgotten War Remembered*, Fern Chandonnet, ed., Fairbanks: University of Alaska Press, 2008, 109-12; Karl Kaoru Kasukabe, "The Escape of the Japanese Garrison from Kiska," from *Alaska at War 1941-1945: The Forgotten War Remembered*, Fern Chandonnet, ed., Fairbanks: University of Alaska Press, 2008, 121-23).

[37] Benjamin B. Talley and Virginia M. Talley, "Building Alaska's Defenses in World War II," from *Alaska at War 1941-1945: The Forgotten War Remembered*, Fern Chandonnet, ed., Fairbanks: University of Alaska Press, 2008, 59-65; Murray and Millett, 197.

[38] Ordnance Bomb Disposal School Headquarters, BD officer roster, 26 November 1942; Dix Fetzer, e-mail to author, 10 April 2004

[39] Ronald Fulcher, *PFC Clarence Fulcher, 1741st Ordnance Company (Bomb Disposal Squad), as told by his son, Ron Fulcher,* unpublished memoir, 7 January 2008; Clarence Fulcher, telephone interview by author, 2 August 2011; Conn, Engleman, and Fairchild, 295).

[40] Possible ramifications of balloon raids launched from Kiska and Attu stem from the author's personal speculations. (Frank A. Parsons to Historical Section, Baltimore, *Report on Bomb Disposal Activities* (1 July 1942 – 30 June 1943), memorandum, 9 July 1943; Robert C. Mikesh, *Japan's World War II Balloon Bomb Attacks on North America*, Washington D.C.: Smithsonian Institution Press, 1973; James S. Russell, "The Aleutian Campaign," from *Alaska at War 1941-1945: The Forgotten War Remembered*, Fern Chandonnet, ed., Fairbanks: University of Alaska Press, 2008, 67-74; Conn, Engleman, and Fairchild, 295).

[41] Fifth U.S. Ordnance Bomb Disposal Squad (Separate) to Commanding Officer of 150th Ordnance Battalion (Headquarters). Ordnance Bomb Disposal School Headquarters; Fern Chandonnet, "The Recapture of Attu," from *Alaska at War 1941-1945: The Forgotten War Remembered*, Fern Chandonnet, ed., Fairbanks: University of Alaska Press, 2008, 81-85.

[42] U.S. Department of the Navy, N. D. Communiqués, May-July 1943, Available from http://www.ibiblio.org/pha/comms.html., Internet; Conn, Engleman, and Fairchild, 295;

[43] Army Corps of Engineers had developed the D-8 Bulldozer, which boasted an armored cab to protect drivers from sniper fire. During the Pacific Campaign, they were used almost like tanks, ramming dugouts and pillboxes. (Clarence Fulcher, *PFC Clarence Fulcher, 1741st Ordnance Company (Bomb Disposal Squad), as told to his son, Ron Fulcher,* unpublished memoir, 7 January 2008; Dod. 514-15.)

[44] Clarence Fulcher, telephone interview by author, 2 August 2011.

[45] U.S. Explosive Ordnance Disposal Technical Manual 60A. *Japanese Explosive Ordnance, 15 Aug. 1945.* Naval Explosive Ordnance Disposal Technology Division, Indian Head, Maryland, 1978; Fulcher memoir.

[46] Positive identification for Rodger has taken some time to achieve, as the EOD Memorial recorded only his rank and surname. Their primary source, 5th BD Squad's official history, was compiled in 1945 after three changes of command, and did not list full names for 2nd Lt. Robert B. Rodger (O-1551300) or T/Sgt. Harry F. Rapp (35032297). I have used Department of Defense and National Archives records available through www.ancestry.com to fill in the vacuum. (5th U.S. Ordnance Bomb Disposal Squad (Separate) to Commanding Officer of 150th Ordnance Battalion (Headquarters), *History of the Fifth Ordnance Bomb Disposal Squad*; U.S. Naturalization Record Indexes, 1791-1992, No. 5458873, dated 6 October 1942; Ordnance Bomb Disposal School Headquarters, roster, 26 November 1942; www.eodmemorial.org/army.html; Hooper, 25.)

[47] Since the official 5th Squad report was not filed until 1945, and Capt. Patrick Hogan offered no details, I cannot as yet determine precisely what killed Rodger and Rapp. To my knowledge, World War II deaths were not classified as "killed in action" unless enemy contact was implicated. I am inclined to accept an explosion, as does Mike Vining, but one could make a compelling case for Japanese snipers. Rodger and Rapp might have been operating beyond infantry protection, and were picked off. Japanese stragglers harassed Army operations until the last group of four was apprehended on July 11. Since most explosion victims left few visible remains, the Army classified these as "DNB," meaning "dead no body," or "dead not buried." Coincidentally, two Army officers stationed in Tunisia had died around the same timeframe (June 18) while disarming an Italian mine. Eyewitnesses reported few remains to be salvaged, and what could be saved was interred over in North Africa. By contrast, Rodger's and Rapp's remains were later sent from Alaska for disposition by next of kin. Harry Rapp had family living in Mahoning County, Ohio, but Rodger did not leave any family in the States. Lt. Rodger's 1942 enlistment profile lists him as divorced with no dependents. Reinterred on October 1, 1948, 2nd Lt. Rodger now rests in Plot D793, Beverly National Cemetery, New Jersey. T/Sgt. Rapp is buried (not memorialized) in Arlington National Cemetery, Arlington, Virginia, Plot: Section: 12, Site: 107. (U.S. Department of the Navy, N. D. Communiqués, May-July 1943, available from http://www.ibiblio.org/pha/comms.html, Internet; *History of the Fifth Ordnance Bomb Disposal Squad*; *Explosive Ordnance Disposal Memorial – U. S. Army*. Mike R. Vining, EOD Memorial Commission, 15 October 2011; www.eodmemorial.org/army.html.)

[48] T/Sgt. Fred Walden and T/5 E. C. Anderson were relieved from their duties after their unit's return to Aberdeen Proving Ground. They were replaced by T/5 (later Sgt.) Ronald W. Woolley and T/5 Donald A. Ware. Additional members of 5th BD Squad included Sgt. William D. Marvin, T/5 Alfred T. Peczynski; T/5 Horace Johnson, T/5 Percy P. Richardson, and T/5 Ernest C. Anderson. (*History of the Fifth Ordnance Bomb Disposal Squad;* Fulcher account.)

[49] First Special Service Force, better known as the Devil's Brigade, were an elite Canadian-American commando unit trained to operate in every possible climate. Forerunners of the Special Forces, the "Forcemen" served with distinction in the Italian Theater, as well as Southern France. Meanwhile, 5th BD Squad participated

in the Normandy campaign, finishing up the war in Germany. They have the distinction of being the only ordnance disposal unit to serve in both Pacific and European Theaters. Some records have erroneously placed them at Salerno and Anzio, but at those times 5th Squad was still in Alaska, or in garrison at Aberdeen Proving Ground. (Alastair Neely, "The First Special Service Force," from *Alaska at War 1941-1945: The Forgotten War Remembered*, Fern Chandonnet, ed., Fairbanks: University of Alaska Press, 2008, 87-95; Galen Roger Perras, "'When We Got There, the Cupboard Was Bare:' Canada's Greenlight Force and the Recapture of Kiska, 1943," from *Alaska at War 1941-1945: The Forgotten War Remembered*, Fern Chandonnet, ed., Fairbanks: University of Alaska Press, 2008, 97-102; Conn, Engleman, and Fairchild, 296-7.)

[50] On August 25, 1943, Capt. Patrick Hogan took over command of 5th Squad on Kiska, where they would remain until January 1944. They were refitted for overseas service, and left for Europe in April 1944. They were present during the latter stages of Normandy. 7th BD Squad also went to France in 1944, landing in Brittany and serving across France and Germany. These were the sole BD units who verifiably served in both Pacific and European Theaters. (Lt. Col. Harry M. Walker, *Special Orders No. 75,* 19 April 1943; 7th Ordnance Bomb Disposal Squad (Separate), unit history, February 1943 to October 1945; *History of the Fifth Ordnance Bomb Disposal Squad;* 1945 BD officer roster; *U.S. Army Campaigns of World War II: Aleutian Islands.* Washington D.C.: Center for Military History, Publication 72-6; Hooper, 25).

[51] Dix Fetzer. [electronic mail] interview by author. 10-14 April 2004; Chad Weihrauch, "Veteran Cop Recalls a World War II Battle;" Conn, Engleman, and Fairchild, 296-7.

[52] Dean C. Allard, "The North Pacific Campaign in Perspective," from *Alaska at War 1941-1945: The Forgotten War Remembered*, Fern Chandonnet, ed., Fairbanks: University of Alaska Press, 2008, 3-11; Fulcher account.

[53] U.S. Explosive Ordnance Disposal Technical Manual 60A, *Japanese Explosive Ordnance, 15 Aug. 1945.* Naval Explosive Ordnance Disposal Technology Division, Indian Head, Maryland, 1978.

[54] War Department Technical Manual E9-1984, *Disposal Methods for Enemy Bombs and Fuzes,* Aberdeen Proving Ground, Maryland: Chief of Ordnance, 12 November 1942; U.S. Explosive Ordnance Disposal Technical Manual 60A, *Japanese Explosive Ordnance, 15 Aug. 1945.* Naval Explosive Ordnance Disposal Technology Division, Indian Head, Maryland, 1978; Mike R. Vining, *Explosive Ordnance Disposal Memorial – U. S. Army,* EOD Memorial Commission, 9 April 2011; Hooper, 17, 26-7, II; http://www.eodmemorial.org/index3.html, Internet.

[55] U.S. Explosive Ordnance Disposal Technical Manual 60A, *Japanese Explosive Ordnance, 15 Aug. 1945.* Naval Explosive Ordnance Disposal Technology Division, Indian Head, Maryland, 1978.

[56] U.S. Explosive Ordnance Disposal Technical Manual 60A, *Japanese Explosive Ordnance, 15 Aug. 1945.* Naval Explosive Ordnance Disposal Technology Division, Indian Head, Maryland, 1978; Army Services Forces Ordnance Department, *Bomb Disposal Technical Information.* (Bulletin No. 25) Aberdeen

Proving Ground, M.D.: Ordnance Bomb Disposal School, 1 April 1944.

[57] Germans did experiment with a piloted V-1 rocket plane, as famously demonstrated by Hanna Freitsch, the Nazi aviatrix. (U.S. Explosive Ordnance Disposal Technical Manual 60A, *Japanese Explosive Ordnance, 15 Aug. 1945* (Naval Explosive Ordnance Disposal Technology Division, Indian Head, Maryland, 1978); Nass, *Bomb Disposal Notes.*)

[58] 4th Marine Division, *Report on Tinian Operations*, Appendix One, Bomb Disposal, Mine Field, and Booby Trap Report (World War II War Diaries, 7 December 1941 to 31 December 1945, NARA Records Group 38); Miller, 126; Hooper, 18-28; See also Frank Durham, *You Only Blow Yourself Up Once* (Lincoln, Nebraska: iUniverse Press, 2003);

[59] James S. Brown III, Telephone interview by author, 28 June 2003; 178th Ordnance Bomb Disposal Squad (Separate), unit history, 1945-46.

[60] 111st Amphibious Corps, *Report of Operations for the Capture and Occupation of Guam Island, Marianas*, 21 July – 10 August 1944 (World War II War Diaries, 7 December 1941 to 31 December 1945, NARA Records Group 38); Neeper interview; Hooper, 26-8.

[61] U.S. Explosive Ordnance Disposal Technical Manual 60A, *Japanese Explosive Ordnance, 15 Aug. 1945* (Naval Explosive Ordnance Disposal Technology Division, Indian Head, Maryland, 1978; Army Services Forces Ordnance Department, *Bomb Disposal Technical Information.* (Bulletin No. 25).

[62] Robert R. Smith, *The War in the Pacific: Triumph in the Philippines*, Washington D.C.: Office of the Chief of Military History, 1963, 694; Department of the Army, *Pamphlet 672-1: Unit Citation and Campaign Participation Credit Register*. Washington D.C.: Government Publishing Office, 1972; Miller, 257.

[63] Army Services Forces Ordnance Department, *Bomb Disposal Technical Information,* Bulletin No. 25, April 1944; *Pamphlet 672-1*; Smith, 88-103; Miller, 196-207.

[64] 100th Ordnance Bomb Disposal Squad (Separate), unit history, 1944-45; Department of the Army, *Pamphlet 672-1: Unit Citation and Campaign Participation Credit Register*. Washington D.C.: Government Publishing Office, 1972; James S. Brown III, transcript, interview by author, 28 June 2003; U.S. Army Enlistment Records, 1939-45, National Archives and Records Administration, www.ancestry.com.

[65] James S. Brown III, transcript, interview by author, 28 June 2003.

[66] 109th Ordnance Bomb Disposal Squad (Separate), unit history, November 1943 to October 1945; Carmel J Cirocco, interview by author, 19 June 2011; Ernest Neeper, interview by author, 14 February 2004.

[67] Williamson Murray and Allen R. Millett, *A War to be Won: Fighting the Second World* War, Cambridge, Massachusetts: Harvard University Press, 2001, 371-72; Miller, 185-90.

[68] Ibid.

[69] According to squad records, the 77th Infantry Division awarded the medals for service against the Japanese on September 4, 1944. Zellmer's award came on September 21. T/5 Elmer J. Craddock was also nominated for the same honor.

(92nd Ordnance Bomb Disposal Squad (Separate), unit history, November 1943 to February 1945).

[70] 92nd Ordnance Bomb Disposal Squad (Separate), unit history, November 1943 to February 1945; Murray and Millett, 371-72.

[71] Devlin, 554-57; Smith, 651-58.

[72] 109th Ordnance Bomb Disposal Squad (Separate), unit history, November 1943 to October 1945; Carmel J Cirocco, interviews by author, 19 June 2011 and 20 July 2011; Ernest Neeper, interview by author, 14 February 2004.

[73] Yamashita lost about 60,000 to Krueger's 3,500 dead and 12,000 wounded. Shortly after his capture, Yamashita was tried and executed by the U.S. Army for war crimes against the Philippines. (92nd Ordnance Bomb Disposal Squad (Separate), unit history, November 1943 to February 1945; Murray and Millett, 371-72; Murray and Millett, 371-72; Miller, 205-06.)

[74] 158th BD Squad, along with 171st through 184th Squads, also received credit for participating in Luzon's assault landings. (James S. Brown III. [transcript] interview by author. 28 June 2003; Army Pamphlet 672-1; Hooper, 28).

[75] Devlin, 556-66; Smith, 211-308.

[76] 109th Ordnance Bomb Disposal Squad (Separate), unit history, November 1943 to October 1945; Carmel J Cirocco, interviews by author, 19 June 2011 and 20 July 2011; Ernest Neeper, interview by author, 14 February 2004; Carmel J. Cirocco, *Certificate of Service,* Form 53-98, 27 June 1945; Army Pamphlet 672-1; Hooper, 27-8.

[77] T/5 Wassil received a commendation and Bronze Star for his actions. Cirocco's discharge took effect one year after his earlier promotion to first lieutenant, so he should have been promoted to captain in due course. However, Carl Cirocco's later efforts to rectify this unintended oversight have been fruitless. (109th Ordnance Bomb Disposal Squad (Separate), unit history, November 1943 to October 1945; Carmel J Cirocco, interviews by author; Ernest Neeper, interview by author; Maj. A. J. Barnett to 2nd Lt. Carmel J. Cirocco, *Special Orders 158*, 7 June 1944; Hooper, 27-8; Devlin, 556-66).

[78] 109th Ordnance Bomb Disposal Squad (Separate), unit history, November 1943 to October 1945; War Department Technical Manual E9-1984, *Disposal Methods for Enemy Bombs and Fuzes,* Aberdeen Proving Ground, Maryland: Chief of Ordnance, 12 November 1942.

[79] "Bomb Disposal," from *Firepower* (Washington D.C.: Army Ordnance Association, August- September 1945), 8-9; Smith, 608; Army Pamphlet 672-1.

[80] Ordnance Bomb Disposal School. [roster of active BD officers] 1 December 1945; Neeper interview; Robert E. Leiendecker, *Bomb Disposal, The Early Years of Explosive Ordnance Disposal (An Informal History)*, Charlottesville, Virginia: NATEODA Press, 2012, 433-4; Mayo, 433-38.

[81] One of Aberdeen's earliest graduates, Starr had served for a time in Boston, as part of the Eastern Defense Command. (176th Ordnance Bomb Disposal Squad (Separate) to Colonel Thomas J. Kane. *Overseas Activities of 176th Ordnance Bomb Disposal Squad,* 21 June 1946; Ordnance Bomb Disposal School Headquarters, BD officer roster, 26 November 1942.)

[82] James S. Brown III. [transcript] interview by author. 28 June 2003; Ordnance Bomb Disposal School. [roster of active BD officers] 1 December 1945.
[83] 178th Ordnance Bomb Disposal Squad (Separate), unit history, 1945-46.
[84] 178th Ordnance Bomb Disposal Squad (Separate), unit history, 1945-46; U.S. Explosive Ordnance Disposal Technical Manual 60A. *Japanese Explosive Ordnance, 15 Aug. 1945.* Naval Explosive Ordnance Disposal Technology Division, Indian Head, Maryland, 1978.
[85] 178th Ordnance Bomb Disposal Squad (Separate), unit history, 1945-46.
[86] 178th Ordnance Bomb Disposal Squad (Separate), unit history, 1945-46; James S. Brown III, transcript, interview by author, 28 June 2003.
[87] 623rd Ammunition Company also sent their provisional bomb squad to Mindanao. (1945 BD officer roster; Mayo, 353-86).
[88] 1942 BD Officer Roster; Ordnance Bomb Disposal School Headquarters, List of B.D. Officers Assigned to Companies, 26 October 1943; Ordnance Bomb Disposal School Headquarters, BD officer roster, 26 October 1943.
[89] During World War II, mixed religious marriages, especially between Jews and Gentiles, had their share of problems, particularly when deciding which traditions children should be raised in. Even today, such unions are strongly discouraged. (Richard E. Metress, National Jewish Welfare Board, Bureau of War Records, 1939-45, NARA, courtesy of www.ancestry.com; Carole P. Carlo, telephone interview by author, 29 July 2011.)
[90] 209th U.S. Ordnance Bomb Disposal (Separate). *Squad History* [unpublished documents] 24 March - 4 August 1945; Robert Leiendecker, *World War II Data [Ordnance Bomb Disposal Squads*, Charlottesville VA; National EOD Association Archives, c. 2003.
[91] 209th U.S. Ordnance Bomb Disposal (Separate). *Squad History* [unpublished documents] (24 March-4 August 1945) Washington D.C.: National Archives; Smith, 308.
[92] 209th U.S. Ordnance Bomb Disposal (Separate). *Squad History* [unpublished documents] (24 March-4 August 1945) Washington D.C.: National Archives.
[93] 209th U.S. Ordnance Bomb Disposal (Separate). *Squad History* [unpublished documents] (24 March-4 August 1945) Washington D.C.: National Archives.
[94] Robert R. Smith, *The War in the Pacific: Triumph in the Philippines.* (Washington D.C.: Office of the Chief of Military History, 1963) 631-34, 692-94.
[95] 209th U.S. Ordnance Bomb Disposal (Separate). *Squad History*; U.S. Explosive Ordnance Disposal Technical Manual 60A. *Japanese Explosive Ordnance, 15 Aug. 1945.* Naval Explosive Ordnance Disposal Technology Division, Indian Head, Maryland, 1978, 16; Smith, 697.
[96] *Japanese Explosive Ordnance, 15 Aug. 1945.* Naval Explosive Ordnance Disposal Technology Division, Indian Head, Maryland, 1978, 16.
[97] *Japanese Explosive Ordnance, 15 Aug. 1945.* Naval Explosive Ordnance Disposal Technology Division, Indian Head, Maryland, 1978, 16.
[98] 209th U.S. Ordnance Bomb Disposal (Separate). *Squad History;* Smith, 631-34.
[99] T/5 Robert Breault and Pfc. Haywood Tolliver were reassigned from 106th BD Squad on June 23. With the addition of Lt. Tarleton, this brought 209th Squad

back up to five total personnel. (209th U.S. Ordnance Bomb Disposal (Separate). *Squad History*; Department of the Army. *Pamphlet 672-1: Unit Citation and Campaign Participation Credit Register.* Washington D.C.: Government Publishing Office, 1972; EOD Memorial: U.S. Army Personnel. Available from http://www.eodmemorial.org/index3.html, Internet).

[100] 156th Ordnance Bomb Disposal Squad to Commandant, Ordnance Bomb Disposal Center. Unit Report of Action on Iwo Jima. 26 June 1945.

[101] Incidentally, Tyree was also credited for preserving a personal diary by Lt. Sugihara Kinru – one of the few surviving records of Iwo Jima. (156th Ordnance Bomb Disposal Squad to Commandant, Ordnance Bomb Disposal Center, Unit Report of Action on Iwo Jima, 26 June 1945; Lewis Tyree Jr., letter, *Journal of Military Affairs.* Vol. 59, No. 3 (July 1995), 576-7).

[102] Roy Appleman, James M. Burns, Russell A. Gugeler, and James Steven, *Okinawa: The Last Battle* (Washington D.C.: Historical Division, Department of the Army, 1948), 84-85. 477-82, 488-90; 176th Ordnance Bomb Disposal Squad (Separate) to Colonel Thomas J. Kane, *Overseas Activities of 176th Ordnance Bomb Disposal Squad,* 21 June 1946; Department of the Army Pamphlet 632-1.

[103] Ibid.

[104] Appleman, etc., 156-73, 479.

[105] 92nd U.S. Ordnance Bomb Disposal Squad to Commandant; http://www.eodmemorial.org/index3.html, Internet; Mike R. Vining, *Explosive Ordnance Disposal Memorial – U. S. Army,* EOD Memorial Commission, 9 April 2011; Appleman, etc., 160-61, 173-83; Hooper 26-7, IV.

[106] The official designation for this Pacific headquarters is quite a mouthful: U.S. Army 6th Pacific Ocean Area Provisional Headquarters Bomb Disposal Detachment. Repeated enquiries at the National Archives have resulted in no progress in finding any documents relative to this unit. (Department of the Army Pamphlet 632-1)

[107] Ordnance Bomb Disposal School, roster of active BD officers, 1 December 1945.

[108] 176th Ordnance Bomb Disposal Squad (Separate) to Colonel Thomas J. Kane, *Overseas Activities of 176th Ordnance Bomb Disposal Squad,* 21 June 1946; Appleman, etc., 453-474.

[109] 178th Ordnance Bomb Disposal Squad (Separate), unit history, 1945-46; James S. Brown III, transcript, interview by author, 28 June 2003.

[110] 178th Ordnance Bomb Disposal Squad (Separate), unit history, 1945-46; James S. Brown III, transcript, interview by author, 28 June 2003.

[111] Japan's propagandistic boast is comparable to Hermann Göring's vainglorious assertions in 1939. (U. S. Navy Technical Mission to Japan, *Japanese Bomb Disposal Methods*, January 1946, 9-16).

[112] U. S. Navy Technical Mission to Japan, *Japanese Bomb Disposal Methods*, January 1946, 7-8; Murray and Millett, 190-91; Hooper, 31.

[113] U. S. Navy Technical Mission to Japan, *Japanese Bomb Disposal Methods*, January 1946, 7-8.

[114] U. S. Navy Technical Mission to Japan, *Japanese Bomb Disposal Methods*, January 1946, 9-16.

[115] U. S. Navy Technical Mission to Japan, *Japanese Bomb Disposal Methods*, January 1946, 7-8; Hooper, 31.
[116] U. S. Navy Technical Mission to Japan, *Japanese Bomb Disposal Methods*, January 1946, 7-8; Hooper, 31.
[117] Robert C. Mikesh, *Japan's World War II Balloon Bomb Attacks on North America*. Washington D.C.: Smithsonian Institution Press, 1973, 1, 28, 69; Conn, Engelman, and Fairchild, 113-4.
[118] Most commonly encountered bomb combinations were 5 kilogram thermite bombs and 12 kilogram (Type 97) explosives. Sometimes, a 15 kilogram (Type 92) HE bomb doubled as an anti-personnel mine, with similar effects to a German SD-2 "Butterfly" Bomb. (Mikesh, 8-24, 43-61, 77).
[119] Stanley W. Davidson, *Military Relations Between United States and Canada*, Washington D.C., Center for Military History, 1959, 200; Mikesh, 25-7.
[120] Mikesh, 67-8.
[121] The victims included Elsie Mitchell (age 26), Edward Engen, (age 13), Jay Gifford, (age 13), Joan Patzke, (age 13), Dick Patzke, (age 14), and Sherman Shoemaker, (age 11). In 1947, Rev. Mitchell later married Betty Patzke, an older sister to two bombing victims. They served for nearly fifteen years as missionaries in Vietnam, where Archie disappeared after being pressed into service by North Vietnamese soldiers on May 30, 1962. (Ibid.)
[122] Some have speculated on the efficacy of Fu-Go weapons, had the Japanese carried out chemical or biological warfare, based on their controversial Unit 731 experiments in Manchuria, where they developed and tested anthrax and bacillus munitions on Chinese and other prisoners of war. Robert Mikesh concluded that Japan's military had not considered using biological contaminants in conjunction with Fu-Go balloons. But questions still linger over Japanese scientists participating in Unit 731, who were granted amnesty by General Douglas MacArthur shortly after the August 1945 surrender. (Ordnance Bomb Disposal School. [roster of active BD officers] 1 December 1945; Mikesh, 25-29, 38-39).
[123] Bradley Biggs, *The Triple Nickles: America's First All-Black Paratroop Unit* (Hamden, Connecticut: Archon Books, 1986), 55-67; Gerard M. Devlin, *Paratrooper!* (St. Martin's Press, New York, 1979), 199-200.
[124] Lieut. Col. John Cannon, panel discussion, 15 February 2005, at West Virginia University; Biggs, 55-67; Devlin, 199-200.
[125] Biggs, 55-67; Brophy and Fisher, 115.

# CHAPTER EIGHT

# PICKING UP

Postwar ordnance removal continued for several years across former Axis nations. To aid reconstruction, the U.S. began training host nation soldiers to safely handle explosives. As previously noted, Germany and Japan both possessed sophisticated networks of bomb disposal teams, which proved quite capable during the Allies' retaliatory bombing raids. Some Americans could not help regretting the damage caused by their own bombers, particularly as they were expected to clear up Allied duds. Describing the German town of Kassel as a "mass of rubble," Lt. Gerald Ledford of 161st Squad made his way through a maze of "twisted iron girders," choked with "piles of broken up concrete and loose bricks." However, Kane's disposaleers were mindful of the war's root cause and took great pleasure at seeing the Axis aggressors humbled. Above all, these soldiers fervently hoped never to see this kind of warfare again.[1]

On September 11, 1945, as the Army's Bomb Disposal Center initiated its drawdown, Lt. Col. Martin Ehrmann spoke on behalf of all disposaleers. Recognizing the "sincere and loyal efforts of each officer and enlisted man," the commandant sagely predicted that they would all someday "look back with pride on [their] insignia." Martin also spared words for those members who had "paid the full price," while recalling other men who were "broken in body." Expressing his wish that "children will never again have to worry about [such things as] Zus-40 and E-1a," Ehrmann nevertheless reminded his colleagues and subordinates alike: "The end is not in sight for bomb disposal personnel."[2]

Before leaving Europe in the autumn, Kane publicly revealed his branch's existence and outlined its postwar goals. He likewise submitted efficiency reports on the various Allied headquarters that provided support for his squads. Except for Patton's uncooperative Third Army, most U.S. headquarters were rated highly. While Kane rated the Eighth and Ninth Air Forces' cooperation as merely satisfactory, the American officer stinted no praise for the combined British services, who shared their resources "freely and completely," offering "additional training [not] available in other theaters."[3]

Kane had an immediate impact on reconstruction efforts in Germany, as well as long-term influence on NATO policy. He urged the creation of an "international Bomb Disposal committee," to oversee future UXB removals. Kane further advocated using surplus materiel to "revitalize [the] European economy. Encouraging the training of select Germans with no Nazi backgrounds, he predicted that such *Sprengkommando* units could presently handle Allied bombs without need for supervision.[4]

Initially, German volunteers were commanded by an American officer known as their *Spreng Leitner.* Even before V-E Day, Capt. Joseph F. Petit (67th BD Squad) had utilized "German bomb disposal squads" to augment his limited manpower. From March 29 to June 13, 1945, the former enemies cleared over two hundred UXBs from Wiesbaden without incident. By 1946, host nation officers had taken complete charge.[5]

During the watchful peace of 1945-46, the Allies still feared that surviving SS or Hitler Youth might regroup and seize unsecured weaponry for a guerilla war in Austria or Southern Germany. Toward this end, American squads continued to dump captured German armaments and munitions in the North Sea or demolish them *in situ.* On June 24, 1946, Col. T. H. Nixon, the new ETO Ordnance Chief, ordered a halt to this practice, instead submitting his plan to "demilitarize" arms and munitions for precious raw materials. Moreover, peacetime required American forces to reduce their stockpiles in West Germany, Austria, and elsewhere. On V-E Day, Col. Nixon had estimated 1,150,000 tons of U. S. munitions remained on the continent. By July 1946, total Army and Air Force arsenals had been reduced by 675,000 tons.[6]

As far back as October 1945, United States Armed Forces Europe (USAFE) commanders had argued for the retention of nine bomb disposal squads, noting their proven efficacy as "highly mobile" teams "under central control," rather than assigning them to limited "geographic areas." After months of stonewalling back in Washington, Kane's argument for centralized administration had finally won out over in Europe. By this point, nearly all of the Army's 212 separate squads were deactivated, while Lt. Col. Ehrmann's Bomb Disposal Center had permanently closed effective November 15, 1945. Before shutting down, Ehrmann's staff had compiled a fairly complete roster of qualified officers, so Ordnance sent out a call for officers to lead reconstituted bomb squads. Since only three original squads remained intact at Aberdeen, almost forty teams were reactivated as regular Army or Reserve components.[7]

In May 1946, the Ninth Air Force opened a new overseas bomb disposal school for Army and Air personnel at Hilpoltstein, Germany. Taught by 1st Lt. Raymond D. Caricofe, the course lasted six weeks.

During the German school's inaugural month, nine veteran Ninth Air Force squads (72nd to 75th, 82nd to 85th, plus the 87th) graduated and dispersed to U. S. Army and Air Force commands across West Germany.[8]

From June 20 to August 31, 1946, five experienced Ninth Air Force teams (72nd, 73rd, 74th, 82nd and 83rd Squads) kept up a weekly disposal rate of 500 tons, chiefly small arms, gunpowder, and munitions. Activities were primarily centered at Roth, Germany – a temporary home to 1st Infantry Division. Acting as both ammunition and bomb disposal officer, Capt. (later Maj.) Willis C. Vaughn (72nd BD Squad) supervised all five squads with assistance from 1st Lt. Dewitt E. Tyler (83rd BD Squad). As 1946 progressed, Capt. Vaughn dealt with shrinking manpower, as squads were redeployed in other critical areas in West Germany. By the autumn, Vaughan's team handled the entire Roth sector by themselves.[9]

Vaughn's soldiers were initially self-conscious, considering themselves as being Air Corps personnel. However, by July 1946, Vaughn reported his team making "many friends" among the "Big Red One," where they found "excellent chow" and good living conditions. Despite "long hours and hard work," Vaughn's men seldom complained about their pace, but their jobs remained hazardous. On August 2, the 72nd Squad held a memorial service for Pvt. Jack V. Austin, who had been killed one week earlier on July 26. Obscured by a "huge concrete wall," Austin had been unloading a cargo truck full of dud German projectiles. Since Pvt. Austin's precise actions were unobserved by his teammates, Vaughn could not offer any further explanation for his soldier's death.[10]

Victims of the same misapprehensions as many Italian citizens, Germans initially thought the disposaleers' badges denoted responsibility for actual bombings and mistrusted the American squads. As a gesture, school instructor Ray Caricofe handled an important June ordnance mission by assuming temporary command of 82nd Squad at Hilpoltstein. Warning the civilian population via their military governors, Caricofe's team shuttled UXBs, rockets, and mortar rounds to a destruction site about five miles northeast of the town. Over 100 tons of ordnance were dispatched in this way, while Hilpoltstein's citizens had a chance to witness the passing of Army vehicles containing hazardous cargo. Germans afterward reported more incidents directly to the U.S. Army.[11]

James J. Casey, a second lieutenant in charge of 73rd BD Squad, interacted with German civilians in the course of duty with Third Army. Casey assumed command over Allendorf Ammunition Depot on July 1, 1946. Charged with sorting and disposing of bad ammunition, Casey's eleven enlisted men, culled from 73rd and 147th Squads, oversaw German civilian workers who had suffered from poor morale. Casey took practical steps by firing uncooperative employees and improving mess facilities with balanced lunches. Casey's leadership contributed toward Allendorf Depot's successful destruction of more than 2,000 tons of ordnance.[12]

While there were fewer opportunities for heroics after V-E Day, U.S. disposaleers nevertheless received credit for jobs well done. On October 9, one Bremerhaven ammo dump at Speckenbuttel Park suffered an explosion, killing four and injuring two 87th Squad members. Clearing Burger Park at the time, 1st Lt. Dewitt E. Tyler split his 83rd Squad in two sections, and successfully cleared both sites in twelve days. Tyler's "courage and effectiveness" were later recognized by his supervisor, Lt. Col. G. C. Masters of 51st Ordnance Service Battalion.[13]

Perhaps the highest decorated bomb disposal soldier of World War II, Capt. Stephen M. Richards "single-handedly defused and dismantled a cave full of German bombs," according to his 2002 obituary. In reality, Capt. Richards' *coup de main* had been achieved with the utmost secrecy. In February 1946, a special multinational team of fourteen specialists had been ordered to find a camouflaged Nazi depository near Stechovice, Czechoslovakia. Their guide, a former SS sergeant, had identified this thirty-foot cave as a repository for documents pertaining to war crimes.[14]

Working hand in glove with a combat engineer section, Richards' bomb expertise came in handy. Together, four men disarmed several detonators, each connected to a main explosive charge weighing a ton. One misstep would have collapsed the cave and killed all the intruders. Having succeeded in their quest to capture the heavy archive crates, Richards' team ran afoul of unfriendly pro-Soviet Czech officials. Fortunately, after a short detention, Prague grudgingly released the men back into Allied custody. Richards eventually received the Soldier's Medal for Valor, in lieu of the wartime Congressional Medal of Honor.[15]

During their six-month mission, nine U.S. bomb squads had cleared approximately 7,000 tons from German cities, such as Regensburg. According to Col. Nixon's original 1946 estimate, about 13,000 tons of non-American explosive ordnance remained for the West German teams. In November 2011, skilled German explosive ordnance technicians disarmed two leftover bombs at Koblenz; one British and one American.[16]

What of the German industrialists and officers responsible for designing and implementing the Luftwaffe's unorthodox array of bombs? Shortly after the war, technicians such as Werner von Braun and Herbert Ruehlemann were recruited by United States agencies for their talents. Whereas von Braun became an important figure in American rocketry and the NASA program, Ruehlemann went to work developing new weapons systems for Aberdeen Proving Ground. Meanwhile, two Luftwaffe generals, Paul Deichmann and Ernst Marquard, were detained in West Germany, where they proved most cooperative with the Allies. By 1954, they had both provided lengthy studies translated into English and incorporated into future bombing doctrines by the U.S. Air Force. Such evolutions are essential at times to win necessary wars, but one also has to contemplate whether such continued efforts might undermine America's efforts to prevent unnecessary wars in the future.[17]

* * *

Back in the States, Col. Thomas J. Kane had become an advocate for peacetime EOD service. In late 1945, Kane had enjoyed a well-deserved reunion with his wife, Margaret, and their two daughters, Kay and Mary Jo. In 1946, Kane served on Aberdeen's Ordnance Board. He also supervised reservist training camps much as he had supervised CCC installations. Capt. Guenther "Gunner" Froebel (135th BD Squad) trained at Aberdeen during the summer, and remembered Kane as a "gregarious, amiable man, who always took an interest in his soldiers." Col. Kane did his utmost to redress certain wartime oversights, such as belated recognition or overdue promotions. Back in France, he had taken slight umbrage when 168th Squad (1st Lt. Floyd E. Welch) received no recognition for disarming "beaucoup bombs" from a crucial Danube River bridge in spring 1945. By contrast, two wrecking truck drivers assigned to Welch's sector each received a Bronze Star for transporting the safe bombs. Kane even tried to gain a retroactive promotion to captain for 1st Lt. Carl Cirocco, but alas, there were limits to the colonel's influence.[18]

In 1947, Kane relocated to Fort Benning, Georgia, where he assumed the role of post ordnance officer. One of Kane's closest confidantes, T/Sgt. Walter "Wally" Korsgaard, recounted an anecdote from their time together at Benning. While driving back in sweltering heat from the post demolition range, they "secured" two watermelons from a large patch. Back at his office, Kane carved a plug out of each melon, and slowly poured vodka inside them. Kane shared these chilled watermelons with his ordnance staff, regardless of rank. Wally never forgot Kane's generosity after they parted ways in 1948. Korsgaard later received a battlefield commission in Korea and retired as a lieutenant colonel.[19]

In 1948, T. J. Kane became Chief Ordnance Officer for the Far Eastern Army and Air Forces. Stationed with the Fifth Air Force at Tokyo, Kane took a particular interest in post-war operations in the Pacific. He supervised bomb removal in Japan, contributing in his own way to Gen. Douglas MacArthur's ambitious reconstruction program. Fortunately, this three-year assignment permitted the colonel to bring his family to Japan. Kay Levering recounted one mirthful Christmas scene from Japan, where their father bought them toy guns as joke gifts, and in return, the girls rewrapped his old neckties as new. Above all, Kay recalled her father loved his job: "Not staying in the Army after the war would have killed him." For three years, Kane shuttled between Japan, South Korea, and the Philippines, observing and training bomb disposal units.[20]

Kay Levering also recalled her father scouring civilian and military newspapers for any reports of injury or death. Whenever anyone – whether soldier or civilian – was reported killed or hurt by unexploded ordnance, Kane "took it very hard." While stationed in Japan, Kane helped to establish a cooperative international movement to patrol the Pacific for leftover ordnance, whether Japanese or Allied.[21]

* * *

Throughout former Japanese-controlled territories, leftover explosives had impeded post-war reconstruction efforts. One August 1945 incident at Guinan, on the Philippine isle of Samar, killed over thirty Army and Navy personnel. They were loading some "corroded" fragmentation bombs onto barges for dumping at sea, when one of the weapons detonated. Toward the end of 1945, 93rd Ordnance Service (Bomb Disposal) Squad lost its commander, 2nd Lt. Leonard Tundermann. Also killed in the December 30 blast were four ordnance privates, Frank T. Sowers, David W. Ekvall, Andrew Fahrenbach, Jr., and James A. Linton. While Tundermann's name appears on the EOD memorial, those of his men as yet do not.[22]

Ordnance removal in Japan itself had continued steadily since 1945. Several Army squads served in the Japanese home islands throughout these post-war years. After a brief stretch on Okinawa, Capt. Robert L. Starr's 176th BD Squad arrived in October 1945, cooperating with the Fifth U.S. Army Air Force based at Tokyo. Capt. Starr personally cleared unexploded American bombs from airfields later used by the Air Force in the Korean War. However, with the Army Bomb Disposal Center's demise in November 1945, several civilian contractors were brought in to augment dwindling numbers of ordnance specialists stationed in Japan. Hence, 178th Squad continued under civilian leadership in 1946, but still answered directly to the 24th Infantry Division's ordnance chief.[23]

Director of "Munitions Disposal" on Kyushu, G.E. Metcalf supervised a combined section of one Army bomb disposal officer, two ordnancemen, plus four untrained privates and six civilian technicians. They were active chiefly in the Nagasaki and Kokura sectors. During two peak months,

November and December 1946, Metcalf reported the destruction of "beached sea mines," "shallow water diving operations" to clear harbors and inland lakes, and inspecting explosives plants before their eventual return to Home Ministry." 178th Squad members also conducted intelligence work on "balloon bombs" at the Sone Bomb Dump. Overall, they destroyed about 160 tons in November, plus 200 tons in December. 115 tons were recovered by Underwater Ammunition Clearance teams.[24]

How well did these civilians and soldiers cooperate? It seems that, given the war's conclusion, ordnancemen and contractors now shared similar goals: removing the war-making abilities of a former enemy, while contributing toward their reconstruction and public safety. According to Metcalf, one civilian had devoted his entire efforts to "clearance of former explosives production concerns," traveling to Honshu to undergo training for this hazardous occupation. Metcalf's operative monitored two plant closures in Sakonoichi, Oita Ken.[25]

178th Squad's soldiers and contractors collaborated with public awareness on the home island of Kyushu. They had little trouble informing their fellow Americans about hazardous explosives; 24th Infantry even had its own newspaper, the *V-Day*, which circulated Metcalf's announcements. However, the director also had to resolve language barriers with his wary Japanese hosts. Fortunately, Metcalf had an ally in the Japanese Police Force, whose reporting system began "working admirably." Accurate descriptions of beached mines and dud bombs came from district police stations through military translators. Japanese guides unerringly brought American technicians to their sites. Yet, despite bilingual safety warnings, Japanese citizens continued to run afoul of surplus war materiel. In late March 1946, six Japanese workers received powder burns at a factory. On November 13, 1946, a Japanese souvenir-chaser was killed while dismantling a 4.7 mm anti-aircraft round near Sasebo. Two others were injured by shrapnel.[26]

By 1948, Col. Kane had successfully recruited new military bomb disposal units in Tokyo. Far removed from Aberdeen Proving Ground, Far East Air Forces required new units to remove lingering wartime armaments, plus rendering service to base organizations. On March 15, 1948, the 7th Ordnance Bomb Disposal Squad was reconstituted under 1st Lt. Richard J. Lane, a veteran officer from the Rhineland campaign. Following a training sequence, Kane awarded the 7th Squad's five junior enlisted men their diplomas on June 26. Over nine months, Lane's soldiers disarmed and removed a wide variety of ordnance, including chemical weapons, sea mines, and even a ton of Japanese fireworks.[27]

Meanwhile, in Hawaii, lethal fireworks had killed several youths on July 4, 1946. Ignoring public warnings, some boys from Oahu had disturbed a live 75mm artillery shell that washed ashore on a nearby islet. Col. R. W. Daniels, Armed Forces ordnance chief for the Middle Pacific, launched "Operation Disposal" shortly after this tragedy. While the Army Corps of Engineers cleared military areas, such as former artillery ranges, Ordnance neutralized explosive souvenirs and duds still in civilian hands. Afterward, both Army teams searched the shallow ocean bottoms and shorelines for hazardous ordnance dumped overboard during wartime. Following a six-month drive, nineteen locations had been rendered safe, with nearly one thousand (977) explosive projectiles destroyed by early 1947. Also noteworthy, the last World War II squad separate ever commissioned, 212$^{th}$ BD Squad, received a Meritorious Service Unit plaque for their conspicuous labors. Lt. Mort Thomas reported his team recovered 111 "live duds" in March and April of 1947.[28]

Like Hawaii, Alaska's outer islands underwent a series of clearance efforts as a precursor to eventual statehood. Since 1945, the U. S. Navy has supervised Aleutian Islands removal, but more recently, private American contractors have taken over this onerous job. In 1998, Foster Wheeler Company started work on Adak. Coincidentally, Dix Fetzer revisited the island that same year with a group of war veterans. After meeting with Foster Wheeler's civilian ordnance team, the former sergeant accompanied them to a site where, fifty-five years before, he had emplaced 25 landmines to protect Canadian positions on Adak Island. Fetzer helped to locate and disarm these still-dangerous armaments.[29]

A retired New Jersey police chief, Dix Fetzer recalled the training he received at Aberdeen Proving Ground. He described the Army's first ordnance disposal instructors as "munitions experts... damned good teachers, and very careful guys." Still bearing the physical and emotional scars of the Aleutian Campaign, Fetzer believed that he "survived through the knowledge gained from [his instructors]... even carried forward to [the] incident [that] happened on Adak in the late '90s." Throughout the next decade, clearance efforts continued across the Aleutian chain until three-quarters of island territory had been declared safe for transfer to the native Aleuts, now a dwindling people owing in part to their capture by Japan in mid-1942. Noting the challenge of resettling these islands, Fetzer warned that "one distant part will *never* be safe, as there is too much [explosive ordnance] that washes ashore regularly." [30]

*  *  *

During the latter stages of World War II, U.S. Army "squads separate" were reclassified as "Ordnance Service Detachments," but this bland title did not last long. After its premature closure in late 1945, the Bomb Disposal Center merged with the Ammunition School, appropriately creating a brand-new military profession known as Explosive Ordnance Disposal (EOD). From April 1946 until April 1950, separate Army and Navy EOD programs evolved at Aberdeen Proving Ground and Indian Head, Maryland. After the Korean War broke out, these programs merged into one program at Indian Head.[31]

During the Korean War, the Army's EOD branch came into its own. 4th EOD Squad covered the U.N. retreat from North Korea, following Chinese intervention in late 1950. 4th Squad's captain, Joseph R. Eszes, had earlier served in Northern Italy. At Kunu-Ri, 98th EOD Squad bravely supported the 2nd Infantry Division against a fierce Chinese offensive. Capt. Robert W. Zinn of 98th Squad, once described as an "unflappable" Pacific Theater veteran, emerged from Korea a highly-decorated colonel. Following widespread reports of their courageous actions, EOD soldiers finally began receiving special hazard pay in early 1951.[32]

At this time, Col. Kane headed the Army's short-lived Ordnance Explosive Disposal Office (OEDO), where he reunited with old friends, such as Maj. Art Keller. Bud Engelhardt described the OEDO as "responsible for a lot of research on tools and methods," resulting in "a lot of technical publications" during the United Nations police action. Bud recalled this organization "was supposed to have become the headquarters for EOD in the Army, but after Col. Kane retired, it fell apart."[33]

In 1953, Col. Kane returned to Pennsylvania, where he commanded Frankford Arsenal. He served as acting post commander at Aberdeen Proving Ground whenever the brigadier left on government business. Frankford turned out a rather sad denouement for Kane's distinguished career. Shortly after the 1954 Korean ceasefire, Kane dismissed two civilian inspectors for fraudulent business practices. He also lost a promising young captain who committed suicide to escape certain embezzlement charges, a tragedy his daughters recalled years later.[34]

Kane retired May 31, 1955. He took a diplomatic assignment to Pakistan, but recurring illnesses forced him to return home in 1958. Kane's last years were spent in Maryland, where he received malaria treatments at Walter Reed Hospital. He remained in touch with Frank Parsons and John Feldman, who enjoyed discussing "the best goddamned war there ever was." Thomas Joseph Kane passed away November 12, 1965 at the untimely age of 65. He was buried with full military honors at Arlington National Cemetery. "During the Arlington funeral," Kay

Levering recalled, "there was a twenty-one gun salute, but not many attended… only the Baltimore and D.C. papers gave it much coverage."[35]

Col. Thomas J. Kane's memorial, which featured regularly at bomb disposal reunions throughout the 1960s and 1970s. (*Kane Collection*).

With Kane's passing, seven of the original Nine from Aberdeen went on with their careers. After retiring in the 1950s with a full colonel's rank, Harry Walker predeceased Kane in 1961. Lt. Col. Arthur E. Keller left Army service shortly before the Vietnam War, but remained in contact with fellow EOD members until his death in 1988. Frank A. Parsons, also a lieutenant colonel, returned to a lucrative engineering career, having completed his master's degree by 1946. Parsons remained a reservist, proud of his decorations from the Battle of the Bulge, which included a Belgian Croix de Guerre and the Legion of Merit. Frank and Dorothy remained friendly with their wartime friends, and were present at Kane's funeral. During the 1980s, their family experienced a double tragedy; one daughter died after a traffic accident in 1982, while a son passed away after suffering a heart attack in 1988. Sadly, Dorothy lost her beloved Frank in 1989, just one year shy of their fiftieth wedding anniversary.[36]

Leaving the military in 1945, Ronald L. Felton went through a period of readjustment, as did many citizen-soldiers wrenched from their previous lives and professions. Not yet thirty, Jobe missed his friends from the bomb disposal branch. However, he soon found constructive ways to deal with his anxieties. First, Jobe began a new career with the U.S. Forest Service, where he won many new friends. Next, he became an avid member of the Veterans of Foreign Wars, receiving honors for recruiting new local members. Twenty years after, Felton could still fit into his captain's uniform, regularly leading Memorial Day and Veteran's Day marches in Sheffield, Pennsylvania. Finally, Jobe kept ties with veteran disposaleers, especially his former squad-mates.[37]

Over the years, Felton organized unit reunions across the entire continent, once touring the Gettysburg National Park. By 1990, nearly every member of 12$^{th}$ BD Squad had sponsored a reunion close to their residence. Al Gardner recalled that although "we tried to meet in everyone's hometown at least once... I don't think we quite made it to Mac's hometown in California." Having participated in several bigger reunions at Aberdeen Proving Ground, Gardner believes his squad holds the record for remaining closest over the years. "If other squads had similar reunions, I've never heard about them." Every squad member remained close to their former commander until his death in 1993. Felton's final reunion took place at Aberdeen in 1989, with six remaining members posing for a group photograph. On Memorial Day of 1993, Capt. Ronald L. Felton passed away after a mercifully short battle with cancer. Mourned by neighbors and friends, Jobe received full military honors as an officer of the United States Army. T/Sgt. George Kramer stunned everyone by arriving in full uniform; he saluted while Felton's casket lowered into the Pennsylvania earth. After a brief illness in 2000, Millie followed her husband. Marsha Frost, Felton's second daughter, continued to keep in touch with the dwindling band of veterans.[38]

12th BD Squad's last full reunion took place at Aberdeen Proving Ground in 1989. From left to right: Kramer, Gardner, Felton, Herrig, Antisdale, and McCluskey.

For the next decade, T/Sgt. James McCluskey sent flowers to his captain's grave on every Memorial Day. Mac and the "Captain's Daughter," as he dubbed Marsha Frost, shared a common cause in preserving the memories of Felton and his small band of disposaleers. Mac had marked the passing of everyone with sadness. The first to go, John Thomson, Jr., had predeceased Felton in the 1980s. Alan Antisdale and Wilbur Herrig died from natural causes over the ensuing decade. However, in 2000, the ex-sergeant was struck by a triple loss. First, Millie Felton passed away, soon followed by Mac's own beloved wife, Mary. Then, just before a pre-arranged visit to Al Gardner in New York City, George Kramer died unexpectedly in Pennsylvania.[39]

When Kramer had returned in 1945, he promptly tied the knot with Dolores, the girl from his optics factory who had sent him kind letters. "From the moment I saw George, I knew he was the one for me," Dee Kramer recalled almost sixty years later. While George's Jewish faith posed a slight complication for his bride's Catholic family, their marriage lasted over fifty years. Both the Kramers remained employed at the same optics factory until their retirements in the 1980s. As Dee remembered, "our company kept most of the women, because not all the men came back." Dee Kramer accompanied her husband to all his reunions, developing friendships with Millie Felton and the other wives.[40]

After his own wife passed away in 2000, Mac went to live with his widowed sister in Arizona. During this period, the author contacted McCluskey through the auspices of Marsha Frost. Over several months, Mac gladly related his wartime experiences with a keen memory for detail. Sadly, Mac's sister died in 2004, forcing him to move into a retirement home. T/Sgt. James McCluskey lived just long enough to witness the escalating Middle Eastern conflict, which he perceived with ambivalence. Shortly after this final interview, Mac died in 2005.[41]

As of this writing, Al Gardner is the last surviving member of Felton's bomb disposal unit from Italy. He still lives with his devoted wife, Peg, surrounded by their children, grandchildren, and great-grandchildren. Their lives were marred only by the loss of a son during the September 11 terrorist attacks. Thomas Gardner, a career firefighter also qualified to handle bombs, perished during the World Trade Center's collapse in 2001. Over the years, Al Gardner has proven an invaluable link to many others within the tight bomb disposal fraternity.[42]

Whereas Ronald Felton had relished his Army memories and connections, Joseph Pilcher spent years trying to forget his experiences. Although proud to have served in World War II, Pilcher had to overcome emotional hurdles, suffering from post-traumatic episodes as time went by. Moving to Pennsylvania, the former New York truck farmer spent thirty years working at Sperry-Univac, an up-and-coming electronics firm. Gradually, life for the Pilchers returned to a state of normality – they were soon joined by a daughter, Patricia. Edith and Joe also received many visits from the Feltons, who lived for a time within close driving distance. Joseph Jr. recalled spending many afternoons with Ron Felton, who took the boy to his first Major League baseball game in Pittsburgh. For a time, "Skip" became close to his father's best friend, who best understood the elder Pilcher's reticence and aloofness. Inspired by both his father and Ron Felton, Joe Pilcher Jr. enlisted in 1962, serving in the infantry during Vietnam before transferring to the Army Corps of Engineers.[43]

Joe and Edith Pilcher about twenty years after World War II. (*Pilcher Collection*)

"Big Joe" showed immense pride in his son, who retired as a major and became a successful artist in Florida. However, the elder Pilcher never came to full terms with his own wartime experiences. While Joe gladly recounted some of his lighter escapades to colleagues at Sperry Univac, he seldom went any deeper. He rarely met his former soldiers, although they frequently exchanged holiday cards. Sgt. Franklin May, terminally ill in 1984, paid a farewell visit to the Pilchers, who had both treated him with such kindness. May bequeathed a few pictures left over from happier times in Havre de Grace. In 1991, T/5 Joseph Olszewski rode a Harley-Davidson to Florida, where the Pilchers had since retired. Edith instantly recognized Olszewski, who wore a large hearing aid.[44]

Toward the end of the century, Joe Pilcher, Sr. developed noticeable symptoms of both Parkinson's and Alzheimer's diseases. He passed away in 1999, preceded by his loving Edith by only a few months. William W. Prichard also died that same year, making Walter R. Nass the last surviving member of Kane's "Nine from Aberdeen."[45]

Shortly after the war ended, Wally and Alice Nass returned to California, where they raised several children. Wally Nass worked at Corvair, and then went into private consultancy. Reluctant to leave the service entirely, Nass finished his military career in the Army Reserves, retiring as a lieutenant colonel in Ordnance. According to Alice, Wally had good memories for his three years at Aberdeen Proving Ground. "At the time," she recollected in 2003, "the U.S. had no experience in bomb disposal, and Wally was proud to have taken part in the beginning of this field." Nass later presented some of his keepsakes to Camp Pendleton, California. Walter R. Nass died in 2002, aged 88.[46]

When Richard "Dick" Metress perished on Mandog Hill, he left behind a young widow, Anita. Still living in Swedesboro, New Jersey, Anita submitted her husband's name to the National Jewish Welfare Board, listing him as deceased. However, Dick's mother and siblings never learned the full truth from the War Department. To Mary Post, her cherished brother would remain living as long as she kept his Army portrait hanging on her wall. Mary Post died in 1979, and all of her correspondence with Dick has vanished over time. However, Mary's eldest daughters still fondly remember their "Uncle Dick," who doted on them as little girls. Significantly, none of Dick's relatives have ever recalled his all-too-brief marriage to the enigmatic Anita, who has vanished from the pages of history like so many others widowed by war. Anita's Jewish heritage may well have been a source of friction among Dick's devoutly Catholic family, but this is solely speculation.[47]

Other World War II bomb disposal veterans went on with their lives, some remaining in the Army, while others returning to the private sector. Dick Walkup served as an EOD squad officer in the Korean War, transferring to general ordnance work afterward. He retired as a lieutenant colonel and still lives as of this writing in Washington State with his wife. Carl Cirocco, having recovered the partial use of his left arm, retired in Pennsylvania surrounded by family. Clarence Fulcher recovered from his injuries in the Aleutian Islands, and still resides in Virginia with his wife. Lastly, Thomas Reece returned to South Bend, Indiana, where he resumed his career and struggled bravely with post-traumatic stress. In 2002, Reece passed away in Florida following a brief illness. T. Dennis Reece, a retired diplomat, published his father's fascinating memoirs in 2005.[48]

With this tale almost told, one last principal in the bomb disposal story needs to be addressed: John Edward Feldman. After V-E Day, Maj. Feldman received the Legion of Merit from the Ordnance Department, recognizing his inventiveness and fearless performance in England. He was then entrusted with organizing divisional papers from the European Theater, paving the way for future historians. Feldman returned to Fort Meade in September 1945, whereupon he left active duty. In July 1946, Major Feldman became an honorary member of the Order of the British Empire (Military Division) for "outstanding service to the Anglo-American Cause… developing new equipment and techniques for bomb disposal. Feldman remained a reserve Army officer throughout the 1950s, being promoted to lieutenant colonel in 1955. He also qualified as an ordnance officer in the field of atomic and nuclear weapons in 1957. [49]

After retirement, John Feldman became a businessman in Fairfield, Ohio. With Martin Ehrmann's passing in 1973, he also became elder statesman for hundreds of World War II bomb disposal veterans. Together with W. G. "Scotty" Calder, Feldman published a veteran's newsletter, and organized the UXB Club. Together with Margaret Kane, John Feldman preserved a sense of *esprit de corps* among World War II disposaleers. After Margaret's death in 1982, Feldman continued to preside over the reunions, which gradually merged with those for EOD veterans serving in later conflicts. During the 1980s, Feldman also campaigned for a museum display in the Aberdeen Proving Ground Ordnance Museum. In 1986, the museum curators created a display for Bomb Disposal and EOD, featuring Col. Kane's original travel journal. However, with the museum's planned relocation to Fort Lee, Virginia, this display's fate remains uncertain. John Feldman died in January 1995, at 85 years of age. His devoted wife, Maria, however, continued to attend bomb disposal veteran meetings until her death in 2007.[50]

* * *

In 1969, the Ordnance Department recognized Kane's leadership in World War II, admitting him to the Ordnance Hall of Fame. In 1980, John Feldman shared in this great honor. They are both respected in EOD circles for their pioneering roles. Since its "golden age," the EOD military specialty has undergone several changes, beginning with its training facilities. For four decades, joint-service EOD training continued at Indian Head, Maryland, supervised by the U.S. Navy. Robert "Ike" Eigell, a respected veteran of Navy operations in the Pacific Theater, directed the Indian Head program until his retirement as Commander in 1964.[51]

Eigell’s new Explosive Ordnance Disposal center emphasized a common foundation for U.S. Army, Air Force, and Navy technicians, thereby resolving one of the chief technical problems of World War II bomb disposal. As a result, Korea and Vietnam-era disposaleers received cross-training in all varieties of mines, shells, and projectiles.[52]

In 1999, EOD indoctrination transferred to Eglin Air Force Base, Florida, where the Marine Corps now shares training responsibilities at the Navy’s modern EOD School (NAVSCOLEOD). Army technicians still comprise the majority of EOD servicemen, and receive supplemental instruction at Fort A.P. Hill, Virginia. Female officers and enlistees have been freely admitted to the EOD services since the Vietnam era, even reaching command rank. Col. Mary G. Goodwin, a distinguished graduate of the Army War College, took command of the 52nd Explosive Ordnance Disposal Group in 1999. Most recently, Col. Marue R. Quick assumed charge of the 52nd EOD Group. Moreover, tasks once allotted solely to commissioned officers have now devolved on NCOs, who comprise the backbone of modern-day EOD. Company grade officers still take part in “hands-on” ordnance work, but they also delegate more authority.[53]

One of the nation’s most distinguished EOD units, the 52nd EOD Group, sustained Army operations during the Global War on Terror. Headquartered at Fort Gillem, Georgia, they received funding for a permanent building. With a sense of history, James Clifford, the ranking sergeant major, suggested naming the building after Col. T. J. Kane. As Clifford recalled: “I developed the idea of calling the building Kane Hall, shepherded the process, and ensured that the building represented the heritage of the EOD community as begun by the ‘Nine from Aberdeen.’”[54]

Clifford’s proposal met with approval from his group commander, Col. Stephen W. Moores. On March 30, 2004, Kane’s 104th birthday, Clifford’s unit held a dedication ceremony for Kane Hall, with Kay Kane Levering attending as guest of honor. During this ceremony, Col. Moores hailed his World War II predecessor as “the man who started it all.” Moores expressed his belief that “Colonel Kane would be very proud of the young men and women in the [EOD] program today.” Subsequently, 52nd EOD Group relocated their headquarters at Fort Campbell, Kentucky, where a second Kane Hall was dedicated on March 29, 2013.[55]

Greek historian Thucydides once described the indiscriminate nature of arrows and stones, killing or maiming every person that they struck. Today’s “arrows and stones” are far more arbitrary and destructive, and so there will always be a need for those who risk their lives to remove them. Kane’s tradition continues in today’s EOD specialists, who will pass on their vital knowledge to future descendants of the “Nine from Aberdeen.”

Kay Levering, Col. Kane's daughter, and CSM Jim Clifford at the Kane Hall dedication on March 31, 2004. Shortly afterward, 52nd EOD Group relocated to Ft. Campbell, Kentucky, and plans are currently in progress for a new Kane Hall. (*Photograph courtesy of Jim Clifford*)

## Notes

[1] 161st Ordnance Bomb Disposal Squad (Separate), unit history, c. 1945; Samuel J. Hooper, *The History of U.S. Army Bomb Disposal and Explosive Ordnance Disposal (1941-1980)* (unpublished manuscript) 1981, 22-24.
[2] Lt. Col. Martin J. Ehrmann to B.D. Personnel, letter, 11 September 1945.
[3] Col. Thomas J. Kane, *Top View of Ordnance Bomb Disposal in ETOUSA*. c. 1945; Ordnance Section, U.S. Forces European Theater (USFET), *Ordnance Section Reveals Work of Bomb Disposal Squads for First Time*, August 1945; Ordnance Section, U.S. Forces European Theater (USFET), *Million Tons of German Ammo Put to Peace Time Usage*, August 1945.
[4] Kane & Feldman, *History of the Ordnance Bomb Disposal Division,* 1-8; Ordnance Section, *Million Tons of German Ammo Put to Peace Time Usage*.
[5] 67th Ordnance Bomb Disposal Squad (Separate) to Commanding General, Special Troops, 12th U.S. Army Group, 13 July 1945; Hooper, 22-24;
[6] Col. T. H. Nixon, U.S. Forces European Theater (USFET), *Ordnance in the European Theater: a Discussion of the Year Following VE Day (*NARA Records Group 156) 1 July 1946; Hooper, 22-24.
[7] According to Sam Hooper, most of these Reservists were kept in country during

the five-year period preceding the Korean War. (United States Armed Forces Europe (USAFE), Weekly Armament and Ordnance Activities Reports (AFHRA 570.11427), 2-9 October 1945; Ordnance Bomb Disposal School, roster of active BD officers, 1 December 1945; Hooper, 29-32).

8 72nd Ordnance Bomb Disposal Squad (Separate) to Commanding Officer, Ansbach Air Depot, 28 May 1946 to 28 January 1947; 73rd Ordnance Bomb Disposal Squad (Separate) to Commanding General, 3rd U.S. Army, 1 May 1946 to 17 January 1947; 74th Ordnance Bomb Disposal Squad (Separate) to Commanding General, 1st U.S. Infantry, 1 June 1946 to 31 December 1946; 75th Ordnance Bomb Disposal Squad (Separate) to Commanding General, Ninth U.S. Air Force, 30 September 1946 to 30 November 1946; 82nd Ordnance Bomb Disposal Squad (Separate), unit history, 30 June 1946 to 31 October 1946; 83rd Ordnance Bomb Disposal Squad (Separate), unit history, 31 May 1946 to 31 January 1947; 84th Ordnance Bomb Disposal Squad (Separate), unit history, 30 June 1946; 87th Ordnance Bomb Disposal Squad (Separate), unit history, 30 June 1946 to 31 January 1947; Hooper, 32.

9 72nd Ordnance Bomb Disposal Squad (Separate) to Commanding Officer, Ansbach Air Depot, 28 May 1946 to 28 January 1947.

10 72nd Ordnance Bomb Disposal Squad (Separate) to Commanding Officer, Ansbach Air Depot, 28 May 1946 to 28 January 1947.

11 82nd Ordnance Bomb Disposal Squad (Separate), unit history, 30 June 1946 to 31 October 1946; Hooper 29-32.

12 73rd Ordnance Bomb Disposal Squad (Separate) to Commanding General, 3rd U.S. Army, 1 May 1946 to 17 January 1947.

13 Tyler's commendation, dated October 31, 1946, was permanently added to 83rd BD Squad's official unit history. By that point, 1st Lt. Theodore R. Saunders had taken command of 83rd BD Squad, which became deactivated on January 17, 1947. (83rd Ordnance Bomb Disposal Squad (Separate), unit history, 30 June 1946 to 31 October 1946; 87th Ordnance Bomb Disposal Squad (Separate), unit history, 30 June 1946 to 31 January 1947; Michael R Vining, *Explosive Ordnance Disposal Memorial – U. S. Army,* EOD Memorial Commission, 9 April 2011).

14 T. Dennis Reece, *Captains of Bomb Disposal*, Lexington, Kentucky: Xlibris Press, 2005, 97-168.

15 Such underground enclaves were considered dangerous by the Allies, who ordered them sealed shut and flooded to minimize chances of ammunition fires. However, modern-day U.S. and German EOD detachments have attempted to clear these sites, sometimes with deadly consequences, according to ordnance historian Sam Hooper. (Marty Clear, "Vet Disarmed Bombs, Helped Develop Port," from *St. Petersburg Times*, 14 June 2003; Hooper, 30, Reece, 97-168.

16 Mark Patton, "Nearly Half of German City to Evacuate Sunday for Defusing of WWII era Bomb," from *Stars and Stripes*, 30 November 2011; Hooper, 31-32.

17 In 1954, Deichmann and Marquard each contributed a study, catalogued at Karlsruhe. Both reports were later translated and annotated by the Americans. Herbert Ruehlemann eventually went to work for Aberdeen Proving Ground. (Paul Deichmann, "Luftwaffe Methods in the Selection of Offensive Weapons,

Volume 1," from *USAF Historical Studies*, No. 187, Manhattan, Kansas: MA/AH Publishing, Sunflower University Press, c. 1985; Ernst A. Marquard, "Luftwaffe Methods in the Selection of Offensive Weapons, Volume 2," USAF *Historical Studies*, No. 187, Manhattan, Kansas: MA/AH Publishing, Sunflower University Press, c. 1985; T. Dennis Reece, *Captains of Bomb Disposal 1942-46*, Lexington, Kentucky: Xlibris Books, 2005, 23-24; for more on Nazi scientists in America, see Thomas Bower, *The Paperclip Conspiracy: The Hunt for the Nazi Scientists*, Boston: Little, Brown and Company, 1987.)

[18] Guenther Froebel, telephone interview by author, 25 May 2003; Guenther Froebel, e-mail to author, 28 May 2003; Carmel J. Cirocco, telephone interviews by author, 19 June 2011, 20 July 2011; Kane & Feldman, *History,* 1-8.

[19] Walter Korsgaard, telephone interview by author, 20 July 2003; *Ordnance Hall of Fame*, Kane biography.

[20] *Ordnance Hall of Fame*; Kane Journal, *1942-43 Itinerary*; Kay Levering interview; Mary Jo Romba, interview with author [transcript] 15 October 2003.

[21] "Bomb Busters," from *Stars and Stripes*, 4 September 1945, 1-2; Kay Levering interview).

[22] Among the dead on August 21, 1945 was Navy Lieut. Edward L. King Jr., whose bereaved father took his grievances straight to the Ordnance Department. The elder King, failing to comprehend the situation, suggested that planes should be used to transport faulty bombs. Congressman Paul H. Maloney of Louisiana also wrote a letter to the Chief of Ordnance. One of Gen. Campbell's aides, John W. Martyn, explained the lesser evil of removing bombs by sea instead of risking a serious air disaster. (Michael R Vining, *Explosive Ordnance Disposal Memorial – U. S. Army,* EOD Memorial Commission, 9 April 2011; Edward L. King Sr. to the Chief of Ordnance, letter, 30 October 1945; John W. Martyn to Hon. Paul H. Maloney, letter, 2 November 1945.)

[23] 176th Ordnance Bomb Disposal Squad (Separate) to Colonel Thomas J. Kane, *Overseas Activities of 176th Ordnance Bomb Disposal Squad,* 21 June 1946; 178th Ordnance Bomb Disposal Squad (Separate), unit history, 1945-47.

[24] 178th Ordnance Bomb Disposal Squad (Separate), unit history, 1945-47.

[25] 178th Ordnance Bomb Disposal Squad (Separate), unit history, 1945-47.

[26] 178th Ordnance Bomb Disposal Squad (Separate), unit history, 1945-47.

[27] Richard Lane had commanded 134th BD Squad in Northern France and the Rhineland. Discharged in 1945, he was evidently reactivated for service in Japan. (7th Ordnance Bomb Disposal Squad (Separate), *Historical Summary Report,* unit history, April-December 1948; Ordnance Bomb Disposal School, roster of active BD officers, 1 December 1945).

[28] Mort Thomas, "Danger – Live Ammo!" from *Ordnance*, Vol. 32, No. 167 (March-April 1948).

[29] Dix Fetzer, [electronic mail] interviews by author. 10-13 April 2004; Paul Roberts. "Return To Adak, Alaska 2000." Accessed 12 April 2004, from http://adak.orneveien.org/contributors/paulroberts/. Internet.

[30] Ibid.

[31] Samuel J. Hooper, *History of U.S. Army Bomb Disposal and Explosive*

*Ordnance Disposal (1941-1980).* [unpublished manuscript] c. 1981; Frank Durham, *You Only Blow Yourself Up Once* (Lincoln, Nebraska: iUniverse Press, 2003), 133-35.

[32] Capt. Joseph Eszes commanded 58th BD Squad in Northern Italy in 1944-45. (Ordnance Bomb Disposal School, roster of active BD officers, 1 December 1945; Charles G. Pritchard, "Ammunition Forward: the U.S. Ordnance Corps at Kunu-Ri, Korea," *Army Magazine*, March 2002).

[33] Bud Engelhardt and Fred Puckett later played a role in establishing a veteran's group, the National EOD Association. (*Ordnance Hall of Fame*, Kane biography; Bud Englehardt to author, [electronic mail] 27 February 2003; Fred J. Puckett, [transcript] interview with author, 15 February 2004.)

[34] Kane's temporary duty as post commander has led some veterans to believe the colonel had been promoted to brigadier general. ("Two Inspectors Fired at Frankford Arsenal," from *Stars and Stripes*, 21 July 1954, 7; *Ordnance Hall of Fame*, Kane biography; Levering interview; Romba interview.)

[35] *Ordnance Hall of Fame*; *Punxsutawney Spirit*. [obituaries] Punxsutawney Area Historical and Genealogical Society Inc.; 12 November 1965; Levering interview; Dorothy Parsons, interview with author, 18 October 2003.

[36] *Punxsutawney Spirit*, obituaries, Punxsutawney Area Historical and Genealogical Society, Inc., 2 March 1961; Dorothy Parsons, interview with author, 18 October 2003; *Firepower Magazine,* Washington D.C.: U.S. Army Signal Corps, June 1945; Social Security Death Index.

[37] Ronald Felton received recognition for increasing veterans' memberships in his state, serving as chapter quartermaster. (Pennsylvania Department of V.F.W. to Ronald L. Felton, Citation of Appreciation [10 April 1953]).

[38] Ronald and Millie Felton had three daughters and a son: Sandra, Marsha, Ron Jr., and Dreena. All are still living save for Dreena, who died in 1987. (McCluskey interviews; Frost interview.)

[39] McCluskey interviews; Gardner interviews.

[40] Dolores Kramer interview, 16 March 2003.

[41] McCluskey interviews; Gardner interviews.

[42] Some years after the 9/11 attacks, a New York street was dedicated to Tom Gardner's memory. (Kramer interview; Gardner interviews; Frost interviews).

[43] Joseph C. Pilcher Jr., interview, 12 July 2003.

[44] Joseph C. Pilcher Jr., interview, 12 July 2003.

[45] "Bombs, Books and Biscuits from Greece," from *Blue Bell News.* [company newsletter] 4A, c. 1976; Pilcher obituary.

[46] Alice Nass, interview by author, 14 October 2003; Social Security Death Index.

[47] Carole P. Carlo, telephone interview by author, 29 July 2011; 209th Ordnance Bomb Disposal (Separate), *Squad History*, 24 March 1945 to 4 August 1945; National Jewish Welfare Board. Bureau of War Records. 1939-45. National Archives and Records Administration. www.ancestry.com.

[48] Clarence Fulcher, telephone interview by author, 2 August 2011; T. Dennis Reece, telephone interview by author, 11 June 2011; Alex Cirocco, telephone interview by author, 19 June 2011; Carmel J. Cirocco, telephone interview by

author, 19 June 2011; Carmel J. Cirocco, telephone interview by author, 20 July 2011; Richard W. Walkup, telephone interview by author; 25 June 2010; Richard W. Walkup, telephone interview by author, 13 November 2010.

[49] *Ordnance Hall of Fame*, Feldman History; Maria Feldman, interview.

[50] Ibid.

[51] *Ordnance Hall of Fame*, Durham, 133-35.

[52] Ibid.

[53] Robert Leiendecker, telephone interview by author, 10 April 2003; Glen Paddie, "52nd EOD has 'Quick' Change of Command," *Fort Campbell Courier*, 11 September 2011; Jim Clifford, e-mail to author, 31 December 2011; *Ordnance Hall of Fame.*

[54] James Clifford, e-mail to author, 16 March 2011.

[55] Edward Brock, "Ordnance Group Gets New Hope," from *Clayton News Daily.* (Clayton, Georgia) 5 April 2004.

# AFTERWORD

# JAMES H. CLIFFORD COMMAND SERGEANT MAJOR U.S. ARMY EOD (RETIRED)

Colonel Thomas J. Kane and his men are among the best of what Tom Brokaw christened our Greatest Generation. These men, volunteers all, stepped into an unknown world in the days following the Japanese attack on Pearl Harbor. They were the first of what has become one of the most respected, revered, and frequently misunderstood disciplines of the military: bomb disposal, now called Explosive Ordnance Disposal.

Like many of the World War II generation, the Nine from Aberdeen saw a need and they filled it. In this case, the need was fraught with perils greater than those faced by most other soldiers. While all soldiers were in harm's way – facing hardships and privations, not to mention physical dangers from combat – the World War II bomb disposal soldier walked toward the hazard of the unexploded bomb while all others avoided them. Why they chose to do so remains a mystery, even to those who have followed in their footsteps. Perhaps there is a sociological or psychological answer to explain why some gravitate toward extremely dangerous pursuits. Practitioners of EOD do not concern themselves with such questions. They do the job for love of the challenge and for their fellow EOD soldier technicians. Others need not understand it; they should merely be grateful that someone else has the daring for the job.

I wonder whether Colonel Kane and his men, if they were to visit a modern Army Explosive Ordnance Disposal company, would they feel at home or would they feel uncomfortably out of place? I think that they would find comfort in the recognition that the heart of today's EOD soldier beats just the same as theirs, with the same motivations as they felt. Today's EOD soldier is outfitted with the latest protective clothing. Each soldier uses a range of protective gear, from body armor and helmets, to full body bomb suits, which provide the best possible - although hardly total - level of protection from explosions and fragmentation. Every EOD unit is equipped with robots employing a variety of sensitive instruments, cameras, and tools. These robots perform reconnaissance, emplace and operate tools, and move unexploded ordnance, providing levels of protection unknown during the WWII era.

The EOD soldier also has access to a wide range of radiography, ordnance disrupters, and techniques unavailable in Colonel Kane's era. Despite the technical advances, it is still the EOD soldiers' lot to regularly take what has become known as "the long walk," tracing their predecessors' boot prints in the mud; a single man or woman approaching unexploded ordnance or improvised explosive device, protected only by manmade clothing, armed only with the tools one can carry, applying training and experience in situations that would cause most others to flee.

Early bomb disposal soldiers practiced discovery learning, the process of "learning on the go." Having no established database to refer to, they conducted field exploitation of ordnance; documenting details in personal notebooks complete with scale drawings; taking exact measurements, noting all markings and colors, and chronicling the outcome when render safe procedures were attempted. These notes were reproduced and disseminated in newsletters throughout the bomb disposal community.

Today's EOD soldier practices the same skills, but unlike his professional forebears, he has a formal research and development institution to lean upon in determining the best actions to take in a given situation. Newly discovered ordnance is exploited by professionals who reverse-engineer them to determine how the item works. Render safe procedures (RSP) are developed and evaluated for effectiveness.

Once this RSP is proven, the information is placed in a database distributed to EOD units using modern communications media. This database is regularly updated to ensure that the EOD soldier has access to the latest available information. Thousands of entries cover domestic and foreign ordnance, and include descriptions, diagrams, that describe functioning, and safety information. The WWII era bomb disposal soldier would not believe the amount of information available to today's EOD soldier. Where yesterday's bomb disposal soldier had only his native ingenuity to guide him, today's model combines that with the collective knowledge of an institution with the sole mission of supporting him.

U.S. Army bomb disposal soldiers trained separately at Aberdeen Proving Ground, Maryland, until the closure of the Ordnance Explosive Disposal Office (OEDO) in the 1950s. After the Korean War, the U.S. Navy became the executive agent for Explosive Ordnance Disposal training and development and continues to function in that capacity today. From the mid-1950s until the late 1990s, Soldiers, Sailors, Airmen, and Marines received instruction at the Naval Explosive Ordnance Disposal

School located at the Naval Ordnance Center in Indian Head, Maryland. During the mid-1970s, Indian Head began training the first women EOD soldiers, who have risen to command positions in this field.

During the 1990s, the EOD School began its relocation to Eglin Air Force Base, Florida, completing the transition in 1999. Consolidation of EOD training has saved money by cutting out redundancies and ensuring that all EOD technicians have the same basic skills. While each service has different traditions, missions, and institutional cultures, EOD personnel talk a common language that translates into smooth operations when they are called to work together on the battlefield.

Although locations and techniques have changed, the essence of the training remains the same. Explosive Ordnance Disposal is still among the hardest specializations in the military. While in EOD School, soldiers learn the basics of ordnance identification, explosive demolition, and the use of EOD tools. They also learn about weapons of mass destruction – nuclear, chemical, and biological ordnance. In the last decade, improvised explosive device (IED) countermeasures, always an important part of EOD School, have taken on an increased level of magnitude and urgency in response to our current needs. The training is tough! While most of those who enter EOD School do graduate, a large number will recycle through various portions of the course to ensure that they meet the high standards of graduation.

Upon graduation, the new EOD soldier is awarded the Basic Explosive Ordnance Disposal Badge, the first of three levels of EOD recognition. These emblems; the Basic, Senior, and Master Explosive Ordnance Disposal badges, denote levels of experience. They are an innovation of the post-World War II era. They were adopted by each of the armed forces and are frequently used as the template for most civilian public safety bomb squad symbols. Upon arrival at their first assignment, newly minted EOD soldiers will continue learning the trade under the leadership of seasoned noncommissioned officers. They will train and operate as junior team members on EOD missions in the United States or overseas, in peace or in war, as the situation dictates. After the passage of time, accomplishment of training objectives, and development of experience, the EOD soldier progresses through positions of increasing responsibility.

At regular intervals, every EOD soldier must reevaluate his future to determine whether he will continue his career. Retention of highly trained EOD soldiers is always a challenge. The EOD soldier pursues a tough and dangerous career. Many will chose to sever ties and move on to other pursuits. Many others will take advantage of his training and experience by accepting lucrative employment offers that regularly come to midgrade EOD noncommissioned officers. For those who continue their EOD careers, there are ample opportunities for promotion and positions of increased responsibilities. The Army has recently begun to recognize the value of experienced EOD noncommissioned officers by offering the very best of them previously unavailable senior leadership positions within the Army's institutions.

The EOD soldier must be well versed in ordnance identification to successfully defeat modern dangers; dangers greater than those faced by his World War II or Korean War counterparts. The availability of robotics and protective gear does not mean that the EOD soldier need not personally approach unexploded ordnance (UXO) or improvised devices. This is still the stock-in-trade of the EOD soldier, the reason that he gets up in the morning. Approaching UXO or IEDs puts the EOD soldier in direct contact with the enemy just as real as any other force-on-force combat situation one can consider. In this case, the threat is modern ordnance, usually incorporating sophisticated electronic fuzing systems unheard of during World War II.

Modern payloads are more complicated than at the dawn of Explosive Ordnance Disposal. Before determining which RSP to perform, the EOD soldier must determine the nature of the payload. Is it explosive, chemical, or biological? Failing to correctly determine the payload may lead to an inadvertent exposure of deadly chemical agents or biological material. Just such a failure by untrained soldiers resulted in the unintentional release of chemical agents in the aftermath of the first Persian Gulf War. Finally, smart bombs of today are often loaded with submunitions that complicate the EOD soldier's job. Where a singular bomb was once encountered, dozens of unexploded bomblets litter wider areas, ready to wreak indiscriminate havoc and create a more problematical equation for the EOD soldier.

Over the last decade, a day has not gone by without multiple media reports of soldiers and civilians being killed or injured by improvised explosive devices (IEDs). No longer the homemade bomb of yesteryear: today, terrorists and insurgents establish full scale workshops and factories dedicated to the manufacture of these death-dispensers. Improvised explosive devices have always been around; their use actually predates the establishment of military or civilian bomb disposal agencies. WWII bomb disposal soldiers in the Pacific and European Theaters were not immune from the threat of what would today be considered rudimentary IEDs.

Having been defeated in stand-up battles, our enemies in Iraq and Afghanistan desperately turned to IEDs as their weapons of choice. These IEDs use the latest in electronic and radio frequency technology, often incorporating unexploded ordnance or commercial chemicals, escalating their lethality. As of this writing, IEDs have taken thousands of lives and injured countless others in Iraq and Afghanistan. While this is a truly tragic aspect of what used to be called the "War on Global Terrorism," the death toll could be much worse. For every coalition soldier or civilian killed or wounded by an IED, a significant number of lives have been saved through the efforts of EOD soldiers. Explosive Ordnance Disposal soldiers of our armed forces and those of our coalition partners have rendered safe thousands of IEDs, saving the lives of untold thousands.

As Dr. Leatherwood has outlined, one of the major hurdles faced by World War II bomb disposal was in gaining its proper place in Army operations. Frequently considered to be a sideshow, bomb disposal was seldom allowed on the midway with the other acts in the Army's "state fair," frequently with disastrous results. Even when allowed to play, credit for its accomplishments was denied or given to others. This is one challenge that EOD has never been fully able to overcome.

In the initial years after the heinous attacks of September 11, 2001, just as their BD forebears did after December 7, 1941, EOD leaders and soldiers have striven boldly to ensure their places on the battlefield. They do not do so for personal or organizational glory, but because their skills are sorely needed in contemporary operations. They have effectively cobbled together efficient combined and joint organizations that have contributed to mission success, overcoming a reputation as an insignificant and ineffective discipline.

Today, EOD operations are considered in all aspects of American military doctrine. Army doctrinal manuals now list EOD as an element of the Protection Warfighting Function, raising EOD to its highest position in doctrinal hierarchy in its 70-year history. This begs the question of what will happen now that operations in Iraq are ended and the end in Afghanistan is in sight. Will EOD once again be relegated to the "wallflower" position at the Army prom, or will we find dancing partners to ensure that when called upon again – as we surely will be – EOD will be ready as an equal partner in the defense of this great nation?

Wherever American EOD soldiers serve, they enjoy a positive and cooperative working relationship with EOD forces of other countries. Our strongest working relationship is also our oldest. American and British EOD soldiers work, train, and share the burdens of war just as they have since World War II. Other coalition partners also provide EOD forces that frequently rely on the guidance and assistance of American EOD soldiers, just as we once relied on the British. Kane's early bomb disposal organization began with no knowledge, no training, no equipment, and no experience. From that relatively obscure start, United States EOD forces have earned recognition as leaders in the EOD fight.

While many EOD soldiers are serving in deployed locations in the Balkans and Middle East, there is still a robust EOD force operating within the United States. Many are just back from the war zone, while others are preparing to go into the fight, but all of them are employed in homeland security. In addition to normal military operations, EOD soldiers respond daily to support requests from civilian authorities to remove UXO items, render safe IEDs, instruct public service agencies, or provide advice regarding crisis and consequence management.

The Nine from Aberdeen have not been forgotten by the Army EOD community. In March 2004, their accomplishments were honored when the Army designated the headquarters of the 52$^{nd}$ Ordnance Group (Explosive Ordnance Disposal) at Fort Gillem, Georgia, as Kane Hall. This modern, yet modest, headquarters was dedicated to the memory of Colonel Thomas J. Kane and all soldiers who served faithfully throughout the 63-year history of Army Bomb Disposal / EOD.

Just inside the door of Kane Hall stood a plaque honoring the fallen soldiers of the 52$^{nd}$ Ordnance Group who had died in the line of duty since the Group was activated in 1993. Kane Hall also had a display for Colonel Kane, as well as a documents archive. However, the physical existence of Kane Hall was short-lived due to the passage of the 2005 Base Realignment and Closure law that slated Fort Gillem for closure in 2011. As a result, the 52$^{nd}$ Ordnance Group soon moved to Fort Campbell, Kentucky – where the concept of Kane Hall still lives. Some day in the future, a new EOD complex will be constructed on Fort Campbell that will accommodate an EOD Group, Battalion, and multiple Company headquarters and facilities. When that occurs, the main building will resurrect the identity of Kane Hall and the other buildings will honor additional notable Army EOD soldiers of the past.

At the EOD School on Eglin Air Force Base, there stands a wall with the U.S. flag and four service flags flying over it. On the wall are mounted four large plaques, one for each service, that were transplanted from their original location in Indian Head. Upon these plaques are memorialized the names of EOD Soldiers, Sailors, Airmen, and Marines killed in the line of duty since World War II. Each year, on the first Saturday in May, active and retired EOD soldiers, families, and friends gather at the EOD Memorial to commemorate more than 200 of their EOD brethren who have made the ultimate sacrifice. At the annual ceremony, the names of lost EOD technicians are added. Each year, the EOD community prays that no more names will be added during the upcoming year. Most years are sadly disappointing, owing to the inherent dangers of the EOD mission and our times.

During the writing of this book nearly 100 EOD technicians from all four of the armed services have been killed in action. The new millennium has proven to be the most dangerous period in the entire 70-year history of Explosive Ordnance Disposal. However, that has not dissuaded the EOD community from continuing the mission just as it has every day since Colonel Kane made his first fateful trip to England. Kane's soldiers could not have known what they were beginning. They only knew that there was a job to do and they were determined to do it. America, indeed the world, is safer thanks to the Nine from Aberdeen and all those who followed them since those early uncertain days in 1941. Uncertainty in all things continues, all things except for the certainty that wherever there is unexploded ordnance or an improvised explosive device there will be an Explosive Ordnance Disposal soldier ready to risk all so that others may live.

James H. Clifford
Command Sergeant Major (ret.)
US Army / EOD
January 24, 2012
McDonough, Georgia

# APPENDICES AND CHARTS

## Selected Campaign Participations for U.S. Army Ordnance Bomb Disposal Units[1]

| CODE | CAMPAIGN | DATES |
|---|---|---|
| M1 | Algeria & Morocco (Ground Campaign) | 8/11/42 to 11/11/42 |
| M2 | Tunisia (Ground) | 11/17/42 to 5/13/43 |
| M3 | Sicily (Ground Campaign) | 7/9/43 to 8/17/43 |
| M4 | Salerno (Assault Landing) | 9/9/43 to 9/10/43 |
| M5 | Naples-Foggia Campaign | 9/9/43 to 1/21/44 |
| M6 | Anzio (Assault Landing) | 1/22/44 to 1/23/44 |
| M7 | Anzio (Ground Campaign) | 1/22/44 to 5/24/44 |
| M8 | Rome-Arno Campaign | 1/22/44 to 9/9/44 |
| M9 | Southern France (Landing) | 8/15/44 to 8/16/44 |
| M10 | Southern France (Ground) | 8/15/44 to 9/14/44 |
| M11 | North Apennines Campaign | 9/10/44 to 4/5/45 |
| M12 | Po Valley Campaign | 4/5/45 to 5/8/45 |
| E1 | U.S. Air Offensive (ETO) | 7/4/42 to 6/5/44 |
| E2 | Normandy (Landing) | 6/7/44 to 6/7/44 |
| E3 | Normandy (Ground) | 6/6/44 to 7/24/44 |
| E4 | Northern France Campaign | 7/25/44 to 7/14/44 |
| E5 | Rhineland Campaign | 7/15/44 to 3/21/45 |
| E6 | Ardennes-Alsace Campaign | 12/16/44 to 1/25/45 |
| E7 | Central Europe Campaign | 3/22/45 to 5/11/45 |

| | | |
|---|---|---|
| **E8** | **Occupation Credit (Germany)** | **5/2/45 to 12/2745** |
| **P1** | **Central Pacific** | **12/7/41 to 12/6/43** |
| **P2** | **U.S. Air Offensive (Japan)** | **4/17/42 to 9/2/45** |
| **P3** | **Aleutian Islands (Alaska)** | **6/3/42 to 8/24/43** |
| **P4** | **Papua Campaign** | **7/23/42 to 1/143** |
| **P5** | **Guadalcanal** | **8/7/42 to 2/21/43** |
| **P6** | **New Guinea** | **1/24/43 to 12/31/44** |
| **P7** | **Northern Solomons** | **2/22/43 – 11/21/44** |
| **P8** | **Bismarck Archipelago** | **12/15 /43 to 11/27/44** |
| **P9** | **Eastern Mandates (Ground Campaign)** | **1/31/44 to 6/14/44** |
| **P10** | **Leyte (Philippine Islands)** | **10/17/44 to 7/1/45** |
| **P11** | **Luzon (Philippine Islands)** | **12/15/44 to 7/4/45** |
| **P12** | **Ryukyu Islands** | **3/23/45 to 7/2/45** |
| **P13** | **Southern Philippines** | **2/27/45 to 7/4/45** |
| **P14** | **Western Pacific (Ground Campaign)** | **6/15/44 to 9/2/45** |
| **P15** | **Occupation Credit (Japan/Okinawa)** | **10/15/45 – 1/4/46** |

| UNIT | CAMPAIGNS | SPECIAL NOTES |
|---|---|---|
| **1st Ordnance BD Squad** | **M2, M5, M9, M11, M12** | **See 55th Squad, 1 KIA** |
| **2nd Ordnance BD Squad** | **E3, E4, E5, E6, E7** | **Meritorious Unit Commendation** |
| **3rd Ordnance BD Squad** | **E3, E4, E7** | |
| **4th Ordnance BD Squad** | **None** | **Present in U.K. (8/43)** |
| **5th Ordnance BD Squad** | **P3, E3, E4, E5, E6, E7** | **2 KIA in Aleutian Islands** |
| **6th Ordnance BD Squad** | **Present in Normandy** | **1 KIA in France (7/44)** |
| **6th Pacific Ocean Area BD Detachment** | **P12 (no further information)** | **Provisional Headquarters for Central Pacific** |
| **7th Ordnance BD Squad** | **P3, E4, E5, E6, E7** | **Reorganized in 1947 for Japan** |
| **8th Ordnance BD Squad** | **E4, E5, E6, E7, E8** | |
| **9th Ordnance BD Squad** | **E3, E4, E5, E7, E8** | **1 KIA** |
| **10th Ordnance BD Squad** | **E4, E7, E8** | |
| **11th Ordnance BD Squad** | **M5, M8, M9, M10, M11** | **12th Army Air Force** |
| **12th Ordnance BD Squad** | **M5, M8, P15 (en route)** | **12th Army Air Force** |
| **13th Ordnance BD Squad** | **M5, M8** | **12th Army Air Force** |
| **14th Ordnance BD Squad** | **E3, E4, E5, E6, E7** | |
| **15th Ordnance BD Squad** | **E2, E3, E4, E5, E6, E7** | **D-Day** |
| **16th Ordnance BD Squad** | **E2, E3, E4, E5, E6, E7** | **D-Day** |
| **17th Ordnance BD Squad** | **E3, E4, E5, E6, E7** | |
| **18th Ordnance BD Squad** | **E3, E4, E5, E6, E7** | |

| | | |
|---|---|---|
| **19th Ordnance BD Squad** | **E3, E4, E5, E6, E7** | |
| **20th Ordnance BD Squad** | **E3, E4, E5, E6, E7** | |
| **21st Ordnance BD Squad** | **E3, E4, E5, E6, E7** | |
| **22nd Ordnance BD Squad** | **E4, E5, E6, E7, E8** | |
| **23rd Ordnance BD Squad** | **E2, E4, E5, E6, E7, E8** | **D-Day, Croix de Guerre** |
| **24th Ordnance BD Squad** | **E4, E8** | |
| **25th Ordnance BD Squad** | **E3, E4, E5, E6, E7, E8** | |
| **26th Ordnance BD Squad** | **E2, E3, E4, E5, E6, E7, E8** | **D-Day, Croix de Guerre, 1 KIA** |
| **27th Ordnance BD Squad** | **E2, E3, E4, E5, E6, E7, E8** | **D-Day, C. de Guerre, Citation** |
| **28th Ordnance BD Squad** | **E4, E5, E6, E7, E8** | |
| **29th Ordnance BD Squad** | **E3, E4, E5, E6, E7, E8** | |
| **30th Ordnance BD Squad** | **E3, E4, E5, E6, E7, E8** | **1 KIA** |
| **31st Ordnance BD Squad** | **E3, E4, E5, E6, E7, E8** | |
| **32nd Ordnance BD Squad** | **E4, E5** | **1 KIA** |
| **33rd Ordnance BD Squad** | **E3, E4, E5, E6, E7, E8** | |
| **34th Ordnance BD Squad** | **E3, E4, E5, E6, E7, E8** | |
| **35th Ordnance BD Squad** | **E3, E4, E5, E6, E7, E8** | |
| **36th Ordnance BD Squad** | **E4, E5, E6, E7, E8** | |
| **37th Ordnance BD Squad** | **E4, E5, E7, E8** | |
| **38th Ordnance BD Squad** | **E4, E5, E6, E7, E8** | |

| | | |
|---|---|---|
| **39th Ordnance BD Squad** | **E4, E5, E6, E7, E8** | |
| **40th Ordnance BD Squad** | **E4, E5, E7, E8** | |
| **41st Ordnance BD Squad** | **E4, E5, E7, E8** | |
| **42nd Ordnance BD Squad** | **E4, E5, E7, E8** | |
| **43rd Ordnance BD Squad** | **E4, E5, E6, E7, E8** | |
| **44th Ordnance BD Squad** | **E4, E5, E7, E8** | |
| **45th Ordnance BD Squad** | **E4, E5, E7, E8** | |
| **46th Ordnance BD Squad** | **E4, E5, E7, E8** | |
| **47th Ordnance BD Squad** | **E2, E3, E4, E5, E8** | **D-Day** |
| **48th Ordnance BD Squad** | **E3, E4, E8** | |
| **49th Ordnance BD Squad** | **E3, E4** | |
| **50th Ordnance BD Squad** | **E4, E5, E7, E8** | |
| **51st Ordnance BD Squad** | **E4, E5, E7, E8** | |
| **52nd Ordnance BD Squad** | **E4, E5, E7, E8** | |
| **53rd Ordnance BD Squad** | **E4, E5, E7, E8** | |
| **54th Ordnance BD Squad** | **E4, E5, E7, E8** | |
| ***55th Ordnance BD Squad** | **M8, M11, M12** | **Casual Detachment "A" (1 KIA)** |
| ***56th Ordnance BD Squad** | **M6, M7, M11, M12** | **Casual Detachment "A"** |
| ***57th Ordnance BD Squad** | **M5, M9, M10, M11, M12** | **Casual Detachment "A" (3 KIA)** |
| ***58th Ordnance BD Squad** | **Present in MTO** | **Casual Detachment "A"** |

| | | |
|---|---|---|
| *59th Ordnance BD Squad | M5, M8 | Casual Detachment "A" |
| 60th Ordnance BD Squad | None | |
| 61st Ordnance BD Squad | None | |
| 62nd Ordnance BD Squad | None | |
| 63rd Ordnance BD Squad | None | |
| 64th Ordnance BD Squad | None | |
| 65th Ordnance BD Squad | None | |
| 66th Ordnance BD Squad | None | |
| 67th Ordnance BD Squad | E3, E4, E5, E6, E7, E8 | |
| 68th Ordnance BD Squad | E4, E5, E6, E7, E8 | |
| 69th Ordnance BD Squad | E3, E4, E8 | |
| 70th Ordnance BD Squad | E3, E4, E8 | |
| 71st Ordnance BD Squad | E4, E5, E6, E7, E8 | |
| 72nd Ordnance BD Squad | E3, E4, E5, E7, E8 | |
| 73rd Ordnance BD Squad | E4, E7, E8 | |
| 74th Ordnance BD Squad | E3, E4, E5, E7, E8 | |
| 75th Ordnance BD Squad | E3, E4, E5, E7, E8 | |
| 76th Ordnance BD Squad | E4, E5, E7, E8 | |
| 77th Ordnance BD Squad | E4, E7, E8 | |
| 78th Ordnance BD Squad | E4, E7, E8 | |

| | | |
|---|---|---|
| **79th Ordnance BD Squad** | **E4, E7, E8** | |
| **80th Ordnance BD Squad** | **E4, E8** | |
| **81st Ordnance BD Squad** | **E4, E7** | |
| **82nd Ordnance BD Squad** | **E4, E5, E7, E8** | |
| **83rd Ordnance BD Squad** | **E4, E7, E8** | |
| **84th Ordnance BD Squad** | **E4, E8** | |
| **85th Ordnance BD Squad** | **E4, E7, E8** | |
| **86th Ordnance BD Squad** | **E3, E4, E5, E6, E7, E8** | |
| **87th Ordnance BD Squad** | **E7, E8** | |
| **88th Ordnance BD Squad** | **E3, E4, E5, E6, E7, E8** | **Meritorious Unit Commendation** |
| **89th Ordnance BD Squad** | **E3, E4, E5, E6, E7, E8** | |
| **90th Ordnance BD Squad** | **E3, E4, E5, E6, E7, E8** | |
| **91st Ordnance BD Squad** | **E4, E5, E6, E7, E8** | |
| **92nd Ordnance BD Squad** | **P10, P12, P14** | **5 KIA, 1 MIA** |
| **93rd Ordnance BD Squad** | **P9, P12** | |
| **94th Ordnance BD Squad** | **P14** | |
| **95th Ordnance BD Squad** | **P12, P14, P15** | |
| **96th Ordnance BD Squad** | **P12, P14, P15** | |
| **97th Ordnance BD Squad** | **P9, P12, P14** | |
| **98th Ordnance BD Squad** | **None** | |

| | | |
|---|---|---|
| **99th Ordnance BD Squad** | **P12, P15** | **Occupation Credit, Korea, 1945** |
| **100th Ordnance BD Squad** | **P6, P7, P10, P11 plus landing** | **Pres. Unit Citation (Philippines)** |
| **101st Ordnance BD Squad** | **P7, P11** | **Pres. Unit Citation (Philippines)** |
| **102nd Ordnance BD Squad** | **P7, P11** | **Pres. Unit Citation (Philippines)** |
| **103rd Ordnance BD Squad** | **P11** | **Pres. Unit Citation (Philippines)** |
| **104th Ordnance BD Squad** | **P14** | **Occupation Credit, Okinawa** |
| **105th Ordnance BD Squad** | **P14** | |
| **106th Ordnance BD Squad** | **P11 plus landing** | **Pres. Unit Citation (Philippines)** |
| **107th Ordnance BD Squad** | **P6, P11 plus landing** | **Pres. Unit Citation (Philippines)** |
| **108th Ordnance BD Squad** | **P6, P7, P8, P11 plus landing, P15** | **Pres. Unit Citation (Philippines)** |
| **109th Ordnance BD Squad** | **P6, P10, P11 plus landing** | **Pres. Unit Citation (Philippines)** |
| **110th Ordnance BD Squad** | **E4, E5, E7, E8** | |
| **111th Ordnance BD Squad** | **E4, E5, E7, E8** | |
| **112th Ordnance BD Squad** | **E5, E6, E8** | |
| **113th Ordnance BD Squad** | **E5, E6, E7, E8** | |
| **114th Ordnance BD Squad** | **E5, E6, E7, E8** | |
| **115th Ordnance BD Squad** | **E5, E6, E8** | |
| **116th Ordnance BD Squad** | **E5, E6, E8** | |
| **117th Ordnance BD Squad** | **E5, E6, E8** | |
| **118th Ordnance BD Squad** | **None** | |

| | | |
|---|---|---|
| **119th Ordnance BD Squad** | **E5, E8** | **Citation from Belgian Army** |
| **120th Ordnance BD Squad** | **E5** | **Citation from Belgian Army** |
| **121st Ordnance BD Squad** | **E7, E8** | **Citation from Belgian Army** |
| **122nd Ordnance BD Squad** | **E5, E6, E8** | |
| **123rd Ordnance BD Squad** | **E5, E6, E7, E8** | |
| **124th Ordnance BD Squad** | **E5, E6, E8** | |
| **125th Ordnance BD Squad** | **E7, E8** | |
| **126th Ordnance BD Squad** | **E5, E6, E7, E8** | |
| **127th Ordnance BD Squad** | **E5** | |
| **128th Ordnance BD Squad** | **E5** | |
| **129th Ordnance BD Squad** | **E5** | |
| **130th Ordnance BD Squad** | **E5** | |
| **131st Ordnance BD Squad** | **E5, E7, E8** | **Orig. 235th Ord. BD Company** |
| **132nd Ordnance BD Squad** | **M8, M10, E5, E7, E8** | **Orig. 235th Ord. BD Company** |
| **133rd Ordnance BD Squad** | **E5, E7, E8** | **Orig. 235th Ord. BD Company** |
| **134th Ordnance BD Squad** | **E5, E7** | **Orig.235th Ord. BD Company** |
| **135th Ordnance BD Squad** | **E5, E7, E8** | **Orig. 235th Ord. BD Company** |
| **136th Ordnance BD Squad** | **M11, M12** | **Orig. 235th Ord. BD Company** |
| **137th Ordnance BD Squad** | **M11, M12** | **Orig. 235th Ord. BD Company** |
| **138th Ordnance BD Squad** | **M11** | **Orig. 235th Ord. BD Company** |

| | | |
|---|---|---|
| **139th Ordnance BD Squad** | **None** | **Orig. 235th Ord. BD Company** |
| **140th Ordnance BD Squad** | **None** | **Orig. 235th Ord. BD Company** |
| **141st Ordnance BD Squad** | **M11** | **Meritorious Unit Commendation** |
| **142nd Ordnance BD Squad** | **M11** | **Orig. 235th Ord. BD Company** |
| **143rd Ordnance BD Squad** | **M9, M10, E5, E6, E7, E8** | **Orig. 236th Ord. BD Company** |
| **144th Ordnance BD Squad** | **M9, M10, E5, E6, E7, E8** | **Orig. 236th Ord. BD Company** |
| **145th Ordnance BD Squad** | **M9, M10, E5, E6, E7, E8** | **Orig. 236th Ord. BD Company** |
| **146th Ordnance BD Squad** | **M9, M10, E5, E6, E7, E8** | **Orig.236th Ord. BD Company** |
| **147th Ordnance BD Squad** | **M5, M8, E5, E6, E7, E8** | **Orig. 236th Ord. BD Company** |
| **148th Ordnance BD Squad** | **M11, M12** | **Orig. 236th Ord. BD Company** |
| **149th Ordnance BD Squad** | **M7, M11** | **Orig. 236th Ord. BD Company** |
| **150th Ordnance BD Squad** | **M7, M11, M12** | **Orig. 236th Ord. BD Company** |
| **151st Ordnance BD Squad** | **M11, M12** | **Orig. 236th Ord. BD Company** |
| **152nd Ordnance BD Squad** | **M11, M12** | **Orig. 236th Ord. BD Company** |
| **153rd Ordnance BD Squad** | **M7, M11, M12** | **Orig. 236th Ord. BD Company** |
| **154th Ordnance BD Squad** | **M7, M11, M12** | **Orig. 236th Ord. BD Company** |
| **155th Ordnance BD Squad** | **E5** | |
| **156th Ordnance BD Squad** | **P2, P15** | **Navy Unit Citation** |
| **157th Ordnance BD Squad** | **E5, E6, E7, E8** | |
| **158th Ordnance BD Squad** | **P10 plus landing, P13** | **Pres. Unit Citation (Philippines)** |

| | | |
|---|---|---|
| **159th Ordnance BD Squad** | **E5, E6, E7, E8** | |
| **160th Ordnance BD Squad** | **E5, E6, E7, E8** | |
| **161st Ordnance BD Squad** | **E5, E6, E7, E8** | |
| **162nd Ordnance BD Squad** | **E5, E6, E7, E8** | |
| **163rd Ordnance BD Squad** | **E5, E6, E7, E8** | |
| **164th Ordnance BD Squad** | **E5, E6, E7, E8** | |
| **165th Ordnance BD Squad** | **E5, E6, E7, E8** | |
| **166th Ordnance BD Squad** | **E5, E6, E7, E8** | |
| **167th Ordnance BD Squad** | **E5, E6, E7, E8** | |
| **168th Ordnance BD Squad** | **E5, E6, E8** | |
| **169th Ordnance BD Squad** | **E5, E6, E8** | |
| **170th Ordnance BD Squad** | **E5, E6, E8** | |
| **171st Ordnance BD Squad** | **P6, P10 plus landing, P11** | **Pres. Unit Citation (Philippines)** |
| **172nd Ordnance BD Squad** | **P6, P10, P11** | **Pres. Unit Citation (Philippines)** |
| **173rd Ordnance BD Squad** | **P6, P10** | **Pres. Unit Citation (Philippines)** |
| **174th Ordnance BD Squad** | **P6, P10, P15** | **Pres. Unit Citation (Philippines)** |
| **175th Ordnance BD Squad** | **P6, P10 plus landing, P11** | **Pres. Unit Citation (Philippines)** |
| **176th Ordnance BD Squad** | **P11** | **Pres. Unit Citation (Philippines)** |
| **177th Ordnance BD Squad** | **P10, P11** | **Pres. Unit Citation (Philippines)** |
| **178th Ordnance BD Squad** | **P11, P15** | **Pres. Unit Citation (Philippines)** |

| | | |
|---|---|---|
| **179th Ordnance BD Squad** | **P11, P15** | **Pres. Unit Citation (Philippines)** |
| **180th Ordnance BD Squad** | **P10, P11** | **Pres. Unit Citation (Philippines)** |
| **181st Ordnance BD Squad** | **P10 plus landing, P13** | **Pres. Unit Citation (Philippines)** |
| **182nd Ordnance BD Squad** | **P10 plus landing, P13** | **Pres. Unit Citation (Philippines)** |
| **183rd Ordnance BD Squad** | **E5** | **ETO only** |
| **183rd Ordnance Svc. Det. (BD)** | **P10** | **Pres. Unit Citation (Philippines)** |
| **184th Ordnance Svc. Det. (BD)** | **P10, P13** | **Pres. Unit Citation (Philippines)** |
| **185th Ordnance BD Squad** | **None** | |
| **186th Ordnance BD Squad** | **None** | |
| **187th Ordnance BD Squad** | **None** | |
| **188th Ordnance BD Squad** | **None** | |
| **189th Ordnance BD Squad** | **None** | |
| **190th Ordnance BD Squad** | **None** | |
| **191st Ordnance BD Squad** | **None** | |
| **192nd Ordnance BD Squad** | **None** | |
| **193rd Ordnance BD Squad** | **None** | |
| **194th Ordnance BD Squad** | **None** | |
| **195th Ordnance BD Squad** | **None** | |
| **196th Ordnance BD Squad** | **None** | |
| **197th Ordnance BD Squad** | **None** | |

| | | |
|---|---|---|
| **198th Ordnance BD Squad** | **None** | |
| **199th Ordnance BD Squad** | **None** | |
| **200th Ordnance BD Squad** | **None** | |
| **201st Ordnance BD Squad** | **None** | |
| **202nd Ordnance BD Squad** | **None** | |
| **203rd Ordnance BD Squad** | **None** | |
| **204th Ordnance BD Squad** | **P10, P12, P15** | **Pres. Unit Citation (Philippines)** |
| **205th Ordnance BD Squad** | **P12, P15** | |
| **206th Ordnance BD Squad** | **P10 plus landing, P12** | **Pres. Unit Citation (Philippines)** |
| **207th Ordnance BD Squad** | **P2** | |
| **208th Ordnance BD Squad** | **P11** | **Pres. Unit Citation (Philippines)** |
| **209th Ordnance BD Squad** | **P10, P11, (P13)** | **4 KIA, Unit Citation (Philippines)** |
| **210th Ordnance BD Squad** | **P11** | **Pres. Unit Citation (Philippines)** |
| **211th Ordnance BD Squad** | **P11** | **Pres. Unit Citation (Philippines)** |
| **212th Ordnance BD Squad** | **Hawaiian Department** | **Meritorious Unit Commendation** |
| **213th Ordnance BD Squad** | **P12, P15** | |
| **214th Ordnance BD Squad** | **P12, P15** | |
| **215th Ordnance BD Squad** | **P15** | |
| **216th Ordnance BD Squad** | **P12, P15** | |
| **217th Ordnance BD Squad** | **P15** | |

| | | |
|---|---|---|
| **218th Ordnance BD Squad** | **P15** | |
| **219th Ordnance BD Squad** | **P15** | |
| **231st Ord. BD Company** | **Western Defense Command** | **Disbanded 10/43** |
| **232nd Ord. BD Company** | **Central Pacific** | **Disbanded 11/43** |
| **233rd Ord. BD Company** | **Panama Canal Zone** | **Disbanded 11/43** |
| **234th Ord. BD Company** | **United Kingdom** | **Disbanded 10/44** |
| **[231st Ord. BD Platoon]** | **E4, E5, E7, E8** | **Formerly 234th BD Company** |
| **[232nd Ord. BD Platoon]** | **E4, E5, E6, E7** | **Formerly 234th BD Company** |
| **[233rd Ord. BD Platoon]** | **E4, E5, E7, E8** | **Formerly 234th BD Company** |
| **[234th Ord. BD Platoon]** | **E4, E5, E6, E7, E8** | **Formerly 234th BD Company** |
| **235th Ord. BD Company** | **M3, M5, M8** | **Disbanded 5/44; 1 KIA, 2 MIA** |
| **236th Ord. BD Company** | **M5, M6 (1st & 2nd Platoons), M8** | **Disbanded 5/44; 3 KIA** |
| **237th Ord. BD Company** | **Southern Pacific** | **Disbanded 11/43** |
| **238th Ord. BD Company** | **Continental United States** | **Disbanded 10/43** |
| **3289th Ord. BD Company** | **E5, E8** | **ETO Bomb Disposal School** |
| **5280th BD Squadron (Prov.)** | **P6** | **Unknown** |

[1] The above listings have been adapted from the official Department of the Army Pamphlet 672-1, plus corrections from War Department General Orders and various unit histories. None of these records are complete with regards to decorations or battle credits, and the Pacific Theater is under-represented owing to poor communications. Some BD units were commissioned but never sent forth. In a few cases, I have noted instances in parentheses where DA Pamphlet 672-1 may have been in error. This is by no means a rebuke of the U.S. Army; only a reminder to all military historians that exact record-keeping was sometimes secondary to winning the Second World War. (Department of the Army, *Pamphlet*

---

*672-1: Bomb Disposal Unit Citation and Campaign Participation Credit Register* (Washington D.C.: Government Publishing Office, 1972); Jerome Krieger to Commander, NAVSCOLEOD, *Fact Sheet*, 5 October 1992.

## Munitions disposed of by *all* squads on the Continent (ETO)

| Month/Year | Allied Bombs | German Bombs | Total Number (UXBs) | Total Tonnage (UXBs) | Misc. Munitions | Total Tonnage |
|---|---|---|---|---|---|---|
| **6/44** | 351 | 10 | 361 | 21.76 | 42.36 | 64.12 |
| **7/44** | 751 | 694 | 1,445 | 114.62 | 344.23 | 458.85 |
| **8/44** | 737 | 4,725 | 5,462 | 145.31 | 409.16 | 554.47 |
| **9/44** | 806 | 8,499 | 9,305 | 221.18 | 530.80 | 751.98 |
| **10/44** | 1,197 | 174,896 | 176,093 | 1,882.00 | 598.00 | 2,480.00 |
| **11/44** | 1,804 | 99,721 | 101,525 | 2,244.00 | 2,113.00 | 4,357.00 |
| **12/44** | 1,853 | 80,154 | 82,007 | 1,353.44 | 3,221.86 | 4,575.30 |
| **1/45** | 1,055 | 130,895 | 131,950 | 670.18 | 3,905.60 | 4,575.78 |
| **2/45** | 1,585 | 71,651 | 73,236 | 924.71 | 4,076.28 | 5,000.79 |
| **3/45** | 2,672 | 12,364 | 15,036 | 811.52 | 8,016.78 | 8,828.30 |
| **4/45** | 2,195 | 12,360 | 14,555 | 775.36 | 7,278.67 | 8,054.03 |
| **5/45** | 379 | 3,061 | 3,440 | 223.49 | 967.27 | 1,190.76 |
| **Totals:** | **15,385** | **599,030** | **614,415** | **9,387.57** | **31,504.01** | **40,891.5** |

Sources: Ordnance Technical Services, *ETO Bomb Disposal History*, NARA Records Group 498, 1942-45; *History of the Ordnance Bomb Disposal Division from D-Day to VE-Day in Europe,* Headquarters Communication Zone ETOUSA, 1945.

## Munitions disposed of by Squads assigned to Armies (ETO)

| Month/Year | Allied Bombs | German Bombs | Total Number (UXBs) | Total Tonnage (UXBs) | Misc. Munitions | Total Tonnage |
|---|---|---|---|---|---|---|
| **6/44** | 351 | 10 | 361 | 21.76 | 42.36 | 64.12 |
| **7/44** | 505 | 37 | 542 | 17.62 | 165.23 | 182.85 |
| **8/44** | 407 | 93 | 500 | 20.31 | 131.23 | 151.47 |
| **9/44** | 383 | 297 | 680 | 44.18 | 146.80 | 190.98 |
| **10/44** | 224 | 349 | 573 | 72.00 | 158.00 | 230.00 |
| **11/44** | 581 | 4,002 | 4,583 | 133.00 | 129.00 | 262.00 |
| **12/44** | 775 | 6,154 | 6,929 | 213.03 | 801.91 | 1,014.94 |
| **1/45** | 386 | 300 | 686 | 94.38 | 1,905.87 | 2,000.25 |
| **2/45** | 325 | 326 | 651 | 150.08 | 2,957.14 | 3,107.22 |
| **3/45** | 1,457 | 4,513` | 5,970 | 354.71 | 5,945.81 | 6,300.52 |
| **4/45** | 927 | 4,778 | 5,705 | 323.18 | 6,153.27 | 6,476.45 |
| **5/45** | 137 | 1,021 | 1,158 | 94.77 | 826.85 | 921.62 |
| **Totals:** | **6,458** | **21,880** | **28,338** | **1,539.00** | **19,363.40** | **20,902.42** |

Sources: Ordnance Technical Services, *ETO Bomb Disposal History*, NARA Records Group 498, 1942-45; *History of the Ordnance Bomb Disposal Division from D-Day to VE-Day in Europe,* Headquarters Communication Zone ETOUSA, 1945.

# Munitions disposed of by Squads assigned to Com Z (ETO)

| Month/Year | Allied Bombs | German Bombs | Total Number (UXBs) | Total Tonnage (UXBs) | Misc. Munitions | Total Tonnage |
|---|---|---|---|---|---|---|
| **6/44** | -- | -- | -- | -- | -- | -- |
| **7/44** | 246 | 657 | 903 | 97.00 | 179.00 | 276.00 |
| **8/44** | 330 | 4,632 | 4,962 | 125.00 | 278.00 | 403.00 |
| **9/44** | 423 | 8,202 | 8,625 | 177.00 | 384.00 | 561.00 |
| **10/44** | 513 | 10,271 | 10,784 | 203.00 | 195.00 | 398.00 |
| **11/44** | 891 | 13,603 | 14,494 | 289.00 | 799.00 | 1,088.00 |
| **12/44** | 685 | 14,898 | 15,583 | 223.27 | 2,240.43 | 2,463.70 |
| **1/45** | 337 | 303 | 640 | 68.92 | 1,903.95 | 1,972.87 |
| **2/45** | 697 | 7,796 | 8,493 | 387.25 | 1,109.58 | 1,496.83 |
| **3/45** | 523 | 6,328 | 6,851 | 302.73 | 2,057.32 | 2,360.05 |
| **4/45** | 446 | 5,226 | 5,672 | 280.12 | 1,110.18 | 1,390.30 |
| **5/45** | 106 | 1,247 | 1,353 | 87.64 | 136.40 | 224.04 |
| **Totals:** | **5,197** | **73,163** | **78,360** | **2,240.93** | **10,392.86** | **12,633.79** |

Sources: Ordnance Technical Services, *ETO Bomb Disposal History*, NARA Records Group 498, 1942-45; *History of the Ordnance Bomb Disposal Division from D-Day to VE-Day in Europe,* Headquarters Communication Zone ETOUSA, 1945.

# Munitions disposed of by Squads assigned to Air Corps (ETO)

| Month/Year | Allied Bombs | German Bombs | Total Number (UXBs) | Total Tonnage (UXBs) | Misc. Munitions | Total Tonnage |
|---|---|---|---|---|---|---|
| **6/44** | -- | -- | -- | -- | -- | -- |
| **7/44** | -- | -- | -- | -- | -- | -- |
| **8/44** | -- | -- | -- | -- | -- | -- |
| **9/44** | -- | -- | -- | -- | -- | -- |
| **10/44** | 460 | 164,276 | 164,736 | 1,607.00 | 245.00 | 1,852.00 |
| **11/44** | 332 | 82,116 | 82,448 | 1,822.00 | 1,185.00 | 3,007.00 |
| **12/44** | 393 | 59,102 | 59,495 | 917.14 | 179.52 | 1,096.66 |
| **1/45** | 332 | 130,292 | 130,624 | 506.88 | 95.78 | 602.66 |
| **2/45** | 563 | 63,529 | 64,092 | 387.38 | 9.56 | 396.94 |
| **3/45** | 692 | 1,523 | 2,215 | 154.08 | 13.65 | 167.73 |
| **4/45** | 822 | 2,356 | 3,178 | 172.06 | 15.22 | 187.28 |
| **5/45** | 136 | 793 | 929 | 41.08 | 4.02 | 45.10 |
| **Totals:** | **3,730** | **503,987** | **507.717** | **5,607.62** | **1,747.75** | **7,355.37** |

Sources: Ordnance Technical Services, *ETO Bomb Disposal History*, NARA Records Group 498, 1942-45; *History of the Ordnance Bomb Disposal Division from D-Day to VE-Day in Europe,* Headquarters Communication Zone ETOUSA, 1945.

## Ninth Air Force Chief Ordnance Bomb Disposal Statistics

| Month/ Year | German Bombs (#) | German UXBs (tons) | American Bombs (#) | American Bombs (tons) | British Bombs (#) | British Bombs (tons) | French Bombs (#) | French Bombs (tons) | Misc. Munitions (tons) |
|---|---|---|---|---|---|---|---|---|---|
| **7/44 to 10/44** | -- | -- | -- | -- | -- | – | -- | -- | -- |
| **11/44** | 91,498 | 13,220.0 | 265 | 51.9 | 68 | 18.5 | 119 | 29.2 | 58.1 |
| **12/44** | 78,345 | 210.8 | 638 | 57.2 | 17 | 4.5 | 50 | 25.6 | 44.8 |
| **1/45** | 118,778 | 248.5 | 257 | 57.36 | 11 | 2.35 | 60 | 14.14 | 79.51 |
| **2/45** | 68,892 | 158.9 | 283 | 46.7 | 6 | 1.5 | -- | -- | 18.5 |
| **3/45** | 1,755 | 61.4 | 686 | 84.7 | 123 | 30.7 | -- | -- | 28.6 |
| **4/45** | 50,711 | 184.75 | 1,017 | 48.49 | 19 | 2.75 | -- | -- | 61.83 |
| **5/45** | 24,429 | 212.5 | 1,148 | 107.85 | 23 | 7.25 | -- | -- | 262.25 |
| **6/45** | 44,473 | 272.3 | 6,950 | 350.6 | 165 | 13 | -- | -- | 229.00 |
| **Subtotals:** | **478,881** | **14,569.15** | **11,244** | **804.8** | **432** | **80.55** | **229** | **68.94** | **781.99** |

| | Allied Bombs | German Bombs | Total UXBs | UXB Tonnage | Munitions | Total Tonnage |
|---|---|---|---|---|---|---|
| **Totals:** | **11,905** | **478,881** | **490,786** | **15,523.44** | **781.99** | **16,305.43** |

Sources: Headquarters, Ninth Air Force, Col. W.R. Maxwell, Office of the Ordnance Officer, *Monthly Ordnance Activities Reports*, August 1944 to June 1945, AFHRA 533.804.

## Common German Incendiary and Explosive Bombs in World War II

| Year | Bomb | Description | Weight | Manufacturer & Location |
|---|---|---|---|---|
| **1933** | **B-1(e)** | Electron Incendiary Bomb | 2.2 lbs. | I.G. Farben |
| | **SD-10** | Fragmentation Bomb | 22 lbs. | Wilhelm Wurl; Weissensee |
| | **SC-50** | High Explosive Bomb | 110 lbs. | Rheinmetall, Dusseldorf |
| | **SC-250** | High Explosive Bomb | 550 lbs. | Rheinmetall, Dusseldorf |
| **1935** | **SC-500** | High Explosive Bomb | 1,100 lbs. | Rheinmetall, Dusseldorf |
| **1936** | **LMA** | Magnetic Parachute “G” Mine | 1,100 lbs. | Experimental Command, Kiel |

| | | | | |
|---|---|---|---|---|
| | **LMB** | Magnetic Parachute "G" Mine | 2,200 lbs. | Experimental Command, Kiel |
| **1938** | **LT-5** | Aircraft Torpedo | 1,760 lbs. | Torpedo Experiment Station |
| | **SD-50** | Multiple Purpose Bomb | 110 lbs. | Vereinigte Oberschlesiche Huetten Werke |
| **1939** | **B-1 (3e)** | Electron Incendiary Bomb | 3 lbs. | I.G. Farben |
| | **SD-500** | Multiple Purpose Bomb | 1,100 lbs. | V.O. Huetten Werke |
| | **PC-500** | Armor Piercing Bomb | 1,100 lbs. | Rheinmetall, Dusseldorf |
| **1940** | **SD-2(t)** | Fighter-Bomber Bomb ("Butterfly") | 4.4 lbs. | V.O., Huetten Werke |
| | **S Be 50** | Concrete Fragmentation Bomb | 110 lbs. | Cologne |
| | **PC-500** | Armor Piercing Bomb (with Rocket) | 1,100 lbs. | Rheinmetall, Dusseldorf |
| | **SC-1000** | High Explosive Bomb | 2,200 lbs. | Rheinmetall, Dusseldorf |
| | **SC-1800** | High Explosive Bomb "Satan" | 4,000 lbs. | Rheinmetall, Dusseldorf |
| | **SD-1700** | Multiple Purpose Bomb | 3,740 lbs. | Rheinmetall, Dusseldorf |
| | **PC-1400** | Armor Piercing Bomb | 3,080 lbs. | Rheinmetall, Dusseldorf |

| | | | | |
|---|---|---|---|---|
| **1940** | **Flam C 250** | Flam Bomb | 550 lbs. | V.O., Huetten Werke |
| | **Flam C 500** | Flam Bomb | 1,100 lbs. | V.O., Huetten Werke |
| **1941** | **B-2 E (Z)** | Electron Incendiary Bomb | 4.4 lbs. | Hagenuk, Kiel |
| | **Sprbrd C-50** | Incendiary-Demolition Bomb | 110 lbs. | Dr. Buck, Goeppingen |
| | **Strbrd C-500** | Scatter Bomb | 1,100 lbs. | Ambi Budd, Johannistal |
| | **SD-250** | Multiple Purpose Bomb | 550 lbs. | Bochumer Verein, Bochum |
| | **PC-1000 (RS)** | Armor Piercing Bomb (with Rocket) | 2,200 lbs. | Rheinmetall, Dusseldorf |
| | **SB-2500** | High Charge Bomb | 5,500 lbs. | Rheinmetall, Dusseldorf |
| | **BM-1000** | Bomb Mine | 2,200 lbs. | A.E.G., Berlin |
| **1942** | **SD-1** | Fragmentation Bomb | 2.2 lbs. | V.O., Huetten Werke |
| | **SD-4 (H1)** | Hollow Charge Bomb | 8.8 lbs. | Wilhelm Wurl; Weissensee |

| | | | | |
|---|---|---|---|---|
| | **SD-70** | Multiple Purpose Bomb | 154 lbs. | Rheinmetall, Dusseldorf |
| **1942** | **SD-1000** | Multiple Purpose Bomb | 220 lbs. | Rheinmetall, Dusseldorf |
| | **PC-1400 X** | Armor Piercing Bomb ("Fritz X") | 3,180 lbs. | Vereinigte Stahlwerke |
| **1943** | **Brand C-50** | Intensive Incendiary Bomb | 110 lbs. | V.O., Huetten Werke |
| | **Brand C-250** | Intensive Incendiary Bomb | 550 lbs. | V.O., Huetten Werke |
| | **SD-9 / SD-15** | Arty. Shells used as Frag. Bombs | 88 /105mm | V.O., Huetten Werke |
| | **Brand 4/10** | Incendiary Bombs (Liquid) | Variable | Wilhelm Wurl; Weissensee |
| | **SB-1000** | High Charge Bomb | 2,200 lbs. | V.O., Huetten Werke |
| | **SC-2000** | High Explosive Bomb | 4,400 lbs. | Rheinmetall, Dusseldorf |
| | **PD-500** | Armor Piercing Bomb | 1,100 lbs. | Rheinmetall, Dusseldorf |
| | **PD-1000** | Armor Piercing Bomb | 2,200 lbs. | Rheinmetall, Dusseldorf |

Sources: Ernst A. Marquard, "Luftwaffe Methods in the Selection of Offensive Weapons, Volume 2," USAF *Historical Studies*, No. 187 (Manhattan, Kansas: MA/AH Publishing, Sunflower University Press, c. 1985), Appendix III.

## Common German Fuze Types (attached to the side unless otherwise noted)

| Fuze Type | Non-Delay | Delayed Action / Ignition Time | Description | For Use With Bomb(s) |
|---|---|---|---|---|
| **E1 AZ 15** | 0.001 sec. | 0.05 / 8 sec. | One of the earliest fuzes | SC-50 / SC-500 |
| **E1 AZ 24** | 0.0005 sec. | None | Fraction Fuze | SB-1000 / SB-2500 |
| **E1 AZ 26** | 0.0005 sec. | None | Used with incendiaries | Flam C 250/500 |
| **E1 AZ 28A** | 0.001 sec. | 0.15 sec. after impact | Used against ships | SC-50 / SC-500 |
| **E1 AZ 28B** | None | 0.12 sec. after impact | Kinetic Fuze | SC-1000 / SC-2000 / SD-1700 |
| **E1 AZ 35** | 0.1 sec. | 0.1 sec. after impact | Used against ships | PC-500 to PC-1400 |

| | | | | |
|---|---|---|---|---|
| **E1 AZ 38** | 0.05 sec. | 0.2 / 5 sec. | Used against ships | All SC bombs |
| **E1 AZ 48** | 0.045 sec. | 0.075 sec. after impact | | PD-500 / PD-1000 / PC-1600 |
| **E1 AZ 55** | 0.001 sec. | 14 sec. | | SD-50 to SD-500 |
| **E1 AZ 55A** | 0.002 | 14 sec. | | SD-50 to SD-500 / Flam C |
| **E1 ZtZ 9** | None | 5-40 sec. | Long-range Remote Control | KC-250 / Brand C-50 |
| **E1 DoppZ 49** | None | 2.7 sec. / 0.04 sec. | Rocket Bomb Ignition Fuze | PC-500 / PC-1000 (RS) |

| | | | | |
|---|---|---|---|---|
| **Uhrw. ZtZ 89** | None | 4-60 sec. | | Brand C-50A |
| **VZ 34** | None | 30 sec. after impact | Typically handled by Navy | "G" Mines |
| **e-AZ 66** | Impact | Highly Sensitive | Electro-dynamic Head Fuze | SD-4 / SD-9 / SD-15 |
| **AZ 3** | Impact | None | Mechanical Head Fuze | SD-10s |
| **AZ 13A** | Impact | None | Mechanical Head Fuze | B-1 E / B-1 (e) Incendiaries |
| **AZ 23A** | Impact | None | Mechanical Base Fuze | Brand 4 / Brand 10 |

| | | | | |
|---|---|---|---|---|
| **AZ 73** | Impact | Highly Sensitive | Head Fuze with Membrane | SD-1 / SD-3 |
| **E1 Stoer Z 50** | None | Vibration Sensitive | Mercury Tilt Switch | For Nose-Spike Bombs |
| **E1 Stoer Z 60** | None | Vibration Sensitive | Mercury Tilt Switch | For Nose-Spike Bombs |
| **E1 Stoer Z 70** | None | Sensitive after Impact | | For use with SD-2 “Butterfly” |
| **Dopp Z 41** | Impact | Optional | Self-winding mechanism | For use with SD-2 “Butterfly” |
| **LZZ 67** | None | 5-30 sec. | Central Fuze | For use with SD-2 “Butterfly” |

| | | | | |
|---|---|---|---|---|
| **Chem. LZZ 77** | None | 6-48 hours | Central Fuze | For use with SD-2 "Butterfly" |
| **ZtZ 59** | None | 13 or 37 sec. | Designed to burst in mid-air | AB-250 / AB-500 Containers |
| **ZtZ 69D** | None | 1.2 sec. | Designed to burst in mid-air | AB-50 / AB-500 Containers |
| **ZtZ 79** | None | 3, 13, or 30 sec. | Designed to burst in mid-air | AB-250 / AB-500 Containers |
| **Chem. LZZ 57** | None | 12 to 100 hours | | SC-250 / SC-500 |
| **LZZ 17A** | None | 2-72 hours | "17" Fuze | SC-250 / SC-500 |

| | | | | |
|---|---|---|---|---|
| **LZZ 17B** | None | 5-120 minutes | “17” Fuze | SC-250 / SC-500 |
| **ZUS-40** | Special | Anti-withdrawal | Mechanical Removal Block | SC-250 / SC-500 |

Sources: Ernst A. Marquard, “Luftwaffe Methods in the Selection of Offensive Weapons, Volume 2,” USAF *Historical Studies*, No. 187 (Manhattan, Kansas: MA/AH Publishing, Sunflower University Press, c. 1985), Appendix III.

# BIBLIOGRAPHY

## Primary Documents

### Air Force Historical Records


Deichmann, Paul. "Luftwaffe Methods in the Selection of Offensive Weapons, Volume 1." *USAF Historical Studies.* No. 187. Manhattan, Kansas: MA/AH Publishing, Sunflower University Press. c. 1985.

Headquarters, Ninth Air Force to Ordnance Department. *Incident Reports.* 20 September 1944.

—. *Disposal of UXBs.* 28 September 1944.

Headquarters, Ninth Air Force, Office of the Ordnance Officer. *Monthly Ordnance Activities Reports.* August 1944 to June 1945. AFHRA 533.804.

Headquarters, Ninth Air Force. *Disposition of Bomb Disposal Units on the Far Shore.* [memorandum] 24 May 1944.

Headquarters, Ninth Air Force to Commanding Officer, 68th Ordnance Bomb Disposal Squad (Separate). *Unit Citation.* 25 November 1944.

Headquarters, Ninth Air Force, Office of the Bomb Disposal Officer. *Consolidated History of Bomb Disposal in the Ninth Air Force.* May 1945.

Marquard, Ernst A. "Luftwaffe Methods in the Selection of Offensive Weapons, Volume 2." *USAF Historical Studies.* No. 187. Manhattan, Kansas: MA/AH Publishing, Sunflower University Press. c. 1985.

Technical Information Bulletins. AFHRA 173.8 through 173.11. Maxwell Air Force Base.

United States Armed Forces Europe (USAFE). Weekly Armament and Ordnance Activities Reports. AFHRA 519.8041-1, AFHRA 533.804, AFHRA 570.11427.

United States Strategic Air Forces (USSTAF). AFHRA 520.673.

United States Army Air Forces. *Passenger Manifest.* 1 December 1944.


### Bomb Disposal Division ETO


Bateman, H.H. to Brigadier General H.B. Sayler. [Commendation for Captain Feldman] 24 January 1944.

Collins, George W. to Commanding General, 50th AAA Brigade. *Propaganda Container in Divers*, 1 February 1945.
Davison, H.G. *Bomb and Munitions School*. 4 October 1944.
—. *Monthly Report of Bomb Disposal Activities, No.2*. 2 December 1944.
De Gaulle, Charles to Joseph C. Pilcher. *Decision No. 341: a l'Ordre du Corps d'Armee*. [letter of citation] 29 January 1945.
—. *Decision No. 341* [certificate] 29 January 1945.
Dunlop, Robert H. *Bomb Disposal Directives*. 9 May 1944.
Eisenhower, Dwight D. to R.B. Lord. *Bomb and Shell Disposal*. [letter of instruction] c. May 1944.
Finley, C.R. to Commanding General, First U.S. Army. *Commendation for First Lieutenant Pilcher*. 4 March 1944.
Gordon, George D. 68th Ordnance Bomb Disposal Squad Sep. *Report on V-1 Attack on Liege, Belgium, 21-29 November 1944*. 7 December 1944.
Headquarters European Theater of Operations, 1st U.S. Army to 1st Lt. Joseph C. Pilcher. [promotion list] 25 May 1944.
Headquarters, Ninth Air Force. *Disposal of UXBs*. 28 September 1944.
Headquarters U.S. Strategic Air Forces in Europe. *Procedure for Giving Assistance to R.A.F Bomb Disposal Organization in Disposal of Bombs*. [letter] 16 June 1943.
Headquarters V Corps U.S. Army. *General Orders No. 57*. [citation] 18 May 1945.
—. *General Orders No. 66*. [citation] 30 May 1945.
Headquarters V Corps U.S. Army to Captain Joseph C. Pilcher. *French Awards*. [memorandum] 9 March 1945.
*History of the Ordnance Bomb Disposal Division from D-Day to VE-Day in Europe*. Headquarters Communication Zone ETOUSA. 1945.
Hodges, Courtney H. to V Corps U.S. Army. [citation] 9 May 1945.
Kane, Thomas J. to Ordnance Officer ETOUSA. *Bomb Disposal Organization Recommended for ETOUSA*. Aberdeen Proving Grounds, MD. [unpublished memo] 11 January 1943.
Kane, Thomas J. to Headquarters ETO, United States Army. [technical report] 16 January 1943.
Kane, Thomas J. to Ordnance Officer ETOUSA. *Bomb Disposal in the Communication Zone*. [unpublished memo] 11 January 1943.
Kane, Thomas J. to Allied Forces Headquarters. *Bomb Disposal Organization*. [unpublished memo] 5 February 1943.
Kane, Thomas J. *Report on Conference with German Bomb Disposal Officer*. 8 October 1944.

Kane, Thomas J. *History of the Bomb Disposal Organization in the ETO.* 4 November 1944.

Kane, Thomas J. to Chief Ordnance Officer ETO. [unused copy] *Report on Operational Activities for October 1944.* 10 November 1944.

Kane, Thomas J. *Monthly Report of Bomb Disposal Activities.* 13 November 1944.

Kane, Thomas J. and John E. Feldman. *History of the Ordnance Bomb Disposal Division From D-Day to VE-Day in Europe.* c. 1945.

Kane, Thomas J. *Top View of Ordnance Bomb Disposal in ETOUSA.* c. 1945.

Kane, Thomas J. to Commanding Officer, 68th Ordnance Bomb Disposal Squad (Separate), IX Air Force. *Bomb Disposal Publicity.* 11 July 1945.

Knight, A.C. *Special Orders No. 24.* [memorandum] 11 March 1944.

Knight, A.C. to 1st Lieutenant Joseph C. Pilcher. [memorandum] 11 March 1944.

Knox, Alan G. to Col. Thomas J. Kane. [undated letter] *Recommendation for Award of Bronze Star Medal*, c. 1946.

Larkin, Schuyler V.C. to Colonel Thomas J. Kane. *Bomb Disposal Training in the United Kingdom*, 1 October 1943.

Larkin, Schuyler V.C. *Bomb Disposal since D-Day.* [unpublished report] 2 January 1945.

*Lightning:* History of 78th Infantry Division, Infantry Journal Press, Washington, D.C., 1947.

Lord, R.B. *Maintenance and Operation of Motor Vehicles*, 15 June 1944.

Medaris, John B. *Overlord Diary.* Ordnance Office, 1st U.S. Army. 25 February 1944.

Ordnance Section. U.S. Forces European Theater (USFET). *Ordnance Section Reveals Work of Bomb Disposal Squads for First Time.* August 1945.

—. *Million Tons of German Ammo Put to Peace Time Usage.* August 1945.

Ordnance Technical Services. *Technical Service Ammunition Ordnance Report.* NARA Records Group 498. 1943-45.

—. *ETO Bomb Disposal History.* NARA Records Group 498. 1942-45.

Racey, Joseph T. *Report of Activities of Ordnance Bomb and Munitions School.* October 1944.

Schiller, George W. to Adjutant, 82nd Ordnance Group. [memorandum] 4 June 1945.

Schiller, George W. to Colonel Thomas J. Kane. [memorandum] 8 June 1945.

Special Observer Section, European Theater of Operations. *Fuze Sterilizing Equipment for Bomb Disposal.* [undated technical report] c. 1942.
V Corps to Captain Joseph C. Pilcher and Technician Fifth Grade Joseph Olszewski, *Citations for Bronze Star*, 30 May 1945.

## Field & Technical Manuals

*Ammunition, General.* Aberdeen Proving Ground, Maryland: Ordnance School. 1942.
*Bomb Fuze Data.* Navy Department, Washington, D.C.: Bureau of Ordnance. 1945.
*Demolitions and Explosives.* Australian Engineer-in-Chief. Intelligence Summary. May 1944.
*Enemy Vehicles and Ordnance.* Aberdeen Proving Ground, Maryland: Chief of Ordnance. 1945.
*Engineer-in-Chief, Bomb Disposal Instructions.* Headquarters, Australian Military Forces. 11 March 1944.
*German Vengeance Weapon, V-2: The Rocket Bomb.* War Department General Staff, Military Intelligence Division G-2. 1944.
*Rockets and Launchers: All Types.* Ordnance School, Aberdeen Proving Ground. February 1944.
Technical Information Bulletins. Ordnance Bomb Disposal Center. Aberdeen Proving Ground. 1944-45.
U.S. Army Field Manual 9-5. *Ordnance in the Field.* GPO: Washington D.C. 1944.
U.S. Army Field Manual 9-40. *Unexploded Bombs: Organization and Operation for Disposal.* GPO: Washington D.C. 1944.
U.S. Explosive Ordnance Disposal Technical Manual 60A. *Japanese Explosive Ordnance, 15 Aug. 1945.* Naval Explosive Ordnance Disposal Technology Division, Indian Head, Maryland. 1978.
War Department Technical Manual E9-1984. *Disposal Methods for Enemy Bombs and Fuzes.* Aberdeen Proving Ground, Maryland: Chief of Ordnance. 12 November 1942.

## Interviews, Letters, and Memoirs

Barry, Edward J. Rutgers Oral History Archives of World War II. Interview conducted by G. Kurt Piehler and Shaun Illingworth in New Brunswick, New Jersey, on October 23, 1998. Transcript by Shaun Illingworth, Edward J. Barry and Sandra Stewart Holyoak.

Brown, James S. III. Telephone interview by author. 28 June 2003.
Calder, W.G. Telephone interview by author. 14 October 2003.
Camm, Frank. Personal Memoirs. Accessed 21 January 2012. From http://62vgd.de/78th/Frank_Camm/. Internet.
Carlo, Carole P. Telephone interview by author. 29 July 2011.
Cirocco, Alex. Telephone interview by author. 19 June 2011.
Cirocco, Carmel J. Telephone interview by author. 19 June 2011.
—. Telephone interview by author. 20 July 2011.
Clifford, James. e-mail to author. 31 December 2011.
Clifford, James. e-mail to author. 16 March 2011.
Collins, Lawrence D. *The 56th Evacuation Hospital.* University of North Texas Press. 1995.
Dillon, Edward. Telephone interview with author. 11 April 2011.
Englehardt, Bud. e-mail. 27 February 2003.
Feldman, Maria. Telephone interview by author. 18 June 2003.
—. Telephone interview by author. 10 August 2003.
Fetzer, Dix. e-mail. 10 April 2004.
Franklin, Robert. *Medic! How I Fought World War II with Morphine, Sulfa, and Iodine Swabs.* Omaha, University of Nebraska Press. 2008.
Froebel, Guenther. Telephone interview by author. 25 May 2003.
—. e-mail. 28 May 2003.
Frost, Marsha Felton. e-mail. 24 February 2003.
—. Telephone interview by author. 1 March 2003.
Fulcher, Clarence. Telephone interview by author. 2 August 2011.
Fulcher, Ronald. *PFC Clarence Fulcher, 1741st Ordnance Company (Bomb Disposal Squad), as told by his son, Ron Fulcher.* unpublished memoir. 7 January 2008.
Gardner, Albert J. Telephone interview by author 6 March 2003.
—. Telephone interview by author. 13 April 2003.
Korsgaard, Walter. Telephone interview by author. 20 July 2003.
Kramer, Dolores. Telephone interview by author. 16 March 2003.
Kuehner, Robert. Telephone interview by author. 6 March 2003.
Leiendecker, Robert. Telephone interview by author. 10 April 2003.
Levering, Kay. Telephone interview by author. 15 October 2003.
McCluskey, James K. Telephone interview by author. 6 March 2003.
—. Telephone interview by author. 30 March 2003.
Metress, Patrick A. Letter to author. 20 February 2004.
Nass, Alice. Telephone interview by author. 14 October 2003.
Neeper, Ernest. Telephone interview by author. 14 February 2004.
Parsons, Dorothy. Telephone interview by author. 18 October 2003.
Pease, Loyal M. Telephone interview by author. 23 May 2003.

Pilcher, Jesse. Telephone interview by author. 2 September 2003.
Pilcher, Joseph C. Jr. Telephone interview by author. 18 April 2003.
—. Telephone interview by author. 12 July 2003.
Puckett, Fred J. Telephone interview by author. 15 February 2004.
Ransted, Chris. E-mail to author. 11 May 2004.
Reece, T. Dennis. Telephone interview by author. 11 June 2011.
Reece, Thomas R. Letter to family. 17 August 1944.
Roberts, Paul. "Return To Adak, Alaska 2000." Accessed 12 April 2004, from http://adak.orneveien.org/contributors/paulroberts/. Internet.
Romba, Mary Jo. Telephone interview by author. 15 October 2003.
Sharman, Thomas D. Letter to author. 26 August 2003.
Tregaskis, Richard. *Invasion Diary*. Lincoln, Nebraska: University of Nebraska. 2004.
Ulio, J. A. to Margaret E. Sarauw. Telegram. 14 June 1945.
Walkup, Richard W. Personal account. 30 March 2000.
—. Telephone interview by author. 25 June 2010.
—. Telephone interview by author. 13 November 2010.
Woodman-Simmons, Gary. e-mail. 4 February 2003.
—. e-mail. 24 September 2003.

## Navy Department

14th Naval District to the Chief of the Bureau of Ordnance. *Report on Unexploded Japanese Bomb No. 1*. 1 January 1942.
Alexander, Harold, Commanding General, Middle East Forces to U.S. Naval Attaché. Memorandum. 18 February 1943.
Cary, R. W. *Proposed Bomb and Mine Disposal Policies for the U. S. Navy and U. S. Army in the Event of an Allied Invasion of Europe*. 11 January 1943.
Montgomery, T. B. to U.S. Pacific Fleet Commander. *Report of Torpedoing U.S.S. L.S.T. 342 – 0130 LOVE July 18, 1943*. 28 July 1943.
U.S. Naval Advanced Amphibious Base Falmouth-Cornwall, *War Diaries*. 1 June 1944
U.S. Department of the Navy. *N. D. Communiqués 1942-45*. Available from http://www.ibiblio.org/pha/comms.html. Internet.
U.S. Navy Bomb Disposal School. *"Mulvaney on Bomb Disposal," Supplement to Intelligence Bulletin No. 85*. 15 September 1945.
U.S. Navy Technical Mission to Japan. *Japanese Bomb Disposal Methods*. January 1946.

## Newspapers, Magazines, and Articles

*Blue Bell News.* [company newsletter] "Bombs, Books and Biscuits from Greece." c. 1976.

Bomb Disposal Reunion Club. Newsletter. January-February 1995.

Brock, Edward. "Ordnance Group Gets New Hope," from *Clayton News Daily.* (Clayton, Georgia) 5 April 2004.

Clear, Marty. "Vet Disarmed Bombs, Helped Develop Port," from *St. Petersburg Times.* 14 June 2003.

Coster, Kurt B. "Boy Finds Lethal WWII Bomb in Qormi Valley." *The Malta Times.* 29 October 2009.

Duin, Julia. "Bomb Squad School." *The Washington Times*, 3 March 2003.

*"ETO Tells All on Bomb Removal."* [unsigned newspaper article] Joseph C. Pilcher Collection. c. 1945.

*Firepower.* "Bomb Disposal." (Washington D.C.: Army Ordnance Association, August- September 1945).

*Flaming Bomb.* newspaper. U.S. Army: Aberdeen Proving Ground, Maryland. 7 January 1943, 8.

Hoge, Tom. "5 GIs Are Wizards on Nazi Arms. *Stars and Stripes.* 25 May 1944.

Kane, Thomas J. "Unexploded Bombs" *Army Ordnance.* September-October 1942.

Kollander, Louis A. "U.S. Carbine, Cal. 30, M2," from *The Ordnance Sergeant.* July 1945.

www.lonesentry.com

Mathews, Tom Jr. "Feldman Was One of Brightest." *Wayne County Press.* (Fairfield, Ill.: The Wayne Country Press Inc., 12 January 1995), Vol. 130, 4.

*V-Mail.* "Artifact Spotlight." Vol. 12, No. 1. National WWII Museum, New Orleans, Louisiana. Spring 2011.

Newman, Al. "Meet the Bomb Killers." (Newsweek 1 May 1944) 23-4.

Paddie, Glen. "52nd EOD has 'Quick' Change of Command." Fort Campbell Courier. 11 September 2011

Patton, Mark. "Nearly Half of German City to Evacuate Sunday for Defusing of WWII era Bomb." *Stars and Stripes.* 30 November 2011.

Pearson, Drew. "Destruction of the Robot." *Mt. Adams Sun.* 21 July 1944, 2.

Pilcher, Edith H. obituary. Yardley, Pennsylvania. 20 January 1999.

Pritchard, Charles G. "Ammunition Forward: the U.S. Ordnance Corps at Kunu-Ri, Korea." *Army Magazine*, March 2002.

*Punxsutawney Spirit.* [obituaries] Punxsutawney Area Historical and Genealogical Society Inc. 18 January 1919; 2 March 1961; 12 November 1965.

Pyle, Ernie. "Ordnance Keeps Army in Trim." *Stars and Stripes.* 27 July 1944.

*Reading Times.* "Realistic War Glimpse Given to City by Army." Reading, Pennsylvania. 13 October 1943.

Rooney, Andrew A. "This is the Eighth Air Force." *Stars and Stripes.* 19 August 1943.

Roper, Edward. "Overseas Ordnance School," in *The Ordnance Sergeant.* July 1945.

Stars and Stripes Press. *Flaming Bomb: The Story of Ordnance in the ETO.* Paris, France: Desfosses-Neogravure. 1945.

—. *The First! The Story of the 1st Infantry Division.* Paris, France: Desfosses-Neogravure. 1945.

—. *The Story of the 36th Infantry Division.* Paris, France: Desfosses-Neogravure. 1945.

—. *The 45th: The Story of the 45th Infantry Division.* Paris, France: Desfosses-Neogravure. 1945.

—. *Lightning: The Story of the 78th Infantry Division.* Paris, France: Desfosses-Neogravure. 1945.

*Time.* "How to Drown a Bomb." 27 July 1942.

*Sheffield Times-Observer.* 16 March 1942.

—. c. July 1945.

*Stars & Stripes.* "Suicide Squadrons." 26 July 1944.

—. "U.S. Army – Redeployment Vets of Italy are spared Pacific Shift." 27 May 1945.

—. "Yanks Scoured Paris Seeking 80-Day Bombs." 15 June 1945.

Swanson, Nancy. "UXB Squads: The Army's Little-Knowns." *The Valley Voice of Sheffield.* 11 November 1983 (pages unknown).

Switzer, George S. *Memorial of Martin L. Ehrmann.* American Mineralogist. Volume 59. 1974.

Thomas, Mort. "Danger – Live Ammo!" *Ordnance*, Vol. 32, No. 167. March-April 1948.

Tyree, Lewis Jr. *The Journal of Military Affairs.* Vol. 59, No. 3. July 1995.

Weihrauch, Chad. "Veteran Cop Recalls a World War II Battle." *Hunterdon Courier News.* 4 April 2004. Available from cnn/story/0,2111,937927,00.html. Internet.

## Ordnance Department


Anderson, Robert E. to Commanding Officer, Ordnance Bomb Disposal Center, *Progress Report of Bomb Disposal Mission.* 29 August 1944.

Army Ordnance Bomb Disposal School. *Bomb Disposal School History.* Aberdeen Proving Ground, Maryland. c. 1942. [unpublished].

—. *List of B.D. Officers Assigned to Staff and Faculty.* Aberdeen Proving Ground, Maryland. 22 March 1943. [unpublished].

Army Services Forces, *Bomb Disposal Technical Information.* (Bulletin No. 25) Aberdeen Proving Ground: Ordnance Bomb Disposal School, 1 April 1944.

Benton, William O. *Procedure for Presentation of the Order of the Purple Heart to Lt. Pilcher* [unpublished letter] 17 December 1942.

Billingsley, John D. to 2nd Lieutenant Joseph Charles Pilcher. [letter of appointment], 28 November 1942.

Campbell, Levin H. (Chief of Ordnance). Ordnance Department Order No. 291. Organization of the Ordnance Department (Field Service Division). 8 July 1942.

Davis, T. J. to Lt. Col. Charles W. McCarthy. *Disposal of Unexploded and Delayed Action Bombs Within Continental United States.* [memorandum] 8 May 1942.

Davis, T. J. to Chief of Chemical Warfare Service. *Disposal of Unexploded and Delayed Action Bombs.* [memorandum] 8 May 1942.

*Detonator* [newsletter] (U.S. Army Bomb Disposal School: Aberdeen Proving Ground, Maryland) 17 September 1943.

—. 22 October 1943.

Doulong, T. R. to Master Sergeant Joseph C. Pilcher. [travel receipt] 13 September 1942.

Ehrmann, Martin J. to all Bomb Disposal Personnel. *Bomb Disposal.* 11 September 1945.

Hatcher, Julian S. to Staff Sergeant Joseph C. Pilcher. *Certificate of Promotion.* [War Department AGO Form 58] 18 July 1941.

Hatcher, Julian S. to Technical Sergeant Joseph C. Pilcher and Staff Sergeant Ronald L. Felton. *Special Orders No. 1.* [unpublished draft] 1 January 1942.

*History of Bomb Disposal in the U.S.A.* Aberdeen Proving Ground. 1942.

Kane, Thomas J. to Colonel F.I. Garforth. [unpublished memorandum] 2 January 1942.

Kane, Thomas J. [unpublished travel itinerary] Aberdeen Proving Ground, MD. 4 January - 9 March 1942.

Kane, Thomas J. to Lt. Col. C. Wingate Reed. [radiogram] 7 January 1942.

Kane, Thomas J. *Statements Relative to Bomb Disposal.* [unpublished journal] Aberdeen Proving Ground, MD. 9 March 1942.

Kane, Thomas J. to Maj. Gen. Levin H. Campbell. *Equipment to be procured for Ordnance Bomb Disposal Companies.* 2 June 1942.

Kane, Thomas J. to Technical Sergeant Joseph C. Pilcher. *Certificate of Promotion.* 9 June 1942.

Kane, Thomas J. to Brig. Gen. J. K. Crain, Chief of Field Service. *Activation of Bomb Disposal Company.* 15 June 1942.

Kane, Thomas J. to Chief of Military Training Division, Aberdeen Proving Ground. *Policy with Regard to Publicity on Bomb Disposal.* 4 August 1942.

Kane, Thomas J. to Chief of U.S. Army Ordnance. *Report of Visit to Ordnance Activities.* Aberdeen Proving Grounds, MD. 19 October 1942.

Kane, Thomas J. *Bomb Disposal Distinctive Badge and Insignia.* 7 December 1942.

Kane, Thomas J. Travel journal and itinerary, U.S. Ordnance Museum, Aberdeen Proving Ground, MD. 1 December 1942 – 25 May 1943.

Kane, Thomas J. to Ninth U.S. Army Air Force Headquarters, Cairo. [unpublished memo] 11 January 1943.

Kane, Thomas J. to Ninth U.S. Army Air Force Headquarters, Cairo. [unpublished memo] 1 March 1943.

Kane, Thomas J. to Ninth U.S. Army Air Force in Middle East. [unpublished memo] 1 March 1943.

Kane, Thomas J. to Ordnance Officer Persian Gulf Service Command. *Bomb Disposal Service.* [unpublished memo] 16 April 1943.

Kane, Thomas J. to Ordnance Officer Persian Gulf Service Command. *Bomb Disposal Training Program.* [unpublished memo] 16 April 1943.

Kane, Thomas J. to 10th U.S. Army Air Force, New Delhi, India. [unpublished memo] 3 May 1943.

Kane, Thomas J. to 14th U.S. Air Force, Kunming, China. [unpublished memo] 7 May 1943.

Kane, Thomas J. to Commanding General, U.S.A.F. in China-Burma-India. [unpublished memorandum] 12 May 1943.

Kane, Thomas J. to Chief of U.S. Army Ordnance. *Report on Bomb Disposal Activities in Various Theatres of Operation.* Aberdeen Proving Grounds, MD. 29 May 1943.

Kane, Thomas J. to 2nd Lieutenants Joseph C. Pilcher and Ronald L. Felton. [memorandum] 9 August 1943.

Kane, Thomas J. *Special Orders No. 183.* [unpublished letter] 30 September 1943.
Kane, Thomas J. to Chief of U.S. Army Ordnance. *Change to T/O & E 9-500.* 3 December 1943.
Kane, Thomas J. to Lt. Col. Martin J. Ehrmann. [personal letter] 20 June 1944.
Kaskin, Lieutenant to Colonel C. Wingate Reed. [memorandum] 15 December 1941.
King Sr., Edward L. to the Chief of Ordnance. [letter] 30 October 1945.
Mack, A.J. to 1st Lieutenant Frank A. Parsons. [instruction letter] 16 January 1942.
Martyn, John W. to Hon. Paul H. Maloney. [letter] 2 November 1945.
McMahon, B.B. to Chief of Ordnance. *Bomb Disposal Liaison.* 3 January 1942.
Minton, Hugh C. to Secretary of General Staff. [memorandum] 9 December 1941.
Nass, Walter R. *Bomb Disposal Technical Notes.* Aberdeen Proving Ground: U.S. Army Ordnance Museum, 1942.
Nixon, T. H. U.S. Forces European Theater (USFET). *Ordnance in the European Theater: a Discussion of the Year Following VE Day.* NARA Records Group 156. 1 July 1946.
Olsen, E. F. to Brigadier General Julian S. Hatcher. [unpublished letter] 30 December 1941.
Ordnance Bomb Disposal School Headquarters. *Bomb Reconnaissance Instructor's Course.* [syllabus] Department of Training. c.1942.
—. [BD officer roster] 26 November 1942.
—. *BDS History* [unit history] c. 1943.
—. *History of Bomb Disposal U.S.A.* c. 1943.
—. *Course BDC-1 Advanced Bomb Reconnaissance.* Department of Training. c.1943.
—. *Course BDM-1 Bomb Disposal Officer's Course.* Department of Training. c.1943.
—. *Course BDM-2 Bomb Reconnaissance Instructor's Course.* Department of Training. c.1943.
—. *Course BDM-3 Military Bomb Reconnaissance Officers and Non-Commissioned Officers Course.* Department of Training. c.1943.
—. *Course BDM-12 Introduction to the Bomb Disposal Problem.* Department of Training. c.1943.
—. *Course BDM-21 N.C.O Bomb Disposal Course.* Department of Training. c.1943.

—. List of B.D. officers Assigned to Companies & Service Commands. 23 March 1943.
—. [assignment index] 23 March 1943.
Ordnance Bomb Disposal School Headquarters to 2nd Lieutenant Ronald L. Felton. [extract] 19 April 1943.
Ordnance Bomb Disposal School Headquarters. *Special Orders No. 114* [weapons qualification roster] 16 June 1943.
—. [BD officer roster] 26 October 1943.
Ordnance Bomb Disposal School Headquarters to First Lieutenant Joseph C. Pilcher. [personnel roster] 26 October 1943.
Ordnance Bomb Disposal School. [roster of active BD officers] 1 December 1945.
Parsons, Frank A. to Historical Section, Baltimore. *Report on Bomb Disposal Activities* (1 July 1942 – 30 June 1943). [memorandum] 9 July 1943.
Pilcher, Joseph C. to 17th Bomb Disposal Squad (Separate). [training schedule]. 18 October 1943.
Pilcher, Joseph C. to Major Edwin F. Trevor. [replacement of command]. 6 April 1944.
Pilcher, Joseph C. *Certificate of Proficiency* [Ordnance School] 31 January 1941.
Reed, C. Wingate to Col. Hugh C. Minton. [memorandum] 8 December 1941.
Reed, C. Wingate to Assistant Chief of Staff G-2. [memorandum] 17 December 1941.
Reed, C. Wingate to Brigadier General Julian S. Hatcher. [memorandum] 17 December 1941.
Reed, C. Wingate to Assistant Chief of Staff G-2. [memorandum] 13 March 1942.
Reed, C. Wingate to Brigadier General Julian S. Hatcher. [memorandum] 18 March 1942.
Saholsky, Bolick A. to Commanding Generals, Overseas Departments. *Delegation of Bomb Disposal Duties*. [memorandum] 21 May 1942.
Saholsky, Bolick A. to Col. H.R. Kutz, Chief of Field Service. *Undesirable Personnel for Bomb Disposal Units*. 15 June 1942.
Saholsky, Bolick A. *Bomb Disposal Activities*. 21 August 1942.
—. [travel itinerary] Aberdeen Proving Ground, MD. 19 October 1942.
Saholsky, Bolick A. to Commanding Generals, Overseas Departments. *Delegation of Bomb Disposal Duties.* [memorandum] 19 October 1942.
Seleen, Paul M. *Activation of Bomb Disposal Companies*. 29 April 1942.

—. *Delegation of Bomb Disposal Duties*. 29 April 1942.
—. *Officers for Bomb Disposal Duty in Foreign Stations*. 25 May 1942.
Seleen, Paul M. to Commanding General, Services of Supply. *The Problem of Bomb Disposal*. 25 May 1942.
Seleen, Paul M. to Ordnance Officer, Western Defense Command. *Activities of the 231st Ordnance Company, Bomb Disposal*. 5 June 1942.
Seleen, Paul M. *Disposal of Unexploded and Delayed Action Bombs*. 5 February 1943.
Somervell, Brehon to Quartermaster General, Aberdeen Proving Ground. *Device for the Bomb Disposal School*. [letter] 29 September 1942.
Somervell, Brehon to Commanding General, Aberdeen Proving Ground. [Award of Purple Heart to Joseph C. Pilcher] 4 December 1942.
Unangst, Austin to T/Sgt. Joseph C. Pilcher. [certificate] 28 May 1942.
Walker, Harry M. *Manpower Survey*. Ordnance BD School, Aberdeen Proving Ground, Maryland. 2 February 1943.
—. *General Orders No. 1* [unpublished document]. 23 February 1943.
—. *Special Orders No. 75* [unpublished document]. 19 April 1943.
Weible, Walter L. (Services of Supply, Training Division) to Maj. Gen. Levin H. Campbell (Chief of Ordnance). *Activation of Bomb Disposal Companies*. 8 May 1942.
Wesson, Charles M. to Private Joseph C. Pilcher. *Certificate of Promotion*. [War Department AGO Form 58] 29 January 1941.
Wesson, Charles M. to Adjutant General Emory S. Adams. [unpublished draft] 13 December 1941.
Wesson, Charles M. to Adjutant General Emory S. Adams. [unpublished draft] 31 December 1941.
Wesson, Charles M. to Major Thomas J. Kane. [radiogram] 13 January 1942.
Wesson, Charles M. (Chief of Ordnance) to Commanding General, Services of Supply. *Delegation of Bomb Disposal Duties*. [memorandum] 29 April 1942.
Westbrook, James A. to 2nd Lieutenant Joseph Pilcher [certificate] 14 January 1943.
Westbrook, James A. *Organization of the Ordnance Bomb Disposal School*. 9 February 1943.
Winningstad, Olaf P. to U.S. Army Ordnance School [memorandum] 19 January 1942.

## Miscellaneous Personal Documents & Records

1st U.S. Army Commander to 1st Lt. Joseph C. Pilcher. [unpublished orders] 20 December 1943.
14th Replacement Depot to Capt. Joseph C. Pilcher. *Special Orders No. 212*. [extract]. 31 July 1945.
150th Ordnance Battalion to Capt. Joseph C. Pilcher. *Special Orders Number 107*. [extract] 10 July 1945.
440th Anti Aircraft Artillery Weapons Battalion to 1st Lt. Joseph C. Pilcher. [rations voucher] 12 May 1944.
1262nd SCU Personnel Center, Fort Dix to Capt. Joseph C. Pilcher. *Special Orders Number 260*. [extract] 18 September 1945.
Barnett, A. J. to Cirocco, Carmel J. *Special Orders 158*. 7 June 1944.
Cirocco, Carmel J. *Certificate of Service* [Form 53-98] 27 June 1945.
—. *Honorable Discharge from the Army of the United States* [War Department AGO Form 55] 27 June 1945.
—. *World War II Scrapbook.* c. 1945.
Coyne Electricians School to Joseph C. Pilcher. [diploma] c. 1936.
Ehrmann, Martin L. *Declaration of Intention.* No. 2293929, 19 October 1928, U.S. Naturalization Record Indexes, 1791-1992. National Archives and Records Administration. www.ancestry.com.
—. *Certificate of Arrival.* No. 2293929, 8 August 1933, U.S. Naturalization Record Indexes, 1791-1992. National Archives and Records Administration. www.ancestry.com.
—. [citizenship records] No. 2293929, 5 December 1933, U.S. Naturalization Record Indexes, 1791-1992. National Archives and Records Administration. www.ancestry.com.
Feldman, John E. *Military History of John Edward Feldman.* [personal data] Aberdeen Proving Ground, Maryland: U.S. Army Ordnance Museum, c. 1945.
—. [bomb disposal officer roster] undated.
Feldman, John E. to Tim Tidwell, Aberdeen Proving Ground, Maryland: U.S. Army Ordnance Museum [letter] undated.
Felton, Ronald L. *Service Journal 1941-43.* [unpublished document].
—. *Army Air Force Officers Qualification Record* [Form 66-2] November 1944.
—. *Certificate of Service* [Form 53-98] 15 December 1945.
—. Travel itinerary [unpublished] c. 1943-45 Sheffield, PA.
Felton, Ronald L. to Marsha Frost. [personal letter] 2 February 1987.
Gardner, Albert J. [travel itinerary] c.1943-45 New York, NY.
Hickerson, Patricia to Carmel J. Cirocco. *Authorization for Issuance of Rewards.* 7 October 1991.

Metress, Patrick A. *Seven Generations of an Irish-American Family: A History of the Hayes-Hickey-Bergin Family.* [unpublished genealogy] 2003.

Mitchell, Samuel C. to Private Joseph C. Pilcher, [pass card], 3 July 1940.

Pennsylvania Department of Veterans of Foreign Wars to Ronald L. Felton. [certificate] 10 April 1953.

Pilcher, Joseph C. *Honorable Discharge from the Army of the United States* [War Department AGO Form 55]. 27 November 1942.

—. *Last Will and Testament* [wartime statement] 24 November 1943.

—. [War Department AGO Form 204]. 25 November 1943.

—. *Officer's Clearance Certificate.* 27 November 1943.

—. *Pay and Allowance Accounts.* December 1943 to July 1945.

—. *World War II Scrapbook.* [unpublished documents] c. 1945.

—. *Overseas Service Rating Form.* [personnel record] c.1945.

—. *Army Separation Qualification Record.* [War Department AGO Form 100]. 5 December 1945.

—. *Certificate of Service* [Form 53-9B]. 5 December 1945.

Reece, Thomas R. [personal letter] 17 August 1944.

Rodger, Robert B. [citizenship records] No. 5458873, 6 October 1942. U.S. Naturalization Record Indexes, 1791-1992. National Archives and Records Administration. www.ancestry.com.

UXB Club to U.S. Army Ordnance Museum. *Nomination for the Ordnance Hall of Fame for John E. Feldman.* c. 1980.

## Royal Engineers Bomb Disposal

Commandant of Army Bomb Disposal School (Lt. Col. S.H. Fisher) to Ronald L. Felton. [certificate] 12 March 1942.

—. (Lt. Col. S.H. Fisher) to Joseph C. Pilcher. [certificate] 12 March 1942.

Phillips, R.M. *Visit of American Army Officers to London.* [program] 26 January 1942.

Royal Army Bomb Disposal School. *Course Syllabus.* Ripon, Yorkshire: Harper Barracks, c. 1942.

—. *Notes on German Bombs.* Ripon, Yorkshire: Harper Barracks, c. 1942.

—. *Principles of Instruction.* Ripon, Yorkshire: Harper Barracks, c. 1942.

## Unit Histories and Citations

1st Ordnance Bomb Disposal Squad (Separate) to II Corps Ordnance. [operation reports] April to October 1943.
3rd Ordnance Bomb Disposal Squad (Separate) to Headquarters, Ninth Air Force. 31 March 1945.
4th Ordnance Bomb Disposal Squad (Separate) to Colonel Thomas J. Kane. 1 June 1945.
5th Ordnance Bomb Disposal Squad (Separate) to Commanding Officer of 150th Ordnance Battalion (Headquarters). *History of the Fifth Ordnance Bomb Disposal Squad.* 28 February 1945.
5th Army Engineer Special Brigade. U.S. Army, U.S. Forces, European Theater, Historical Division: Records, 1941-1946. NARA Record Group 498.
6th Ordnance Bomb Disposal Squad (Separate) to Headquarters, Ninth Air Force. 31 March 1945.
7th Ordnance Bomb Disposal Squad (Separate) [unit history] February 1943 to October 1945.
7th Ordnance Bomb Disposal Squad (Separate). *Historical Summary Report.* [unit history] April-December 1948.
8th Ordnance Bomb Disposal Squad (Separate) to Commanding General Ninth Air Force Engineer Command. [unit history] January-April 1945.
9th Ordnance Bomb Disposal Squad (Separate) to Headquarters, Ninth Air Force. 31 March 1945.
10th Ordnance Bomb Disposal Squad (Separate) to Headquarters, Ninth Air Force. [unit history] 15 February 1945 to 28 June 1945.
11th Ordnance Bomb Disposal Squad (Separate) to Headquarters, Twelfth Air Force. *Daily Journals.* [unit history] October 1943 to June 1944.
12th Ordnance Bomb Disposal Squad (Separate) to Commanding General of Twelfth Air Force. *Special Accounts May 1944-July 1945.*
15th Ordnance Bomb Disposal Squad (Separate) to Adjutant General. *Action Against Enemy.* [After Action Report]. 20 July 1944.
16th Ordnance Bomb Disposal Squad (Separate) to Colonel Thomas J. Kane. *Squad History Jan. 1944 to June 1945.* 8 June 1945.
17th Ordnance Bomb Disposal Squad (Separate) to Colonel Thomas J. Kane. *Squad History 1944-1945.* 8 June 1945.
27th Ordnance Bomb Disposal Squad (Separate). *Squad History.* 11 June 1945.
30th Ordnance Bomb Disposal Squad (Separate). [unit history] c. 1945.
31st Ordnance Bomb Disposal Squad (Separate). [unit history] c. 1945.

32nd Ordnance Bomb Disposal Squad (Separate). *Squad History*. 20 June 1945.
35th Ordnance Bomb Disposal Squad (Separate). [unit history] c. 12 June 1945.
37th Ordnance Bomb Disposal Squad (Separate). [unit history] 23 June 1945.
41st Ordnance Bomb Disposal Squad (Separate). [unit history] May 1944.
42nd Ordnance Bomb Disposal Squad (Separate) to Headquarters, Ninth Air Force. 31 March 1945.
43rd Ordnance Bomb Disposal Squad (Separate). [unit history] 11 August 1943 to 14 December 1945.
44th Ordnance Bomb Disposal Squad (Separate) to Headquarters, Ninth Air Force. 31 March 1945.
45th Ordnance Bomb Disposal Squad (Separate) to Headquarters, Ninth Air Force. 31 March 1945.
46th Ordnance Bomb Disposal Squad (Separate). [unit history] 6 March 1944 to 26 May 1945.
47th Ordnance Bomb Disposal Squad (Separate). [unit history] 14 December 1945.
48th Ordnance Bomb Disposal Squad (Separate). [unit history] 1 June 1945 to 14 December 1945.
51st Ordnance Bomb Disposal Squad (Separate). [unit history] June to August 1945.
54th Ordnance Bomb Disposal Squad (Separate). [unit history] 1943-45.
55th Ordnance Bomb Disposal Squad (Separate). [unit history] 1943-45.
56th Ordnance Bomb Disposal Squad (Separate). [unit history] 1944-45.
57th Ordnance Bomb Disposal Squad (Separate). [unit histories] February 1943 to June 1945.
58th Ordnance Bomb Disposal Squad (Separate). [unit histories] October 1944 to April 1945.
67th Ordnance Bomb Disposal Squad (Separate) to Commanding General, Special Troops, 12th U.S. Army Group. *Unit History*. 13 July 1945.
68th Ordnance Bomb Disposal Squad (Separate). [unit history] 16 December 1945.
68th Ordnance Bomb Disposal Squad (Separate) to Headquarters, Ninth Air Force. *Report on V-1 Attack on Liege, Belgium*. 7 December 1944.
68th Ordnance Bomb Disposal Squad (Separate). *Commendation*. James B. Newman to T/Sgt. Walter Haasis, 12 June 1945.
69th Ordnance Bomb Disposal Squad (Separate). [unit history] 16 December 1945.

70th Ordnance Bomb Disposal Squad (Separate). [unit history] 16 December 1945.
71st Ordnance Bomb Disposal Squad (Separate). [unit history] 16 December 1945.
72nd Ordnance Bomb Disposal Squad (Separate) to Headquarters, Ninth Air Force. 31 March 1945.
72nd Ordnance Bomb Disposal Squad (Separate) to Commanding Officer, Ansbach Air Depot. 28 May 1946 to 28 January 1947.
73rd Ordnance Bomb Disposal Squad (Separate) to Headquarters, Ninth Air Force. 31 March 1945.
73rd Ordnance Bomb Disposal Squad (Separate) to Commanding General, 3rd U.S. Army. 1 May 1946 to 17 January 1947.
74th Ordnance Bomb Disposal Squad (Separate) to Headquarters, Ninth Air Force. 31 March 1945.
74th Ordnance Bomb Disposal Squad (Separate) to Commanding General, 1st U.S. Infantry. 1 June 1946 to 31 December 1946.
75th Ordnance Bomb Disposal Squad (Separate) to Headquarters, Ninth Air Force. 31 March 1945.
75th Ordnance Bomb Disposal Squad (Separate) to Commanding General, Ninth U.S. Air Force. 30 September 1946 to 30 November 1946.
76th Ordnance Bomb Disposal Squad (Separate). [unit history] 5 April 1944 to 17 December 1945.
77th Ordnance Bomb Disposal Squad (Separate). [unit history] 3 March 1945 to 15 December 1945.
78th Ordnance Bomb Disposal Squad (Separate). [unit history] 17 December 1945.
79th Ordnance Bomb Disposal Squad (Separate). [unit history] 31 May 1944 to 30 June 1944.
80th Ordnance Bomb Disposal Squad (Separate). [unit history] 29 May 1944 to 11 December 1945.
81st Ordnance Bomb Disposal Squad (Separate). [unit history] 14 December 1945.
82nd Ordnance Bomb Disposal Squad (Separate) to Headquarters, Ninth Air Force. 31 March 1945.
82nd Ordnance Bomb Disposal Squad (Separate). [unit history] 30 June 1946 to 31 October 1946.
83rd Ordnance Bomb Disposal Squad (Separate) to Headquarters, Ninth Air Force. 31 March 1945.
83rd Ordnance Bomb Disposal Squad (Separate). [unit history] 31 May 1946 to 31 January 1947.

84th Ordnance Bomb Disposal Squad (Separate) to Headquarters, Ninth Air Force. 31 March 1945.

84th Ordnance Bomb Disposal Squad (Separate). [unit history] 30 June 1946.

85th Ordnance Bomb Disposal Squad (Separate) to Headquarters, Ninth Air Force. 31 March 1945.

86th Ordnance Bomb Disposal Squad (Separate). [unit history] 14 December 1945.

87th Ordnance Ammunition Battalion. [unit history] 1944-45.

87th Ordnance Bomb Disposal Squad (Separate). [unit history] 14 December 1945.

87th Ordnance Bomb Disposal Squad (Separate). [unit history] 30 June 1946 to 31 January 1947.

88th Ordnance Bomb Disposal Squad (Separate). [unit history] 23 March 1945.

90th Ordnance Bomb Disposal Squad (Separate). [unit history] 26 March 1945.

92nd Ordnance Bomb Disposal Squad to Commandant, Ordnance Bomb Disposal School. [operation report] 1 February 1944.

92nd Ordnance Bomb Disposal Squad to Commandant, Ordnance Bomb Disposal School. [unit history] November 1943 to February 1945.

100th Ordnance Bomb Disposal Squad (Separate). [unit history] 1944-45.

109th Ordnance Bomb Disposal Squad (Separate). [unit history] November 1943 to October 1945.

136th Ordnance Bomb Disposal Squad (Separate). [unit history] May-June 1944.

138th Ordnance Bomb Disposal Squad (Separate). [unit history] 7 May 1944.

142nd Ordnance Bomb Disposal Squad (Separate). [unit history] June 1944

143rd Ordnance Bomb Disposal Squad (Separate). [unit history] 7 May 1944.

156th Ordnance Bomb Disposal Squad to Commandant, Ordnance Bomb Disposal Center. *Unit Report of Action on Iwo Jima.* 26 June 1945.

161st Ordnance Bomb Disposal Squad (Separate). [unit history] 1944-45.

163rd Ordnance Bomb Disposal Squad to Colonel Thomas J. Kane. *Recommendation for Award of Bronze Star Medal.* c. 1945.

176th Ordnance Bomb Disposal Squad (Separate) to Colonel Thomas J. Kane. *Overseas Activities of 176th Ordnance Bomb Disposal Squad.* 21 June 1946.

178th Ordnance Bomb Disposal Squad (Separate). [unit history] 1945-46.

209th Ordnance Bomb Disposal (Separate). *Squad History.* 24 March 1945 to 4 August 1945.
233rd Ordnance Bomb Disposal Platoon. [unit history] April-May 1945.
234th Ordnance Bomb Disposal Company. [travel journal]. 2 October 1943- 8 February 1945.
235th Ordnance Bomb Disposal Company, 3rd Platoon. *American Bomb Disposal in the Sicilian Campaign.* September 1943.
Barry, Edward J. to 17th U.S. Ordnance Bomb Disposal Squad (Separate) [memorandum] 13 July 1945.
Bowyer (Colonel) to 11th, 12th, 13th Bomb Disposal Squads [transfer orders]. 13 September 1943.
Engel, Albert J. to Ninth Air Force Headquarters. *Unexploded Enemy Ammunition.* 9 October 1944.
Gordon, George D. to 68th Ordnance Bomb Disposal Squad (Separate). *Unit Citation.* 25 November 1944.
Gordon, George D. to Commanding General, Engineer Command, U.S. Strategic Air Forces in Europe. *Commendation of Enlisted Man.* 14 April 1945.
Gordon, George D. to Commanding General, Engineer Command, U.S. Strategic Air Forces in Europe. *Commendation of Enlisted Man.* 5 June 1945.
Headquarters Peninsular Base Section. *General Orders No. 83.* Disbandment of 235th Ordnance Bomb Disposal Company, 6 May 1944.
—. *General Orders No. 85.* Disbandment of 235th Ordnance Bomb Disposal Company, 6 May 1944.
Krieger, Jerome to Commander, NAVSCOLEOD. *Fact Sheet.* 5 October 1992.
Leiendecker, Robert. *World War II Statistics [Army Ordnance Bomb Disposal Squads].* (Charlottesville VA; Library of National EOD Association, c. 2003).
Ninth Army Headquarters. *General Orders 103.* 9 April 1945.
IX TAC U.S. Army Air Force Bomb Disposal Squad Histories, NARA Records Group 338.

## U.S. Government Documents & Sources

Department of the Army. *Pamphlet 672-1: Bomb Disposal Unit Citation and Campaign Participation Credit Register.* Washington D.C.: Government Publishing Office, 1972.

National Jewish Welfare Board. Bureau of War Records. 1939-45. National Archives and Records Administration. www.ancestry.com.

U.S. Army Enlistment Records, 1939-45. National Archives and Records Administration. www.ancestry.com.

U.S. Army, U.S. Forces, European Theater, Historical Division. Records, 1941-1946. Staff Section Reports. www.Fold3.com.

U.S. Army, U.S. Forces, European Theater, Historical Division. Records, 1941-1946. Miscellaneous Reports. www.Fold3.com.

U.S. Bureau of the Census, Department of Commerce, 1880-1930. National Archives and Records Administration. www.ancestry.com.

U.S. Department of Labor, Immigration and Naturalization Service Records. National Archives and Records Administration. www.ancestry.com.

World War II War Diaries. 7 December 1941 to 31 December 1945. National Archives and Records Administration. Record Group 38.

www.dtic.mil/dpmo/wwii

www.eodmemorial.org

## War Department

Adjutant General (Major General J.A. Ulio). *Delegation of Bomb Disposal Duties*. [memoranda] 5 February 1943.

Adjutant General (Major General J.A. Ulio) to Defense Commands. *Disposal of Unexploded and Delayed Action Bombs within the Continental Limits of the United States*. 30 May 1942.

Adjutant General (Major General Emory S. Adams) to Chief of Ordnance. *Disposal of Unexploded and Delayed Action Bombs*. [memorandum] 12 December 1941.

Adjutant General (Major General Emory S. Adams) to Brig. Gen. Julian S. Hatcher. *Bomb Demolition Course.* [memorandum] 30 December 1941.

Adjutant General (Major General Emory S. Adams) to Brig. Gen. Julian S. Hatcher. *Bomb Demolition Course.* [amendment to orders] 16 January 1942.

Edwards, Idwal H. *Activation of Bomb Disposal Companies.* 20 June 1942.

—. Assistant Chief of Staff to the War Department, Chief of Staff. *Unexploded Bomb Disposal*. 16 August 1942.

Eisenhower, Dwight D. to the Commanding Generals. *Defense of Continental United States.* [memorandum] 22 April 1942.

Eisenhower, Dwight D. to Chief of Ordnance. *Disposal of Unexploded and Delayed Action Bombs Within Continental United States.* [memorandum] 13 May 1942.

Goodwin, S. R. (Adjutant General) to Chief of Ordnance (Lt. Gen. Levin Campbell). *Officers for Bomb Disposal Duty in Foreign Stations.* 4 June 1942.

Guisinger, Earl C. to Emory S. Adams (Adjutant General). *Officers for Bomb Demolition Course.* [unpublished memorandum] 23 December 1941.

Harris, John P. *Special Orders No. 180.* 29 July 1943.

Headquarters USFET MIS Center. *Final Interrogation Report No. 28.* Hanz Heinz Manderscheid. 5 September 1945.

Huebner, Clarence R. to Assistant Chief of Staff, War Department. *Unexploded Bomb Disposal.* (Adjutant General Letters 471.6). 10 August 1942 – 2 September 1942.

Kane, Thomas J. to U.S. War Department. *Bomb Disposal, U. S. A.* [unpublished report] c.1942.

London to United States War Department. [cablegram] 7 December 1941.

—. [cablegram] 12 December 1941.

London to United States War Department. [cablegram] 7 January 1942.

Lutes, Leroy. *Activation of Bomb Disposal Companies.* 15 June 1942.

O'Leary A.E., Adjutant General's Office, War Department. *Disposal of Unexploded and Delayed Action Bombs.* (Adjutant General Letters 471.6). 5 February 1943.

Third Service Command Headquarters. *Activation of the 1st to 13th Ord. Bomb Disp. Sqd., Sep.* 4 February 1943.

U.S. War Department to Colonel C. Wingate Reed. [memorandum] 15 December 1941.

U.S. War Department to the Adjutant General. *Disposal of Unexploded and Delayed-Action Bombs.* 7 January 1942.

U.S. War Department to the Adjutant General. *Ordnance Training Center General Order #7.* 4 February 1942.

U.S. War Department to the Adjutant General. *Constitution and Activation of the 231st Ordnance Company, Bomb Disposal.* Ordnance Department, Washington D.C. 11 May 1942.

U.S. War Department. *Liaison Bulletin No. 75.* Bureau of Public Relations, Washington, D.C. 1942.

—. *Table of Organization No. 9 Bomb Disposal Company.* Ordnance Department, Washington D.C. 1942.

U.S. War Department to 2nd Lieutenant Joseph C. Pilcher. *Special Orders No 256.* 13 September 1943.
U.S. War Department. *Missing Air Crew Report 1102. File 42-6451.* 27 October 1943.
U.S. War Department to Commandant, Bomb Disposal School, Aberdeen Proving Ground, Maryland. *Bomb Disposal Directives.* 16 May 1944.
U.S. War Department to Commanding General, North African Theater of Operations. *Constitution, Activation and Disbandment of Ordnance Bomb Disposal Units.* AG 322. 11 January 1944.
U.S. War Department. *U.S. Army Casualty Reports.* 1945.

## Photographs

Aberdeen Proving Ground Ordnance Museum
German Bundesarchiv
German Luftarchiv
National Archives and Records Administration
National EOD Association
Royal Engineers Association
U.S. Army Ordnance Hall of Fame
Carmel J. Cirocco Collection
Ronald L. Felton Collection
Marsha F. Frost Collection
Alfred J. Gardner Collection
Thomas J. Kane Collection
Joseph C. Pilcher Collection
Thomas R. Reece Collection
George C. Sarauw Collection
Mike R. Vining Collection

## Secondary Sources

Ambrose, Stephen E. *Eisenhower: Soldier, General of the Army, President-Elect, 1890-1952, Vol. 1.* New York: Simon & Schuster, 1983.
—. *D-Day, June 6, 1944: The Climactic Battle of World War II.* New York: Simon & Schuster, 1994.
—. *Citizen Soldiers.* New York: Simon and Schuster, 1997.
Appleman, Roy, James M. Burns, Russell A. Gugeler, and James Steven. *Okinawa: The Last Battle.* Washington D.C.: Historical Division, Department of the Army, 1948.

Atkinson, Rick. *An Army at Dawn*. New York: Henry Holt, 2002.
—. *The Day of Battle*. New York: Henry Holt, 2007.
Bailey, Ronald H. *The Home Front USA*. Alexandria, VA: WWII Time-Life, 1977.
Beevor, Antony. *D-Day: The Battle for Normandy*. London: Penguin Books. 2009.
Biggs, Bradley. *The Triple Nickles: America's First All-Black Paratroop Unit*. (Hamden, Conn.: Archon Books, 1986).
Blumenson, Martin. *European Theater of Operations: Breakout and Pursuit*. Washington D.C.: Office of the Chief of Military History, 1961.
Blumenson, Martin. *Mediterranean Theater of Operations: Salerno to Cassino*. Washington D.C.: Office of the Center for Military History, 1969.
—. *The Patton Papers*. Boston: Houghton Mifflin, 1974.
Bower, Thomas. *The Paperclip Conspiracy: The Hunt for the Nazi Scientists*. Boston: Little, Brown and Company. 1987.
Brooks, Thomas R. *The War North of Rome*. New York: Sarpedon Publishers, 1996.
Bradley, Omar N. and Clay Blair. *A General's Life*. Simon and Schuster, New York, 1983.
Breyer, Siegfried. *The German Aircraft Carrier Graf Zeppelin*. Atglen, Pennsylvania: Schiffer Publishing Ltd. 1989.
Brophy, Leo P., and George J. Fisher. *Chemical Warfare Service: Organizing For War*. Washington D.C.: Office of the Chief of Military History, 1959.
Campbell, Levin H. Jr. *The Industry-Ordnance Team*. New York: Whittlesey House & McGraw-Hill Inc., 1946.
Chandonnet, Fern, ed. *Alaska at War 1941-1945: The Forgotten War Remembered*. Fairbanks: University of Alaska Press, 2008.
Churchill, Winston S. *Their Finest Hour*. 6 vols. Boston: Houghton-Mifflin, 1949.
Cole, Hugh M. *European Theater of Operations: The Ardennes: Battle of the Bulge*. Washington D.C.: Office of the Chief of Military History, 1965.
Collins, Larry and Dominique LaPierre. *Is Paris Burning?* New York: Simon and Schuster, 1965.
Conn, Stetson, Rose C. Engleman, and Byron Fairchild. *Guarding the United States and its Outposts*. Washington D.C.: Chief of Military History, 1946.

Cooling, B. Franklin. "U.S. Army Support of Civil Defense: The Formative Years," from *Military Affairs*, Vol. 35, No. 1 (February 1971).

Crowl, Philip A. *Campaign in the Marianas*. Washington D.C.: Chief of Military History, 1960.

Davidson, Stanley W. *Military Relations Between United States and Canada*. Washington D.C.: Center for Military History, 1959.

D'Este, Carlo. *Patton: a Genius for War*. New York: Harper Collins, 1995.

—. *Eisenhower: a Soldier's Life*. New York, Henry Holt, 2002.

Dod, Karl C., *The Corps of Engineers: The War Against Japan*. Washington D.C.: Center for Military History, 1966.

Durham, J. Frank. *You Only Blow Yourself Up Once: Confessions of a World War Two Bomb Disposaleer.* Lincoln, Nebraska: iUniverse, 2003.

Explosive Ordnance Disposal Division, *"A History of U.S. Bomb Disposal,"* [pamphlet] (Redstone Arsenal Press, AL: n.d.). National Explosive Ordnance Association Collection.

Green, Constance M., Peter C. Root, and Harry C. Thomson, *The Ordnance Department: Planning Munitions for War.* Washington D.C.: Department of the Army, 1955.

Griffith, Samuel B. *The Battle for Guadalcanal.* Champaign, Illinois: University of Illinois Press. 1963.

Hartley, A.B. *Unexploded Bomb*. New York: W.W. Norton Co., 1958.

Hewes, James E., Jr. *From Root to McNamara: Army Organization and Administration.* Washington D.C.: Center of Military History, U.S. Army, 1975.

Hooper, Samuel J. *The History of U.S. Army Bomb Disposal and Explosive Ordnance Disposal (1941-1980).* [unpublished manuscript ] c.1981.

Howarth, Stephen. *To Shining Sea: a History of the United States Navy, 1775-1991.* New York: Random House, 1991.

Jackson, W.G.F. *The Battle for Italy*. New York: Harper & Row, 1967.

Jappy, Melissa J. *Danger UXB*. London: Macmillan Publishers Ltd., 2001.

Johnson, David. *V-1 V-2: Hitler's Vengeance on London.* New York: Stein & Day, 1981.

Kuehner, Robert. "The Deadly 88," in *UXB Volume II*, Jim Jenkinson, ed. Sussex, Eng.: Woodfield Publishing Co., 2001.

Larew, Karl G. "December 7, 1941: The Day No One Bombed Panama," from *The Historian*. (Tampa, Florida: Blackwell Publishing) Volume 66, Number 2 (Summer 2004).

Leiendecker, Robert E. *Bomb Disposal, The Early Years of Explosive Ordnance Disposal (An Informal History).* (Charlottesville, Virginia: NATEODA Press, 2012).

Lenz, Robert R. and Fred Philcox. *History of Explosive Ordnance Disposal.* c. 1960.

Mauldin, Bill. *Bill Mauldin's Up Front,* New York: W.W. Norton, 1945.

Mayo, Lida. The *Ordnance Department: On Beachhead and Battlefront.* Washington D.C.: Department of Defense, 1991.

McDonald, Charles B. *European Theater of Operations: The Siegfried Line Campaign.* Washington D.C.: Office of the Chief of Military History, 1963.

—. *European Theater of Operations: The Last Offensive.* Washington D.C.: Office of the Chief of Military History, 1973.

Mikesh, Robert C. *Japan's World War II Balloon Bomb Attacks on North America.* Washington D.C.: Smithsonian Institution Press, 1973.

Miller, Donald L. *D-Days in the Pacific.* New York City, New York: Simon & Schuster, 2005.

Montgomery, Bernard L. *The Memoirs of Field Marshal Montgomery.* Cleveland & New York: World Publishing Company, 1958.

Morison, Samuel E. "The Struggle for Guadalcanal, August 1942 – February 1943." *The History of United States Naval Operations in World War II*, Vol. 5. Boston: Little, Brown and Company, 1958.

Murray, Williamson and Allen R. Millett. *A War to be Won: Fighting the Second World War.* Cambridge, Massachusetts: Harvard University Press, 2001.

Palmer, Robert, Bell I. Wiley, and William R. Keast, *Procurement and Training of Ground Combat Troops.* Washington D.C.: Center of Military History [1948] 2003.

Pritchard, Charles G. "A Yank on Bomb Disposal with the RAF," in *UXB Volume II.* Jim Jenkinson, ed. Sussex, Eng.: Woodfield Publishing Co., 2001.

Ransted, Chris. *Bomb Disposal and the British Casualties of WW2.* United Kingdom. Royal Engineers Association. 2004.

Reece, T. Dennis. *Captains of Bomb Disposal 1942-46.* Lexington, Kentucky: Xlibris Books, 2005.

Romanus, Charles F., and Riley Sunderland. *Time Runs Out in CBI.* Washington D.C.: Center For Military History, 1985.

Ross, Robert Smith. *The Approach to the Philippines.* Washington: United States Center for Military History. 1953.

Ryan, Cornelius. *A Bridge Too Far.* New York: Simon & Schuster, 1974.

Shirley, Orville C. *Americans: the Story of the 442$^{nd}$ Combat Team.* Washington: Infantry Journal Press, 1946.

Simon, Leslie E. *German Research in World War II.* London: Chapman & Hall, Limited, 1947.

Smith, Robert R. *The War in the Pacific: Triumph in the Philippines.* Washington D.C.: Office of the Chief of Military History, 1963.

Smith, W. H. B. *A Basic Manual of Small Arms.* Harrisburg, Pennsylvania: Military Publishing Company, 1943.

Strawson, John. *The Italian Campaign.* New York: Carroll & Graf Publishers, 1988.

Super, Carl and David E. Stuart. "Japanese Artillery," from *Ordnance Sergeant* (July 1945).

*U.S. Army Campaigns of World War II: Aleutian Islands.* Washington D.C.: Center for Military History, Publication 72-6.

*V Corps Operation in the ETO 6 January 1942 – 9 May 1945.* (U. S. Army Historical Section: GPO, Washington D.C.) 1945.

Vining, Mike R. *Army Bomb Disposal & EOD Heraldry and Badges.* National EOD Association, 9 April 2011.

—. *Explosive Ordnance Disposal Memorial – U. S. Army.* Submitted to the EOD Memorial Commission, 15 October 2011.

Wakeling, Eric E. *A Short History of Royal Engineer Bomb Disposal.* Buckinghamshire, England: B.D. Publishing, 1997.

Weigley, Russell F. *Eisenhower's Lieutenants: The Campaign of France and Germany 1944-1945.* Bloomington, Ind.: Indiana University Press, 1981.

Wright, Gordon. *The Ordeal of Total War.* New York: Harper & Row, 1997.

# INDEX

F



G



H



I



J



K



M

W